WOODROW WILSON
AS I KNOW HIM

Mr. Tumulty with the President at the Signing of a Treaty

WOODROW WILSON AS I KNOW HIM

BY
JOSEPH P. TUMULTY

AMS PRESS
NEW YORK

Reprinted from the edition of 1921, Garden City
First AMS EDITION published 1970
Manufactured in the United States of America

International Standard Book Number: 0-404-06527-9
Library of Congress Number: 71-127912   30Au. 9   30Aug'79

AMS PRESS INC.
NEW YORK, N.Y. 10003

TO THE MEMORY OF
MY DEAR MOTHER
ALICIA TUMULTY
WHOSE SPIRIT OF
GENEROSITY, LOYALTY, AND TOLERANCE
I TRUST WILL BE FOUND IN
THE LINES OF THIS BOOK

ACKNOWLEDGMENT

In preparing this volume I have made use of portions of the following books: "The War The World and Wilson" by George Creel; "What Wilson Did at Paris," by Ray Stannard Baker; "Woodrow Wilson and His Work" by William E. Dodd; "The Panama Canal Tolls Controversy" by Hugh Gordon Miller and Joseph C. Freehoff; "Woodrow Wilson the Man and His Work" by Henry Jones Ford; "The Real Colonel House" by Arthur D. Howden Smith; "The Foreign Policy of Woodrow Wilson" by Edgar E. Robinson and Victor J. West. In addition, I wish to make acknowledgment to the following books for incidental assistance: "My Four Years in Germany" by James W. Gerard; "Woodrow Wilson, An Interpretation" by A. Maurice Low; "A People Awakened" by Charles Reade Bacon; "Woodrow Wilson" by Hester E. Hosford; "What Really Happened at Paris," edited by Edward Mandell House and Charles Seymour, and above all, to the public addresses of Woodrow Wilson. I myself had furnished considerable data for various books on Woodrow Wilson and have felt at liberty to make liberal use of some portions of these sources as guide posts for my own narrative.

PREFACE

WOODROW WILSON prefers not to be written about. His enemies may, and of course will, say what they please, but he would like to have his friends hold their peace. He seems to think and feel that if he himself can keep silent while his foes are talking, his friends should be equally stoical. He made this plain in October, 1920, when he learned that I had slipped away from my office at the White House one night shortly before the election and made a speech about him in a little Maryland town, Bethesda. He did not read the speech, I am sure he has never read it, but the fact that I had made any sort of speech about him, displeased him. That was one of the few times in my long association with him that I found him distinctly cold. He said nothing, but his silence was vocal.

I suspect this book will share the fate of the Bethesda speech, will not be read by Mr. Wilson. If this seems strange to those who do not know him personally, I can only say that "Woodrow Wilson is made that way." He cannot dramatize himself and shrinks from attempts of others to dramatize him. "I will not write about myself," is his invariable retort to friends who urge him to publish his own story of the Paris Peace Conference. He craves the silence from others which he imposes upon himself. He is quite willing to leave the assessment and interpretation of himself to time and posterity. Knowing all this I have not consulted him about this book. Yet I

have felt that the book should be written, because I am
anxious that his contemporaries should know him as I
have known him, not only as an individual but also as the
advocate of a set of great ideas and as the leader of great
movements. If I can picture him, even imperfectly, as I
have found him to be, both in himself and in his relationship to important events, I must believe that the portrait
will correct some curious misapprehensions about him.

For instance, there is a prevalent idea, an innocently
ignorant opinion in some quarters, an all too sedulously
cultivated report in other quarters, that he has been
uniformly headstrong, impatient of advice, his mind
hermetically closed to counsel from others. This book
will expose the error of that opinion; will show how, in his
own words, his mind was "open and to let," how he
welcomed suggestions and criticism. Indeed I fear that
unless the reader ponders carefully what I have written
he may glean the opposite idea, that sometimes the President had to be prodded to action, and that I represent
myself as the chief prodder.

The superficial reader may find countenance lent to
this latter view in the many notes of information and advice which I addressed to the President and in the record
of his subsequent actions which were more or less in accord with the counsel contained in some of these notes.
If the reader deduces from this the conclusion that I
was the instigator of some of the President's important
policies, he will misinterpret the facts and the President's
character and mental processes; if he concludes that I
am trying to represent myself as the instigator he will
misunderstand my motives in publishing these notes.

These motives are: first, to tell the story of my association with Mr. Wilson, and part of the record is con-

tained in these notes; secondly, to show what liberty he allowed me to suggest and criticize; how, so far from being offended, he welcomed counsel. Having this privilege I exercised it. I conceived it as part of my duty as his secretary and friend to report to him my own interpretations of facts and public opinion as I gathered these from newspapers and conversations, and sometimes to suggest modes of action. These notes were memoranda for my chief's consideration.

The reader will see how frankly critical some of these notes are. The mere fact that the President permitted me to continue to write to him in a vein of candour that was frequently brusque and blunt, is the conclusive answer to the charge that he resented criticism.

Contrary to the misrepresentations, he had from time to time many advisers. In most instances, I do not possess written reports of what others said orally and in writing, and therefore in this record, which is essentially concerned with my own official and personal relations with him, I may seem to represent myself as a preponderating influence. This is neither the fact nor my intention. The public acts of Mr. Wilson were frequently mosaics, made up of his own ideas and those of others. My written notes were merely stones offered for the mosaic. Sometimes the stones were rejected, sometimes accepted and shaped by the master builder into the pattern.

It was a habit of Mr. Wilson's to meditate before taking action, to listen to advice without comment, frequently without indicating whether or not the idea broached by others had already occurred to him. We who knew him best knew that often the idea had occurred to him and had been thought out more lucidly than any adviser could state it. But he would test his own views by the touchstone of other minds' reactions to the situations and problems which he was facing and would get the "slant" of other minds.

He was always ahead of us all in his thinking. An admirer once said: "You could shut him up in an hermetically sealed room and trust him to reach the right decision," but as a matter of fact he did not work that way. He sought counsel and considered it and acted on it or dismissed it according to his best judgment, for the responsibility for the final action was his, and he was boldly prepared to accept that responsibility and conscientiously careful not to abuse it by acting rashly. While he would on occasion make momentous decisions quickly and decisively, the habitual character of his mind was deliberative. He wanted all the facts and so far as possible the contingencies. Younger men like myself could counsel immediate and drastic action, but even while we were advising we knew that he would, without haste and without waste, calmly calculate his course. What, coming from us, were merely words, would, coming from him, constitute acts and a nation's destiny. He regarded himself as the "trustee of the people," who should not act until he was sure he was right and should then act with the decision and finality of fate itself.

Of another misapprehension, namely, that Mr. Wilson lacks human warmth, I shall let the book speak without much prefatory comment. I have done my work ill indeed if there does not emerge from the pages a human-hearted man, a man whose passion it was to serve mankind. In his daily intercourse with individuals he showed uniform consideration, at times deep tenderness, though he did not have in his possession the little bag of tricks which some politicians use so effectively: he did not clap men on their backs, call them by their first names, and profess to each individual he met that of all the men in the world this was the man whom he most yearned to see. Perhaps he was too sincere for that; perhaps by nature too reserved; but I am convinced that he who reads this book will feel that he has met a man whose public career was governed not merely by a great brain, but also by a great heart. I did not invent this character. I observed him for eleven years.

CONTENTS

WOODROW WILSON
AS I KNOW HIM

Woodrow Wilson As I Know Him

CHAPTER I

THE POLITICAL LABORATORY

MY INTRODUCTION to politics was in the Fifth Ward of Jersey City, New Jersey, which for many years was the "Bloody Angle" of politics of the city in which I lived. Always Democratic, it had been for many years the heart and centre of what New Jersey Democrats were pleased to call the great Gibraltar of Democracy. The ward in which I lived was made up of the plainest sort of people, a veritable melting pot of all races, but with a predominance of Irish, Germans, and Italians, between whom it was, like ancient Gaul, divided into three parts.

My dear father, Philip Tumulty, a wounded soldier of the Civil War, after serving an apprenticeship as an iron moulder under a delightful, whole-souled Englishman, opened a little grocery store on Wayne Street, Jersey City, where were laid the foundation stones of his modest fortune and where, by his fine common sense, poise, and judgment, he soon established himself as the leader of a Democratic faction in that neighbourhood. This modest little place soon became a political laboratory for me. In the evening, around the plain, old-fashioned counters, seated upon barrels and boxes, the interesting characters of the neighbourhood gathered, representing as they did

1

the leading active political forces in that quaint cosmopolitan community.

No matter how far back my memory turns, I cannot recall when I did not hear politics discussed—not ward politics only, but frequently the politics of the nation and the world. In that grocery store, from the lips of the plainest folk who came there, were carried on serious discussions of the tariff, the money question, our foreign relations, and all phases of the then famous Venezuelan question, which in those days threatened to set two continents on fire.

The make-up of the little "cabinet" or group which surrounded my father was most interesting. There was Mr. Alexander Hamill, the father of Congressman Hamill of Jersey City, a student of Queen's College in Ireland and who afterward taught in the National Schools of Ireland, a well-read, highly cultured, broad-minded man of affairs; and dear Uncle Jimmie Kelter, almost a centenarian, whose fine old gray hair gave him the appearance of a patriarch. Uncle Jimmie nightly revelled in the recital to those who were present as ready listeners, his experience when he was present at a session of the House of Parliament in London and heard the famous Irish statesman, Daniel O'Connell, denounce England's attitude of injustice toward Catholic emancipation. He loved to regale the little group that encircled him by reciting from memory the great speech of Robert Emmett from the dock, and excerpts from the classic speeches of the leading Irish orators like Curran, Sheridan, and Fox.

While these discussions in the little store wended their uneasy way along, a spark of humour was often injected into them by the delightful banter of a rollicking, good-natured Irishman, a big two-fisted fellow, generous-hearted and lovable, whom we affectionately called "Big Phil." I can see him now, standing like a great pyramid in the midst of the little group, every now and then throwing his head back in good-natured abandon, recounting wild and fantastic tales about the fairies and banshees of the Old Land from whence he had come. When his listeners would turn away, with skepticism written all over their countenances, he would turn to me, whose youthful enthusiasm made me an easy victim upon which to work his magic spell in the stories which he told of the wonders of the Old Land across the sea.

I loved these delightful little gatherings in whose deliberations my dear father played so notable a part. Those kind folk, now off the stage, never allowed the spirit of provincialism to guide their judgment or their attitude toward great public affairs. I recall with pleasure their tolerance, their largeness of view, and fine magnanimity which raised every question they discussed to a high level. They were a very simple folk, but independent in their political actions and views. Into that little group of free, independent political thinkers would often come a warning from the Democratic boss of the city that they must follow with undivided allegiance the organization's dictum in political matters and not seek to lead opinion in the community in which they lived. Supremely indifferent were these fine old chaps to those warnings, and unmindful of political consequences. They felt that they had left behind them a land of oppression and they would not submit to tyrannous dictation in this free land of ours, no matter who sought to exert it.

In this political laboratory I came in contact with the raw materials of political life that, as an older man, I was soon to see moulded into political action in a larger

way in the years to come. I found in politics that the
great policies of a nation are simply the policies and passions of the ward extended. In the little discussions that
took place in that store, I was, even as a youth, looking
on from the side-lines, struck by the fine, wholesome,
generous spirit of my own father. Never would he permit, for instance, in the matter of the discussion of Ireland—so dear to his heart—a shade of resentment or
bitterness toward England to influence his judgment in
the least, for he believed that no man could be a just judge
in any matter where his mind was filled with passion; and
so in this matter, the subject of such fierce controversy,
as in every other, he held a judgment free and far away
from his passionate antagonisms. I found in the simple
life of the community where I was brought up the same
human things, in a small way, that I was subsequently
to come in contact with in a larger way in the whirligig
of political life in the Capitol of the Nation. I found the
same relative bigness and the same relative smallness,
the same petty jealousies and rivalries which manifest
themselves in the larger fields of a great nation's life;
the same good nature, and the same deep humanity expressing itself in the same way, only differently ap-
parelled.

One of the most interesting places in the world for the
study of human character is the country store or the city
grocery. I was able as a boy standing behind the counter
of the little grocery store to study people; and intimately
to become acquainted with them and their daily lives
and the lives of their women and children. I never came
in contact with their daily routine, their joys and sorrows,
their bitter actualities and deep tragedies, without feeling rise in me a desire to be of service. I remember many

years ago, seated hehind the counter of my father's
grocery store, with what passionate resentment I read the
vivid headlines of the metropolitan newspapers and the
ghastly accounts of the now famous Homestead Strike of
1892.   Of course, I came to realize in after years that
the headlines of a newspaper are not always in agreement
with the actual facts; but I do recall how intently I pored
over every detail of this tragic story of industrial war
and how, deep in my heart, I resented the efforts of a
capitalistic system that would use its power in this unjust, inhuman way.   Little did I realize as I pored over
the story of this tragedy in that far-off day that some
time, seated at my desk at the White House in the office
of the secretary to the President of the United States,
I would have the pleasure of meeting face to face the
leading actor in this lurid drama, Mr. Andrew Carnegie
himself, and of hearing from his own lips a human and
intelligent recital of the events which formed the interesting background of the Homestead Strike.

CHAPTER II

DOING THE POLITICAL CHORES

FOR the young man who wishes to rise in the politics of a great city there is no royal road to preferment but only a plain path of modest service uncomplainingly rendered. Of course, there seem to be exceptions to this rule. At times it is possible for the scion of a great family to rise to temporary distinction in politics without a preliminary course in the school of local politics, for as a Democratic boss once said to me: "Great family names are fine window-dressers," but in my own experience I have seen the disappointing end of careers thus begun and have found that sometimes after a great name has been temporarily used to meet certain political emergencies, the would-be politician is quickly thrust aside to make way for the less-pretentious but more capable man. There is nothing permanent or lasting about a place in politics gained in this adventitious way. Of course, there sometimes come to high office men from military careers, or men, like the distinguished subject of this book, from fields apparently remote from practical politics, but such successes are due to an appealing personal force, or to exceptional genius which the young aspirant had better not assume that he possesses. The general rule holds good that a political apprenticeship is as necessary and valuable as an industrial apprenticeship.

My first official connection with politics was as the

financial secretary of the Fifth Ward Democratic Club of
Jersey City.   My father had told me that if I intended to
play an active part in politics, it would be necessary to
begin modestly at the bottom of the ladder, to do the
political chores, as it were, which are a necessary part of
ward organization work.   I recall those days with singular pleasure, for my work gave me an unusual opportunity
to meet the privates in the ranks and to make friendships
that were permanent.

The meetings of the Club were held each week in a
modest club house, with part of the meeting given over
to addresses made by what were then considered the
leading men in the Democratic party.   It is queer how the
average political worker favours the senator, or the ex-
judge, or the ex-Congressman, as a speaker on these
occasions.   Ex-Congressman Gray, of Texas (I doubt
whether there ever was a congressman by that name),
would often be the headliner and he could be depended
upon to draw a crowded and enthusiastic house.   The
knowledge and experience I gained at these inspirational
meetings were mighty helpful to me in the political life
I had carved out for myself.   I found that when you had
convinced these plain, everyday fellows that, although
you were a college man, you were not necessarily a high-
brow, they were willing to serve you to the end.   It was a
valuable course in a great university.   It was not very
long until I was given my first opportunity, in 1896, to
make my first political speech in behalf of Mr. Bryan,
then the Democratic candidate for President.   I was not
able at that time to disentangle the intricacies of the
difficult money problems, but I endeavoured, imperfectly
at least, in the speeches I made, to lay my finger on what
I considered the great moral issue that lay behind the

silver question in that memorable campaign—the attempt by eastern financial interests to dominate the Government of the United States.

After my apprenticeship, begun as secretary of the Fifth Ward Democratic Club, an incident happened which caused a sudden rise in my political stock. At a county convention I was given the opportunity of making the nominating speech for the Fifth Ward's candidate for street and water commissioner—a bricklayer and a fine fellow—who was opposing the machine candidate. It was a real effort on my part and caused me days and nights of worry and preparation. Indeed, it seemed to me to be the great moment of my life. I vividly recall the incidents of what to me was a memorable occasion. I distinctly remember that on the night of the Convention, with the delegates from my ward, I faced an unfriendly and hostile audience, our candidate having aroused the opposition of the boss and his satellites. While I felt that the attitude of the Convention was one of opposition to our candidate, there was no evidence of unfriendliness or hostility to myself as the humble spokesman of the Fifth Ward. When I stood up to speak I realized that I had to "play up" to the spirit of generosity which is always latent in a crowd such as I was addressing. I believe I won, although my candidate, unfortunately, lost. My Irish buoyancy and good nature brought me over the line. I felt that the audience in the gallery and the delegates on the floor were with me, but unfortunately for my cause, the boss, who was always the dominating influence of the Convention, was against me, and so we lost in the spirited fight we made. In this first skirmish of my political career I made up my mind to meet defeat with good grace and, if possible, smilingly, and no sore spot or resentment over our defeat ever showed itself in my attitude toward the men who saw fit to oppose us. Evidently, the boss and his friends appreciated this attitude, for it was reported to me shortly after the Convention that I was to be given recognition and by the boss's orders would soon be placed on the eligible list for future consideration in connection with a place on the legislative ticket.

One lesson I learned was not to be embittered by defeat. Since then I have seen too many cases of men so disgruntled at being worsted in their first battles that their political careers ended when they should have been just beginning.

CHAPTER III

AFTER serving my apprenticeship as a ward worker, devoted friends from my home ward urged my name upon the Democratic leader, Mr. Robert Davis, for a place upon the Democratic legislative ticket for Hudson County. I had grown to have a deep regard and affection for this fine old fellow. While he was a boss in every sense, maintaining close relations with the Public Service Corporations of the state, he had an engaging human side. He never pretended nor deceived. With his friends he was open, frank, generous, and honourable in all his dealings, and especially kind to and considerate of the young men who became part of his working force. With his political enemies he was fair and decent. Many a time during a legislative session, when I was a member of the House of Assembly, word would come to us of the boss's desire that we should support this or that bill, behind which certain corporate interests lay. The orders, however, were clean and without a threat of any kind. He took no unfair advantage and made no reprisals when we failed to carry out his desires.

While a member of the New Jersey Legislature, the name of Woodrow Wilson began to be first discussed in the political world of New Jersey. It came about in this way: By reason of the normal Republican majority of the state the nomination by the Legislature in those days of a Democratic candidate for the United States senatorship was a mere compliment, a courtesy, a very meagre one indeed, and was generally paid to the old war horses of democracy like James E. Martine, of Plainfield, New Jersey; but the appearance of the doughty Colonel Harvey on the scene, at the 1907 session of the New Jersey Legislature, gave a new turn to this custom. A request was made by Colonel Harvey and diplomatically conveyed by his friends to the Democratic members of the Legislature, that the honorary nomination for the United States senatorship at this session of the Legislature should be given to President Wilson of Princeton. It may be added that I learned years afterward that Mr. Wilson was not a party to Colonel Harvey's plans; that once he even sent a friend as an emissary to explain to the Colonel that Mr. Wilson did not believe that the use of his name in connection with political office was a service to him or to Princeton University.

The suggestion that Woodrow Wilson be given the nomination was hotly resented by young men like myself in the Legislature. Frankly, I led the opposition to the man I was afterward to serve for eleven years in the capacity of private secretary. The basis of my opposition to Mr. Wilson for this empty honour was the rumour that had been industriously circulated in the state House and elsewhere, that there was, as Mr. Dooley says, "a plan afoot" by the big interests of New Jersey and New York to nominate Woodrow Wilson for the senatorship and then nominate him for governor of the state as a preliminary start for the Presidency. I remember now, with the deepest chagrin and regret, having bitterly assailed Woodrow Wilson's candidacy in a Democratic caucus which I attended and how I denounced him for his alleged opposition to labour. In view of my

subsequent intimacy with Mr. Wilson and the knowledge
gained of his great heart and his big vision in all matters
affecting labour, I cannot now point with pride to the
speech I then made attacking him.   I am sure the dear
doctor, away off in Princeton, never even heard of my
opposition to him, although in my conceit I thought the
state reverberated with the report of my unqualified and
bitter opposition to him.   In my poor vanity I thought
that perhaps what I had said in my speech of opposition
to him had reached the cloisters of Princeton.   As a matter of fact, he never heard about me or my speech, and
afterward in the years of our association he "joshed" me
about my opposition to him and would often make me
very uncomfortable by recounting to his friends at the
White House how even his own secretary had opposed
him when his name was first under consideration for
the United States senatorship in New Jersey.

To me was given the honour of nominating at a joint
session of the Senate and House Assembly the candidate
opposed to Woodrow Wilson for the Senate, the Honourable Edwin E. Stevens.   I recall the comparison I made
between the claims of Colonel Stevens, the strict party
man, and those of Woodrow Wilson, the Princeton professor.   The speech nominating Woodrow Wilson at
the joint session of the Legislature was the shortest on
record.   It was delivered by a big generous fellow, John
Baader, one of the Smith-Nugent men from Essex County.
When Essex County was called, he slowly rose to his feet
and almost shamefacedly addressing the Speaker of the
House, said, tremulously: "I nominate for the United
States Senate Woodrow Wilson, of Princeton," and
then, amid silence, sat down.   No applause greeted the
name of the man he nominated.   It seemed as if the col-

lege professor had no friends in the Legislature except the man who had put his name forward for the nomination.

Colonel Stevens won the honorary nomination and Woodrow Wilson was defeated. Colonel Harvey, disgruntled but not discouraged, packed up his kit and left on the next train for New York.

CHAPTER IV

COLONEL HARVEY ON THE SCENE

ALTHOUGH the intrepid Colonel Harvey was defeated in the first skirmish to advance the cause of Woodrow Wilson, he continued to pursue his purpose to force his personal choice upon the New Jersey Democracy. The approaching gubernatorial election in 1910 gave the Colonel his opportunity and he took full advantage of it.

Rumours began to circulate that the machine run by Davis, Smith, and Ross, the great Democratic triumvirate of the state, was determined to nominate the Princeton president at any cost. Young men like Mark Sullivan, John Treacy, and myself, all of Hudson County, representing the liberal wing of our party, were bitterly opposed to this effort. We suspected that the "Old Gang" was up to its old trick of foisting upon the Democrats of the state a tool which they could use for their own advantage, who, under the name of the Democratic party, would do the bidding of the corporate interests which had, under both the "regular" organizations, Democratic and Republican, found in New Jersey their most nutritious pastures. At a meeting held at the Lawyers' Club in New York, younger Democrats, like Judge Silzer of Middlesex and myself, "plighted our political troth" and pledged our undying opposition to the candidacy of the Princeton president. As a result of our conferences we set in motion the progressive machinery of the state in an in-

14

tensive effort to force the nomination of Judge Silzer in opposition to that of Woodrow Wilson.

As soon as the Democratic boss of Hudson County, Bob Davis, one of the leaders in the Wilson movement in North Jersey, was apprized of the proposed action on our part, he set about to head it off, and as part of his plan of opposition he sent for me in an effort to wean me away from the Silzer candidacy. I refused to yield. Upon being interrogated by me as to his interest in Woodrow Wilson, Boss Davis stated that if we nominated Woodrow Wilson there would be a big campaign fund put up for him by Moses Taylor Pyne, a trustee of Princeton University. Never before was the ignorance of a boss made more manifest. As a matter of fact, at that very time there was no more implacable foe of Woodrow Wilson in the state of New Jersey than Moses Taylor Pyne, who headed the opposition to Mr. Wilson in the Princeton fight.

Years after this incident the President and I often laughed at what must have been the surprise and discomfiture of Boss Davis when he finally learned the facts as to Moses Taylor Pyne's real feelings toward Woodrow Wilson. Previous to the gubernatorial campaign I asked Boss Davis if he thought Woodrow Wilson would make a good governor. His reply was characteristic of the point of view of the boss in dealing with these matters of moment to the people of the state. "How the hell do I know whether he'll make a good governor?" he replied; "he will make a good candidate, and that is the only thing that interests me."

Shortly after, those of us who banded together to oppose the bosses in their efforts to force Doctor Wilson upon us began to feel the pressure of the organization's influence. Many of our friends left us in despair and in fear of the power of the machine. The movement toward Woodrow Wilson in the state was soon in full swing. The Davis-Smith-Nugent-Ross machine was in fine working order on the day and the night of the Convention.

I was not even a delegate to the Convention, but I was present and kept in close touch by contact with my friends with every phase of the convention fight. Colonel Harvey was again on the scene as the generalissimo of the Wilson forces, quietly and stealthily moving about, lining up his forces for the memorable battle of the morrow. There was bitter but unorganized opposition to the favourite son of the state machine, Woodrow Wilson. The Convention itself presented an unusual situation and demonstrated more than anything I ever saw the power of the "Old Gang" to do the thing its masters had in mind. As I look back upon the great event of this convention, the nomination of Woodrow Wilson for the governorship of New Jersey, I feel that destiny was inscrutably engaged there, working in mysterious ways its wonders to perform, working perhaps through strange, incongruous instrumentalities to bring the man of destiny into action, led by those who were opposed to everything Woodrow Wilson stood for, opposed by those who were yearning for and striving for just the dawn of political liberalism that his advent in politics heralded. The conflict of the Trenton Convention about to be enacted was an illustration of the poet's line, "Where ignorant armies clash by night." The successful side of the Convention was fighting for what they least wanted; the defeated against what they most wanted. Here in this convention, in truth, were present in aggressive action the incongruities of politics

and in full display were witnessed the sardonic contrasts
between the visible and the invisible situations in politics.   All the Old Guard moving with Prussian precision
to the nomination of the man who was to destroy for a
time the machine rule in New Jersey and inaugurate a
new national era in political liberalism while all the
liberal elements of the state, including fine old Judge
Westcott of Camden and young men like myself were
sullen, helpless.   Every progressive Democrat in the
Convention was opposed to the nomination of the Princetonian, and every standpatter and Old Guardsman was
in favour of Woodrow Wilson.   On the convention floor,
dominating the whole affair, stood ex-Senator James
Smith, Jr., of New Jersey, the spokesman of the "high-
brow" candidate for governor, controlling the delegates
from south and west Jersey.   Handsome, cool, dignified,
he rose from the floor of the convention hall, and in rich,
low tones, seconded the nomination of the man "he had
never met," the man he would not "presume" to claim acquaintance with, the man whose life had lain in other
fields than his.   Very close to him, "taking his orders,"
and acting upon every suggestion that came to him, sat
Jim Nugent, grim, big-jawed, the giant full-back of
Smith's invincible team, the rising star of machine
politics in New Jersey.   Down the aisle sat the "Little
Napoleon" of Hudson County, Bob Davis, wearing a
sardonic smile on his usually placid face, with his big
eyes riveted upon those in the Convention who were
fighting desperately and against great odds the effort of
the state machine to nominate President Wilson.   Across
the aisle from me sat "Plank-Shad" Thompson, of Gloucester, big and debonair, a thoroughly fine fellow socially,
but always ready to act upon and carry out every tip that

came to him from the master minds in the Convention—
Davis and Smith.

These were the leading actors in this political drama.
Behind the lines, in the "offing," was the Insurgent
Group, young men like Mark Sullivan and John Treacy
of Hudson, stout defenders of the liberal wing in the
Convention, feeling sullen, beaten, and hopelessly impotent
against the mass attack of the machine forces. What a
political medley was present in this convention—plebeian
and patrician, machine man and political idealist—all
gathered together and fighting as leading characters and
supernumeraries in the political drama about to be
enacted.

Not three men outside of the leading actors in this
great political drama had ever seen the Princeton professor, although many had doubtless read his speeches.
I watched every move from the side-lines. The bosses,
with consummate precision, moved to the doing of the
job in hand, working their spell of threats and coercion
upon a beaten, sullen, spiritless body of delegates. One
could easily discern that there was no heart in the delegates for the job on hand. To them, the active forces in
the Convention, the Princeton president was, indeed, a
man of mystery. Who could solve the riddle of this
political Sphinx? Who was this man Wilson? What
were his purposes? What his ideals? These questions
were troubling and perplexing the delegates. Colonel
Harvey, the commander-in-chief of the Wilson forces,
when interrogated by us, refused to answer. How master-
fully the Old Guard staged every act of the drama, and
thus brought about the nomination of the Princeton
president. The Convention is at an end. Wilson has
been nominated by a narrow margin; the delegates,

bitter and resentful, are about to withdraw; the curtain is about to roll down on the last scene. The chairman, Mr. John R. Hardin, the distinguished lawyer of Essex, is about to announce the final vote, when the clerk of the Convention, in a tone of voice that reached every part of the hall, announces in a most dramatic fashion: "We have just received word that Mr. Wilson, the candidate for the governorship, *and the next President of the United States*, has received word of his nomination; has left Princeton, and is now on his way to the Convention." Excellent stage work. The voice of the secretary making this dramatic statement was the voice of Jacob, but the deft hand behind this clever move was that of Colonel Harvey. This announcement literally sets the Convention on fire. Bedlam breaks loose. The only sullen and indifferent ones in the hall are those of us who met defeat a few hours before. For us, at least, the mystery is about to be solved. The Princeton professor has left the shades of the University to enter the Elysian Fields of politics.

At the time the secretary's announcement was made I was in the rear of the convention hall, trying to become reconciled to our defeat. I then wended my weary way to the stage and stood close to the band, which was busy entertaining the crowd until the arrival of Mr. Wilson. I wanted to obtain what newspaper men call a "close-up" of this man of mystery.

What were my own feelings as I saw the candidate quietly walk to the speakers' stand? I was now to see almost face to face for the first time the man I had openly and bitterly denounced only a few hours before. What reaction of regret or pleasure did I experience as I beheld the vigorous, clean-cut, plainly garbed man, who now

stood before me, cool and smiling? My first reaction
of regret came when he uttered these words:

I feel the responsibility of the occasion. Responsibility is proportionate to opportunity. It is a great opportunity to serve the
State and Nation. I did not seek this nomination, I have made no
pledge and have given no promises. If elected, I am left absolutely
free to serve you with all singleness of purpose. It is a new era
when these things can be said, and in connection with this I feel that
the dominant idea of the moment is the responsibility of deserving.
I will have to serve the state very well in order to deserve the honour
of being at its head. . . .

Did you ever experience the elation of a great hope, that you
desire to do right because it is right and without thought of doing it
for your own interest? At that period your hopes are unselfish.

This in particular is a day of unselfish purpose for Democracy.
The country has been universally misled and the people have begun
to believe that there is something radically wrong. And now we
should make this era of hope one of realization through the Democratic party.

I had another reaction of regret when he said:
"Government is not a warfare of interests. We shall
not gain our ends by heat and bitterness." How simple
the man, how modest, how cultured! Attempting none
of the cheap "plays" of the old campaign orator, he
impressively proceeded with his thrilling speech, carrying
his audience with him under the spell of his eloquent
words. How tense the moment! His words, spoken
in tones so soft, so fine, in voice so well modulated, so
heart-stirring. Only a few sentences are uttered and our
souls are stirred to their very depths. It was not only what
he said, but the simple heart-stirring way in which he said
it. The great climax came when he uttered these moving
words: "The future is not for parties 'playing politics'
but for measures conceived in the largest spirit, pushed by

parties whose leaders are statesmen, not demagogues, who love not their offices but their duty and their opportunity for service. We are witnessing a renaissance of public spirit, a reawakening of sober public opinion, a revival of the power of the people, the beginning of an age of thoughtful reconstruction that makes our thoughts hark back to the age in which democracy was set up in America. With the new age we shall show a new spirit. We shall serve justice and candour and all things that make for the right. Is not our own party disciplined and made ready for this great task? Shall we not forget ourselves in making it the instrument of righteousness for the state and for the nation?"

After this climax there was a short pause. "Go on, go on," eagerly cried the crowd. The personal magnetism of the man, his winning smile, so frank and so sincere, the light of his gray eyes, the fine poise of his well-shaped head, the beautiful rhythm of his vigorous sentences, held the men in the Convention breathless under their mystic spell. Men all about me cried in a frenzy: "Thank God, at last, a leader has come!"

Then, the great ending. Turning to the flag that hung over the speakers' stand, he said, in words so impressive as to bring almost a sob from his hearers:

When I think of the flag which our ships carry, the only touch of colour about them, the only thing that moves as if it had a settled spirit in it—in their solid structure, it seems to me I see alternate strips of parchment upon which are written the rights of liberty and justice and strips of blood spilled to vindicate those rights and then— in the corner—a prediction of the blue serene into which every nation may swim which stands for these great things.

The speech is over. Around me there is a swirling mass of men whose hearts had been touched by the great speech which is just at an end. Men stood about me with tears streaming from their eyes. Realizing that they had just stood in the presence of greatness, it seemed as if they had been lifted out of the selfish miasma of politics, and, in the spirit of the Crusaders, were ready to dedicate themselves to the cause of liberating their state from the bondage of special interests.

As I turned to leave the convention hall there stood at my side old John Crandall, of Atlantic City, like myself a bitter, implacable foe of Woodrow Wilson, in the Convention. I watched him intently to see what effect the speech had had upon him. For a minute he was silent, as if in a dream, and then, drawing himself up to his full height, with a cynical smile on his face, waving his hat and cane in the air, and at the same time shaking his head in a self-accusing way, yelled at the top of his voice, "I am sixty-five years old, and still a damn fool!"

CHAPTER V

NO CAMPAIGN in New Jersey caused so great an interest as the gubernatorial campaign of 1910. The introduction of a Princeton professor into the political mêlée in New Jersey had given a novel touch to what ordinarily would have been a routine affair. The prologue to the great drama, the various scenes of which were now to unfold before the voters of the state, had been enacted at the Democratic Convention at Trenton under the masterly direction of the members of the Democratic Old Guard of the state. New Jersey had long been noted throughout the country as the "Mother of Trusts" and the nesting place of Privilege. Through their alliance and partnership with the political bosses of both parties the so-called corporate interests had been for many years successful, against the greatest pressure of public opinion, in blocking the passage of progressive legislation.

Liberal-minded men in the state had for many years been carrying on an agitation for the enactment into law of legislation that would make possible the following great needs:

1. The passage of a Direct Primary Act.
2. The passage of an Employers' Liability Act.
3. The regulation of Public Utilities.
4. The passage of a Corrupt Practices Act.

These were matters within the scope of state legislation, and to these was added an agitation for a fifth reform, which, of course, could be accomplished only through an amendment to the Constitution of the United States, the election of United States senators by vote of the people.

In the old days in New Jersey, now happily gone, the days when the granting of special corporation charters was the vogue, a sort of political suzerainty was set up by Railroad and Public Service interests. Every election was, in its last analysis, a solemn referendum upon the question as to which corporate interest should control legislation—whether the Pennsylvania Railroad, whose master mind was the Republican leader of the state, United States Senator Sewall, or the Public Service interests, whose votaries and friends were Senator Smith of New Jersey, and Milan Ross, Sr., of Middlesex County.

While these corporate interests fought among themselves over the matter of a United States senatorship or the governorship of a state, they were at one in their unrelenting, bitter, and highly organized opposition to the passage of what in this day we call by the highly dignified name of Social Welfare Legislation. The voices of those liberal-minded men and women of the state, who, year after year, fought for this legislation, were like voices crying in the wilderness. An illustration of corporate opposition was the unrelenting attitude of the Special Interest group of the state to the passage of the Employers' Liability Act. Every decent, progressive, humane man in the state felt that the old, barbaric, Fellow-Servant doctrine should be changed and that there should be substituted for it a more humane, wholesome, modern doctrine. Nearly every state in the Union had already recognized the injustice of the old rule, but the privileged interests in New Jersey could not be moved in their bitter

and implacable opposition to it, and for over half a century
they had succeeded in preventing its enactment into law.
Progressives or New Idea Republicans, high in the
councils of that party, had fought with their Democratic
brethren to pass this legislation, but always without
result. At last there came a revolt in the Republican
party, brought about and led by sturdy Republicans like
Everett Colby of Essex, and William P. Martin of the
same county; George Record and Mark M. Fagan of my
own county, Hudson. Out of this split came the establishment in the ranks of the Republican party itself of a
faction which called itself the New Idea branch of the
Republican party. The campaign for humane legislation
within the ranks of the G.O.P. was at last begun in real
fighting fashion. It was the irrepressible conflict between
the old and the new, between those who believed human
rights are superior to and take precedence over property
rights. The conflict could not be stayed; its leaders
could not be restrained. These men, Colby, Record,
Martin, and Fagan, were the sowers of the Progressive
seed which Woodrow Wilson, by his genius for leadership
and constructive action along humane lines, was soon to
harvest. His candidacy, therefore, admirably fitted into
the interesting situation.

When the convention that nominated Woodrow Wilson had adjourned, a convention wholly dominated by
reactionary bosses, it seemed as if progress and every fine
thing for which the Progressives had worked had been
put finally to sleep. Behind the selection of the Princetonian and his candidacy lay the Old Guard who thought
the Professor could be used as a shield for their strategy.
The Progressives, both Democratic and Republican, had
witnessed the scenes enacted at the Democratic Conven-

tion at Trenton with breaking hearts. They were about
to lose hope. They did not know that the candidate had
at the outset served notice on the Old Guard that if he
were nominated he must be a free man to do nobody's
bidding, to serve no interests except those of the people
of the state; but the Old Guard had not published this.

The Republican candidate, nominated at the time
Woodrow Wilson was selected, was a most pleasant,
kindly, genial man from Passaic, Mr. Vivian M. Lewis,
who had just retired as banking commissioner for the
state. By clever plays to the Progressives he had, at
least temporarily, brought together the various progressive elements of the state. This movement apparently was aided by the Democratic candidate's reluctance
in the early days of the campaign to speak out boldly
against the domination of the Democratic party by the
bosses or the Old Guard.

CHAPTER VI

SOMETHING NEW IN POLITICAL CAMPAIGNS

WOODROW WILSON opened his gubernatorial campaign with a speech in Jersey City, my home town. It was a distinct disappointment to those who attended the meeting. His speech in accepting the nomination had touched us deeply and had aroused in us great expectations, but after the Jersey City speech we were depressed in spirit, for it seemed to us that he was evading the real issues of the campaign. I was most anxious to meet the candidate and give him, if he invited it, my impressions of this speech. A dinner given to complete the ceremonies attendant upon the purchase of the Caldwell residence of Grover Cleveland gave me the first opportunity to meet the president of Princeton in an intimate way. Mr. Wilson's first wife, a most delightful woman, made the introduction possible. As I fondly look back upon this meeting, I vividly recall my impressions of the man who had just been nominated for the governorship of the state in a convention in which I had bitterly opposed him.

The democratic bearing of the man, his warmth of manner, charm, and kindly bearing were the first things that attracted me to him. There was no coldness or austerity about him, nor was he what the politicians would call "high-browish." He impressed me as a plain, unaffected, affable gentleman, who was most anxious to receive advice and suggestion from any quarter. He

made us doubly welcome by saying that he had heard
a great deal of favourable comment about the work of
Judge Sullivan and myself in the Legislature. This made
us feel perfectly at home, and this frank manner of dealing
with us opened the way for the suggestions we desired to
make to him as to the attitude we younger Democrats
thought he should assume on what we believed were the
vital, progressive issues of the campaign.

When he was informed that I was present at his first
meeting a few nights before in Jersey City, he came over
to me and in a most friendly way said: "What did you
really think of my speech?" For a moment I was embarrassed, and yet the frankness of the man was compelling and so I said: "Doctor, do you really desire an
honest opinion of that speech? I really want to
serve you but I can do so only by speaking frankly."
He replied: "That is what I most desire." "Well," I said,
"your speech was most disappointing." I stopped
suddenly, feeling that I had done enough damage to the
Professor's feelings. But he urged: "Please tell me what
your criticism is. What I most need is honesty and
frankness. You cannot hurt my feelings by truthfully
expressing your opinion. Don't forget that I am an
amateur at this game and need advice and guidance."
Encouraged by this suggestion, I proceeded to tell him
what I considered the principal defects of his opening
speech at Jersey City. I told him that there was a lack
of definiteness in it which gave rise to the impression that
he was trying to evade a discussion of the moral issues of
the campaign, among them, of major importance, being
the regulation of Public Utilities and the passage of an
Employers' Liability Act. Briefly sketching for him our
legislative situation, I gave him the facts with reference to

CORNISH, N. H.,
July 3, 1915

My dear Tumulty:

I am heartily obliged to you for
your telegrams. It is characteristic of you
to keep my mind free by such messages. I am
really having a most refreshing and rewarding
time and am very thankful to get it. I hope
that you are not having depressing weather in
Washington and that you are finding it possible
to make satisfactory arrangements for the family,
so that we can have the pleasure of having you
with us at the White House when I get back.

With warmest messages from us all,

Affectionately yours,

Woodrow Wilson

Hon. Joseph P. Tumulty,

Washington, D. C.

This letter reveals the warm personal relations between the President
and his secretary

those large measures of public interest; how, for many years, in face of constant agitation, the Old Guard had prevented the enactment of these measures into law, and how, therefore, his failure to discuss these matters in his first speech had caused a grave feeling of unrest in the progressive ranks of both parties in New Jersey.

He listened with keen attention and then modestly remarked: "I value very highly this tip and you may rest assured I shall cover these matters in my next speech. I meant that speech to be general."

In my ignorance of things past I did not know that the candidate had himself written the platform adopted by the Trenton Convention, and in my ignorance of the future I did not then know that one of the boldest and most remarkable political campaigns in America was to be conducted on that platform, and that after the election and inauguration of the nominee the chief business of the legislation was destined to be the enactment into law of each of the planks of the platform, a complete and itemized fulfilment of preëlection promises, unusual in the history of American politics. At the time of my first conversation with the nominee I only knew that the Convention had been dominated by the reactionary elements in the party, that under this domination it had stolen the thunder of the progressive elements of the party and of the New Idea Republicans, and that the platform had been practically ignored by the candidate in his first campaign speech. In these circumstances, and smarting as I was under the recollection of recent defeat, it is not strange that I thought I detected the old political ruse of dressing the wolf in sheep's clothing, of using handsome pledges as a mask to deceive the gullible, and that I assumed that this scholarly amateur in politics was being

used for their own purposes by masters and veterans in
the old game of thimblerig.

The candidate soon struck his gait and astonished me
and all New Jersey with the vigour, frankness, and
lucidity of his speeches of exposition and appeal. No
campaign in years in New Jersey had roused such universal interest. There was no mistaking the character and
enthusiasm of the greeting the candidate received every
place he spoke, nor the response his thrilling speeches
evoked all over the state. Those who had gathered the
idea that the head of the great university would appear
pedantic and stand stiff-necked upon an academic pedestal
from which he would talk over the heads of the common
people were forced, by the fighting, aggressive attitude of
the Doctor, to revise their old estimates. The campaign
had only begun when the leading newspapers of the
country, particularly the large dailies of New York, were
taking an interest in the New Jersey fight.

Those of us who doubted Woodrow Wilson's sincerity
and his sympathy for the great progressive measures for
which we had been fighting in the New Jersey Legislature
were soon put at ease by the developments of his campaign and his sympathetic attitude toward the things
we had so much at heart.

No candidate for governor in New Jersey had ever
made so striking and moving an appeal. Forgetting and
ignoring the old slogans and shibboleths, he appealed to
the hearts and consciences of the people of the state. His
homely illustrations evoked expressions of delight, until
it seemed as if this newcomer in the politics of our state
had a better knowledge of the psychology of the ordinary
crowd than the old stagers who had spent their lives in
politics. His illustrations always went home.

For instance, speaking of progress, Doctor Wilson said
that much depended upon the action of the one who is
supposed to be progressive. "I can recall," he would say in
trying to make his point, "the picture of a poor devil of a
donkey on a treadmill. He keeps on tramping, tramping,
tramping, but he never gets anywhere. But," he
continued, "there is a certain elephant that's tramping,
too, and how much progress is it making?" And then,
again, he would grow solemn when he spoke of the
average man. Turning aside from the humorous, he
would strike a serious note like this one:

You know that communities are not distinguished by exceptional
men. They are distinguished by the average of their citizenship.
. . . I often think of the poor man when he goes to vote: a moral
unit in his lonely dignity.

The deepest conviction and passion of my heart is that the common people, by which I mean all of us, are to be absolutely trusted.
The peculiarity of some representatives, particularly those of the
Republican party, is that when they talk about the people, they obviously do not include themselves. Now if, when you think of the
people, you are not thinking about yourself, then you do not belong
in America.

When I look back at the processes of history, when I look back
at the genesis of America, I see this written over every page, that the
nations are renewed from the bottom, not from the top; that the
genius which springs up from the ranks of unknown men is the genius
which renews the youth and the energy of the people; and in every
age of the world, where you stop the courses of the blood from the
roots, you injure the great, useful structure to the extent that at-
rophy, death, and decay are sure to ensue. This is the reason that an
hereditary monarchy does not work; that is the reason that an hereditary aristocracy does not work; that is the reason that everything
of that sort is full of corruption and ready to decay.

So I say that our challenge of to-day is to include in the partnership
all those great bodies of unnamed men who are going to produce our

future leaders and renew the future energies of America. And as I confess that, as I confess my belief in the common man, I know what I am saying. The man who is swimming against the stream knows the strength of it. The man who is in the mêlée knows what blows are being struck and what blood is being drawn. The man who is on the make is a judge of what is happening in America, not the man who has made; not the man who has emerged from the flood, not the man who is standing on the bank, looking on, but the man who is struggling for his life and for the lives of those who are dearer to him than himself. That is the man whose judgment will tell you what is going on in America, and that is the man by whose judgment I for one wish to be guided—so that as the tasks multiply and the days come when all will seem confusion and dismay, we may lift up our eyes to the hills out of these dark valleys where the crags of special privilege overshadow and darken our path, to where the sun gleams through the great passage in the broken cliffs, the sun of God, the sun meant to regenerate men, the sun meant to liberate them from their passion and despair and to lift us to those uplands which are the promised land of every man who desires liberty and achievement.

Speaking for the necessity of corporate reform in business, he said:

I am not objecting to the size of these corporations. Nothing is big enough to scare me. What I am objecting to is that the Government should give them exceptional advantages, which enables them to succeed and does not put them on the same footing as other people. I think those great touring cars, for example, which are labelled "Seeing New York," are too big for the streets. You have almost to walk around the block to get away from them, and size has a great deal to do with the trouble if you are trying to get out of the way. But I have no objection on that account to the ordinary automobile properly handled by a man of conscience who is also a gentleman. I have no objection to the size, power, and beauty of an automobile. I am interested, however, in the size and conscience of the men who handle them, and what I object to is that some corporation men are taking "joy-rides" in their corporations.

Time and time again men were reminded of the great speeches of Lincoln and thought they saw his fine spirit breathing through sentences like these:

Gentlemen, we are not working for to-day, we are not working for our own interest, we are all going to pass away. But think of what is involved. Here are the tradition, and the fame, and the prosperity, and the purity, and the peace of a great nation involved. For the time being we are that nation, but the generations that are behind us are pointing us forward to the path and saying:"Remember the great traditions of the American people," and all those unborn children that will constitute the generations that are ahead will look back to us, either at those who serve them or at those who betray them. Will any man in such circumstances think it worthy to stand and not try to do what is possible in so great a cause, to save a country, to purify a polity, to set up vast reforms which will increase the happiness of mankind? God forbid that I should either be daunted or turned away from a great task like this.

Speaking of the candidate who opposed him:

I have been informed that he has the best of me in looks. Now, it is not always the useful horse that is most beautiful. If I had a big load to be drawn some distance I should select one of those big, shaggy kinds of horses, not much for beauty but strong of pull.

On one occasion, when he had been talking about his and Mr. Lewis's different conceptions of the "constitutional governor", and telling his audience how he, if elected, would interpret the election as a mandate from the people to assist in and direct legislation in the interests of the people of New Jersey at large, he paused an instant and then in those incisive tones and with that compression of the lips which marked his more bellicose words, he said curtly: "If you don't want that kind of a governor, don't elect me."

Excerpts from the speeches cannot do justice to this remarkable campaign, which Woodrow Wilson himself, after he had been twice elected President of the United States, considered the most satisfying of his political campaigns, because the most systematic and basic. As Presidential candidate he had to cover a wide territory and touch only the high spots in the national issues, but in his gubernatorial campaign he spoke in every county of the state and in some counties several times, and his speeches grew out of each other and were connected with each other in a way that made them a popular treatise on self-government. He used no technical jargon and none of the stereotyped bombast of the usual political campaign. He had a theme which he wanted to expound to the people of New Jersey, which theme was the nature and character of free government, how it had been lost in New Jersey through the complicated involvements of invisible government, manipulated from behind the scenes by adroit representatives of the corporate interest working in conjunction with the old political machines; how under this clever manipulation legislators had ceased to represent the electorate and were, as he called them, only "errand boys" to do the bidding of the real rulers of New Jersey, many of whom were not even residents of the state, and how free government could be restored to New Jersey through responsible leadership. He was making an application to practical politics of the fundamental principles of responsible government which he had analyzed in his earlier writings, including the book on "Congressional Government." Beneath the concrete campaign issues in New Jersey he saw the fundamental principles of Magna Charta and the Bill of Rights and the Declaration of Independence and the Constitution of the

United States. His trained habit of thinking through concrete facts to basic principles was serving him well in this campaign; his trained habit of clear exposition in the Princeton lecture hall was serving him well. People heard from him political speaking of a new kind; full of weighty instruction and yet so simply phrased and so aptly illustrated that the simplest minded could follow the train of reasoning; profound in political philosophy and yet at every step humanized by one who believed government the most human of things because concerned with the happiness and welfare of individuals; sometimes he spoke in parables, homely anecdotes so applied that all could understand; sometimes he was caustic when he commented on the excessive zeal of corporations for strict constitutionalism, meaning thereby only such legislation and judicial interpretations as would defend their property rights—how they had secured those rights being a question not discussed by these gentlemen; sometimes, though not frequently, there would be purple patches of eloquence, particularly when descanting on the long struggle of the inarticulate masses for political representation. One of the surprises of the campaign to those who had known him as an orator of classic eloquence was the comparative infrequency of rhetorical periods. It was as if he were now too deeply engaged with actualities to chisel and polish his sentences. Of the many anecdotes which he told during the campaign one of his favourites was of the Irishman digging a cellar, who when asked what he was doing said: "I'm letting the darkness out." Woodrow Wilson told the people of New Jersey that he was "letting the darkness out" of the New Jersey political situation. "Pitiless publicity" was one of his many phrases coined in the campaign which quickly found currency, not only in New Jersey but throughout the country, for presently the United States at large began to realize that what was going on in New Jersey was symbolical of the situation throughout the country, a tremendous struggle to restore popular government to the people. Since the founders of the Republic expounded free institutions to the first electorates of this country there had probably been no political campaign which went so directly to the roots of free representative government and how to get it as that campaign which Woodrow Wilson conducted in New Jersey in the autumn of 1910.

CHAPTER VII

THE CRISIS OF THE CAMPAIGN

THE crisis of the campaign came when George L. Record, Progressive leader in the ranks of the Republican party in Hudson County, uttered a ringing challenge to the Democratic candidate to debate the issues of the campaign with him. The challenge contained an alternative proposition that the Democratic candidate either meet Mr. Record in joint debate in various parts of the state or that he answer certain questions with reference to the control of the Democratic party by what Mr. Record called the "Old Guard." Mr. Record's letter and challenge created a profound sensation throughout the state and brought hope and comfort to the ranks of the Republican party.

Record emphasized the Old Guard's control of the convention at which Wilson was nominated, basing most of his questions upon this character of political control, and openly challenging Wilson, the Democratic candidate, to say whether the elements that were dominant at Trenton in the Convention would be permitted by him, in case of his election, to influence his action as governor.

For several days after the letter containing the challenge reached the Democratic candidate, there was a great deal of apprehension in the ranks of the Democratic party lest the candidate should decide to ignore the Record challenge, thus giving aid and comfort to the enemies of progressivism in the state, or, on the other hand, that he would accept it and thus give Mr. Record, who was a most resourceful public speaker and a leading exponent of liberalism in the state, a chance to outwit him in public debate. The latter practically demanded of the Democratic candidate that he repudiate not only the Old Guard but the active management of his campaign which had been taken over by James R. Nugent, one of the leaders of Essex County, who daily accompanied the Democratic candidate on his tour of the state.

For a time it looked as if Doctor Wilson would ignore entirely the Record challenge. It was plainly evident from all sides that what appeared to be his reluctance to take a stand in the matter had turned support away at a time when the sentiment of the state was rapidly flowing his way.

I accompanied the candidate on an automobile tour of the state and in our little talks I sought to find out, in a diplomatic way, just how his mind was running on the Record challenge and how he intended to meet it. In the automobile with us on this tour was James R. Nugent, then the state chairman of the Democratic Committee. I ascertained that even he knew nothing about the Princetonian's attitude toward the Record challenge. A significant remark which the candidate dropped "between meetings" gave me the first intimation that the Democratic candidate was, to use a baseball expression, "on to the Record curve" and that he would answer him in so emphatic and overwhelming a fashion that the Republican campaign would never entirely recover from the blow.

One day while we were seated in the tonneau of the automobile discussing the Record challenge, Mr. Wilson pointed his finger at Jim Nugent and said, very significantly: "I intend to reply to Mr. Record, but I am sure that it will hurt the feelings of this fine fellow."

A few days later, without consulting any one, Mr. Wilson replied to Record's challenge. It was a definite, clean-cut, unequivocal repudiation of the Old Guard's control of the Democratic party, and a convincing answer to every question that had been put to him. It rang true. Old-line Republicans, after reading this conclusive reply, shook their heads and said, regretfully, "Damn Record; the campaign's over."

It was plainly evident that the crisis of the campaign had been safely passed and that Mr. Wilson was on his way to the governorship.

In his challenge Mr. Record had addressed to Doctor Wilson nineteen questions. Mr. Wilson's reply was in part as follows:

You wish to know what my relations would be with the Democrats whose power and influence you fear should I be elected governor, particularly in such important matters as appointments and the signing of bills, and I am very glad to tell you. If elected I shall not either in the matter of appointments to office, or assent to legislation, or in shaping any part of the policy of my administration, submit to the dictation of any person, or persons, "special interests," or organizations. I will always welcome advice and suggestions from any citizens, whether boss, leader, organization man, or plain citizen, and I shall confidently seek the advice of influential and disinterested men representative of the communities and disconnected from political organizations entirely; but all suggestions and all advice will be considered on its merits and no additional weight will be given to any man's advice because of his exercising, or supposing that he exercises, some sort of political influence or control. I should deem myself for ever disgraced should I, in even the slightest degree, coöperate in any such system. I regard myself as pledged to the regeneration of the Democratic party.

Mr. Record also inquired: "Do you admit that the boss system exists as I have described it?" "If so, how do you propose to abolish it?"

Mr. Wilson said:

Of course I admit it. Its existence is notorious. I have made it my business for many years to observe and understand that system, and I hate it as thoroughly as I understand it. You are quite right in saying that the system is bipartisan; that it constitutes "the most dangerous condition in the public life of our state and nation to-day"; and that it has virtually, for the time being, "destroyed representative government and in its place set up a government of privilege." I would propose to abolish it by the reforms suggested in the Democratic platform, by the election to office of men who will refuse to submit to it, and who will lend all their energies to break it up, and by pitiless publicity.

Still hoping to corner the Governor, Mr. Record named the bosses:

In referring to the Board of Guardians, do you mean such Republican leaders as Baird, Murphy, Kean, and Stokes? Wherein do the relations to the special interests of such leaders differ from the relation to the same interests of such Democratic leaders as Smith, Nugent, and Davis?

Mr. Wilson, answering this, said:

I refer to the men you name. They [meaning Baird, Murphy, Kean, Stokes] differ from the others in this, that they are in control of the government of the state while the others are not, and cannot be if the present Democratic ticket is elected.

In reply to Mr. Record's question: "Will you join me in denouncing the Democratic 'overlords' as parties to a political boss system?" Doctor Wilson replied: "Certainly I will join you in denouncing them—or any one of either party who attempts any outrages against the Government and public morality."

At this time I was in close touch with the managers of the Wilson campaign, including Smith, Nugent, and Davis. While they admired the fine strategy that lay back of the Democratic candidate's reply to Mr. Record, they looked upon it as a mere gesture upon the part of Mr. Wilson and scorned to believe that his reply to Mr. Record constituted a challenge to their leadership. They did not show any evidences of dismay or chagrin at the courageous attitude taken by Doctor Wilson. They simply smiled and shrugged their shoulders and said: "This is a great campaign play."

CHAPTER VIII

THE END OF THE CAMPAIGN

THE final meeting of the gubernatorial campaign was held in a large auditorium in Newark, New Jersey, where the last appeal was made by the Democratic candidate. It was a meeting filled with emotionalism such as I had never seen in a campaign before. The Democratic candidate, Woodrow Wilson, had covered every section of the state and it was easy for even the casual observer to note the rising tide in his favour. The campaign had, indeed, become a crusade; his eloquence and sledge-hammer blows at the opposition having cut our party lines asunder. I was present at the final meeting and took my place in the wings of the theatre or auditorium, alongside of Senator Smith, the Democratic chieftain who a few weeks before had, in a masterful fashion, manipulated the workings of the Convention at Trenton in such a way as to make the Doctor's nomination possible. Mr. Wilson's speech on this occasion was a profession of faith in the people, in the plain people, those "whose names never emerged into the headlines of newspapers." When he said in a delightful sort of banter to his audience, "I want you to take a sportsman's chance on me," there went up a shout of approval which could be heard as far as the hills of old Bergen.

The peroration of his final speech, spoken in a tone of

voice that seemed not only to reach every ear but, in fact, to touch every heart, was as follows:

We have begun a fight that, it may be, will take many a generation to complete, the fight against privilege; but you know that men are not put into this world to go the path of ease. They are put into this world to go the path of pain and struggle. No man would wish to sit idly by and lose the opportunity to take part in such a struggle. All through the centuries there has been this slow, painful struggle forward, forward, up, up, a little at a time, along the entire incline, the interminable way which leads to the perfection of force, to the real seat of justice and honour.

There are men who have fallen by the way; blood without stint has been shed; men have sacrificed everything in this sometimes blind, but always instinctive and constant struggle, and America has undertaken to lead the way; America has undertaken to be the haven of hope, the opportunity for all men.

Don't look forward too much. Don't look at the road ahead of you in dismay. Look at the road behind you. Don't you see how far up the hill we have come? Don't you see what those low and damp miasmatic levels were from which we have slowly led the way? Don't you see the rows of men come, not upon the lower level, but upon the upper, like the rays of the rising sun? Don't you see the light starting and don't you see the light illuminating all nations?

Don't you know that you are coming more and more into the beauty of its radiance? Don't you know that the past is for ever behind us, that we have passed many kinds of evils no longer possible, that we have achieved great ends and have almost seen their fruition in free America? Don't forget the road that you have trod, but, remembering it and looking back for reassurance, look forward with confidence and charity to your fellow men one at a time as you pass them along the road, and see those who are willing to lead you, and say, "We do not believe you know the whole road. We know that you are no prophet, we know that you are no seer, but we believe that you know the direction and are leading us in that direction, though it costs you your life, provided it does not cost you your honour."

And then trust your guides, imperfect as they are, and some day, when we all are dead, men will come and point at the distant upland with a great shout of joy and triumph and thank God that there were men who undertook to lead in the struggle. What difference does it make if we ourselves do not reach the uplands? We have given our lives to the enterprise. The world is made happier and humankind better because we have lived.

At the end of this memorable and touching speech old Senator James Smith, seated alongside of me, pulled me by the coat and, in a voice just above a whisper and with tears in his eyes, said: "That is a great man, Mr. Tumulty. He is destined for great things."

It did not seem possible on this memorable night that within a few days these two Democratic chieftains would be challenging each other and engaging in a desperate struggle to decide the question of Democratic leadership in the state.

CHAPTER IX

A PARTY SPLIT

ALL the prophecies and predictions of the political seers and philosophers of New Jersey, many of them of course feeling their own partisan pulse, were annihilated and set adrift by the happenings in New Jersey on the first Tuesday in November, 1910. Woodrow Wilson, college professor, man of mystery, political recluse, the nominee of the most standpat Democratic convention of many years, had been chosen the leader of the people of the state by the unprecedented majority of 39,000, and was wearing the laurels of victory. The old bosses and leaders chuckled and smiled; they were soon to have a Roman holiday under the aegis of the Wilson Administration.

There were many surprises in the Wilson victory. The Democrats awoke on the day after the election to find that they had not only won the governorship of the state, but their joy was unbounded to find that they had captured the Lower House of the Legislature that would have the election, under the preferential primary system just adopted, of a United States senator. Therein lay the fly in the ointment.

Never in their wildest dreams or vain imaginings did the leaders of the Democratic party believe that there was the slightest chance even under the most favourable circumstances of carrying a majority of the vote of the state for the Democratic choice, James E. Martine, of Plainfield.

The suggestion that it was possible to elect a Democrat to the United States Senate was considered a form of political heresy. The nomination for the Senate had been thrown about the state until torn and tattered almost beyond repair; it was finally taken up and salvaged by that sturdy old Democrat of Union County, Jim Martine. Even I had received the offer of the senatorial toga, but the one who brought the nomination to me was rudely cast out of my office. The question was: What would be the attitude of the new Democratic leader, Woodrow Wilson, toward the preferential choice, Martine? Would the vote at the election be considered as having the full virtue and vigour of a solemn referendum or was it to be considered as Senator Smith would have it, a sort of practical joke perpetrated upon the electors? Soon the opinion of the people of the state began to express itself in no uncertain way, demanding the carrying out of the "solemn covenant" of the election, only to be answered by the challenge of Senator Smith and his friends to enter the field against Martine, the choice at the election.

This business pitchforked the Governor-elect prematurely into the rough-and-tumble of "politics as she is," not always a dainty game. As I review in retrospect this famous chapter of state history, which, because of the subsequent supreme distinction of one of the parties to the contest, became a chapter in national history, I realize the almost pathetic situation of Mr. Wilson. He had called himself an amateur in politics, and such he was in the practical details and involutions of the great American game, though in his campaign he had shown himself a master of political debate. In the ordinary course of events he would have been allowed two months

between his election and inauguration to begin an orderly
adjustment to the new life, to make a gradual transition
from the comely proprieties of an academic chair to the
catch-as-catch-can methods of the political wrestling mat,
to get acquainted with the men and problems of the new
career. But the Smith-Martine affair gave birth prematurely to an immediate occasion for a fight.

As president of Princeton, Doctor Wilson had proved
that he was not averse to a fight when a fight was necessary
and when it was distinctly his affair, but he may well have
paused to consider whether the Smith-Martine business
was his affair. One of his favourite stories in later years
was of the Irishman who entered a saloon and seeing two
men in a tangle of fists and writhing legs and bloody heads
on the floor at the rear of the saloon, turned to the bar-
keeper and asked: "Is this a private fight, or can anybody
git into it?" A more politic man than Woodrow Wilson
and one less sensitive to moral duty, might well have argued that this contest was the business of the Legislature,
not of the Governor. Many a governor-elect would have
avoided the issue on this unquestionably sound legal
principle, and friends in Princeton were in fact advising
Mr. Wilson to precisely this course, the course of neutrality. It would not be strange if neutrality, aloofness,
had presented a rather attractive picture at times to Mr.
Wilson's mind. Why should he gratuitously take a
partisan position between the factions which would
inevitably win for him the enmity of a strong element
within the party? Which would also win for him the
unpleasant reputation of ingratitude? For though he
had at the first overtures from Senator Smith and his
friends made it as clear as language can make anything
that he could accept the nomination only with the

explicit understanding that acceptance should establish
no obligations of political favours to anybody, it would
be impossible to make it appear that opposition to Smith's
darling desire to become senator was not an ungracious
return to the man who had led the forces which had
nominated Wilson at Trenton.

On the other hand, there was his distinct pledge to the
people during his campaign, that if they elected him governor he would make himself the leader of the party, would
broadly and not with pettifogging legalism interpret his
constitutional relationship to the Legislature, would
undertake to assist in legislative action, and not wait
supinely for the Legislature to do something, and then
sign or veto the thing done. Moreover, he had insisted
on the principle of the preferential primary as one means
by which the people should participate in their own
government and convey an expression of their will and
purpose to the law-making body. The people had voted
for Martine. The fact that Senator Smith had scorned
to have his name placed on the ballot, the fact that human
imagination could picture a stronger senator from New
Jersey than genial "Jim" Martine did not affect the
argument. A great majority had voted for Martine
and for nobody else. Was the use of the preferential
primary for the first time in the selection of a United
States senator to be ignored, and all the arguments that
Candidate Wilson and others had made in behalf of the
system to be taken "in a Pickwickian sense," as not
meaning anything?

There was a real dilemma doubtless much more acutely
realized by the Governor-elect than by the hot-heads,
including myself, who were clamorous for an immediate
proclamation of support of Martine, on progressive

principles, and for an ultimatum of war-to-the-knife against Smith and the old crowd.

It seemed as if Mr. Wilson were hesitating and holding off, reluctant to accept the gage of battle thrown down by the challenge of the Smith wing. The leading Democratic and Independent journals of the state were most insistent that immediate proof be given by Governor-elect Wilson of his leadership and control over the party and that a test should be made as to which influence, reactionary or progressive, was to control the destinies of our party in the state. Those of us who had followed. the candidate throughout the campaign and who had been heartened by his progressive attitude were sorely disappointed at his failure immediately to act. It was painfully evident to us that behind the scenes at Princeton the new governor's friends, particularly Colonel Harvey, were urging upon him cautious and well-considered action and what mayhap might be called "a policy of watchful waiting," picturing to him the insurmountable difficulties that would lie in his path in case he exercised his leadership in the matter of Martine's selection to the United States Senate. They suggested that the vote for Martine had no binding force; that it was a mere perfunctory expression of preference in the matter of the United States senatorship which the Legislature was free to ignore. The only man, therefore, who could make the vote effective was the Governor-elect himself. What he would do in these circumstances was for days after the election a matter of perplexing doubt to his many friends. Disappointment and chagrin at the candidate's silence brooded over the ranks of the progressives of the state. In my law office in Jersey City I tried to convince those who came to confer with me regarding the matter that

they must be patient; that, ultimately, everything would
be all right and that Doctor Wilson would soon assert his
leadership over the party and take his proper place at the
head of those who worked to make the preferential vote
an effective instrumentality. Frankly, though I did not
give expression to my doubts, I was profoundly and deeply
disappointed at the apparently hesitant, uncertain attitude
of the Governor-elect. Feeling certain that popular opinion would be with him in case he decided to lead in this
struggle, I was convinced that the delay in announcing
his attitude toward the Smith-Nugent "defi" was dampen-
ing the ardour and enthusiasm of many of his friends.

The progressive Democrats of the state waited with
patience the word of command and counsel from the
Princeton professor to initiate the fight that would settle
for all time in the state of New Jersey the question
whether the referendum on the question of the election
of United States senators should be treated as "a scrap
of paper," or whether it was to be upheld and vindicated
by the action of the Legislature. No direct word came to
me of the Governor-elect's attitude on this vital question.
Rumours of his position toward Senator Smith's candidacy
filtered "through the lines" from Princeton; various
stories and intimations that seemed to indicate that the
Governor-elect would allow Martine's selection to go by
default; that he would not interfere in any way to carry
out the mandate of the election.

Things were in this unsatisfactory condition when to my
surprise I received a call in my modest Jersey City law
offices from the Governor-elect. Knowing him as I know
him, I can see that in his deliberate fashion he was taking
testimony from both sides and slowly arriving at his own
decision. Having heard from the cautious who counselled

neutrality, he was now seeking the arguments of the impetuous who demanded action and wanted it "hot off the bat." But at that time, not knowing him as I now know him, he seemed, in this interview, to be vacillating between two opinions, for he did what I have often known him to do subsequently: stated with lucidity the arguments of the other side, and with the air of one quite open-minded, without opinions of his own, seemed to seek my arguments in rebuttal. I was sorely disappointed by what then seemed to me his negative attitude, so unlike the militant debater whom I had come to admire in the campaign which had recently been brought to a brilliant and victorious close. In my youthful impetuosity I felt that we had been deceived in our man, a bold talker but timid in action. I simply did not then know the man and the mixed elements in him. Later, in close association, I was to see this phase of him not infrequently, the canny Scot, listening without comment and apparently with mind to let to conflicting arguments while his own mind was slowly moving to its own position, where it would stand fixed and immovable as Gibraltar.

Almost as if it were an academic question, with which he had no personal concern, he propounded the alternatives: Should he lead the fight against Senator Smith, or should he stand aloof and permit the Legislature to act without any suggestion from him? He summarized the arguments of his friends at Princeton who were advising him to steer clear of this fight and not permit himself to be drawn into it by young, impetuous people like myself. He said that certain overtures and suggestions of compromises had been made to him by Senator Smith's friends, to the effect that if he would not play a leading part in the fight and allow the Legislature to act without interference from him, Senator Smith and his friends in the state would agree not to oppose his legislative programme at the coming session. It was further suggested that Senator Smith had the necessary votes to elect himself and that it would be futile to attempt to elect Jim Martine; and that his intervention in this family quarrel would result in a bitter and humiliating defeat for him at the very outset of his administration. When the Governor-elect had concluded this preliminary statement, I was depressed and disappointed. I did not think there should be a moment's hesitation on his part in at once accepting the challenge so defiantly addressed to him by the Democratic bosses of the state.

Frankly, I laid the whole case before him in words to this effect: "My dear Doctor Wilson, there is no way I can better serve you than by frankly dealing with the question. Your friends away off in Princeton probably do not know how for years our party and its destinies have been in the hands of these very men, enemies of liberalism in New Jersey, who by your silence or indifference as to the United States senatorship are to be given a new lease on life. The issue involved in this fight is fundamental and goes far beyond the senatorship. The action you take will have a far-reaching effect upon our party's fortunes and no one can calculate the effect it will undoubtedly have on your own political future. In urging you not to take part in this fight your friends are acting unwisely. You cannot afford not to fight and not to have an immediate test of your leadership in this matter. The question of Mr. Martine's fitness, as your friends urge, is not an issue seriously to be considered. 47,454 votes in the state have decided that matter and you cannot reverse their verdict. Your friends have placed too much emphasis on Martine's alleged unfitness and too little on the duty you owe the party and the state as *leader*."

I called to his attention the fact that men like myself had been heartened and encouraged by his speeches in the campaign; how we felt that at last we had found in him a leader, bold and fearless, and that now, when the first real test of leadership came, it appeared that we were to be disappointed and that by his silence and inaction he would permit Senator Smith to win and allow Martine, the popular choice, to be defeated, thus setting aside the verdict of the election. He listened intently but without comment to all I had to say. Proceeding with my argument, I said: "The people of New Jersey accepted your word and, to employ your own phrase, 'took a sportsman's chance on you' and they must not be disappointed. Your failure to make this fight will mean that you have not only surrendered your leadership as governor in this matter, but by the same act you will have abdicated your leadership in favour of the Old Guard all along the line. They have set a trap for you, and I know you will not permit yourself to be caught in it." In conclusion I said: "They say they will support your reform programme. What assurance have you that, having defeated you in this your first big fight, they will not turn on you and defeat your whole legislative programme? As governor, you have the power to lead us to a great victory in this vital matter. Exercise it now, and opinion throughout the state will strongly and enthusiastically support you. You have but to announce your willingness to lead and the people of the state will rally to your standard. The fight, in any event, will be made and we wish you to lead it. This is really the first step to the Presidency. That is what is really involved. Not only the people of New Jersey but

the people of America are interested in this fight. They
are clamouring for leadership, and I am sure you are the
man to lead, and that you will not fail."

When the Governor-elect rose to leave my office, he
turned to me and asked, still in a non-committal manner,
whether in my opinion we could win the fight in case he
should decide to enter upon it. I at once assured him
that while the various political machines of the state
would oppose him at every turn, their so-called organizations were made of cardboard and that they would
immediately disintegrate and fall the moment he assumed
leadership and announced that the fight was on.

In his own time and by his own processes Mr. Wilson
arrived at his decision. It was the first of my many
experiences of his deliberative processes in making up his
mind and of the fire and granite in him after he had made
his decision. He informed me that he would support
Martine and use all his force, official and personal, to have
the Legislature accept the preferential primary as the
people's mandate.

With prudence and caution, with a political sense that
challenged the admiration of every practical politician in
the state, the Princetonian began to set the stage for the
preliminary test. There was nothing dramatic about
these preliminaries. Quickly assuming the offensive, he
went about the task of mobilizing his political forces in
the most patient, practical way. No statement to the
people of his purposes to accept the challenge of the
Democratic bosses was made by him. Certain things in
the way of accommodation were necessary to be done before
this definite step was taken. It was decided that until
the Governor-elect had conferred with the Democratic
bosses in an effort to persuade them that the course they

had adopted was wrong, it would be best not to make an immediate issue by the Governor-elect's announcement. We thought that by tactfully handling Smith and Davis we would be able by this method of conciliation to convince their friends, at least those in the party organization, that we were not ruthlessly bent upon leading a revolt, but that we were attempting peacefully a settlement that would prevent a split in our party ranks.

We were convinced that in the great body of organization Democrats there were many fine men who resented this attempt of the bosses to force Jim Smith again on the party and that there were many who silently wished us success, although they were not free to come to our side in open espousal. Thus we began patiently to build our back-fire in the ranks of the Democratic organization itself, to unhorse the Essex boss.

The first thing to carry out the programme was a visit paid to the sick room of the Democratic boss of the Hudson wing, Bob Davis, who lay dangerously ill in his modest home on Grove Street, Jersey City. The visit itself of the Governor-elect to the home of the stricken boss had a marked psychological effect in conciliating and winning over to our side the active party workers in the Davis machine. To many of the privates in the ranks the boss was a veritable hero and they witnessed with pleasure the personal visit of the new Governor-elect to the boss at his home and looked upon it as a genuine act of obeisance and deference to their stricken leader. They thought this a generous and a big thing to do, and so it naturally turned their sympathies to the Governor-elect. It gave further proof to them that the man elected Governor was not "high-browish" or inclined to fight unless he had previously laid all his cards on the table. We also

realized that to have ignored the boss would have been
to give strength and comfort to the enemy, and so we
deliberately set out to cultivate his friends in a spirit of
honourable and frank dealing. The visit to the boss was
a part of this plan. The meeting between these two men
—one, the Governor-elect and until recently the president of Princeton; the other, a Democratic boss, old and
battle-scarred—in the little sick room of the humble
home, was a most interesting affair and at times a most
touching and pathetic one. Both men were frank in
dealing with each other. There was no formality or coldness in the meeting. The Governor-elect quickly placed
the whole situation before the boss, showing how the
Democratic party had for many years advocated the very
system—the election of United States senators by the
people—that the Democratic bosses of the state were
now attacking and repudiating. Briefly, he sketched
the disastrous effects upon our party and its prestige in
the state and the nation if a Democratic legislature should
be the first, after advocating it, to cast it aside in order to
satisfy the selfish ambition and vanity of one of the Old
Guard. In a sincere manly fashion, so characteristic
of him, Boss Davis then proceeded to state *his* case.
Briefly, it was this: He had given his solemn promise
and had entered into a gentleman's agreement with Smith
to deliver to him the twelve legislative votes from Hudson.
He would not violate his agreement. Laughingly, he
said to the Governor-elect: "If the Pope of Rome, of
whose Church I am a member, should come to this room
to urge me to change my attitude, I would refuse to do so.
I have given my promise and you would not have me
break it, would you, Doctor?" With real feeling and a
show of appreciation of the boss's frankness and loyalty

to his friends, the Governor-elect quickly replied: "Of course, I would not have you break your promise, but you must not feel aggrieved if I shall find it necessary to fight you and Smith in the open for the Hudson votes." "Go on, Doctor," said the sick man, "I am a game sport and I am sure that with you there will be no hitting below the belt." And thus the first conference between the Governor-elect and the political boss ended.

Mr. Wilson's next visit was to Senator Smith himself at the Senator's home in Newark, a meeting entirely friendly in character and frank in expressions of the unalterable determination of the two men, of Senator Smith not to withdraw from the race, of Doctor Wilson to oppose his candidacy and place the issue before the people of the state. Senator Smith with engaging candour gave Mr. Wilson his strong personal reasons for wishing to return to the United States Senate: he said that he had left the Senate under a cloud due to the investigations of the Sugar Trust and that for the sake of his children he wanted to reinstate himself in the Senate. Mr. Wilson expressed his sympathy for this motive, more appealing than mere personal ambition, but declared that he could not permit his sympathy as an individual to interfere with his duty as he conceived it, as an official pledged by all his public utterances to support progressive principles, among which was the preferential primary system, and committed to a course of active leadership in matters which concerned the state at large, in which category the selection of a United States senator certainly fell. He made a personal appeal to the Senator for the sake of the party to forego his desire and by a noble act of renunciation to win the regard of all the citizens of the state, saying: "Why, Senator, you have it in your power to become

instantly the biggest man in the state." But the Senator
was firm. And so, though the visit was conducted with
the dignity and courtesy characteristic of both men, it
ended with their frank acknowledgment to each other
that from now on there existed between them a state of
war.

Returning to Princeton from Newark, the formal
announcement of the Governor's entrance into the fight
was made and the contest for the senatorship and the
leadership of the Democratic party was on. The announcement was as follows:

WOODROW WILSON'S CHALLENGE TO THE BOSSES
Friday Evening, Dec. 9, 1910.

The question who should be chosen by the incoming legislature of
the state to occupy the seat in the Senate of the United States
which will presently be made vacant by the expiration of the term
of Mr. Kean is of such vital importance to the people of the
state, both as a question of political good faith and as a question of
genuine representation in the Senate, that I feel constrained to express my own opinion with regard to it in terms which cannot be
misunderstood. I had hoped that it would not be necessary for me
to speak; but it is.

I realize the delicacy of taking any part in the discussion of the
matter. As Governor of New Jersey I shall have no part in the choice
of a Senator. Legally speaking, it is not my duty even to give
advice with regard to the choice. But there are other duties besides
legal duties. The recent campaign has put me in an unusual position.
I offered, if elected, to be the political spokesman and adviser of
the people. I even asked those who did not care to make their
choice of governor upon that understanding not to vote for me.
I believe that the choice was made upon that undertaking; and I
cannot escape the responsibility involved. I have no desire to escape
it. It is my duty to say, with a full sense of the peculiar responsibility of my position, what I deem it to be the obligation of the Legislature to do in this gravely important matter.

I know that the people of New Jersey do not desire Mr. James Smith, Jr., to be sent again to the Senate. If he should be, he will not go as their representative. The only means I have of knowing whom they do desire to represent them is the vote at the recent primaries, where 48,000 Democratic voters, a majority of the whole number who voted at the primaries, declared their preference for Mr. Martine, of Union County. For me that vote is conclusive. I think it should be for every member of the Legislature.

Absolute good faith in dealing with the people, an unhesitating fidelity to every principle avowed, is the highest law of political morality under a constitutional government. The Democratic party has been given a majority in the Legislature; the Democratic voters of the state have expressed their preference under a law advocated and supported by the opinion of their party, declared alike in platforms and in enacted law. It is clearly the duty of every Democratic legislator who would keep faith with the law of the state with the avowed principles of his party to vote for Mr. Martine. It is my duty to advocate his election—to urge it by every honourable means at my command.

Immediately the work of organizing our forces for the fight was set in motion. I had been designated by the Governor-elect to handle the fight in Hudson County, the Davis stronghold. Meetings were arranged for at what were considered the strategic points in the fight: Jersey City and Newark. The announcement of the Governor-elect's acceptance of the challenge had given a thrill to the whole state and immediately the reaction against the Old Guard's attempt to discredit the primary choice was evident. The bitterness in the ranks of the contesting factions began to express itself in charges and counter-charges that were made. Speeches for and against the candidates were addressed to the ears of the unwary voter. The state was soon up in arms. There was no doubt of the attitude of the people. This was made plain in so many ways that our task was to impress

this opinion upon the members of the Legislature, whose
vote, in the last analysis, would be the determining factor
in this contest. While we were laying down a barrage
in the way of organization work and making preparations
for our meetings throughout the state, the Governor-
elect was conferring nightly with members of the Legislature at the University Club in New York. From day to
day could be observed the rising tide in favour of our
cause, and slowly its effect upon the members of the
Legislature was made manifest. The first meeting in the
senatorial contest was held in Jersey City. As chairman
of the committee, I had arranged the details for this
first speech of the Governor-elect. I had adopted a
plan in making the arrangements that I felt would remove
from the minds of the organization workers, to whom we
desired to appeal, the idea that this was a revolt or
secessionist movement in the ranks of the Democratic
party. The committee in charge of the meeting had
selected the finest, cleanest men in our party's ranks to
preside over and take part in the meeting.

There was never such an outpouring of people. Men
and women from outside the state, and, particularly, men
and women from New York and Connecticut, had come
all the way to New Jersey to witness this first skirmish in
the political upheaval that was soon to take place. The
metropolitan dailies had sent their best men to write up
the story and to give a "size-up" of the new Governor-
elect in fighting action. They were not disappointed.
He was in rare form. His speech was filled with epigrams
that carried the fight home to those upon whom we
were trying to make an impression. When he warned
his friends not to be afraid of the machine which the
bosses controlled he said, with biting irony: "We do

not fear their fortresses [meaning the political machines] that frown and look down upon us from their shining heights." Smiling deprecatingly and waving his hand, he continued: "They are but made of paste-board and when you approach them they fall at your very touch."

Ridiculing and belittling the power of the bosses, he called them "warts upon the body politic." "It is not," said the new chief of Democracy, "a capital process to cut off a wart. You don't have to go to the hospital and take an anæsthetic. The thing can be done while you wait, and it is being done. The clinic is open, and every man can witness the operation."

The meeting was a triumph and strikingly demonstrated the power of brain and fine leadership over brawn and selfish politics.

The final appeal to the voters on the United States senatorship was made in the heart of the enemy's country, the stronghold of the Smith-Nugent faction at Newark, New Jersey. The same enthusiastic, whole-souled response that characterized the Jersey City meeting was repeated. The same defiant challenge to the Old Guard was uttered by the new Governor. Sarcasm, bitter irony, delightful humour, and good-natured flings at the Old Guard were found in this his final appeal. In a tone of voice that carried the deep emotion he felt, he said, as his final word:

Do you know what is true of the special interests at this moment? They have got all their baggage packed and they are ready to strike camp over night, provided they think it is profitable for them to come over to the Democratic party. They are waiting to come over bag and baggage and take possession of the Democratic party. Will they be welcome? Do you want them? I pray God we may never wake up some fine morning and find them encamped on our side.

The response was thrilling. The two meetings just held, one in Jersey City and the other in Newark, convinced those of us in charge of the Martine campaign that we had made the right impression in the state and, having deeply aroused the voters, all we had to do was to harvest the crop, the seed of which had been planted in the soil of public opinion by the speeches the new Governor had made. It was plain that the machine crowd was stunned and reeling from the frequent and telling blows that had been so vigorously delivered by him. Suggestions of compromise came from the enemy's ranks, but no armistice would be granted, except upon the basis of an absolute and unconditional surrender. Offers and suggested proposals from the Old Guard to the Governor-elect were thrust aside as valueless and not worthy his consideration. There was nothing to do but play for a "knock-out." Soon the full pressure of the opinion of the state began to be felt. Members of the Legislature from the various counties began to feel its influence upon them. Our ranks began to be strengthened by additions from the other side. The Governor's speeches and his nightly conferences were having their full effect. The bosses, now in panic, were each day borne down by the news brought to them of the innumerable defections in their quickly dwindling forces. However, the bosses showed a bold front and declared that their man had the votes. But their confidence waned as election day approached. Realizing the fact that we were dealing with the best-trained minds in the Democratic party, we gave no news to the outside world of the strength in number of our own ranks, knowing full well that if we did so imprudent a thing, the active men in the ranks of the enemy would pull every wire of influence and use every method of threats and coercion to wean the votes away from us. We "stood pat" and watched with interest every move made by the other side. In his final statement before the joint meeting of the Legislature Smith boldly announced his election to the Senate on the strength of the number of legislative votes pledged to him, but those of us who were in the midst of this political mêlée knew that he was licked and that he was only whistling to keep up his courage.

In the meantime, the Governor-elect had tendered to me the post of secretary to the Governor, and I accepted this office which brought me into more intimate association with him and his plans.

CHAPTER X

THE conferences and meetings in preparation for the great senatorial fight having been concluded, the scene of activities was transferred to Trenton, where shortly after the Inauguration plans were laid for the final battle.

Immediately upon the conclusion of the Inaugural ceremonies, the hand-to-hand contests for the great prize and incidentally the leadership of the Democrats, was on in full swing. At the beginning of the fight the bosses counted upon the active support of the influential Democratic leaders throughout the state, like Robert S. Hudspeth of Hudson County, Johnston Cornish of Warren County, Edward E. Grosscup of Gloucester County, Barney Gannon and Peter Daley of Middlesex County, old Doctor Barber of Warren County, Otto Wittpenn of Hudson County, Billy French and Judge Westcott of Camden, Dave Crater of Monmouth, and minor bosses or leaders in south and middle Jersey. But in utter amazement they found that we had captured these fine pieces of heavy political artillery and that through them we had acquired and taken over some of the most valuable political salients in the state.

A little incident in the campaign is worth reciting. In managing the campaign I found that for some unaccountable reason the so-called Irish vote of the state was massed solidly behind ex-Senator Smith and in bitter opposition to Governor Wilson. We were constantly coming in contact with these currents of opposition, and how to overcome them and bring the Irish vote into our fold was the task that devolved upon me as the manager of Martine's campaign. Seated in my office one day I recalled that years before I had read in the *Congressional Record* an account of a speech delivered in the United States Senate by James Smith, upholding in terms of highest praise the famous Hay-Pauncefote Treaty. The speech in all its details, particularly the argument it contained calling for closer relations between the United States and Great Britain, was still fresh in my memory. Evidently Senator Smith and his Irish friends had forgotten it, for he was now trying to mobilize the Irish vote of the state in his favour. On re-reading this speech of the old Senator, I smiled with satisfaction, realizing the campaign use that could be made of it. After considering the matter carefully, I sent for a devoted friend of mine, a fine, clean-cut Irishman, who stood high in the ranks of the Clan-na-Gael and other Irish societies in our county. After he had read the speech, we discussed the method of using it, for we felt sure that our Irish friends, when they became acquainted with this speech upon reading it, would not find themselves in agreement with Smith's attitude toward England and the Treaty. My friend consented to write letters to the leading papers, particularly the Irish papers of the state, setting forth Smith's attitude toward the Treaty. The effect upon the Irish vote was immediate and soon resolutions began to be adopted by the various Irish societies throughout the state, denouncing Smith for having advocated the much-despised "Anglo-Saxon Alliance."

While I opposed Senator Smith in this contest there was nothing personally antagonistic in my attitude. We were, I hope, friends throughout the conflict, and many times since then we have discussed the events leading up to Martine's election to the United States Senate. It was only a few months ago, while seated at a table at the Shoreham Hotel in Washington, that the old Senator, genial and debonair as ever, was discussing the fights of the old days, and particularly the events leading up to his defeat for the United States senatorship. In discussing the New Jersey campaign, he told me of the use that had been made by "someone" in the Wilson ranks of his Senate speech on the Hay-Pauncefote Treaty. He said that his reason for making this speech was his sincere desire as an Irish-American to bring about more amicable relations between the United States and England, and as I listened to this frank recital I felt that, although the use I had made of his speech was legitimate in the circumstances, there was nothing to be proud of in having exploited the Senator's really fine speech for political purposes.

The State House at Trenton on the night previous to the balloting for the senatorship was a place of feverish activity. The Essex ex-Chieftain, Smith, kept "open house" in the then famous Room 100 of the Trenton House. The Governor-elect, calm and apparently undisturbed, but anxious and ready for a contest, quietly moved about the Executive offices attending to official matters.

We felt confident of the result of the vote if the members of the Legislature were left free, but we were certain that every kind of pressure would be put upon them to change the votes of the wobblers in our ranks. All night long and until four or five o'clock in the morning the Governor-elect and I remained in the Executive office, keeping in close contact with our friends both by telephone and

personal conference. Senator Smith never knew it, but
some of the men close to him and participating in his own
conferences on this fateful night hourly brought to us
information as to what would be the real line-up of his
forces on the day set for balloting. We found a spy in our
own ranks—a leading lawyer and politician from my own
county—who, while pretending to be our friend, was
supplying the enemy with what he thought was useful
information. We, however, were already aware of this
gentleman's duplicity and, although he never suspected
it, whenever he left the Executive office he was followed
by a professional detective, who heard and reported to us
every bit of information he had supplied to our political
foes.

On the night before the election the Smith-Nugent
leaders had gathered their forces and, headed by a band,
paraded through the streets of Trenton, passing in review
before Senator Smith who stood upon the steps of the
Trenton House and greeted them in most generous
fashion. The purpose of this demonstration was obvious
to the Governor-elect and his friends. It was simply to
give to the arriving legislators an impression of great
strength behind the Smith-Nugent forces.

On the morning of the balloting the corridors and lobby
of the State House were crowded with the henchmen of
the Essex chieftain. The surface indications were that
Smith had the necessary number of votes, but to those of
us who were able accurately to analyze the situation it
was apparent that the froth would soon pass away. The
parade and the demonstration of the Nugent followers had
deeply impressed some of the men in our ranks, particularly the editor of a Trenton newspaper, who came to the
Executive offices and urged upon the Governor the

publication of a statement which he had prepared, filled
with grandiloquent phrase, warning the people of the
state that the members of the Legislature were about to
be coerced and threatened by the strong-arm methods of
the Smith-Nugent organization.

Frankly, the suggestion which this Trenton editor made
to the new Governor impressed him. The Governor made
certain changes in the statement and then sent for me to
read it, asking my advice upon it. The first test of my
official connection with the Governor was at hand. Upon
reading the editor's article I saw at once that its issuance
would be most unwise, and I frankly said so. My
practical and political objection to it, however, was that
if published it would give to the people of the state the
impression that our forces were in a panic and that we
were in grave fear of the result. I further argued that it
was an attempt at executive coercion of the Legislature
that would meet with bitter resentment. I felt that we
had already won the fight; that the Legislature, which
was the jury in the case, was inclined to favour us if
we did not seek to influence its members by such foolish
action as the Trenton editor advised. The statement
was not published.

I found in this little argument with the new Governor
that he was open-minded and anxious for advice and I
thereafter felt free to discuss matters with him in the
frankest way.

The first ballot showed Martine leading heavily. In
the following ballots he gained strength at every count.
The Legislature adjourned the first day without reaching
a decision. As we surveyed the field after the first day's
balloting it was clear to us that if we hoped to win the
fight we would have to have Hudson County's legislative

vote. The Democratic boss, Bob Davis, had died a few
days previous, and had entrusted his affairs to the hands
of a fine, clean-cut, wholesome Irish-American, James
Hennessy, then chairman of the Hudson County Demc-
cratic Committee. He was one of the squarest men I
ever met in politics and had been an intimate associate of
my father in the old days in Jersey City. On the day of
the final balloting we were sorely pressed. When it
seemed as if we had reached the limit of our strength, it
occurred to me that a final appeal to Hennessy by the
Governor might have some effect. We decided to send
for Hennessy to come to the Executive offices. It was
clear from his attitude when he arrived that, while his
sympathies lay with us, he was bound in honour to carry
out the instructions of his chief and deliver the Hudson
County vote to Smith. The Governor, getting very
close to him and discussing the campaign in the most
intimate way, told him that if Martine was rejected, the
political effect on our party's fortunes would be disastrous;
that we were sure we had the votes and that the next
ballot would give proof of this, and that it was only a
question, to use a campaign phrase, of "getting on the
band wagon" and making Martine's nomination unanimous. When the Governor concluded his talk, I turned
to Hennessy in the most familiar way, and spoke of the
Governor's desire to elect Martine and of the unselfish
purpose he had in mind and how he, Hennessy, was blocking the way. I said to him: "You have it in your power
to do a big thing. You may never have the chance
again." He finally stood up and said to me: "What
do you want me to do?" I told him that we wanted
him to go to the Hudson delegates and give word that
the "jig" was up and that they must throw their

support to Martine. Shortly after this meeting the Hudson delegation met in caucus and agreed to support Martine,

When Smith and Nugent heard of this message they practically surrendered. The balloting which began at ten o'clock was a mere formal affair for it was plainly evident from the changes in the early balloting that Martine's election was assured. Martine's election was a fact; and Woodrow Wilson was the victor in the first battle for the Presidency.

I have stated that I am not proud of the way I used Senator Smith's speech on the Hay-Pauncefote Treaty. We were fighting veterans in the political game, men who knew all the tricks and who did not scruple to play any of them. In the rough school of practical politics I had been taught that "you must fight the devil with fire" and that it is as legitimate in politics as in war to deceive the enemy about your resources. But we conducted politics on higher levels during the eight years in the White House, when my chief, no longer an amateur, taught me, by precept and example, that effective fighting can be conducted without resort to the tricks and duplicities of those who place political advantage above principle. Woodrow Wilson made new rules for the game, and they were the rules which men of honour adopt when conducting their private business on principles of good faith and truth-telling.

CHAPTER XI

THE election of Martine having been settled and the preferential vote having been validated through the courageous handling of a delicate situation, the new Governor was firmly in the saddle. His leadership had been tested and only the fragments of the Old Guard machine were left. The road was thus cleared of all obstacles in his own party that might be put in the way of his programme of constructive legislation.

Having delivered his first message, which contained a full and detailed discussion of his whole programme, he applied himself with great energy and industry to the task of preparing bills for introduction in the Senate and House. Not content with the mere delivery of his message, he put himself entirely at the disposal of the members of the Legislature and industriously applied himself to the task of preparation until the following measures: *Regulation of Public Utilities, Corrupt Practices Act, Direct Primaries Act,* and the *Employers' Liability Act,* were in shape to be introduced.

While his leadership was vindicated as a result of the Smith-Martine fight, the contest had undoubtedly left many bitter scars and enmities which soon manifested themselves in the unfriendly attitude of the Smith men in the Legislature toward the new Governor and particularly toward his programme of constructive legislation. For awhile after the election of Martine they seemed subdued and cheerfully resigned to defeat; but when the new Governor launched his legislative programme they began eagerly to attack it in many subtle ways. While there were some members of this group who honestly opposed the Governor's programme because of their conservative tendencies, the majority of the opposition were bent upon "putting it to sleep," because, forsooth, it bore the Wilson label. The new Governor quickly grasped the full significance of the situation and openly challenged the opposition. To accomplish his purpose, he did an unprecedented thing. He invited the Democratic members of the Legislature to meet him in the Supreme Court Room of the State House and there, face to face, he laid before them various items of his programme and challenged the opposition to lay their cards on the table. In the course of this conference one of the leaders of the Smith-Nugent faction expressed his dissatisfaction with the whole programme, challenging the new Governor's right to be present at the conference; even intimating that his presence was an unconstitutional act which might subject him to impeachment. The new Governor, undisturbed by this criticism, turned to the gentleman who had challenged his right to be present at the conference, and said:

You can turn aside from the measure if you choose; you can decline to follow me; you can deprive me of office and turn away from me, but you cannot deprive me of power so long as I steadfastly stand for what I believe to be the interests and legitimate demands of the people themselves. I beg you to remember, in this which promises to be an historic conference, you are settling the question of the power or impotence, the distinction or the ignominy of the party to which the people with singular generosity have offered the conduct of their affairs

Some of the members of the Legislature came to my
office after this conference and told me of the great speech
the Governor had just delivered and how defiantly he had
met the attack of his enemies. This caucus gave an
emphatic endorsement of his legislative programme and
in a few weeks the House of Assembly had acted
upon it, and the various bills that constituted his
entire programme were on their way to the Republican
Senate. How to induce favourable action at the hands
of the Republican Senate was a problem. There were
very few members of the Senate whose ideals and purposes
were in agreement with those of the Governor.

When the bills reached the Senate, the Governor began
daily conferences with the Republican members of that
body, discussing with them the items of his programme
and urging speedy action upon them. As a part of the
programme of inducing the Republicans to support him, a
friend of mine who was on the inside of the Republican
situation reported to me that it was the opinion in the
Republican ranks that the new Governor was too much
a professor and doctrinaire; that he was lacking in good-
fellowship and companionship; that while the members
of the Legislature who had conferred with him had found
him open and frank, they thought there was a coldness
and an austerity about him which held the Governor
aloof and prevented that intimate contact that was
so necessary in working out the programme we had outlined.

We finally decided that the fault lay in the lack of
social intimacy between the new Governor and the
members of the Legislature. In my social and official
contact with Mr. Wilson I always found him most
genial and agreeable. When we were at luncheon or

dinner at the old Sterling Hotel in Trenton he would never burden our little talks by any weighty discussion of important matters that were pending before him. He entirely forgot all business and gave himself over to the telling of delightful stories. How to make the real good-fellowship of the man an asset in dealing with the members of the Senate was a problem. I very frankly told him one day at luncheon that many members of both legislative bodies felt that he was too stiff and academic and that they were anxious to find out for themselves if there was a more human side to him. In order to give him an opportunity to overcome this false impression we arranged a delightful dinner at the Trenton Country Club, to which we invited both Democratic and Republican members of the Senate. The evening was a delightful one. In the corner of the little room where the dinner was served sat three darky musicians who regaled the little group with fine old southern melodies. It was real fun to watch the new Governor's conduct in this environment. He was like a boy out of school. He was no longer the college professor or the cold man of affairs. He delighted the members of the Senate who sat about him with amusing stories, witty remarks, and delightful bits of sarcasm. At the close of the dinner, Senator Frelinghuysen walked over and challenged him to a Virginia Reel. He accepted this invitation and the crowd of men were soon delighted to see the Somerset senator lead the new Governor out on the floor and his long legs were soon moving in rhythm with the music.

After all, men are just boys, and this bringing together of these practical men on so happy and free an occasion did much to convince the members of the Senate that the new Governor after all was like themselves, a plain,

TELEGRAM.

The White House, Washington.

3 RN JM 75 Govt.

Windsor, Vermont, July 5,1915

Hon. Jos. P. Tumulty,
The White House,
Washington, D.C.

▓▓▓▓▓▓▓▓▓ is down and out in his newspaper work and desperately in
need of employment. Says there is a vacancy as foreign trade adviser in the
State Department and also one in the District Play Grounds department. Would
be very much obliged if you would see if something can be done for him in
either place. His address 221 A. Street, Northeast.

                                        Woodrow Wilson.

Dear Tumulty,

    I want to issue this statement
to help Mr. Hoover and his Commission in the splendid work they are
doing, and head off mischief-makers
(or, rather, one particular mischief-
maker who is a little out of his
mind) on this side the water.

    Will you not please read it to
Lansing over the 'phone and, if he
has no objection to offer, give it
out?

                    W. W.

A glimpse at the President's human side

76

simple man, modestly trying to serve the interests of a great state.

This affair broke the ice, and after that there was a close intimacy between the Governor and the members of the Legislature, both Democrats and Republicans, and this coöperation soon brought about the enactment of the whole Wilson programme. Never before had so comprehensive a programme been so expeditiously acted upon by a legislative body. The Legislature had convened in January and by the middle of April every campaign pledge that the Governor had made had been kept, although the Senate with which he had to deal was largely Republican.

As the legislative session progressed it appeared that certain Democratic senators were reluctant to follow his leadership. Indeed it was also apparent that the Republicans were alike unwilling to act favourably upon his legislative suggestions. In this situation he summoned the Democratic senators and reminded them of the party pledges in the platform and served notice that if they did not vote for these measures they would have to explain to their constituents. He then summoned the Republican senators and said to them, in effect, this: "The legislation proposed was promised in the Democratic platform. That is not your platform. Therefore, you are not pledged to this action. But if you obstruct the action I shall have to trouble you to go with me to your districts and discuss these matters with your constituents and tell them why you consider this bad legislation and why you resisted it."

The newspapers of the country soon began to discuss the achievements of the Wilson administration in New Jersey and immediately the name of the Governor began to be mentioned in connection with the Presidency.

One of the matters of national importance with which he was called upon to deal during this legislative session was the passage of railroad grade-crossing legislation. In response to the agitation that had long existed in New Jersey for the elimination of grade crossings, the Democrats had inserted a radical plank in their platform in reference to it, and, acting upon this, the Legislature had passed a grade-crossing bill, to which the railroads of the state strenuously objected. It was a matter of the greatest public interest and importance that for many years had been the subject of bitter controversies throughout the state. While the bill was before the Governor for consideration, the railroad attorneys had prepared long, comprehensive briefs attacking the bill as unjust to the railroads and as containing many features which in their essence were confiscatory. When the bill came before the Governor for final action no one considered for a moment the possibility of a veto, first, because of the traditional attitude of the Democratic party of New Jersey in the matter of grade crossings; and, secondly, because of the effect a veto would have upon the progressive thought of the country. I recall very well my discussion with him in regard to this most important bill. Realizing that he was at this time looming up as a national figure, and knowing that the Progressives of the country were awaiting with keen interest his action on the bill, I feared the effect upon his political fortunes that a veto of the bill would undoubtedly have.

The Baltimore Convention was only a few months away and it was clear to me that no matter how safe and sane were the grounds upon which he would veto this legislation, his enemies in the Democratic party would charge him with being influenced by the New Jersey railroad interests who were engaged in a most vigorous campaign against the passage of this legislation. In fact, when we came to discuss the matter, I frankly called this phase of it to his attention. I tried to make him see the effects such a veto would have upon his political fortunes, but he soon made it clear to me that he was unmindful of all such consequences. After thoroughly considering the matter, he finally decided to veto the bill. In discussing the matter with me, he said: "I realize the unjust and unfortunate inference that will be drawn by my political enemies from a veto of this bill, but the bill, as drawn, is unjust and unfair to the railroads and I ought not to be afraid to say so publicly. I cannot consider the effect of a veto upon my own political fortunes. If I should sign this bill it would mean practically a confiscation of railroad property and I would not be worthy of the trust of a single man in the state or in the country were I afraid to do my duty and to protect private property by my act." His attitude toward the bill was clearly set forth in the veto, part of which is as follows:

I know the seriousness and great consequence of the question affected by this important measure. There is a demand, well grounded and imperative, throughout the state that some practicable legislation should be adopted whereby the grade crossings of railways which everywhere threaten life and interfere with the convenience of both city and rural communities should as rapidly as possible be abolished. But there is certainly not a demand in New Jersey for legislation which is unjust and impracticable.

* * * * * * *

The non-enactment of this bill into law will, of course, be a serious disappointment to the people of the state, but it will only concentrate their attention upon the just and equitable way of accomplishing the end in view. I do not believe that the people of the state are in such haste as to be willing to work a gross injustice, either to the railroads or to private owners of property, or to the several communities affected.

Of course his political enemies made free use of this veto in an effort to injure him throughout the country in every state campaign where his fortunes as candidate were involved. As a matter of fact, his veto of this bill did shock the people of the state, but when they seriously considered the matter in all its aspects, they felt that their governor had, at least, done an honourable and a courageous thing in refusing to approve it.

Discussion of him as a strong Presidential possibility was steadily growing. I had felt a delicacy about talking of this with him, but in a walk that we were accustomed to take along the banks of the Delaware and Raritan Canal between office hours, I, one day, made bold to open the subject in this way: "It is evident from the newspapers, Governor, that you are being considered for the Presidency." I could plainly see from the way he met the suggestion that he did not resent my boldness in opening the discussion. I told him that we were receiving letters at the Executive offices from various parts of the country in praise of the programme he had just put through the Legislature. As we discussed the possibilities of the Presidential situation, he turned to me in the most solemn way, and putting his hand to his mouth, as if to whisper something, said: "I do not know, Tumulty, that I would care to be President during the next four years." And then looking around as if he were afraid uninvited ears might be listening, he continued: "For the next President will have a war on his hands, and I am not sure that I would make a good war President." This reply greatly excited my curiosity and interest and I said: "With what nation do you think we will have a war?" Very cautiously he said: "I do not care to name the nation," and our little talk ended. This statement was made to me in April, 1911. Was it a prophecy of the war that was to burst upon the world in August, 1914?

CHAPTER XII

COLONEL HARVEY

U PON the completion of the legislative work of the first session of the New Jersey Legislature the name of Woodrow Wilson quickly forged to the front as a strong Presidential possibility. Intimate friends, including Walter Hines Page, afterward United States Ambassador to Great Britain; Cleveland H. Dodge and Robert Bridges, the two latter old friends and classmates of the Governor in the famous class of '79 at Princeton, set about by conferences to launch the Presidential boom of their friend, and selected for the task of the actual management of the campaign the young Princetonian, William F. McCombs, then an active and rising young lawyer of New York. These gentlemen, and other devoted friends and advisers of the Governor, made up the first Wilson contingent, and at once initiated a plan of publicity and organization throughout the country. They arranged to have the New Jersey Governor visit strategic points in the country to make addresses on a variety of public questions. Whether Colonel Harvey was behind the scenes as the adviser of this little group I have never ascertained, but *Harper's Weekly*, then edited by the Colonel, was his leading supporter in the magazine world, carrying the name of the Princetonian at its mast-head as a candidate for the Presidency. There were frequent conferences between the Colonel and the Governor at the Executive offices, and as a result of these conferences the Wilson boom soon became a thing to be reckoned with by the Old Guard in control of party affairs in the nation.

Wilson stock from the moment of the adjournment of the Legislature began to rise, and his candidacy spread with great rapidity, until in nearly every state in the Union "Wilson Clubs" were being established. The New Jersey primaries, where again he met and defeated the Smith forces; the Ohio primaries, where he split the delegates with the favourite son, Governor Harmon, a distinguished Democrat; and the Wisconsin primaries, at which he swept the state, gave a tremendous impetus to the already growing movement for the "Reform" Governor of New Jersey.

Everything was serenely moving in the Wilson camp, when like a thunderclap out of a clear sky broke the story of the disagreement between Colonel Harvey, Marse Henry Watterson, and the Governor of New Jersey. I recall my conversation with Governor Wilson on the day following the Harvey-Watterson conference at a New York club. As private secretary to the Governor, I always made it a rule to keep in close touch with every conference then being held regarding the political situation, and in this way I first learned about the Harvey-Watterson meeting which for a few weeks threatened to destroy all the lines of support that had been built up throughout the past months of diligent work and organization.

The Governor and I were seated in a trolley car on our way from the State Capitol to the railroad station in Trenton when he informed me, in the most casual way and without seeming to understand the possible damage he had done his own cause, of what followed the conference

the previous day. It was like this: the conference had
ended and they were leaving the room when Colonel
Harvey put his hand on Woodrow Wilson's shoulder and
said: "Governor, I want to ask you a frank question, and
I want you to give me a frank answer. In your opinion
is the support of *Harper's Weekly* helping or hurting you?"
In telling me of it Woodrow Wilson said: "I was most
embarrassed, and replied: 'Colonel, I wish you had not
asked me that question.' 'Well, what is the answer?'
Colonel Harvey insisted pleasantly. 'Why, Colonel, some
of my friends tell me it is not helping me in the West.'
Colonel Harvey said: 'I was afraid you might feel that way
about it, and we shall have to soft-pedal a bit'." Mr.
Wilson was so serenely unconscious that any offence had
been taken that when informed by me a little later that
his name had disappeared from the head of the editorial
column of *Harper's Weekly* he did not connect this with
the interview. "Was Colonel Harvey offended?" I asked.
"He didn't seem to be," was the Governor's answer.

I immediately scented the danger of the situation and
the possibilities of disaster to his political fortunes that
lay in his reply, and I told him very frankly that I was
afraid he had deeply wounded Colonel Harvey and that
it might result in a serious break in their relations. The
Governor seemed grieved at this and said that he hoped
such was not the case; that even after he had expressed
himself so freely, Colonel Harvey had been most kind and
agreeable to him and that they had continued to discuss
in the most friendly way the plans for the campaign and
that the little conference had ended without apparent
evidence that anything untoward had happened that
might lead to a break in their relations. We then discussed at length the seriousness of the situation, and as

a result of our talk the Governor wrote Colonel Harvey and endeavoured to make clear what he had in mind when he answered the question put to him by the Colonel at the club conference a few days before, not, indeed, by way of apology, but simply by way of explanation. This letter to the Colonel and a subsequent one went a long way toward softening the unfortunate impression that had been created by the publication of the Harvey-Watterson correspondence. The letters are as follows:

(Personal)

University Club
Fifth Avenue and Fifty-Fourth Street
December 21, 1911.

MY DEAR COLONEL:

Every day I am confirmed in the judgment that my mind is a one-track road and can run only one train of thought at a time! A long time after that interview with you and Marse Henry at the Manhattan Club it came over me that when (at the close of the interview) you asked me that question about the *Weekly* I answered it simply as a matter of fact and of business, and said never a word of my sincere gratitude to you for all your generous support, or of my hope that it might be continued. Forgive me, and forget my manners!

Faithfully, yours,
WOODROW WILSON.

To which letter Colonel Harvey sent the following reply:

(Personal)

Franklin Square
New York, January 4, 1912.

MY DEAR WILSON:

Replying to your note from the University Club, I think it should go without saying that no purely personal issue could arise between you and me. Whatever anybody else may surmise, you surely must know that in trying to arouse and further your political aspirations during the past few years I have been actuated solely by the belief that I was rendering a distinct public service.

The real point at the time of our interview was, as you aptly put it, one simply "of fact and of business," and when you stated the fact to be that my support was hurting your candidacy, and that you were experiencing difficulty in finding a way to counteract its harmful effect, the only thing possible for me to do, in simple fairness to you, no less than in consideration of my own self-respect, was to relieve you of your embarrassment so far as it lay within my power to do so, by ceasing to advocate your nomination. That, I think, was fully understood between us at the time, and, acting accordingly, I took down your name from the head of the *Weekly's* editorial page some days before your letter was written. That seems to be all there is to it.

Whatever little hurt I may have felt as a consequence of the unexpected peremptoriness of your attitude toward me is, of course, wholly eliminated by your gracious words.

> Very truly yours,
> GEORGE HARVEY.

To Colonel Harvey's letter Governor Wilson replied as follows:

(Personal)

> Hotel Astor
> New York, January 11, 1912.

MY DEAR COL. HARVEY:

Generous and cordial as was your letter written in reply to my note from the University Club, it has left me uneasy, because, in its perfect frankness, it shows that I did hurt you by what I so tactlessly said at the Knickerbocker Club. I am very much ashamed of myself, for there is nothing I am more ashamed of than hurting a true friend, however unintentional the hurt may have been. I wanted very much to see you in Washington, but was absolutely captured by callers every minute I was in my rooms, and when I was not there was fulfilling public engagements. I saw you at the dinner but could not get at you, and after the dinner was surrounded and prevented from getting at you. I am in town to-day, to speak this evening, and came in early in the hope of catching you at your office.

For I owe it to you and to my own thought and feeling to tell you how grateful I am for all your generous praise and support of me (no one has described me more nearly as I would like myself to be than you have); how I have admired you for the independence and unhesitating courage and individuality of your course; and how far I was from desiring that you should cease your support of me in the *Weekly*. You will think me very stupid—but I did not think of that as the result of my blunt answer to your question. I thought only of the means of convincing people of the real independence of the *Weekly's* position. You will remember that that was what we discussed. And now that I have unintentionally put you in a false and embarrassing position you heap coals of fire on my head by continuing to give out interviews favourable to my candidacy! All that I can say is that you have proved yourself very big, and that I wish I might have an early opportunity to tell you face to face how I really feel about it all. With warm regard,

Cordially and faithfully, yours,

WOODROW WILSON.

For a while it seemed as if the old relations between the Colonel and the New Jersey Governor would be resumed, but some unfriendly influence, bent upon the Governor's undoing, thrust itself into the affair, and soon the story of the Manhattan Club incident broke about the Princetonian's head with a fury and bitterness that deeply distressed many of Mr. Wilson's friends throughout the country. The immediate effect upon his candidacy was almost disastrous. Charges of ingratitude to the "original Wilson man" flew thick and fast. Mr. Wilson's enemies throughout the country took up the charge of ingratitude and soon the stock of the New Jersey man began to fall, until his immediate friends almost lost heart. The bad effect of the publication of the Harvey-Watterson correspondence and the bitter attacks upon the sincerity of the New Jersey Governor were soon perceptible in the falling away of contributions so necessary to keep alive the campaign then being carried on throughout the country. The "band-wagon" crowd began to leave us and jump aboard the Clark, Underwood, and Harmon booms.

Suddenly, as if over night, a reaction in favour of Governor Wilson began to set in. The continued pounding and attacks of the reactionary press soon convinced the progressives in the ranks of the Democratic party that Wilson was being unjustly condemned, because he had courageously spoken what many believed to be the truth. At this critical stage of affairs a thing happened which routed his enemies. One of the leading publicity men of the Wilson forces in Washington, realizing the damage that was being done his chief, inspired a story, through his Washington newspaper friends, that Wilson was being gibbeted because he refused to accept the support of Wall Street interests which Harvey and Watterson had offered him, and that his refusal to accept their offer was the real cause of the break. This new angle of the Harvey-Watterson episode worked a complete reversal of opinion.

The clever work of this publicity man in turning the light on what he conceived to be the real purpose of the Harvey-Watterson conference probably did injustice to these two gentlemen, but at all events it gave weight to the impression in the minds of many people throughout the country that the real reason for the break was Mr. Wilson's refusal to bow the knee to certain eastern financial interests that were understood to be behind *Harper's Weekly*.

The tide quickly turned against Colonel Harvey and Marse Henry Watterson. Marse Henry, alone in his suite at the New Willard Hotel at Washington, and the Colonel, away off in his tower at Deal, New Jersey, were busily engaged in explaining to the public and attempting, in heroic fashion, to extricate themselves from the unfortunate implications created by the story of the Wilson publicity man. What appeared at first blush to be a thing that would destroy the candidacy of the New Jersey Governor had been, by clever newspaper manipulation, turned to his advantage and aid.

When the bitterness and rancour caused by this unfortunate incident had happily passed away Colonel Watterson and I met at a delightful dinner at Harvey's Restaurant in Washington and discussed the "old fight." The young fellow who had inspired the story which so grievously distressed Marse Henry and Colonel Harvey was present at this dinner. Marse Henry was in fine spirits, and without showing the slightest trace of the old bitterness, rehearsed the details of this now-famous incident in a witty, sportsmanlike, and good-natured way, and at its conclusion he turned to my newspaper friend and laughingly said: "You damn rascal, you are the scoundrel who sent out the story that Harvey and I were trying to force Wall Street money on Wilson. However, old man, it did the trick. If it had not been for the clever use you made of this incident, Wilson never would have been President."

In a beautiful letter addressed to the President by Marse Henry on September 24, 1914, conveying his expressions of regret at the death of the President's first wife, appears the following statement with reference to the famous Harvey-Watterson controversy:

I hope that hereafter you and I will better understand one another; in any event that the single disagreeable episode will vanish and never be thought of more. In Paris last winter I went over the whole matter with Mr. McCombs and we quite settled and blotted out our end of it. I very much regret the use of any rude word—too much the characteristic of our rough-and-tumble political combats—and can truly say that I have not only earnestly wished the success of your administration but have sought to find points of agreement, not of disagreement.

I am writing as an old man—old enough to be your father—who has the claim upon your consideration that all his life he has pursued the ends you yourself have aimed at, if at times too zealously and exactingly, yet without self-seeking or rancor.

Your friend,
HENRY WATTERSON.

The President's acknowledgment of this letter is as follows:

September 28, 1914.
MY DEAR COLONEL WATTERSON:
Your kind letter has gratified me very deeply. You may be sure that any feeling I may have had has long since disappeared and that I feel only gratified that you should again and again have come to my support in the columns of the *Courier-Journal*. The whole thing was a great misunderstanding.

Sincerely yours,
WOODROW WILSON.

While the Harvey-Watterson episode ended as above related, there is no doubt that Woodrow Wilson deeply regretted the whole matter, and, so far as he was concerned, there was no feeling on his part of unfriendliness or bitterness toward Colonel Harvey. Indeed, he felt that Colonel Harvey had unselfishly devoted himself to his cause in the early and trying days of his candidacy, and that Harvey's support of him was untouched by selfish interests of any kind. In every way he tried to soften the unfortunate impression that had been made on the country by what many thought was an abrupt, ungracious way of treating a friend. An incident in connection with this matter is worth relating:

One day at the conclusion of the regular Tuesday cabinet meeting the President and I lingered at the table, as was our custom, and gossiped about the affairs of the Administration and the country. These discussions were intimate and frank in every way.

A note in the social column of one of the leading papers of Washington carried the story that Colonel Harvey's daughter, Miss Dorothy Harvey, was in town and was a guest at the home of Mrs. Champ Clark. I took occasion to mention this to the President, suggesting that it would be a gracious thing on his part and on the part of Mrs. Wilson to invite Miss Harvey to the Sayre-Wilson wedding which was scheduled to take place a few days later, hoping that in this way an opening might be made for the resumption of the old relationship between the Colonel and Mr. Wilson. The President appeared greatly interested in the suggestion, saying that he would take it up with Mrs. Wilson at once, assuring me that it could be arranged. When I saw how readily he acted upon this suggestion, I felt that this was an opening for a full, frank discussion of his relations with Colonel Harvey. I approached the subject in this way: "For a long time I have wanted to discuss Colonel Harvey with you. There is no doubt, Governor, that this unfortunate episode did not sit well on the stomachs of the American people. Whether you believe it or not, the country resented your attitude toward your old friend, and out of this incident an impression has grown which is becoming stronger with each day, that you pay little regard to friendship and the obligations that grow out of it. I have been hoping that in some way the old relationship could

be resumed and that you would feel free at some time in a
public way to attest your real feeling for Colonel Harvey,
at least by way of reciprocation for the genuine way he
stood by you in the old days in New Jersey." The President
looked at me in the most serious way, apparently weighing
every word I had uttered, and said: "You are right,
Tumulty; unfortunate impressions have been created.
What can I do for Colonel Harvey to attest in some public
way my appreciation of what he did for me in the old
days?" I asked why, inasmuch as McCombs had declined the French Ambassadorship, this post might not be
offered to Colonel Harvey, adding that I believed he
coveted and would appreciate such an appointment.
The President said that this was an admirable suggestion
and authorized me to get in touch with Colonel Harvey at
once and make him the offer of the French post.

While my relations with Colonel Harvey were at no
time strained, and, in fact, up to this day our friendship
has been uninterrupted, I thought it would be more tactful if I should approach him through the junior senator
from New York, James O'Gorman. Immediately upon
leaving the President I went to the Army and Navy Club,
where Senator O'Gorman was living, and told him of my
conversation with the President in reference to Colonel
Harvey. He was enthusiastic and immediately got in
touch with Colonel Harvey at his home at Deal, New
Jersey, told him of the President's offer, and asked for a
conference. Then a thing happened which completely
destroyed these plans for a reconciliation. The following
Sunday an interview signed by Colonel Harvey, bitterly
assailing the President, appeared in the New York *Times*.
The fat was in the fire. Senator O'Gorman and I were
silenced. When I approached the President on Monday

morning to discuss further the matter with him, he said:
"I greatly regret this interview of Colonel Harvey. How
can I now with propriety offer him any post? Knowing
Harvey as I do, he would be reluctant to take it, for the
country might be of the opinion that he had yielded in his
criticism of me by the offer of this appointment, and I
could not in honour make the appointment now, for it
might appear to the country that by this method I was
trying to purchase the silence of the Colonel. I am very
sorry, indeed, that the plan we discussed has fallen to the
ground."

And thus the efforts of Mr. Wilson to bring about a
reconciliation with his old friend ended in dismal failure.

CHAPTER XIII

THE "COCKED-HAT" INCIDENT

WHILE Governor Wilson came out of this controversy with the two Colonels, Harvey and Watterson, with flying colours, he was by no means beyond the danger line. His enemies both within and without the party hotly contested his leadership, and the bitterness of the opposition grew in proportion as his candidacy gained daily advantages. Everything possible was done to block his progress and to make more difficult his road to the Presidency. Everything he had ever said or written, especially his "History of the American People," was carefully examined in the hope of finding some way to discredit him. All the guns of the opposition were turned upon him, but nothing seemed sufficient to block his progress. All the charges, intimations, insinuations, and slanders that were industriously circulated by his enemies were without effect, and the trained political minds in his own camp were apprehensive lest his candidacy had reached its climax too long before the convention. How to maintain the present advantage was the problem that perplexed them. They were hopefully looking forward to the benefits that would accrue to their candidate in the round-up of candidates at the famous Jackson Day dinner, scheduled for early January, 1912. This dinner was an annual affair and was eagerly looked forward to. It was expected that the leading lights of the Democratic party would attend this dinner, including Colonel W. J. Bryan, Champ Clark, Oscar Underwood, ex-Governor Folk of Missouri, Roger Sullivan of Illinois, and the New Jersey Governor's friends were confident that because of his ability as a public speaker he would make a strong and favourable impression. They were not disappointed.

We were awaiting the Jackson Day dinner with great expectations, and congratulating ourselves that we were now safely "out of the woods," and that things would move smoothly for our candidate, when like a bolt from the blue came the publication of the famous Joline "cocked-hat" letter, which caused another panic in the ranks of the too-optimistic Wilson forces.

This letter was written by Mr. Wilson to Mr. Adrian Joline, a Princeton alumnus and prominent New York lawyer at the time of the split in the Democratic party over the silver question. The letter is as follows:

Princeton, New Jersey,
April 29, 1907.

MY DEAR MR. JOLINE:

Thank you very much for sending me your address at Parsons, Kan., before the board of directors of the Missouri, Kansas & Texas Railway Company. I have read it with relish and entire agreement. Would that we could do something, at once dignified and effective, to knock Mr. Bryan once for all into a cocked hat!

Cordially and sincerely yours,
WOODROW WILSON.

The publication of this letter came at a most inopportune time for the Wilson candidacy, and how to meet it was one of the most difficult problems that the Wilson forces had to face. Our enemies were jubilant. They felt that at last they had broken our lines and that we would not be able to "come back."

At this time I was at the State House at Trenton and I received a telegram from the Governor, requesting that I come at once to Washington, where he was conferring with the leaders of his forces in an effort to find some way to neutralize the bad effects of the Joline cocked-hat story in advance of the Jackson Day banquet, at which Mr. Bryan would be present. On my arrival in Washington I went to the Willard Hotel and found the Governor in a conference with William F. McCombs, Tom Pence, Senator O'Gorman, and Dudley Field Malone. We discussed the situation fully and the character of reply the Governor should make by way of explanation of the Joline letter. Mr. Josephus Daniels, a friend and associate of Mr. Bryan, was sent to confer with Mr. Bryan in order that Mr. Wilson might have a close friend at hand who could interpret the motives which lay back of the Joline letter and impress upon Mr. Bryan the present favourable attitude of Mr. Wilson toward him. Mr. McCombs suggested that the Governor address an open letter to Mr. Bryan, voicing his regret over the publication of this letter and assuring him of his present kindly feelings toward him. I vigorously opposed Mr. McCombs' suggestion, arguing that no explanation of the Joline letter could be made to Mr. Bryan that would wear the appearance of sincerity, or be convincing, and that the letter having been written there was nothing to do to extenuate it in any way and that the wise thing was to make a virtue of necessity. I suggested that on the following night, when the Governor was to deliver his address at the Jackson Day dinner, he could, in the most generous and kindly way, pay a handsome tribute to Mr. Bryan for his unselfish service to the Democratic party throughout the dark years he had been its leader; that I felt that he would appreciate a tribute of this kind and that he would resent any explanation of this incident which would appear to be truckling or apologetic in character. This plan was finally agreed upon. In the very beginning of his speech, in the most tactful way, Governor Wilson paid a tribute to the Great Commoner by saying, as he turned to Mr. Bryan: "When others were faint-hearted, Colonel Bryan carried the Democratic standard. He kept the 'fires burning' which have heartened and encouraged the democracy of the country."

The speech at the Jackson Day dinner was a triumph for Woodrow Wilson. While it was a tempestuous voyage for him, with many dangerous eddies to be avoided, he emerged from the experience with his prestige enhanced and with his candidacy throughout the country strengthened. The Bryan-Joline crisis was safely passed. In the presence of the newspaper men at the banquet, Mr. Bryan put his arm around Mr. Wilson's shoulders in an affectionate way, and thus happily concluded the incident which for a time threatened to wreck a great enterprise.

On his return from Washington to Trenton, Governor Wilson told me that Mr. Bryan had bidden him not to worry about the publication of the Joline letter, saying: "I, of course, knew that you were not with me in my position on the currency," and Woodrow Wilson replied: "All I can say, Mr. Bryan, is that you are a great, big man."

CHAPTER XIV

O LD line politicians, like Roger Sullivan of Illinois
and Tom Taggart of Indiana, were turned to the
Princetonian by his notable speech at the Jackson
Day dinner and now gave sympathetic ear to the New
Jersey Governor's claims for the nomination. An incident which happened at the conclusion of the banquet,
as the Governor was on his way to make his train for
New Jersey, illustrates the character of the victory he had
won over difficulties which at the time seemed insurmountable. The old Illinois leader, Roger Sullivan,
greeted the candidate in the most friendly way as he left
the banquet hall, saying to him as he grasped his hand:
"That was a great speech, Governor," and then, drawing
closer to him, added: "I cannot say to you now just what
the Illinois delegation will do, but you may rely upon it,
I will be there when you need me." This remark did not
seem of importance at the time, but when we discussed
the incident the next day at the Capitol at Trenton we
both felt that, at a critical moment of the convention
Roger Sullivan could be relied upon to support us and to
throw the vote of Illinois our way. Sullivan kept his
promise in real, generous fashion. When it seemed as if
the Baltimore Convention was at the point of deadlock,
and after the Illinois delegation had voted many times for
Champ Clark, Sullivan threw the full support of Illinois
to the New Jersey Governor, and thus the tide was

quickly turned in favour of Mr. Wilson's candidacy for the Presidency.

I had often wondered what influence beyond this Jackson Day banquet speech had induced this grizzly old political warrior to support Woodrow Wilson. Afterward I learned the real cause of it from men who kept in close touch with the Illinois delegation during the trying days of the Baltimore Convention.

Everyone who knew Roger Sullivan knew the great influence which both his fine wife and devoted son wielded over him. His son, Boetius, a Harvard graduate, had early become a Wilson devotee and supporter, and the correspondence between father, mother, and son, contained a spirited discussion of the availability of the New Jersey man for the Democratic nomination. The interest of Mrs. Sullivan and her son continued throughout the days of the Convention, which they both attended, and at the most critical moment in the proceedings of the Convention when a point was arrived at when the Illinois vote was decisive, the Illinois leader left a conference where he was being strongly urged by Mr. Wilson's friends to support the New Jersey Governor, to have a final conference with Mrs. Sullivan and their son before he would finally agree to throw his support to Wilson. Everyone at Baltimore knows the result of this conference and how the inner councils of the Sullivan family prevailed. Illinois swung to Wilson and he was soon nominated. It was said, after the New Jersey man's nomination and election, that he showed base ingratitude to Roger Sullivan, the man who more than any other single individual in the Convention had brought about his nomination. Mr. Sullivan's devoted friends in Illinois were particularly bitter at the apparent coldness of Mr.

Wilson toward their friend and idol. The President, as a matter of fact, was never unmindful of his obligation to Sullivan for the personally loyal way he had stood by him at Baltimore, and in every way while he was President he let those associated with him know that Sullivan and his friends, wherever it was possible, should be preferred in the matter of the distribution of patronage in Illinois.

The thing, however, which irritated Sullivan's friends and made many of them irreconcilable foes of Woodrow Wilson was his apparent unwillingness to say a good word for Sullivan when he announced his candidacy for the United States senatorship of Illinois. This presented an opportunity for President Wilson to pay the old debt and "even up" things with Roger. Realizing the delicacy of the situation and how deeply the progressive element in the Democratic party throughout the country might misunderstand and even resent his putting his "okeh" on the candidacy of the Illinois leader for the senatorship, nevertheless, upon considering the matter, he decided to do so and prepared a generous and wholehearted letter of endorsement of Sullivan. He felt that as a good sportsman he was bound in honour to do this for the man whose influence and support, thrown to him at the right moment of the Convention, had brought about his nomination for the Presidency. But there were other and deeper reasons urging him on to endorse his old friend. He knew how eagerly and earnestly Sullivan had fought for him at Baltimore and how in doing so he had won the enmity of the eastern wing of the Democratic party. The old bosses in the party, like Smith and Murphy, had often twitted Sullivan on his support of Wilson and threatened reprisals. Sullivan, however, stood like adamant against these influences and showed an allegiance to the New Jerseyman which earned the admiration and affection of every Wilsonite in the country. The President felt confident that should Roger Sullivan be elected to the Senate, he could count upon him to stand by and loyally support him and the Administration. At this very time the President was beginning to realize in the keenest way the necessity for real, loyal backing in the Senate. Many of the men whom he had personally supported for the Senate in the various senatorial fights throughout the country, especially those who were known as progressive senators, like Hardwick and Smith of Georgia, O'Gorman of New York, and Martine of New Jersey, had grown indifferent and were reluctant to follow his leadership in anything. The so-called Old Guard in the Senate, made up of men like Mark Smith of Arizona, Senators Martin and Swanson of Virginia, Ollie James of Kentucky, John Sharp Williams of Mississippi, Joe Robinson of Arkansas, Billy Hughes of New Jersey, Senator Culberson of Texas, Senator Simmons of North Carolina, and Senator Smith of Maryland, contrary to every prophecy and prediction made by their enemies, stood with the President through every fight in the finest and handsomest way, never deserting his leadership for a moment. Often he would say to me when we were discussing the senatorial situation: "My head is with the progressives in the Democratic party, but my heart, because of the way they stood by me, is with the so-called Old Guard in the Senate. They stand without hitching." He knew that, while Roger Sullivan was a conservative, he could be relied upon in every emergency to back him up even to the point of sacrifice. What President Wilson wanted more than anything else, as he often said, was a team that would work with him. Sullivan was just this type of man, and beyond everything else his loyalty had been tested and could be relied upon in every emergency.

In the light of these circumstances, the President decided finally to throw his hat in the ring in favour of the boss of Illinois for the United States senatorship. The letter advocating Sullivan's election was dictated and signed by the President, and is as follows:

THE WHITE HOUSE
WASHINGTON

October 12, 1914.

MY DEAR MR. RAINEY:

I have read with the greatest interest the account you were kind enough to send me of the Illinois Democratic State Convention. It is full of fine promise for the party; for it shows all the elements of the party heartily drawing together for a successful campaign; and with this union success is sure to come.

You call my attention to the fact that some Democrats are urging voters to cast their ballots for the Progressive candidate for the Senate of the United States rather than for the nominee of the Democratic primaries. You ask me if I approve of this. I do not. I have held myself very strictly to the principle that as a party man I am bound by the free choice of the people at the polls. I have always stood by the result of the primaries; I shall always do so; and I think it the duty of every Democrat to do so who cares for the success and sincerity of his party. Mr. Sullivan has been selected in a fair primary, and therefore he is entitled to the support of his party.

Sincerely yours,
WOODROW WILSON.

HON. HENRY T. RAINEY,
House of Representatives.

This letter and the contents of it will be a matter of news to Sullivan's friends throughout the country. Many, doubtless, will inquire why it was not published at the time. The reason it failed to reach the stage of publication can in no way be attributed to Woodrow Wilson. He never recalled it and the original is in my files. This may be surprising news to the friends of the dead leader, Roger Sullivan, but it is only fair to Mr. Wilson to say that he never hesitated in rushing to the defence of his old friend in the most generous way. He wrote this letter with the full realization of just how much it might personally injure him with the progressive thought of the country. The letter, after being written and signed by the President, was held in reserve by me until Sullivan's friends in Chicago, those in close touch with his affairs there, felt free to advise its publication. I was directed by them to release it, but the order for its release was countermanded by one of the advisers close to Sullivan, who telephoned me that it was thought inadvisable to have the President come into the campaign in Sullivan's behalf, the reason being that the publication of Wilson's letter might arouse the passionate antagonism of Theodore Roosevelt, who was about to begin a tour of Illinois in behalf of Sullivan's opponent. I was advised later that the individual with whom I dealt in this matter and upon whose direction the letter was withheld from publication had no authority to act for Sullivan in the matter and that Sullivan and his friends were deeply disappointed at Mr. Wilson's apparent unwillingness to take up the cudgel for his old friend. Many times I tried to make clear to Sullivan's friends just what the attitude of the President was, but whether I succeeded I do not know. The President, secluded in the White House, away from the madding crowd, never realized the basis of Sullivan's disappointment, for he felt that he had "gone through" for his friend and had not forgotten for a moment Sullivan's advocacy of him at Baltimore. When the news of Sullivan's death was brought to him at a time when he, also, was seriously ill, his lips quivered, great tears stood in his eyes, and turning to Mrs. Wilson, who stood beside his bed, he said: "Roger Sullivan was a wonderful and devoted friend at Baltimore," and then, turning to me, he said: "Tumulty, I sincerely hope that you will personally go to Chicago and attend the funeral and tell Mrs. Sullivan how deeply I grieve over the death of my old friend."

CHAPTER XV

THE contests for the delegates to the National Convention were on in full swing throughout the various states. In the early contests, particularly in the far western states, like Utah, South Dakota, North Dakota, and Montana, the Wilson candidacy, according to primary returns, began to take on the appearance of a real, robust boom. As the critical days of the Convention approached, evidences of a recession of the favourable tide to Wilson began to manifest themselves, particularly in the states of Massachusetts and Illinois, both of which swung to Clark, with New York in the offing quietly favouring Champ Clark. It was clear to the campaign managers of Wilson that from a psychological standpoint the pivotal states were New Jersey and Ohio; New Jersey, because ex-Senator Smith had again challenged the leadership of Wilson and had notified his friends throughout the country that New Jersey could be relied upon to repudiate its governor in an overwhelming fashion. Smith had made deals and combinations with all the disgruntled elements of the state, and with powerful financial backing from the so-called interests in New Jersey and New York and the mighty support of the Hearst newspapers, he was pressing the New Jersey man closely, until at times it seemed as if he might succeed in at least splitting the delegation. The friends of the New

Jersey man, therefore, realizing the effect upon the
democracy of the country of an adverse verdict in his
home state, concentrated all possible forces at this
critical point. In the meantime, and before the actual
determination of the issue in New Jersey, Wisconsin and
Pennsylvania swung into the Wilson column, and the
Ohio primaries resulted in a split delegation between
Wilson and Harmon, in Harmon's home state. All eyes
were, therefore, intently watching New Jersey. A repudiation would be disastrous, although the old-timers in
the Wilson camp tried to encourage us by saying that even
though New Jersey might turn against its governor,
Grover Cleveland, under similar circumstances in 1892,
despite the opposition of his home state, had been nominated and elected President. But, fortunately for us,
New Jersey in the handsomest way stood by her favourite
son. The news of New Jersey's endorsement was flashed
through the country, and there was jubilation in every
Wilson camp. The day following the New Jersey
primaries the New York *World*, the great Democratic
paper, carried a striking editorial under the caption of
"WOODROW WILSON FOR PRESIDENT." The New Jersey
primaries and the Ohio results were great feathers in the
caps of the Wilson men, and with enthusiasm and ardour
they followed up this advantage.

As the days for the opening of the Baltimore Convention approached the New Jersey Governor and his
family left Princeton for Sea Girt, a delightful place along
the Atlantic seaboard, where the state of New Jersey had
provided for its governor an executive mansion, a
charming cottage, a replica of General Washington's
headquarters at Morristown. With us to these headquarters, to keep vigil as it were over the New Jersey

Governor, went a galaxy of newspaper men, representing the leading papers of the country.

The first, and indeed the most important, situation the candidate was called upon to handle at Sea Girt as a preliminary to the Convention was his reply to the now famous Bryan-Parker telegrams, which played so important a part in the deliberations and indeed in the character of the whole Convention. It will be recalled that Mr. Bryan, who was in attendance at the Republican Convention at Chicago as a special correspondent, had telegraphed an identic telegram to each of the Democratic candidates, Messrs. Clark, Underwood, Wilson, and Harmon, as follows:

Chicago, June, 1912.

In the interest of harmony, I suggest to the sub-committee of the Democratic National Committee the advisability of recommending as temporary chairman some progressive acceptable to the leading progressive candidates for the Presidential nomination. I take it for granted that no committeeman interested in Democratic success would desire to offend the members of a convention overwhelmingly progressive by naming a reactionary to sound the keynote of the campaign.

Eight members of the sub-committee, however, have, over the protest of the remaining eight, agreed upon not only a Reactionary but upon the one Democrat who, among those not candidates for the Presidential nomination, is, in the eyes of the public, most conspicuously identified with the reactionary element of the party. I shall be pleased to join you and your friends in opposing his selection by the full committee or by the Convention. Kindly answer here.

W. J. BRYAN.

I was on my way from New York to Sea Girt when I read a copy of this telegram in the evening papers. I believe that I grasped the full significance of this move on the part of Mr. Bryan. In fact, I became so anxious about it that I left the train before reaching my destination, in order to say to Governor Wilson over the 'phone how important I thought the message really was and how cautiously it should be handled. I tried to impress upon him the importance of the answer he was called upon to make to Mr. Bryan. He calmly informed me that he had not yet received the telegram and that he would, of course, give me an opportunity to discuss the matter with him before making his reply.

It was clear that Mr. Bryan, whose influence in the councils of the Democratic party at that time was very great, was seeking by this method to ascertain from leading Presidential candidates like Wilson, Underwood, Clark, and Harmon, just how they felt about the efforts of the New York delegation, led by the Tammany boss, Charlie Murphy, and the conservative element of the Democratic party in the East, to control the Convention and to give it the most conservative and standpat appearance by controlling the preliminary organization and nominating Alton B. Parker as temporary chairman. For many weeks previous to the Convention it had been rumoured that that was the programme and that the real purpose which lay behind it was to unhorse Bryan and to end for all time his control and that of the radicals of the West over the affairs of the Democratic party. It was a recrudescence of the old fight of 1896, between the conservative East and the radical West—Bryan assuming, of course, the leadership of the radicals of the West, and Charlie Murphy and his group acting as the spokesmen of the conservative East.

It was clear to me that Bryan anticipated just what replies Underwood, Clark, and Harmon would make to his inquiry. Whether he was certain of what the New Jersey Governor would say in answer to his telegram, I never could ascertain. Indeed, many of the New Jersey Governor's supporters were ungenerous enough to say that behind the inquiry lay a selfish purpose; that Mr. Bryan took this method to reëstablish his leadership and to place himself at the forefront of the liberal, progressive forces of the Convention.

It is clear, as one looks back upon this incident, that a misstep in the handling of this inquiry from Mr. Bryan might have been fatal to the New Jersey man's candidacy.

When I arrived at Sea Girt to discuss the matter with Governor Wilson, I was surprised to find that he had not even read the telegram, although a copy of it lay upon his desk, and when he did read it and we were discussing it he did not share my view of its great importance. In attempting to emphasize its importance I experienced one of the most difficult jobs I ever had in the eleven years I was associated with Woodrow Wilson. In vain I tried to impress upon him what I believed to be the purpose which lay behind the whole business; that his reply would determine the question as to whether he was going to line up with the progressive element which was strong in the West, or whether he would take sides with those of the conservative East, many of whom were bitterly opposed to him. He finally informed me that he was in touch with Mr. McCombs, his campaign manager at Baltimore, and that he would not reply to Mr. Bryan's telegram until he received some word from the former as to what his opinion was in regard to handling this difficult matter. I left him, after impressing upon him the necessity of early action, lest our progressive friends both at Baltimore and throughout the country who were awaiting word from us should be disappointed by his apparent unwillingness to take his position with the progressives.

The newspaper correspondents at Sea Girt, realizing the importance of the candidate's decision, industriously kept upon our trail to find out what reply would be made to Mr. Bryan. The direct wire between Baltimore and Sea Girt was kept busy with inquiries from our friends as to what attitude we were taking in the matter. While my relations with McCombs at the time were of the friendliest sort, I feared that the Eastern environment in which he lived, and his attempt to bring Tammany into camp for the New Jersey Governor, would necessarily play a large part in influencing his judgment, and I was apprehensive lest Governor Wilson should be too much inclined to accept Mr. McCombs' final judgment in the matter.

On June 21, 1912, the following telegram came from Mr. McCombs, as the basis of a proposed reply to Mr. Bryan by the New Jersey Governor:

Baltimore, June 21, 1912.

Hon. William J. Bryan
Lincoln, Nebraska.

I quite agree with you that the temporary chairman of the Convention should voice the sentiments of the democracy of the nation which I am convinced is distinctly progressive. However, before receiving your telegram I had given the following statement for publication in the Baltimore *Evening Sun:* My friends in Baltimore are on the people's side in everything that affects the organization of the Convention. They are certain not to forget their standards as they have already shown. It is not necessary that I should remind them of these standards from New Jersey and I have neither the right nor the desire to direct the organization of a convention of which I am not even a member.

(signed) McCombs,

I was greatly disappointed, of course, at the character
of reply suggested by McCombs and argued with the
Governor at length on what I considered would be the
disastrous effects of making a reply such as the one contained in the above telegram. Clearly, Mr. McCombs'
suggested reply was a rebuke to Mr. Bryan and a bid for
the Eastern vote in the convention. Of course, Governor
Wilson was most reluctant to disregard the advice of
McCombs. He felt that he (McCombs) was "on the
job" at Baltimore and more intimately in touch with the
situation than he himself could be at Sea Girt. After a
long discussion of the matter, the proposed reply prepared by McCombs was ignored and the following telegram was prepared and sent by Woodrow Wilson:

W. J. BRYAN, Chicago:
    You are quite right. Before hearing of your message I clearly
stated my position in answer to a question from the Baltimore
Evening Sun. The Baltimore Convention is to be a convention
of Progressives, of men who are progressive in principle and by conviction. It must, if it is not to be put in a wrong light before the
country, express its convictions in its organization and in its choice
of the men who are to speak for it. You are to be a member of the
Convention and are entirely within your rights in doing everything
within your power to bring that result about. No one will doubt
where my sympathies lie and you will, I am sure, find my friends in
the Convention acting upon clear conviction and always in the interest of the people's cause. I am happy in the confidence that
they need no suggestion from me.
                            (Signed) WOODROW WILSON.

This reply, more than any other single thing, changed
the whole attitude and temper of the Convention toward
Woodrow Wilson. The progressive forces in it were seeking leadership and Mr. Bryan, by his inquiry, had pro-

vided an opportunity, of which Mr. Wilson took full advantage.

An interesting incident occurred in connection with this affair. Being unable to induce the Governor quickly to reply to Mr. Bryan, and realizing that our friends at Baltimore would expect him to agree with Mr. Bryan, and thus take his place with the progressive element in the Convention, I was firmly convinced that he would at the end be found in agreement with Mr. Bryan. I, therefore, took the liberty of saying to the newspaper men in our group—those who were favourably disposed to us—that when Mr. Wilson did reply to Mr. Bryan he would be found in harmony with the Commoner's ideas. This unofficial tip was immediately conveyed to Baltimore and our friends, after returning from the Convention, told me how this piece of inspired information had put heart in our men, and that on a bulletin board before the Baltimore *Sun* offices there was posted the announcement "WILSON AGREES WITH BRYAN" and before it hundreds of Wilson men gathered, cheering the message of the New Jersey Governor.

The reply of the New Jersey Governor was prepared by him while he was seated on the side of a little bed in one of the rooms of the Sea Girt cottage. He looked at me intently, holding a pad and pencil in his hands, and then wrote these significant words to Mr. Bryan: "*You are right.*"

I have often wondered what effect on the Convention McCombs' proposed reply, which contained a rebuke to Mr. Bryan, would have had. From that time on Mr. Bryan was the devoted friend of the New Jersey Governor. Mr. Wilson's reply had convinced the Nebraskan that the Governor was not afraid to accept the issue and that he was in favour of supporting a preliminary organization that was to be progressive both in principle and by conviction.

McCombs was obsessed with the idea that the New York delegation must be won; that everything else was negligible compared with that. Therefore he wished Mr. Wilson in his reply to say something that would be considered by the New York delegation as a public rebuke to Mr. Bryan. I afterward learned that McCombs, nervous, incapable of standing the strain and excitement of the Convention, had retired to a friend's house at Baltimore where, after the Woodrow Wilson telegram to William Jennings Bryan, he was found in a room, lying across a bed, crying miserably. To the inquiries of his friends as to what was the matter with him McCombs replied, weeping, that the Governor had spoiled everything by his telegram to Bryan; that had the Governor followed his [McCombs'] advice, he could have been nominated.

The direct wire between the Sea Girt cottage and the Wilson headquarters at Baltimore was kept busy from early morning until late at night. The telephone exchange in the cottage was so arranged that a branch telephone was kept in the little room under the stairway, which constituted a sort of listening post, which permitted me, in accordance with the suggestion of the Governor himself, to listen in on conversations, not by way of eavesdropping, but in order that we might intelligently confer after each conversation on the various matters that might have to be decided upon with reference to the organization of the convention. Many of the momentous questions having to do with the conduct of the Convention were discussed and settled over this 'phone. The most frequent users of the 'phone during these days were Colonel Bryan and Mr. McCombs, our campaign manager. During the opening days of the Convention I made it my business to keep in close touch with Baltimore both by conversations over the 'phone with the active managers of the Wilson boom and by carefully reading each morning the news items appearing in the New York *Times*, New York *World*, and the Baltimore *Sun*, this last-named paper being one of the leading advocates of the Wilson candidacy in the country.

I was personally, and in some cases intimately, acquainted with the special writers on these great journals and knew from previous contact with them that they were on the "inside" of the situation at Baltimore, and in this way much information was gleaned which proved helpful in keeping us in touch with the many happenings at the Convention.

Having successfully passed through the Bryan-Parker crisis, we decided upon a kind of strategy that would win to our side the various progressive elements in the Convention. In line with this idea, we suggested to our managers at Baltimore the advisability of putting forward the name of Ollie M. James of Kentucky for permanent chairman of the Convention. While he was a staunch Clark man and a devoted follower of Mr. Bryan, we knew he could be relied upon to give us a fair deal as the presiding officer of the Convention. There was another reason, too. Away off in Sea Girt we gathered the impression that the sober second thought of the Convention favoured his selection and that even though we might fail in our attempt to nominate him for this office, our efforts at least in this regard would give the impression to those who looked with favour upon Wilson as their second choice. Another reason was this: We were not

afraid to trust our cause to a Clark man, and Ollie James
for many years had been the idol of convention crowds.
When, upon the conclusion of the Bryan-Parker episode,
Mr. Bryan telephoned Sea Girt to discuss with the
Governor the matter of the chairmanship, he was
greatly surprised and pleased to have the Governor say,
in the most hearty way that, upon canvassing the whole
situation, he felt it would be an admirable and just thing
to select Ollie James of Kentucky. Mr. Bryan said:
"But, Governor Wilson, Mr. James is in the Convention
as a Clark man." "It does not matter," was the Governor's reply. "He is our kind of a fellow, and I am sure
my friends can rely upon him to treat our cause well."
From Mr. Bryan's subsequent conversations over the
telephone it clearly appeared that he was delighted at the
suggestion of his own intimate friend, and it was plain
that he was being convinced from moves of this kind by
the New Jersey Governor that Woodrow Wilson was
willing to stand or fall with him in attempting to organize
the Convention along progressive lines.

Years after the Convention the senator from Kentucky,
who became my closest and dearest friend, and who
distinguished himself as a member of the Senate, and who
was one of the staunchest defenders of the President and
the Administration, told me of the wisdom which he
thought lay behind the suggestion of himself for the
chairmanship; that we, at Sea Girt, rightly sensed the
situation and that the suggestion of his name had done
more than anything else to convince the men in the
Convention of the genuine character of the New Jersey
Governor's progressiveness. We felt that strategic
moves of this kind appealed to the progressive thought
in the Convention and went far to remove the strange

impression many of the delegates had that Wilson was a rank conservative. It was plainly perceptible that these acts were quickly turning the progressives in the Convention toward our candidate.

In following these suggestions, we were, in fact, acting independently of the New Jersey Governor's advisers at Baltimore. It was plain to be seen that the battle at Baltimore would finally simmer down to a contest between the reactionaries and the progressives, and we decided at Sea Girt that in every move that was to be made our purpose should be to win the progressive support in the Convention. McCombs was at no time found in harmony with this action, his principal activities at Baltimore being given over to an attempt to win for the New Jersey Governor the support of the conservatives of the East, and, particularly, New York, whose seventy-six votes he thought the great prize of the Convention.

CHAPTER XVI

THE BALTIMORE CONVENTION

A T SEA GIRT we kept in close touch with our friends at Baltimore, so that after each ballot the New Jersey candidate was apprised of the result. During the trying days and nights of the Convention the only eager and anxious ones in the family group, besides myself, were Mrs. Wilson and the Wilson girls. The candidate himself indeed seemed to take only perfunctory interest in what was happening at Baltimore. He never allowed a single ballot or the changes those ballots reflected to ruffle or disturb him. Never before was the equable disposition of the man better manifested than during these trying days. Only once did he show evidences of irritation. It was upon the receipt of word from Baltimore, carried through the daily press, that his manager Mr. McCombs was indulging in patronage deals to secure blocks of delegates. Upon considering this news he immediately issued a public statement saying that no one was authorized to make any offer of a Cabinet post for him and that those who had done so were acting without authority from him. This caused a flurry in the ranks of our friends in Baltimore and the statement was the subject of heated discussion between the Governor and Mr. McCombs over the telephone. Of course, I did not hear what was said at the other end of the wire, but I remember that the Governor said: "I am sorry, McCombs, but my statement must stand as I have issued it. There must be no conditions whatever attached to the nomination." And there the conversation ended. While this colloquy took place I was seated just outside of the telephone booth. When the Governor came out he told me of the talk he had had with McCombs, and that their principal discussion was the attempt by McCombs and his friends at Baltimore to exact from him a promise that in case of his nomination William Jennings Bryan should not be named for the post of Secretary of State; that a great deal in the way of delegates' votes from the Eastern states depended upon his giving this promise. The Governor then said to me: "I will not bargain for this office. It would be foolish for me at this time to decide upon a Cabinet officer, and it would be outrageous to eliminate anybody from consideration now, particularly Mr. Bryan, who has rendered such fine service to the party in all seasons."

The candidacy of the New Jersey Governor gained with each ballot—only slightly, however—but he was the only candidate who showed an increased vote at each stage of the Convention proceedings. The critical period was reached on Thursday night. In the early afternoon we had received intimations from Baltimore that on that night the New York delegation would throw its support to Champ Clark, and our friends at Baltimore were afraid that if this purpose was carried out it would result in a stampede to Clark. We discussed the possibilities of the situation that night after dinner, but up to ten o'clock, when the Governor retired for the night, New York was still voting for Harmon. I left the Sea Girt cottage and went out to the newspaper men's tent to await word from Baltimore. The telegrapher in charge of the Associated Press wire was a devoted friend and admirer of the New Jersey candidate. There was no one in the tent but the telegrapher and myself. Everything was quiet. Suddenly the telegraph instrument began to register. The operator looked up from the instrument, and I could tell from his expression that something big was coming. He took his pad and quickly began to record the message. In a tone of voice that indicated its seriousness, he read to me the following message: "New York casts its seventy-six votes for Champ Clark. Great demonstration on." And then the instrument stopped recording. It looked as if the "jig was up." Frankly, I almost collapsed at the news. I had been up for many nights and had had only a few hours' sleep. I left the tent, almost in despair, about eleven o'clock, and returned to the Sea Girt cottage, preparatory to going to my home at Avon, New Jersey. As I was leaving the cottage the Governor appeared at one of the upper windows, clad in his pajamas, and looking at me in the most serious way, said: "Tumulty, is there any news from Baltimore?" I replied: "Nothing new, Governor." When we were breakfasting together the next morning, he laughingly said to me: "You thought you could fool me last night when I asked if there was any word from Baltimore; but I could tell from the serious expression on your face that something had gone wrong." This was about the first evidence of real interest he had shown in the Baltimore proceedings.

As will be recalled, the thing that prevented Champ Clark from gathering the full benefit which would have come to him from the casting of the New York vote in his favour was a question by "Alfalfa Bill" Murray, a delegate from Oklahoma. He said: "Is this convention going to surrender its leadership to the Tammany Tiger?"

This stemmed the tide toward Mr. Clark, and changed the whole face of the Convention.

It was evident that on Friday night the deadlock stage of the Convention had been finally reached. The Wilson vote had risen to 354, and there remained without perceptible change. It began to look as if the candidacy of the New Jersey Governor had reached its full strength. The frantic efforts of the Wilson men to win additional votes were unavailing. Indeed, Wilson's case appeared to be hopeless. On Saturday morning, McCombs telephoned Sea Girt and asked for the Governor. The Governor took up the 'phone and for a long time listened intently to what was being said at the other end. I afterward learned that McCombs had conveyed word to the Governor that his case was hopeless and that it was useless to continue the fight, and asked for instructions. Whereupon, the following conversation took place in my presence: "So, McCombs, you feel it is hopeless to make further endeavours?" When McCombs asked the Governor if he would instruct his friends to support Mr. Underwood, Mr. Wilson said: "No, that would not be fair. I ought not to try to influence my friends in behalf of another candidate. They have been mighty loyal and kind to me. Please say to them how greatly I appreciate their generous support and that they are now free to support any candidate they choose."

In the room at the time of this conversation between McCombs and the New Jersey Governor sat Mrs. Wilson and myself. When the Governor said to McCombs, "So you think it is hopeless?" great tears stood in the eyes of Mrs. Wilson, and as the Governor put down the telephone, she walked over to him and in the most tender way put her arms around his neck, saying:

"My dear Woodrow, I am sorry, indeed, that you have failed." Looking at her, with a smile that carried no evidence of the disappointment or chagrin he felt at the news he had just received, he said: "My dear, of course I am disappointed, but we must not complain. We must be sportsmen. After all, it is God's will, and I feel that a great load has been lifted from my shoulders." With a smile he remarked that this failure would make it possible for them, when his term as Governor of New Jersey was completed, to go for a vacation to the English Lake country—a region loved by them both, where they had previously spent happy summers. Turning to me, he asked for a pencil and pad and informed me that he would prepare a message of congratulation to Champ Clark, saying as he left the room: "Champ Clark will be nominated and I will give you the message in a few minutes."

I afterward learned that McCombs was about to release the delegates when Roger Sullivan, who had been informed of McCombs' message to the New Jersey Governor, rushed over to McCombs and said to him, "Damn you, don't you do that. Sit steady in the boat."

This is the true story of the occurrence so strangely distorted by Mr. McCombs in the book he left for publication after his death, wherein he would make it appear that Governor Wilson had got in a panic and tried to withdraw from the race; whereas the panic was all in the troubled breast of Mr. McCombs, a physically frail, morally timid person, constitutionally unfit for the task of conducting such a fight as was being waged in Baltimore. More sturdy friends of Governor Wilson at the Convention were busy trying to brace up the halting manager and persuade him to continue the fight, even against the desperate odds that faced them. But for

these stronger natures, among whom were old Roger
Sullivan of Illinois and W. G. McAdoo, the battle would
have been lost.

The message of congratulation to Champ Clark was
prepared and ready to be put on the wire for transmission
to him when the Baltimore Convention assembled again
on Saturday, June 29, 1912. I had argued with the
Governor that despite what McCombs had said to him
over the 'phone on the previous day I felt that there was
still a great deal of latent strength in the Wilson forces in
the Convention which was ready to jump into action as
soon as it appeared that Champ Clark's case was hopeless.
The first ballot on Saturday gave weight to my view, for
upon that ballot Wilson gained fifteen or twenty votes,
which injected new hope into our forces in the Convention.
From that time on Wilson steadily moved forward, and
then came Bryan's resolutions, opposing any candidate
who received the support of the "privilege-hunting"
class, and attempting the expulsion of a certain Eastern
group from the Convention. Pandemonium reigned in
the Convention Hall, but the vote upon the resolutions
themselves showed the temper of the delegates. This
made the Clark nomination hopeless. Bryan's rôle as an
exponent of outraged public opinion and as a master of
great conventions was superbly played. When he finally
threw his tremendous influence to Wilson, the struggle
was over. Indiana jumped to Wilson, then Illinois, and
the fight was won. Wilson received the necessary two-
third vote and was proclaimed the candidate.

The progressive element of the Democratic party had
triumphed after a long, stubborn fight by what at first was
a minority in the Convention for enlightened progressivism, with Woodrow Wilson as the standard bearer. To

those like myself far away from the Convention there was the sense of a great issue at stake at Baltimore. One old gentleman who visited Sea Girt after the Convention compared the stand of the Liberals in the Convention to the handful at Thermopylæ; others compared their heroic determination to the struggle of Garibaldi and his troops. To the outside world it was plain that a great battle for the right was being waged at Baltimore, under the inspiration of a new leadership. At times it appeared that the raw Wilson recruits would have to surrender, that they could not withstand the smashing blows delivered by the trained army which the Conservatives had mobilized. But they stood firm, for there was in the ranks of the Liberal group in the Baltimore Convention an unconquerable spirit, akin to that of the Crusaders, and a leadership of ardent men who were convinced that they were fighting, not merely for a man but for a principle which this man symbolized. Among these were men like W. G. McAdoo of New York, A. Mitchell Palmer, Joseph Guffey, and Vance McCormick of Pennsylvania, Senator "Billy" Hughes of New Jersey, and Angus McLean of North Carolina.

Although the Wilson forces were largely made up of "new" men, some of whom had never before been actively interested in politics, comparatively young men like McAdoo, Palmer, McCormick, McLean, Guffey, and old men like Judge Westcott of New Jersey, yet they were drawn to the light that had dawned in New Jersey and were eager and anxious to have that light of inspired leadership given to the nation. Judge Westcott fired the Convention with his eloquence and brought showers of applause when he quoted at length from a speech Mr. Wilson had made when president of Princeton, and for which he had been hissed, lampooned, and derided by the Princeton opposition. Judge Westcott said:

Men are known by what they say and do. Men are known by those who hate them and those who oppose them. Many years ago the great executive of New Jersey said: "No man is great who thinks himself so, and no man is good who does not strive to secure the happiness and comfort, of others." This is the secret of his life. This is, in the last analysis, the explanation of his power. Later, in his memorable effort to retain high scholarship and simple democracy in Princeton University, he declared: "The great voice of America does not come from seats of learning. It comes in a murmur from the hills and woods, and the farms and factories and the mills, rolling on and gaining volume until it comes to us from the homes of common men. Do these murmurs echo in the corridors of our universities? I have not heard them." A clarion call to the spirit that now moves America. Still later he shouted: "I will not cry peace so long as social injustice and political wrong exist in the state of New Jersey." Here is the very soul of the silent revolution now solidifying sentiment and purpose in our common country.

Men in the Convention, overwhelmed with the emotion of the great hour and the vindication of the bold liberal, Woodrow Wilson, bowed their heads and sobbed aloud. The "amateurs" of that convention had met the onslaughts of the Old Guard and had won, and thus was brought about, through their efforts, their courage, and their devotion, the dawn of a new day in the politics of the nation.

CHAPTER XVII

SHORTLY after the Democratic National Convention I gave a dinner at the newspaper men's cottage at Sea Girt, to which I invited the Democratic candidate and the newspaper men, in order that they might be given a chance to meet him in the most intimate way and obtain from him what he was pleased to call the "inside" of his mind. Upon the conclusion of the dinner, the Democratic candidate opened his heart in a little talk of the most intimate and interesting character. It contained not only his views of the Presidency, but also a frank discussion of the great problems that would confront the next administration. In referring to Mr. Roosevelt, he said that he had done a great service in rousing the country from its lethargy, and in that work he had rendered admirable and lasting service, but beyond that he had failed, for he had not, during his administrations, attacked two of the major problems: the tariff and the currency, which he, Wilson, considered to be the heart and centre of the whole movement for lasting and permanent reform in America. Discussing Mr. Roosevelt, he said:

He promised too often the millennium. No public man has a right to go so far afield. You have no right to promise Heaven unless you can bring us to it, for, in making promises, you create too much expectation and your failure brings with it only disappointment and sometimes despair. As a candidate for the Presidency I do not want to promise Heaven unless I can bring you to it. I can only see a little distance up the road. I cannot tell you what is around the corner. The successful leader ought not to keep too far in advance of the mass he is seeking to lead, for he will soon lose contact with them. No unusual expectation ought to be created by him. When messages are brought to me by my friends of what is expected of the next President, I am sometimes terrified at the task that would await me in case I should be elected. For instance, my daughter, who is engaged in social-welfare work in Philadelphia, told me of a visit she paid a humble home in that city where the head of a large family told her that her husband was going to vote for me because it would mean cheaper bread. My God, gentlemen, just think of the responsibility an expectation of that kind creates! I can't reduce the price of bread. I can only strive in the few years I shall have in office to remove the noxious growths that have been planted in our soil and try to clear the way for the new adjustment which is necessary. That adjustment cannot be brought about suddenly. We cannot arbitrarily turn right about face and pull one policy up by the roots and cast it aside, while we plant another in virgin soil. A great industrial system has been built up in this country under the fosterage of the Government, behind a wall of unproductive taxes. Changes must be brought about, first here, then there, and then there again. We must move from step to step with as much prudence as resolution. In other words, we are called upon to perform a delicate operation, and in performing a delicate operation it is necessary for the surgeon who uses the knife to know where the foundation of vitality is, so that in cutting out the excrescence he shall not interfere with the vital tissues.

And while we do so we must create by absolute fairness and open-mindedness the atmosphere of mutual concession. There are no old scores to be paid off; there are no resentments to be satisfied; there is no revolution to be attempted. Men of every interest must be drawn into conference as to what it behooves us to do, and what it is possible for us to do. No one should be excluded from the conference except those who will not come in upon terms of equality and the common interest. We deal with great and delicate matters. We should deal with them with pure and elevated purpose, without fear, without excitement, without undue haste, like men dealing with the sacred fortunes of a great country, and not like those who play for political advantage, or seek to reverse any policy in their own behalf.

CHAPTER XVIII

THE election being over, the President-elect proceeded with the selection of his Cabinet and with
that end in view immediately began those conferences with his friends throughout the country in an effort
to gather information upon which to base a final selection.
All sorts of suggestions began to flow into the Executive
offices at Trenton. Tentative slates were prepared for
consideration, and the records and antecedents of the
men whose names appeared on them were subjected to a
searching scrutiny. Every now and then during this
period the President-elect would discuss with me the
various candidates and ask me to investigate this or that
phase of the character of certain men under consideration.

One day as we were leaving the Executive offices at
Trenton, the Governor said: "Tumulty, you have read
Gideon Wells's 'Diary of the Civil War', have you not?"
I told him that some months before he had generously
presented me with those three interesting volumes that
contained a most accurate and comprehensive inside view
of Mr. Lincoln's Cabinet. "Who," he said, "in Wells's
discussion of the Lincoln Cabinet reminds you of William
F. McCombs?" I replied that, in some respects, William
A. Seward, Mr. Lincoln's Secretary of State. Not, of
course, in the bigness of Seward's mind, for I was not
attempting to make any comparison between the intellects
of the two men, but in the effort of Seward to dominate

Lincoln and thus creating jealousies in other members of the Cabinet that were the cause of continual embarrassment to Mr. Lincoln. Mr. Wilson turned to me and said: "You are absolutely right, and that is one reason why I have not seriously considered the claims of Mr. McCombs for a Cabinet post. I am sure that if I did put him in my Cabinet, I should find him interfering with the administration of the other departments in the same way that Seward sought to interfere, for instance, with the Treasury Department under Salmon P. Chase. McCombs is a man of fine intellect, but he is never satisfied unless he plays the stellar rôle, and I am afraid he cannot work in harness with other men and that I should never get any real team work from him. There is another serious objection to McCombs for a place in my Cabinet. A few days ago he boldly informed me that he desired to have the post of Attorney General. When I asked him why he preferred to be Attorney General, he informed me that, being a lawyer, the Attorney Generalship would help him professionally after his term of office expired. What a surprising statement for any man to make! Why, Tumulty, many of the scandals of previous administrations have come about in this way, Cabinet officers using their posts to advance their own personal fortunes. It must not be done in our administration. It would constitute a grave scandal to appoint such a man to so high an office."

It has often been charged by Mr. McCombs' friends that Mr. Wilson showed a lack of appreciation of his services and an utter disregard of the fine things McCombs did in his behalf. Those of us who were on the inside and witnessed the patience of Woodrow Wilson in handling this most difficult person know how untrue such statements are. I personally know that during the trying days preceding the election most of Mr. Wilson's time was given over to straightening out McCombs and attempting to satisfy his mind that neither Mr. McAdoo, Colonel House, nor any other friends of Mr. Wilson were seeking to unhorse him and to take his place in the candidate's affections. Never did any man show greater patience than did Woodrow Wilson in his attitude toward McCombs. The illness of McCombs during the campaign fed fuel to the fires of his naturally jealous disposition. He suspected everybody; trusted no one, and suspected that the President's friends were engaged in a conspiracy to destroy him. Of course, it is true that Mr. Wilson refused to give him the post of Attorney General which he greatly coveted, for reasons I have fully stated above; but at the very time when McCombs' friends were saying that the President had ignored him and failed to offer him any place in his administration, the President had already tendered McCombs his choice of two of the most important diplomatic posts at his disposal—the Ambassadorship to Germany and the Ambassadorship to France. An interesting incident in connection with the offer of the French post to McCombs and his acceptance of it is worth relating.

The President arrived in Washington on the third of March and went to the Shoreham Hotel. McCombs had already received Mr. Wilson's offer of the French Ambassadorship, and on the night of the third of March he concluded he would accept it. He sent a messenger to the Shoreham Hotel with his letter of acceptance. Before the arrival of McCombs' letter at the Shoreham the President had retired for the night, and the message was inserted under the door of his room. However, it seems that shortly after sending the message of acceptance McCombs changed his mind and sent a friend to the Shoreham to recover the letter, and at twelve o'clock at night I found him outside of the President's room on his knees, busily engaged in digging out McCombs' letter of acceptance from underneath the door.

From that time on, with every changing wind, McCombs would first accept and then reject the offer of the French post. By his vacillation he prevented the appointment of an Ambassador to France for four months. He had easy access to the President and saw him frequently. As he left the White House after calling on the President one day, Mr. Wilson showed sharp irritation and said to me: "If McCombs would only discuss somebody else for office save himself I would be more interested."

That the offer of the French post was made by the President and rejected by McCombs is evidenced by the following letter, addressed to the President by McCombs, under date of April 3, 1913:

WILLIAM F. McCOMBS

COUNSELLOR AT LAW

96 BROADWAY & 6 WALL STREET

NEW YORK

April 3, 1913.

MY DEAR MR. PRESIDENT:

Since I saw you on Saturday, I have been making continuous efforts to dispose of my affairs so that I might accept your very flattering offer. I have been in touch with Tumulty from day to day to find out whether my delay was embarrassing you in any way, and he told me it was not. Of course, I did not want to inconvenience you.

As I have told you before, my difficulty in accepting the post has lain in the adjustments of my financial affairs here and in the forming

WILLIAM F. Mc COMBS
COUNSELLOR AT LAW
46 BROADWAY & 6 WALL STREET
NEW YORK

TELEPHONE 245 RECTOR

April 3, 1913.

My dear Mr. President:

Since I saw you on Saturday, I have been making continuous efforts to dispose of my affairs so that I might accept your very flattering offer. I have been in touch with Tumulty from day to day to find out whether my delay was embarrassing you in any way, and he told me it was not. Of course, I did not want to inconvenience you.

As I have told you before, my difficulty in accepting the post has lain in the adjustment of my financial affairs here and in the forming of a connection which would continue, in some degree, my practice. The clientele which my lawyer has is very largely personal to himself, and it is almost impossible to arrange that the affairs of such a clientele be handled by others. This is the difficulty under which I have labored.

After intimations to my clients, I find my clients would, in their view, be prejudicial to their interests and that they would each seek separate counsel. This would mean my return to New York without any clientele whatsoever and a new start. After the statement which you so kindly issued, it occurred to me that I might make an arrangement under which my affairs could be handled. I am convinced now that it is impossible, and that I must remain here to maintain myself. During the past two

WILLIAM F. Mc COMBS
COUNSELLOR AT LAW
46 BROADWAY & 6 WALL STREET
NEW YORK

TELEPHONE 245 RECTOR

years, I have been compelled to neglect my business to a very large extent and I feel that it is absolutely essential for me to recoup. In view of the very great honor of the French post, I was quite willing to sacrifice almost anything. I now know that the sacrifice would be complete.

I was sorry to see in the New York papers of yesterday, under Washington date line, that I had accepted the embassy. It has placed me in a most embarrassing position, and has caused general comment of vacillation. I cannot imagine how the fact that I was re-considering the matter became public. The press clippings I get in the matter are most annoying to me, and must be to you. I suppose the only thing to say in the matter is that my position is the same as it was when my statement was given out in Washington.

Let me again thank you very deeply for the great honor you have conferred upon me. I sincerely wish it were within my power to accept. It is such a thing as rarely comes in a man's lifetime.

Believe me as ever,

Always yours to command,

Wm. F. McCombs

Hon. Woodrow Wilson,
The White House,
Washington, D. C.

A letter from the man who could not make up his mind

of a connection which would continue, in some degree, my practice. The clientèle which any lawyer has is very largely personal to himself, and it is almost impossible to arrange that the affairs of such a clientèle be handled by others. This is the difficulty under which I have labored.

After intimations to my clients, I find my absence would, in their view, be prejudicial to their interests and that they would each seek separate counsel. This would mean my return to New York without any clientèle whatsoever and a new start. After the statement which you so kindly issued, it occurred to me that I might make an arrangement under which my affairs could be handled. I am convinced now that it is impossible, and that I must remain here to maintain myself. During the past two years I have been compelled to neglect my business to a very large extent, and I feel that it is absolutely essential for me to recoup. In view of the very great honor of the French post, I was quite willing to sacrifice almost anything. I now know that the sacrifice would be complete.

I was sorry to see in the New York papers of yesterday, under Washington date line, that I had accepted the embassy. It has placed me in a most embarrassing position, and has caused general comment of vacillation. I cannot imagine how the fact that I was re-considering became public. The press clippings I get in the matter are most annoying to me, and must be to you. I suppose the only thing to say in the matter is that my position is the same as it was when my statement was given out in Washington.

Let me again thank you very deeply for the great honor you have conferred upon me. I sincerely wish it were within my power to accept. It is such a thing as rarely comes in a man's lifetime.

Believe me as ever,

Always yours to command,

WM. F. McCOMBS.

HON. WOODROW WILSON,
The White House,
Washington, D. C.

Even after McCombs had declined the French post, as recited in the above letter to the President, he continued to vacillate, and addressed the following telegrams and cables to me in regard to the French Ambassadorship:

New York, April·4, 1913.
HON. JOS. P. TUMULTY,
   Washington, D. C.
Confidentially, expect to come tomorrow. Please suspend on matter until I see you.

W. F. M.

New York April 25, 1913.
JOS. P. TUMULTY,
   Washington, D. C.
Confirm understanding that nothing be done for the present and nothing sent in.

W. F. M

Sagaponac, N. Y., May 3, 1913.
Radio S. S. *Olympic.*
JOS. P. TUMULTY,
   White House,
      Washington, D. C.
Will cable about time sending name in when I reach Paris in *acceptance* our understanding.

W. F. M.

Paris, Via French, May 13, 1913.
JOS. P. TUMULTY,
   White House,
      Washington.
Have been ill, improving. Cable you Thursday in matter.

W. F. M.

Paris, June 1, 1913.
J. P. TUMULTY,
   Washington.
Some better. Operation doubtful. Question delayed a few days.

W. F. M.

Then came the following cable to the President from Col. E. M. House:

Paris, June 12, 1913.

THE PRESIDENT
    Washington.

Damon [code name for McCombs] requests me to say that after he sees present incumbent tomorrow he will cable you. He is much improved.

EMHOUSE.

Paris, June 18, 1913.

Jos. P. TUMULTY,
    Washington.

Am sending conclusive message through usual channel so you get it tomorrow morning. This confirms message today which was incomplete. Hope everything will be o. k.

Mc.

Paris, July 6, 1913.

J. P. TUMULTY,
    Washington.

Accept if no previous arrangement cable at once care Monroe Banquier Paris.

W.

Paris, July 7, 1913.

TUMULTY,
    Washington.

Better wait a little or leave out for another strictly confidential.

W.

By this last message McCombs meant that the President had better wait a little for him to make up his mind, or to select another for the French post, which the President refused to do.

The kindest explanation of Mr. McCombs' distorted and entirely untruthful story is that his sensitive mind had brooded so long on fancied injuries that he had come to believe that what he deposed was true. He was sensitive to a pathological degree, jealous, suspicious of everybody, and consumed with ambition to appear as the sole maker of President Wilson politically. He is dead, and it would have been pleasanter to keep silent about him. I should have remained silent had he not left his embittered manuscript in the hands of friends, with directions to publish it after his death, when those whom he attacks in its various chapters would feel a hesitancy about challenging his statements and attempting in any way to asperse his memory. That he was abnormal was known to all who came into intimate contact with him during the campaign and after. His suspicions and spites manifested themselves in ways so small that he would have been laughable had he not been pitiable. The simple fact is that both the nomination and the election of Governor Wilson were in spite of Mr. McCombs, not because of him. Mr. McCombs was ill during most of the campaign, which had to be directed by the assistant chairman, Mr. McAdoo, with all possible embarrassing interference from the chairman's sick room.

The full force of McCombs' petty spite, malice, and jealousy was expended upon Mr. William G. McAdoo of New York, who at the time had established a high reputation for his courage and intrepidity in building the famous Manhattan and Hudson tunnels. Mr. McAdoo, in the early days of Woodrow Wilson's candidacy, took his place at the fore-front of the Wilson forces. At the time of his espousal of the Wilson cause he was the only leader in the New York financial world ready and courageous enough to take up the cudgels for Mr. Wilson. His influence thrown to the Wilson side strengthened the Wilson cause in every part of the country. Every

intimation that reached McCombs during the campaign
that Mr. McAdoo, as vice-chairman of the National
Committee, was engaged in doing this or that thing in
connection with his duties as vice-chairman, was always
calculated to stir anew the fires of envy and jealousy
which seemed always burning in the breast of McCombs.

I was in close touch with Mr. Wilson and all the phases
of his campaign at the time, and on several occasions was
asked to act as mediator in the differences between Mr.
McAdoo and Mr. McCombs, and I am, therefore, in a
position calmly to analyze and assess the reasons for
McCombs' implacable hatred of Mr. McAdoo. I found
that the motives which actuated McCombs were of the
pettiest and meanest sort. At their base lay the realization that Mr. McAdoo had, by his gallant and helpful
support of Mr. Wilson, won his admiration and deep respect, and now everything must be done by McCombs and
his friends to destroy Mr. McAdoo in the estimation of the
Democratic candidate for the Presidency. In the efforts
put forth by McCombs and his friends to destroy Mr.
Wilson's high opinion of Mr. McAdoo every contemptible
and underhanded method was resorted to. Mr. McAdoo
re-acted to these unfair attacks in the most kindly and magnanimous way. Never for a single moment did he allow
the McCombs campaign against him to stand in the way
of Woodrow Wilson's advancement to the Presidency.

During the whole time that Mr. McCombs was engaged
in his vendetta, Mr. McAdoo was generous, gallant, big,
and forgiving, even suggesting to the Democratic candidate, in my presence, that it might be wiser for him
(McAdoo) to withdraw from the campaign, so that
"things at headquarters might run easier and more
smoothly." Mr. Wilson would not by any act of his

permit the sniping methods of McCombs to be rewarded in the withdrawal of McAdoo from his campaign.

After the election and when it was certain that McAdoo was being seriously considered for the post of Secretary of the Treasury, McCombs' jealousy began to exert itself in the most venomous way. He tried to persuade Mr. Wilson that the selection of Mr. McAdoo for the post of Secretary of the Treasury would be too much a recognition of the Wall Street point of view, and would be considered a repudiation of McCombs' leadership in the National Committee.

The campaign of McCombs to prevent the nomination of Mr. McAdoo for a post in the Cabinet failed utterly. His poison brigade then gathered at the Shoreham Hotel in Washington on the day of the Inauguration and, attempting to reform their broken lines, now sought to prevent his confirmation at the hands of the Senate. Every agency of opposition that McCombs could invoke to accomplish this purpose was put into action, but like all his efforts against Mr. McAdoo they met with failure. Mr. McAdoo was confirmed and took his place as Secretary of the Treasury, where his constructive genius in matters of finance was soon brought into play, and under his magnificent leadership the foundation stones of the Federal Reserve system were laid, the fruitage of which is now being realized in every business throughout the country.

Frequent conferences were held at Princeton with reference to the selection of the President's Cabinet, and in these conferences Colonel House and I participated. At a luncheon at the Sterling Hotel at Trenton Mr. Bryan was offered the post of Secretary of State.

On the first of March the post of Secretary of War was

still open. It had been offered to Mr. A. Mitchell Palmer of Pennsylvania and had been declined by him for an unusual reason. The President requested Mr. Palmer to meet him at Colonel House's apartment in New York. When the President tendered him the position of Secretary of War, Mr. Palmer frankly told the President that he was a Quaker and that the tenets of his religion prevented his acceptance of any position having to do with the conduct of war. The President tried to overcome these scruples, but his efforts were unavailing. The President then telephoned me and informed me of Palmer's declination and asked if I had any suggestion regarding the vacancy in his Cabinet. I told him that I was anxious to see a New Jersey man occupy a place at his Cabinet table, and we discussed the various possibilities over the 'phone, but without reaching any definite conclusion. I informed the President that I would suggest the name of someone within a few hours. I then went to the library in my home in New Jersey and in looking over the *Lawyers' Diary* I ran across the name of Lindley Garrison, who at the time was vice-chancellor of the state of New Jersey. Mr. Garrison was a resident of my home town and although I had only met him casually and had tried a few cases before him, he had made a deep impression upon me as a high type of equity judge.

I telephoned the President-elect that night and suggested the name of Lindley Garrison, whose reputation as a distinguished judge of the Chancery Court was known to the President-elect. He was invited to Trenton the next day and without having the slightest knowledge of the purpose of this summons, he arrived and was offered the post of Secretary of War in Mr. Wilson's Cabinet, which he accepted.

CHAPTER XIX

A PRESIDENTIAL inauguration is a picturesque affair even when the weather is stormy, as it frequently is on the fourth of March in Washington. It is a brilliant affair when the sun shines bright and the air is balmy, as happened on March 4, 1913, when Woodrow Wilson took the oath of office at noon, delivered his inaugural address a few minutes later, reviewed the parade immediately after luncheon, and before nightfall was at his desk in the White House transacting the business of the Government. To the popular imagination Inauguration Day represents crowds and hurrahs, brass bands and processions. The hotels, restaurants, and boarding houses of Washington overflow with people from all parts of the country who have come to "see the show." The pavements, windows, and housetops along Pennsylvania Avenue from the east front of the Capitol to the western gate of the White House are crowded with folk eager to see the procession with its military column and marching clubs. From an improvised stand in front of the White House, surrounded by his friends, the new President reviews the parade.

Every four years the newspaper boys describe Inauguration Day, but I am not aware of any novelist who has put it in a book. Why not? It offers material of a high order for literary description. "Human interest" material also in abundance, not merely in the aspects of the retiring and incoming Presidents with their respective retinues of important officials, but in the comedies and tragedies of the lesser figures of the motley political world. Familiar faces vanish, new faces appear—especially when a change of administration brings a change of party control. An evacuating column of ousted and dejected office-holders, prophesying national disaster at the hands of parvenus, meets an advancing column of would-be office-holders rejoicing in general over their party's success and palpitantly eager for individual advantage. As in life, so in Washington on Inauguration Day, humour and pathos mingle. Inauguration Day is the beginning of a period of uprooting and transplanting.

So it was when the Democrats came into office on March 4, 1913, after sixteen years of uninterrupted Republican control and for only the third time in the fifty-two years since Buchanan had walked out of the White House and Lincoln had walked in. Hungry Democrats flocked to Washington, dismayed Republicans looked on in silence or with sardonic comment. Democratic old-timers who had been waiting, like Mr. Micawber, for "something to turn up" through long lean years, mingled in the hotel lobbies with youths flushed with the excitement of a first experience in the political game and discussed the "prospects," each confident that he was indispensable to the new administration. Minor office-holders who had, so they said, been political neutrals during the past administration, anxiously scanned the horizon for signs that they would be retained. "Original Wilson men" from various parts of the country were introducing themselves or being introduced by their friends. And there were the thousands, with no axes to grind, who had come simply to look on, or to participate in a long-postponed Democratic rejoicing, or to wish the new President Godspeed for his and the country's sake.

It is not my business in a book wholly concerned with the personal side of Woodrow Wilson's political career to attempt a description of Inauguration Day, with its clamours and its heartaches and its hopes. To the new President the day was, as he himself said, not one of "triumph" but of "dedication." For him the occasion had a significance beyond the fortunes of individuals and parties. Something more had happened than a replacement of Republicans by Democrats. He believed that he had been elected as a result of a stirring of the American conscience against thinly masked "privilege" and a reawakening of American aspiration for government which should more nearly meet the needs of the plain people of the country. He knew that he would have to disappoint many a hungry office-seeker, whose chief claim to preferment lay in his boast that he "had always voted the . Democratic ticket." Among the new President's first duties would be the selection of men to fill offices and, of course, in loyalty to his party, he would give preference to Democrats, but it did not please him to think of this in terms of "patronage" and "spoils." With the concentration of a purposeful man he was anxious chiefly to find the best people for the various offices, those capable of doing a day's work and those who could sense the opportunities for service in whole-hearted devotion to the country's common cause. His inaugural address met the expectations of thoughtful hearers. It was on a high plane of statesmanship, uncoloured by partisanship. It was the announcement of a programme in the interest of the country at large, with the idea of trusteeship strongly stressed. There was nothing very radical in the address:

nothing to terrify those who were apprehensive lest property rights should be violated. The President gave specific assurance that there would be due attention to "the old-fashioned, never-to-be-neglected, safeguarding of property," but he also immediately added "and of individual right." Legitimate property claims would be scrupulously respected, but it was clear that they who conceived that the chief business of government is the promotion of their private or corporate interests would get little aid and comfort from this administration. The underlying meaning of the President's progressivism was clear: the recovery of old things which through long neglect or misuse had been lost, a return to the starting point of our Government, government in the interest of the many, not of the few: "Our work is a work of restoration"; "We have been refreshed by a new insight into our life."

A deep humanity pervaded the message. To the thoughtful hearer it must have been clear that the President's mind was more occupied with the masses than with special classes. He was not hostile to the classes. He was simply less interested in them. He suggested a social as well as a political programme: "Men and women and children" must be "shielded in their lives, their very vitality, from the consequences of great industrial and social processes which they cannot alter, control, or singly cope with." "The first duty of law is to keep sound the society it serves." Such was the first utterance of the President who in a few weeks was to appear as the champion, not of the special interests, native and foreign, in Mexico, but of the fifteen million Mexican people, groping blindly, through blood and confusion, after some form of self-government, and who in a few years was to appear as the champion of small nations and the masses throughout the world in a titanic struggle against the old principles of autocracy.

Mingled with the high and human tone of it all was a clear and itemized forecast of proposed legislation: a revised tariff, a federal reserve banking system, a farmers' loan bank. And all who knew Woodrow Wilson's record in New Jersey were aware that the Executive would be the leader in the enactment of legislation. The executive and legislative branches of the Government in this administration would, all informed people knew, be in partnership in the promotion of an enterprise as practical as it was inspiring.

After Chief Justice White administered the oath of office, the President read the brief address, of which the following are the concluding words:

This is not a day of triumph; it is a day of dedication. Here muster, not the forces of party, but the forces of humanity. Men's hearts wait upon us; men's lives hang in the balance; men's hopes call upon us to say what we will do. Who shall live up to the great trust? Who dares fail to try? I summon all honest men, all patriotic, all forward-looking men, to my side. God helping me, I will not fail them, if they will but counsel and sustain me!

CHAPTER XX

MEXICO

MANY grave matters inherited from the Taft régime pressed upon the new Administration for immediate solution. One of the most serious was the situation in Mexico, growing out of the revolution against the Madero Government which broke out in Mexico City on February 9, 1913. The murder of ex-President Madero and Vice-President Suarez, and the usurpation of presidential authority by General Victoriano Huerta, Minister of Foreign Affairs, and the general industrial and social chaos of Mexico, made it necessary for the new administration, only a month in power, quickly to act and to declare its policy with reference to the question then pending as to the recognition of the provisional government, the head of which was Huerta. After becoming "President" of Mexico, the usurper had brazenly addressed the following telegram to President Taft: "I have overthrown the Government and, therefore, peace and order will reign," and boldly asserted a claim to recognition by the Government of the United States. This was the state of affairs in Mexico when President Wilson was inaugurated. The duly-elected President of Mexico, Francisco Madero, had been overthrown by a band of conspirators headed by Huerta. Were the fruits of the hard-won fight of the Mexican masses against the arbitrary rule of the favoured few to be wasted? President Wilson answered this question in his formal statement of March 12, 1913, eight days after his inauguration. With respect to Latin-American affairs, he said:

One of the chief objects of my administration will be to cultivate the friendship and deserve the confidence of our sister republics of Central and South America, and to promote in every proper and honorable way the interests which are common to the peoples of the two continents. I earnestly desire the most cordial understanding and coöperation between the peoples and leaders of America, and, therefore, deem it my duty to make this brief statement:

"Coöperation is possible only when supported at every turn by the orderly processes of just government based upon law, not upon arbitrary or irregular force. We hold, as I am sure all thoughtful leaders of republican governments everywhere hold, that just government rests always upon the consent of the governed, and that there can be no freedom without order based upon law and upon the public conscience and approval. We shall look to make these principles the basis of mutual intercourse, respect, and helpfulness between our sister republics and ourselves. . . . *We can have no sympathy with those who seek to seize the power of government to advance their own personal interests or ambition.*"

Two considerations animated the President in the formulation of his Mexican policy and compelled his adherence in it throughout his administration, namely:

The firm conviction that all nations, both the weak and the powerful, have the inviolable right to control their internal affairs.

The belief, established from the history of the world, that Mexico will never become a peaceful and law-abiding neighbour of the United States until she has been permitted to achieve a permanent and basic settlement of her troubles without outside interference.

Steadfastly, Woodrow Wilson refused to recognize Huerta as the Provisional President of Mexico. He said: "Huerta, the bitter, implacable foe of everything progressive and humane in Mexico, boldly defending the privileges of the old scientifico group which he represented, openly defied the authority of the United States and sneered at the much-ridiculed policy of 'watchful waiting' proclaimed by the new administration, and laughed to scorn the high idealism which lay behind it." To him the declaration of the American President that "we can have no sympathy with those who seek to seize the power of government to advance their own personal interests or ambition" was a mere gesture, too puerile to be seriously considered.

While Huerta in Mexico was blatantly denouncing this benevolent policy of coöperation and helpfulness, aid and comfort were rendered the usurper by the jingoistic criticisms of the President's enemies in the United States Congress and throughout the country, many of whom, urged on by the oil interests, in their mad delirium, cried out for a blood-and-iron policy toward Mexico. Resisting the American interests in Mexico was a part of the President's task. Those who cried loudest for intervention were they who had land, mineral, and industrial investments in Mexico. The "vigorous American policy" which they demanded was a policy for personal enrichment. It was with this phase of the matter in mind that the President said: "I have to pause and remind myself that I am President of the United States and not of a small group of Americans with vested interests in Mexico."

But the new President, having mapped out the course he was to follow, a course fraught with a great deal of danger to his administration, seeking to bring about the moral isolation of Huerta himself, calmly moved on, apparently unmindful of the jeers and ridicule of his critics in America and elsewhere. "I am willing," he said, "no matter what my personal fortunes may be, to play for the verdict of mankind. Personally, it will be a matter of indifference to me what the verdict on the 7th of November is, provided I feel any degree of confidence that when a later jury sits I shall get their judgment in my favour. Not my favour personally—what difference does that make?—but my favour as an honest and conscientious spokesman of a great nation.

What an utterly foolish thing, said his critics, it is to attempt in this day to oust a Mexican dictator by mere rhetoric and high-sounding phrases!

When Wilson said: "The situation must be given a little more time to work itself out in the new circumstances; I believe that only a little while will be necessary. . . : We must exercise the self-restraint of a really great nation which realizes its own strength and scorns to misuse it," his enemies smugly shrugged their shoulders and said, with disgust: "Well, what's the use? what can you expect from a dreamer of dreams, a mere doctrinaire? Doesn't Wilson, the historian, know that force and force alone can bring that grizzly old warrior Huerta to his senses?"

What was the President seeking to do in proclaiming his policy of "watchful waiting"? He was merely seeking to establish in Pan-American affairs the principle that no president of a South American republic who came to power by usurpation and assassination should receive, while he was president, the recognition of the United States. This doctrine was not only good statesmanship, but it was likewise sound in morals.

It was disheartening to find bitter criticism of this policy from the outside, and depressing to find the enemies of watchful waiting "boring from within" through

his own Cabinet officers. Lindley Garrison, his own
Secretary of War, had no sympathy for this idealistic
policy. His only antidote for what was happening in
Mexico was force and intervention and he honourably
urged this view upon the President, but without succeeding in bringing about the consummation so dear to his
heart.

> And one denies, and one forsakes, and still
> unquestioning he goes, who has his lonely thoughts.

But the President stood firm in his resolve that the
people of Mexico should not be punished for the male-
factions of their usurping president, and steadily, against
great odds, he moved forward to vindicate his policy,
unmindful of the jeers and criticisms of his enemies.
The heart of that policy he eloquently exposed when he
said: "I am more interested in the fortunes of oppressed
men, pitiful women and children, than in any property
rights whatever. The people of Mexico are striving
for the rights that are fundamental to life and happiness
—fifteen million oppressed men, overburdened women,
and pitiful children in virtual bondage in their own home
of fertile lands and inexhaustible treasure! Some of
the leaders of the revolution may often have been mistaken and violent and selfish, but the revolution itself
was inevitable and is right. The unspeakable Huerta
betrayed the very comrades he served, traitorously over-
threw the government of which he was a trusted part,
impudently spoke for the very forces that had driven
his people to rebellion with which he had pretended to
sympathize. The men who overcame him and drove
him out represent at least the fierce passion of reconstruc-

tion which lies at the very heart of liberty; and so long
as they represent, however imperfectly, such a struggle
for deliverance, I am ready to serve their ends when I
can. So long as the power of recognition rests with me
the Government of the United States will refuse to extend
the hand of welcome to any one who obtains power in
a sister republic by treachery and violence."

But the President's policy of watchful waiting did
win. The days of the Huerta régime slowly wended
their uneasy way. Huerta suspended the Mexican Constitution and, having imprisoned half of the Mexican
Congress, proceeded to administer the Government as
an arbitrary ruler. Slowly but surely he began to feel
the mighty pressure of the unfriendly Government of
the United States upon him. Still defiant, he sought to
unite behind him the Mexican people, hoping to provoke
them to military action against the United States. To
hold his power he was willing to run the risk of making
his own country a bloody shamble, but President Wilson
had the measure of the tyrant Huerta from the beginning,
and soon his efforts to isolate him began to bear fruit.
Even now his bitter critics gave a listening ear to the oft-
repeated statement of the American President, as if it
contained the germ of a prophecy:

The steady pressure of moral force will before many days break
the barriers of pride and prejudice down, and we shall triumph as
Mexico's friends sooner than we could triumph as her enemy—and
how much more handsomely and with how much higher and finer
satisfactions of conscience and of honour!

Little by little the usurper was being isolated. By
moral pressure every day his power and prestige were
perceptibly crumbling. His collapse was not far away

when the President declared: "We shall not, I believe,
be obliged to alter our policy of watchful waiting."
The campaign of Woodrow Wilson to force Huerta
finally triumphed. On July 15th, Huerta resigned and
departed from Mexico. Wilson's humanity and broad
statesmanship had won over the system of cruel oppression for which the "unspeakable Huerta" had stood.

During the Huerta controversy a thing happened which
aggravated the Mexican affair, and which culminated
in the now-famous Tampico incident.

On April 9, 1914, a paymaster of the United States
steamship *Dolphin* landed at the Iturbide bridge at
Tampico with a whaleboat and boat's crew to obtain
supplies needed aboard the *Dolphin*. While loading these
supplies the paymaster and his men were arrested by
an officer and squad of the army of General Huerta.
Neither the paymaster nor any of the boat's crew were
armed. The boat flew the United States flag both at the
bow and stern. Two of the men were in the boat when
arrested and hence were taken from United States
"soil." Admiral Mayo, senior American officer stationed off Tampico, immediately demanded the release
of the sailors. Release was ordered after the paymaster
and the sailors had been detained about an hour.
Not only did Admiral Mayo demand the release of the
sailors but insisted on a formal apology by the Huerta Government consisting of a twenty-one-gun salute to the flag.

During the critical days following the refusal of Huerta
to accede to Admiral Mayo's request the State Department was notified that there would arrive at Vera Cruz
the German steamship *Ypirango* about to deliver to
Huerta 15,000,000 rounds of ammunition and 500 rapid-
fire guns.

About 2.30 o'clock in the morning of the 21st day of
April, 1914, the telephone operator at the White House
called me at my home, and rousing me from bed, informed
me that the Secretary of State, Mr. Bryan, desired to
speak to me at once upon a very urgent and serious
matter. I went to the telephone and was informed by
Mr. Bryan that he had just received a wireless informing him that the German steamship *Ypirango,* carrying
munitions would arrive at Vera Cruz that morning about
ten o'clock and that he thought the President ought to be
notified and that, in his opinion, drastic measures should
at once be taken to prevent the delivery of these munitions
to the Customs House at Vera Cruz. While Mr. Bryan
and I were talking, Mr. Daniels, the Secretary of the
Navy, got on the wire and confirmed all that Mr. Bryan
had just told me. Soon the President was on the 'phone,
and in a voice indicating that he had just been aroused
from sleep, carried on the following conversation with
Messrs. Bryan, Daniels, and myself: Mr. Bryan reported
to him the situation at Vera Cruz and informed him of the
receipt of the wireless:

"Mr. President, I am sorry to inform you that I have
just received a wireless that a German ship will arrive
at Vera Cruz this morning at ten o'clock, containing large
supplies of munitions and arms for the Mexicans and I
want your judgment as to how we shall handle the
situation."

Replying to Mr. Bryan, the President said: "Of course,
Mr. Bryan, you understand what drastic action in this matter might ultimately mean in our relations with Mexico?"

Mr. Bryan said, by way of reply:

"I thoroughly appreciate this, Mr. President, and

fully considered it before telephoning you." For a second there was a slight pause and then the President asked Mr. Daniels his opinion in regard to the matter. Mr. Daniels frankly agreed with Mr. Bryan that immediate action should be taken to prevent the German ship from landing its cargo. Without a moment's delay the President said to Mr. Daniels:

"Daniels, send this message to Admiral Fletcher: '*Take Vera Cruz at Once*'."

As I sat at the 'phone on this fateful morning, away from the hurly-burly world outside, clad only in my pajamas, and listened to this discussion, the tenseness of the whole situation and its grave possibilities of war with all its tragedy gripped me. Here were three men quietly gathered about a 'phone, pacifists at heart, men who had been criticized and lampooned throughout the whole country as being anti-militarist, now without hesitation of any kind agreeing on a course of action that might result in bringing two nations to war. They were pacifists no longer, but plain, simple men, bent upon discharging the duty they owed their country and utterly disregarding their own personal feelings of antagonism to every phase of war.

After Mr. Bryan and Mr. Daniels had left the telephone the President said: "Tumulty, are you there? What did you think of my message?" I replied that there was nothing else to do under the circumstances. He then said: "It is too bad, isn't it, but we could not allow that cargo to land. The Mexicans intend using those guns upon our own boys. It is hard to take action of this kind. I have tried to keep out of this Mexican mess, but we are now on the brink of war and there is no alternative."

Discussing this vital matter that morning with the Commander-in-Chief of the Army and Navy, I could visualize the possible tragedy of the whole affair. I pictured the flagship of Admiral Fletcher with its fine cargo of sturdy young marines, riding serenely at anchor off Vera Cruz, and those aboard the vessel utterly unmindful of the message that was now on its way through the air, an ominous message which to some of them would be a portent of death. When the President concluded his conversation with me his voice was husky. It indicated to me that he felt the solemnity of the whole delicate business he was now handling, while the people of America, whose spokesman he was, were at this hour quietly sleeping in their beds, unaware and unmindful of the grave import of this message which was already on its way to Vera Cruz.

When I arrived at the White House the next morning I found the newspaper correspondents attached to the Executive offices uninformed of what had happened in the early morning, but when I notified them that the President had ordered Admiral Fletcher at 2.30 o'clock in the morning to take Vera Cruz, they jumped, as one man, to the door, to flash this significant news to the country and the world.

With Huerta's abdication Venustiano Carranza took hold, but the Mexican troubles were not at an end. The constant raiding expeditions of Villa across the American border were a source of great irritation and threatened every few days a conflagration. While Villa stood with Carranza as a companion in arms to depose Huerta, the "*entente cordiale*" was at an end as soon as Huerta passed off the stage. With these expeditions of Villa and his motley crew across the border our relations with our neighbour to the south were again seriously

threatened. With Villa carrying on his raids and Carranza
always misunderstanding the purpose and attitude of
our Government and spurning its offer of helpful co-
operation, difficulties of various sorts arose with each
day, until popular opinion became insistent in its demand
for vigorous action on the part of the American President.
Every ounce of reserve patience of the President was called
into action to keep the situation steady. How to do it,
with many incidents happening each day to intensify and
aggravate an already acute situation, was the problem
that met the President at every turn. At this time the
President was the loneliest figure in Washington.

> Grotesque uncertain shapes infest the dark
>   And wings of bats are heard in aimless flight;
> Discordant voices cry and serpents hiss,
>   No friendly star, no beacon's beckoning ray.

Even the members of his own party in the Senate and
House were left without an apology or excuse for the
seeming indifference of the President to affairs in Mexico.
Day after day from outraged senators would come
vigorous demands for firm action on the part of America,
insistent that something radical be done to establish.
conditions of peace along our southern borders. From
many of them came the unqualified demand for intervention, so that the Mexican question should be once and
for all settled.

In the Cabinet, the Secretary of War, the vigorous
spokesman of the Cabinet group, demanding radical
action in the way of intervention, was insisting that we
intervene and put an end to the pusillanimous rule of
Carranza and "clean up" Mexico. Even I, who had
stood with the President during the critical days of the

Dear Tumulty:

can't talk less than half an hour to save his life, and when he is through he has talked on so many different subjects that I never can remember what he said. It is literally impossible for me with the present pressure upon me to see him, and I hope you will ask him if he can't submit a memorandum.

The President.

C.L.S.

Dear Tumulty:

I should like to see Mr.   but just now it does not seem possible because I know he is a gentleman who needs a good deal of sea room. I am taking his suggestions up with the Secretary of the Navy.

The President.

C.L.S.

Dealing with bores

Mexican imbroglio, for a while grew faint hearted in my devotion to the policy of watchful waiting. To me, the attack of Villa on Columbus, and the killing of some of our soldiers while asleep, was the last straw. The continuance of this impossible situation along the border was unthinkable. To force the President's hand, if possible, I expressed my feelings in the following letters to him:

THE WHITE HOUSE
WASHINGTON

March 15, 1916.

MY DEAR GOVERNOR:

I have been thinking over what we discussed this morning with reference to the Mexican situation.

I am not acting on impulse and without a full realization, I hope, of everything that is involved. I am convinced that we should pursue to the end the declared purpose announced by you last Friday and endorsed by Congress and the people of the United States of "getting Villa." If the *de facto* government is going to resist the entrance of our troops, a new situation will be presented. I feel that you ought to advise Congress at the earliest possible moment of what the situation really is in order to secure its support and coöperation in whatever action is needed to accomplish the purpose you have in mind. To retrace our steps now would be not only disastrous to our party and humiliating to the country, but would be destructive of our influence in international affairs and make it forever impossible to deal in any effective way with Mexican affairs.

Your appeal to Congress ought to deal with this matter in an affirmative way, asking for the requisite power which you may feel assured will be granted you in ungrudging fashion.

My apology for writing you is my distress of mind and my deep interest in everything that affects you and your future and, I hope, the country's welfare. I would not be your friend if I did not tell you frankly how I feel.

Faithfully,
TUMULTY.

THE PRESIDENT,
The White House.

June 24, 1916.

DEAR GOVERNOR:

The Mexican authorities admit that they have taken American soldiers and incarcerated them. The people feel that a demand should be made for their immediate release, and that it should not take the form of an elaborate note. Only firmness and an unflinching insistence upon our part will bring the gentlemen in Mexico City to their senses.

If I were President at this moment, or acting as Secretary of State, my message to Carranza would be the following:

"Release those American soldiers or take the consequences." This would ring around the world.

Faithfully,
TUMULTY.

THE PRESIDENT,
    The White House.

After reading these letters, the President sent for me one day to visit with him in his study, and to discuss "the present situation in Mexico." As I sat down, he turned to me in the most serious way and said: "Tumulty, you are Irish, and, therefore, full of fight. I know how deeply you feel about this Columbus affair. Of course, it is tragical and deeply regrettable from every standpoint, but in the last analysis I, and not the Cabinet or you, must bear the responsibility for every action that is to be taken. I have to sleep with my conscience in these matters and I shall be held responsible for every drop of blood that may be spent in the enterprise of intervention. I am seriously considering every phase of this difficult matter, and I can say frankly to you, and you may inform the Cabinet officers who discuss it with you, that 'there won't be any war with Mexico if I can prevent it,' no matter how loud the gentlemen on the hill yell for it and demand it. It is not a difficult thing for a president to declare war, especially against a weak and defenceless nation like Mexico. In a republic like ours, the man on horseback is always an idol, and were I considering the matter from the standpoint of my own political fortunes, and its influence upon the result of the next election, I should at once grasp this opportunity and invade Mexico, for it would mean the triumph of my administration. But this has never been in my thoughts for a single moment. The thing that daunts me and holds me back is the aftermath of war, with all its tears and tragedies. I came from the South and I know what war is, for I have seen its wreckage and terrible ruin. It is easy for me as President to declare war. I do not have to fight, and neither do the gentlemen on the Hill who now clamour for it. It is some poor farmer's boy, or the son of some poor widow away off in some modest community, or perhaps the scion of a great family, who will have to do the fighting and the dying. I will not resort to war against Mexico until I have exhausted every means to keep out of this mess. I know they will call me a coward and a quitter, but that will not disturb me. Time, the great solvent, will, I am sure, vindicate this policy of humanity and forbearance. Men forget what is back of this struggle in Mexico. It is the age-long struggle of a people to come into their own, and while we look upon the incidents in the foreground, let us not forget the tragic reality in the background which towers above this whole sad picture. The gentlemen who criticize me speak as if America were afraid to fight Mexico. Poor Mexico, with its pitiful men, women, and children, fighting to gain a foothold in their own land! They speak of the valour of America. What is true valour? I would be just as much ashamed to be rash as I would to be a coward. Valour is self-respecting. Valour is circumspect. Valour strikes only when it is right to strike. Valour withholds itself from all small implications and entanglements and waits for the great opportunity when the sword will flash as if it carried the light of heaven upon its blade."

As the President spoke, his eyes flashed and his lips quivered with the deep emotion he felt. It was the first time he had unburdened himself and laid bare his real feelings toward Mexico. Rising from his chair, he walked toward the window of his study, the very window out of which Lincoln had looked upon the Potomac and the hills of Virginia during the critical days of the Civil War when he was receiving bad news about the defeat of the Northern army. Continuing his talk, he said: "Tumulty, some day the people of America will know why I hesitated to intervene in Mexico. I cannot tell them now for we are at peace with the great power whose poisonous propaganda is responsible for the present terrible condition of affairs in Mexico. German propagandists are there now, fomenting strife and trouble between our countries. Germany is anxious to have us at war with Mexico, so that our minds and our energies will be taken off the great war across the sea. She wishes an uninterrupted opportunity to carry on her submarine warfare and believes that war with Mexico will keep our hands off her and thus give her liberty of action to do as she pleases on the high seas. It begins to look as if war with Germany is inevitable. If it should come— I pray God it may not—I do not wish America's energies and forces divided, for we will need every ounce of reserve we have to lick Germany. Tumulty, we must try patience a little longer and await the development of the whole plot in Mexico."

Did not the publication of the famous Zimmerman note show that German intrigue was busy in Mexico?

Berlin, January 19, 1917.

On the first of February we intend to begin submarine warfare unrestricted. In spite of this it is our intention to keep neutral with the United States of America. If this attempt is not successful, we propose an alliance with Mexico on the following basis: That we shall make war together and together make peace. We shall give general financial support and it is understood that Mexico is to reconquer the lost territory in New Mexico, Texas and Arizona. The details are left to you for settlement.

You are instructed to inform the President of Mexico of the above in the greatest confidence as soon as it is certain that there will be an outbreak of war with the United States, and suggest that the President of Mexico, on his own initiative, should communicate with Japan, suggesting adherence at once to this plan; at the same time offer to mediate between Germany and Japan.

Please call to the attention of the President of Mexico that the employment of ruthless submarine warfare now promises to compel England to make peace in a few months.

ZIMMERMAN.

To GERMAN MINISTER VON ECKHARDT,
Mexico City.

In the President's Flag Day address, delivered at Washington on June 14, 1917, appeared the following:

They [meaning Germany] sought by violence to destroy our industries and arrest our commerce. They tried to incite Mexico to take up arms against us and to draw Japan into an hostile alliance with her; and that, not by indirection, but by direct suggestion *from the Foreign Office at Berlin.*

As the storm of ridicule and criticism of his policy of watchful waiting beat fiercely upon him, I often wondered if he felt the petty meanness which underlay it, or was disturbed or dispirited by it. As the unkind blows fell upon him, thick and fast from every quarter, he gave no evidence to those who were close to him of any irritation, or of the deep anger he must have felt at what appeared to be a lack of sympathy on the part of the country toward the idealistic policy in the treatment of Mexican affairs. Never for a single moment was he driven from the course he had mapped out for himself. He had given his heart and soul to a great humane task and he moved toward its consummation amid a hurricane of protests and criticisms.

There was a time, however, when I thought he displayed chagrin and disappointment at the obstacles placed in his path in settling the affairs of Mexico. It was in a little speech delivered at the Brooklyn Navy Yard on the occasion of the burial of the Marines who fell at Vera Cruz. The following paragraph contained a note of sadness and even depression. Perhaps, in the following words, he pictured his own loneliness and utter dejection:

I never went into battle; I never was under fire; but I fancy there are some things just as hard to do as to go under fire. I fancy that it is just as hard to do your duty when men are sneering at you as when they are shooting at you. When they shoot at you, they can only take your natural life; when they sneer at you, they can wound your living heart, and men who are brave enough, steadfast enough, steady in their principles enough, to go about their duty with regard to their fellow-men, no matter whether there are hisses or cheers, men who can do what Rudyard Kipling in one of his poems wrote, "Meet with triumph and disaster and treat those two imposters just the same," are men for a nation to be proud of. Morally speaking, disaster and triumph are imposters. The cheers of the moment are not what a man ought to think about, but the verdict of his conscience and of the consciences of mankind.

CHAPTER XXI

IN AN introduction to "The Panama Canal Tolls
Controversy," edited by Hugh Gordon Miller and
Joseph C. Freehoff, Mr. Oscar S. Straus wrote:
"There is no more honourable chapter in the highly
creditable history of the diplomacy of our country than
the repeal of the Panama Tolls Act under the present administration. Being a controversy affecting our inter-
nâtional relations, it is gratifying that, aside from the
leadership of the President, the repeal was effected not
solely by the party in power, but by the help of leaders in
all three parties, rising above the plane of partisan politics
to the higher reaches of broad statesmanship, guided by a
scrupulous regard for our international character in accord with 'a decent respect for the opinions of mankind,'
as expressed in the Declaration of Independence." President Wilson himself, after the repealing act had been
passed, remarked, "When everything else about this
Administration has been forgotten, its attitude on the
Panama Tolls treaty will be remembered as a long forward step in the process of making the conduct between
nations the same as that which obtains between honourable individuals dealing with each other, scrupulously
respecting their contracts, no matter what the cost."

In making his recommendations to Congress he, almost
with high disdain, ignored legal technicalities and diplomatic quibbles and took high moral ground. Said he,

"The large thing to do is the only thing we can afford to do, a voluntary withdrawal from a position everywhere quoted and misunderstood. We ought to reverse our action without raising the question whether we were right or wrong, and so once more deserve our reputation for generosity and for the redemption of our every obligation without quibble or hesitation."

An act passed in 1912 had exempted American coastwise shipping passing through the Canal from the tolls assessed on other vessels, and the British Government had protested against this on the ground that it violated the Hay-Pauncefote treaty of 1901, which had stipulated that the Canal should be open to the vessels of all nations "on terms of entire equality." Other nations than England had an interest in this question, and there was a suspicion that some of them were even more keenly if not more heavily interested; but England took the initiative, and the struggle to save the exemption was turned, in the United States, into a demonstration by the Irish, Germans, and other anti-British elements. Innate hostility to England and coastwise shipping interests formed the backbone of the opposition to any repeal of this exemption, but the Taft Administration had held that the exemption did not conflict with the treaty (on the ground that the words "all nations" meant all nations except the United States), and British opposition to the fortification of the Canal, as well as the attitude of a section of the British press during the Canadian elections of 1911, had created a distrust of British motives which was heightened by the conviction of many that the Hay-Pauncefote Treaty had been a bad bargain.

It was understood early in President Wilson's Administration that he believed the exemption was in violation

of the treaty, but not until October did he make formal
announcement that he intended to ask Congress to repeal it. The question did not come into the foreground,
however, until March 5, 1914, when the President addressed this request to Congress in ominous language,
which to this day remains unexplained. "No communication I addressed to Congress," he said, "has carried with
it more grave and far-reaching implications to the interests
of the country." After expressing his belief that the
law as it stood violated the treaty and should be repealed
as a point of honour, he continued: "I ask this of you
in support of the foreign policy of the Administration.
I shall not know how to deal with other matters of even
greater delicacy and nearer consequence if you do not
grant it to me in ungrudging measure."

The first word I received that the President contemplated addressing Congress, asking for the repeal of
Panama Tolls, came about in this way: I was notified
after dinner one evening that the President wished to
confer with me in his study. When I arrived at the
White House Mrs. Wilson met me and informed me of
the plan which the President had in mind with reference
to this matter and of his decision to issue a statement
that night which would be carried in the newspapers
the following morning, and of his determination to address Congress, asking for a repeal of the Panama Tolls.
Mrs. Wilson showed considerable excitement over the
President's proposed step when she discussed the matter
with me as I arrived at the White House. She said she
had argued with the President and had tried to persuade
him that if he intended to do so unusual a thing that
now was the inopportune moment for it for the reason
that it would create a party crisis and probably a split,

the result of which we could not foresee. When I went
into the President's study, he read me the announcement
he had prepared for the papers. The full significance
and the possible danger which lay in the proposed move
that the President was about to make struck me at once.
Frankly I put the whole political situation in the country
before him as it would be affected by his attitude in this
matter, saying to him that the stand he was about to
take would irritate large blocks of Irish, Germans, and
other anti-British elements in the country, and that we
might expect that the leaders in our own party, the heads
of the various committees, like Fitzgerald of Appropria-
tions, Underwood of the Ways and Means, and Clark,
the Speaker of the House, would be found in solid opposition, and that, at a time when we needed every bit
of strength to put our party programme of domestic legislation into effect, it seemed to me unwise to inject this
matter, which could only be a disturbing element, into
our party's councils. In discussing the matter with me,
after I had presented the objections to it, which I did with
great feeling and probably some irritation, he said:
"I knew the view you would take of it, but, unfortunately,
every argument you lay before me in opposition to the
programme I have outlined in this statement is purely a
partisan one and one whose value I cannot recognize at
this time. I must not count the effect of a move of this
kind upon my own personal political fortunes. I am
the trustee of the people and I am bound to take cognizance of the fact that by reason of our attitude on
Panama Tolls our treaties are discredited in every chan-
cellery of Europe, where we are looked upon as a nation that does not live up to its plighted word. We
may have made a very bad bargain with England on

Panama Tolls, but it will be all the more credit to us if we stand by an agreement even when it entails a sacrifice on our part. The men who were parties to this treaty, like Joseph Choate, all agree that we have been indulging in hair-splitting and that we have done a great injustice to England. I ought not, therefore, to be afraid, because of the antagonisms that will be created, to do my duty and risk my political future if necessary in righting a great wrong. We cannot expect to hold the friendship of the world, especially of England, France, and Japan, if we are to treat agreements not as inviolable contracts, but as mere matters of convenience, whose plain terms are to be ignored when matters of expediency dictate. I know that the Irish, through the Hearst newspapers, will cry out that I have surrendered to England, that I am attempting to hand over to Europe a quasi-control over the Panama Canal. As a matter of fact, we are in bad by reason of our attitude on Panama Tolls with various leading nations of Europe, and some unforeseen contingency may arise where it will be found that the reason for their withdrawal of friendship for us was our petty attitude in this matter. I realize, as you urge, that the leaders of our party will be found in opposition, but I must forget this and try to work the matter out so that at least I shall have cleared my skirts and have done what is possible for me to do to right a great wrong."

When the President concluded his statement I put before him the possible reaction against his administration and him personally which might be reflected in the returns of the Congressional elections to be held that year. He replied by saying: "I have calculated every element in the situation and I have concluded where the path of duty lies. If we begin to consider the effect upon our own political fortunes of every step we take in these delicate matters of our foreign relations, America will be set adrift and her word questioned in every court in Europe. It is important that every agreement that America subscribes her name to shall be carried out in the spirit of those who negotiated it."

On March 5, 1914, the President addressed Congress and asked for a repeal of Panama Tolls and immediately the fierce fires of party opposition began to burn. His party leaders expressed their opposition to the repeal in open, honourable, and vigorous fashion and the fight was on. Now that the leading Democrats in the Senate and House had left us, it was necessary for us to reorganize our forces at once. This task devolved upon me and I immediately got in touch with younger men of the House, like Mitchell Palmer, Judge Covington, and that sturdy Republican from Minnesota, Fred Stevens, and over night we had a militant organization in the trenches, prepared to meet the onslaught of our enemies.

The President was adamant under the bitterest criticism. His attitude brought down on him a shower of personal abuse and vituperation from Irish organs and from a group of newspapers which presently were to appear as the chief supporters of Germany. The arguments against the repeal were unusually bitter, and even though Elihu Root, leading Republican senator, in a brilliant and effective speech took his stand by the President and against the recent Republican Administration, partisan criticism seized upon the opening. Nevertheless, the tolls exemption was repealed in June and the events of July and August, 1914, and especially after Von Bethmann-Hollweg stood up in the German Reichstag and characterized the treaty between Germany and Belgium as a mere scrap of paper, gave a certain satisfaction to those who stood by the President for the sanctity of treaties.

Sir Edward Grey, then Secretary of State for Foreign Affairs, commenting upon the action in the House of Commons said: "It has not been done to please us, or in the interest of good relations, but I believe from a much greater motive—the feeling that a government which is to use its influence among nations to make relations better must never, when the occasion arises, flinch or quail from interpreting treaty rights in a strictly fair spirit."

CHAPTER XXII

I HAVE bitterly resented at times the imputation and charge that Woodrow Wilson is so egotistical, self-willed, and so wedded to his own ideas that he not only does not invite suggestion from the outside but that he resents it and refuses to be guided by it.

I feel that my daily intimacy with him for eleven years gives me the right to speak frankly in the matter. Of course, like every great man, he is firmly set in his opinions. He holds and cleaves to them with a passionate devotion and tenacity but only after the fullest consideration of all the facts and information upon which he bases a final conviction. Time and again I have seen him gallantly retreat under the fire of a better argument in a matter that he had been previously disposed to favour.

And what of his attitude toward those who came to the Executive offices to argue with him on some vital matter in which he had formed what appeared to be an unalterable judgment? Never did he assume the unfriendly or unyielding attitude of the doctrinaire or the man of a single idea. I recall a case in point. He was discussing the revenue situation with Representative Claude Kitchin of North Carolina, at a time when it was the subject of bitter controversy in the ranks of the Democratic party. The President and Mr. Kitchin held radically divergent views on this matter; the President sought to lead the party in one direction and Mr. Kitchin openly pursued an opposite course. I was present at this conference. No warm friendship existed between these two men; but there was never any evidence of hostility in the President's attitude toward Mr. Kitchin. He listened politely and with patience to every argument that Mr. Kitchin vigorously put forward to sustain his contention in the matter, and took without wincing the sledge-hammer blows often dealt by Mr. Kitchin. The President replied to Mr. Kitchin's arguments in an open, frank manner and invited him to the fullest possible discussion of the matter.

I recall the conclusion of this interview, when it seemed that, having driven the President from point to point, Mr. Kitchin was the victor. There was no disappointment or chagrin evident in the President's manner as he faced Mr. Kitchin to accept his defeat. He met it in true sportsmanlike fashion. At the conclusion of Mr. Kitchin's argument the President literally threw up his hands and said, quietly, without showing a trace of disappointment: "I surrender, Mr. Kitchin. You have beaten me. I shall inform my friends on the Hill that I was mistaken and shall instruct them, of course, to follow you in this matter."

I could crowd this chapter with similar incidents, but it would be a work of supererogation.

Never before was Mr. Wilson's open-minded desire to apply in practice the principle of common counsel better illustrated than in his handling of the important work in connection with the establishment of the Federal Reserve Act, the keystone of the great arch of the Democratic Administration. It was the first item in his programme to set business free in America and to establish it upon a firm and permanent basis. He aptly said to me, when he first discussed the basic reason for the legislation, he wished not only to set business free in America, but he desired also to take away from certain financial interests in the country the power they had unjustly exercised of "hazing" the Democratic party at every Presidential election.

Shortly after the Presidential election in 1912, while he was burdened with the responsibilities of the Executive office at Trenton, New Jersey, he began, in collaboration with that fine, able, resourceful Virginian, Representative Carter Glass, then chairman of the Banking and Currency Committee of the House, the preparation of the Federal Reserve Banking and Currency Act. For hours at the Executive office in Trenton the Virginia Congressman conferred with the Governor of New Jersey over the preliminary drafts of this most vital piece of legislation. For days the work of preparation was carried on, so that when Mr. Wilson arrived in Washington to take up the duties of the Presidency, the Banking and Currency Bill was in shape and ready for immediate introduction in the Senate and House.

Looking back over the struggle that ensued from the time this measure was introduced into the Senate and House, I often wonder if the people "back home," especially the various business interests of the country, who have been saved from financial disaster by this admirable and wholesome piece of legislation, ever realized the painstaking labour and industry, night and day, which Woodrow Wilson, in addition to his other multitudinous duties, put upon this task. Could they but understand the character of the opposition he faced even in his own party ranks, and how in the midst of one of Washington's most trying summers, without vacation or recreation of any kind, he grappled with this problem in the face of stubborn opposition, they would, perhaps, be willing to pay tribute to the earnestness and sincerity of this man who finally placed upon the statute books one of the greatest constructive pieces of legislation of half a century. Having given his heart to this important task, whose enactment into law was a boon to business and established for the first time in America a "Democracy of Credit," as he was pleased to call it, he relentlessly pursued his object until senators and representatives yielded to his insistent request for the enactment of this law, not under the stress of the party whip, but through arguments which he passionately presented to those who sought his counsel in this matter.

During this time I gladly accepted the President's invitation to spend the summer with him at the White House, where I occupied the bedroom that had been used as Mr. Lincoln's Cabinet Room, and where Mr. Lincoln had signed his famous Emancipation Proclamation. My presence, during that summer, as a member of the President's family, gave me a good opportunity to see him in action in his conferences in regard to the Federal Reserve Act. Never was greater patience, forbearance, or fortitude, shown by a chief executive under such trying circumstances. Day after day, when it seemed as if real progress was being made, unexpected opposition would develop and make it necessary to rebuild our shattered lines, until finally the bill was out of the House and on its way to the Senate.

Its arrival in the Senate was but the beginning of what appeared an almost interminable struggle. The President's stalwart adviser in the Treasury, Mr. McAdoo, was always at hand to rally and give encouragement

to our forces, many of whom at times were in despair over
the prospects of the bill. The leaders of the opposition
on the committee were Senator Root on the Republican
side and Senators O'Gorman and Reed on the Democratic.

It seemed at times as if they had succeeded in blocking
an agreement on the Conference Report. At last word
was brought to the President by Representative Glass
that the opposition of these gentlemen might succeed
in killing the bill. The President up to this time, although
fighting against great odds, showed no impatience or
petulancy, but the message brought by Mr. Glass was the
last straw. Looking at Mr. Glass, with a show of fire
and in a voice that indicated the impatience he felt, the
President said: "Glass, have you got the votes in the
committee to override these gentlemen [meaning O'Gorman and Reed]?" Glass replied that he had. "Then,"
said the President, "outvote them, damn them, outvote
them!"

Mr. McAdoo came to the White House a few days later
to make a report about the situation in the Senate, with
reference to the Federal Reserve Act. His report was
most discouraging as to the final passage of the bill.
He said that his information from the Hill was that the
leaders of the opposition in the Senate were bent upon
a filibuster and that the probabilities were that the Senate
would finally adjourn without any action being taken
on the Federal Reserve Act.

This conversation took place on the White House
portico, which overlooks the beautiful Potomac and the
hills of Virginia. It was one of the hottest days in June,
a day which left all of us who were about the President
low in spirit. Only those who know the depressing character of Washington's midsummer heat can understand

the full significance of this statement. The President
on this occasion was seated in an old-fashioned rocker,
attired in a comfortable, cool-looking Palm Beach suit.
Mr. McAdoo reported the situation in detail and said
that, in his opinion, it was hopeless to try to do more with
the bill: that an impasse had been reached between the
Senate and the House. The President quickly interrupted Mr. McAdoo, saying, with a smile: "Mac, when
the boys at Princeton came to me and told me they were
going to lose a football game, they always lost. We
must not lose this game; too much is involved. Please
say to the gentlemen on the Hill who urge a postponement
of this matter that Washington weather, especially in
these days, fully agrees with me and that unless final
action is taken on this measure at this session I will
immediately call Congress in extraordinary session to
act upon this matter." This challenge, brought to the
Hill by Mr. McAdoo, quickly did the job and the bill was
soon on its way to the White House.

Mr. Wilson conducted the conferences in this matter
with friends and foes alike with a quiet mastery and good
temper diametrically contrary to the reports sedulously
circulated for political purposes, that he was autocratic
and refused to coöperate with the members of the Senate
and House in an effort to pass legislation in which the
whole country was interested.

We have only to recall the previous attempts made by
former administrations to legislate upon the currency
question, especially the efforts of the Harrison and
Cleveland administrations, to understand and appreciate the difficulties that lay in the path of Woodrow
Wilson in his efforts to free the credit of the country from
selfish control and to push this vital legislation to enact-

ment. Previous attempts had always resulted in failure
and sometimes in disaster to the administrations in control
at the time. The only evidences of these frequent but
abortive efforts to pass currency legislation were large and
bulky volumes containing the hearings of the expensive
Monetary Commission that had been set up by Senator
Aldrich of Rhode Island. As an historian and man of
affairs, Woodrow Wilson realized the difficulties and
obstacles that lay in his path in attempting to reform the
currency, but he was not in the least daunted by the
magnitude of the task which confronted him. He moved
cautiously forward and pressed for early action at the
first session of the Congress following his inauguration.
He realized that with the passage of the tariff legislation,
which always acts as a business depressant, it was necessary at the same time to have the stimulus the Currency
Bill would afford when enacted into law. The split of
'96 in the Democratic ranks over the money question was
an additional reason for cautious and well-considered
action if the Federal Reserve Bill was to become a reality.

The presence of Mr. Bryan in the Cabinet and his well-
known views on this question were strong reasons for
watchful and careful prevision. It was obvious to Mr.
Wilson from the outset that insurmountable difficulties
lay in his path, but he brushed them aside as if they were
inconsequential.

In the Committee on Banking and Currency, in both
the Senate and House, were many ardent and devoted
friends of Mr. Bryan, who thought that his radical views
on the money question could be used as a rallying point
for opposition to the President's plan for currency reform.
But those who counted on Mr. Bryan's antagonism were
doomed to disappointment and failure, for while it is

true that Mr. Bryan found serious objections to certain parts of the bill, when these were eliminated he moved forward with the President in the most generous fashion and remained with him until the Federal Reserve Act was made part of the law of the land.

It was in a conference with members of the Banking and Currency Committee that I first saw the President in action with the gentlemen of the Senate and House. He had invited the Democratic members of the Banking and Currency Committee to confer with him in the Cabinet Room in the White House offices. From my desk in an ante-room I heard all the discussions of the bill. There was full, open discussion of the bill in all its phases at this conference in which were collected the conservatives of the East, the radicalists of the West, and those who came to be known as the "corn tassel" representatives of the South, all holding widely divergent views and representing every shade of opinion, some of it sharply antagonistic to the President's views. Some of the members were openly hostile to the President, even in a personal way, particularly one representative from the South, and some of the questions addressed to the President were ungracious to the verge of open insult. It was an exasperating experience, but Mr. Wilson stood the test with patience, betraying no resentment to impertinent questions, replying to every query with Chesterfieldian grace and affability, parrying every blow with courtesy and gentleness, gallantly ignoring the unfriendly tone and manifest unfairness of some of the questions, keeping himself strictly to the merits of the discussion, subordinating his personal feelings to the important public business under consideration, until all his interrogators were convinced of his sincerity and fair-

mindedness and some were ashamed of their own ungracious bearing.

It was clear to me as I watched this great man in
action on this trying occasion that in the cause he was
defending he saw, with a vision unimpaired and a judgment unclouded by prejudice or prepossessions, far beyond the little room in which he was conferring. He
saw the varied and pressing needs of a great nation
labouring now under a currency system that held its
resources as if in a strait-jacket. He saw in the old
monetary system which had prevailed in the country
for many years a prolific breeder of panic and financial
distress. He saw the farmer of the West and South a
plaything of Eastern financial interests. And thus, under
the leadership of Woodrow Wilson was begun the first
skirmish in the great battle to free the credit of the country from selfish control, a movement which led to the
establishment of a financial system that ended for all
time the danger or possibility of financial panic.

There was an interesting incident in connection with the
handling of the currency legislation that brought about
what threatened to be the first rift in the President's
Cabinet. It concerned Mr. Bryan's attitude of opposition
to certain features of the bill as drafted by the Banking
and Currency Committee of the House. My connection
with this particular affair arose in this way: In the early
stages of the discussion of the Federal Reserve Act, and
while Mr. Glass's committee was considering the matter,
a messenger from the White House informed me that the
President wished to confer with me in his study. As I
walked into the room, I saw at once from his general
attitude and expression that something serious was afoot
and that he was very much distressed. Turning around

in his chair he said: "It begins to look as if W. J. B. [he thus referred to Mr. Bryan] and I have come to the parting of the ways on the Currency Bill. He is opposed to the bank-note feature of the bill as drawn. We had a long discussion about the matter after Cabinet meeting to-day. In thoroughly kindly way Mr. Bryan informed me that he was opposed to that feature of the bill. Of course, you know, W. J. B. and I have never been in agreement on the money question. It is only fair, however, to say that in our discussion Mr. Bryan conducted himself in the most generous way, and I was deeply touched by his personal attitude of friendliness toward me. He even went so far as to say that in order that I might not be embarrassed in the handling of the bill, he was willing to resign and leave the country and make no public criticism of the measure. In the meantime, Mr. Bryan has promised to say nothing to any one about the matter until he has a further discussion with me."

The President then frankly discussed with me the effect of the possible resignation of Mr. Bryan. The President suggested that I drop in on Mr. Bryan very soon and if possible casually invite a discussion of the Federal Reserve Act, telling Mr. Bryan of his [the President's] interests in it, and how much he appreciated Mr. Bryan's personal attitude toward him.

I realized the seriousness and delicacy of the situation I was asked to handle, and, being on the friendliest terms with Mr. Bryan, I telephoned him and invited myself to his home—the old Logan Mansion, a beautiful place in the northwest part of Washington. I found Mr. Bryan alone when I arrived. We went at once to his library and, in a boyish way, he showed me a picture which the President had autographed for him only a few days previ-

ous. As we stood before this picture Mr. Bryan gave
expression to his sincere admiration and affection for the
President. He related, with deep feeling, how much Mr.
Bryan had enjoyed his contact and official companionship
with him and how he had come to have a very deep affection for him. As we turned away from the picture, he
grew serious and began the discussion of the very thing the
President and I had conferred on only a few hours before.
He freely discussed his differences with the President
over the Federal Reserve Act, and asked me the direct
question: "Who from Wall Street has been discussing
this bill with the President? I am afraid that some of the
President's friends have been emphasizing too much the
view of Wall Street in their conferences with the President
on this bill." I frankly told Mr. Bryan that this imputation did a great injustice to the fine men with whom the
President conferred on the matter of banking reform and
that I was certain that the President's only intimate
advisers in this matter were Mr. McAdoo, Senator Owen
of Oklahoma, and Mr. Glass of Virginia, and that I
personally knew that in their discussions the President
never argued the point of view of the Eastern financial
interests. Mr. Bryan was reassured by my statement
and proceeded to lay before me his objections to the
character of the currency issue provided for in the bill.
He then took from the library shelves a volume containing all the Democratic National platforms and read
excerpts from them bearing upon the question of currency
reform. He soon convinced me that there was great
merit in his contention. Before leaving him, I told him
of my interview with the President and how deeply distressed he [the President] was that Mr. Bryan was not
disposed to support him in the matter of the Federal

Reserve Act. It was evident that Mr. Bryan felt a keen sympathy for the President and that he was honestly trying to find a way out of his difficulties that would enable him to give the President his whole-hearted support. He showed real emotion when I disclosed to him the personal feelings of the President toward him, and I feel sure I left him in a more agreeable frame of mind. I told him that I would talk with the President, Mr. McAdoo, and Mr. Glass and report to him on the following day.

I returned to the President's study and reported to him in detail the results of my conference with Mr. Bryan. I called his attention to Mr. Bryan's criticism of the bill and then ventured the opinion that Mr. Bryan, according to the traditional policy of the Democratic party, was right in his attitude and that I felt that he [Mr. Wilson] was wrong. For a moment the President showed a little impatience with this statement and asked me to point out to him where the party in the National platforms had ever taken the view Mr. Bryan indicated in his discussion with me. I then showed him the book Mr. Bryan had given me, containing the Democratic platforms, and he read very carefully plank after plank on the currency. He finally closed the book, placed it on his desk, and said: "I am convinced there is a great deal in what Mr. Bryan says." We then discussed ways of adjusting the matter. I finally suggested that the President allow me to talk with Mr. Glass and place before him Mr. Bryan's position and that he have Mr. Glass confer with Secretary McAdoo and Senator Owen. This was arranged. I had no way of ascertaining just what took place at this conference, but after the Cabinet meeting on the following Tuesday Mr. Bryan walked around to where the President was sitting, and said to him: "Mr. President, we have settled our differences and you may rely upon me to remain with you to the end of the fight." The President thanked him cordially, and thus the first break in the Cabinet line was averted.

CHAPTER XXIII

A S THE days of the 1916 Convention at St. Louis approached, it was a foregone conclusion that there would be no serious contender against the President for the nomination and that he would win the prize by a practically unanimous vote. While at times the friends of Mr. Bryan and Mr. Clark were hopeful that the President might withdraw from the contest, after the Democrats at the Convention were assured that the President was ready to accept a renomination, the field was made clear for the setting of the Convention stage to accomplish that end.

It was thought that the St. Louis Convention would be a trite affair; that there would be no enthusiasm in it. This anticipation arose from the idea expressed by many of the devoted friends of the Democratic party, that the cause of Democracy in 1916 was little less than hopeless. Much of this feeling came from the inordinately high estimate which many placed upon Mr. Justice Hughes both as a candidate and as a campaigner. Indeed, many Democrats who had canvassed the national situation felt that without a continuation of the split in the ranks of the Republican party the road to Democratic success was indeed a hard and difficult one to travel.

There is no doubt that in the opinion of the country Mr. Justice Hughes was the strongest man the Republicans could put forward. The fact that he was resigning from the Supreme Court bench and that he had a remarkably progressive record as Governor of New York added a glamour and prestige to this nomination. I, myself, never lost confidence, however, in our ability to win. The Congressional elections of 1914, when the Democratic majority in the House was reduced to thirty-five, had dispirited Democratic friends throughout the country and made them feel that the nomination at St. Louis would be a purely formal matter and without fruitful results.

In a letter addressed to Colonel Harvey in 1914 I had expressed the opinion that the reduced Democratic majority in the Congressional elections of 1914, which was being construed as an apparent defeat of the party, was not a final judgment upon the work of the President and the achievements of his administration; that it was not a reversal irretrievable in character; that it should not depress the Democratic workers throughout the country, and that the field of conquest for the Democratic party in 1916 *was the West and the Pacific coast.* A calm analysis of the election results in 1914 convinced me that if the Presidential election of 1916 was to be won, our efforts for victory had to be concentrated upon a cultivation of sentiment throughout the West in favour of the Democratic cause.

My letter to Colonel Harvey is as follows:

THE WHITE HOUSE,
WASHINGTON

November 7, 1914.
DEAR COLONEL HARVEY:

Now that the clouds have cleared away, let me send you just a line or two expressing an opinion of last Tuesday's election.

It is my feeling that we are making unmistakable gains in sections of the country where Democratic hopes never ran high before this time. Note the results in the states of Utah, Michigan, Minnesota,

Wisconsin, South Dakota, North Dakota, Washington and California. It now appears from the returns, regardless of what the Eastern papers may say, that our majority in the House will be approximately from thirty-five to forty; that our majority in the Senate will be sixteen.

We have elected for the first time in the history of the Democratic party, so far as I can recall, Democratic Senators in the great Republican States of California, Wisconsin and South Dakota. The gains we have made in the West, along the Pacific coast, are mighty interesting and show a new field of conquest for the Democratic party in 1916. To elect a congress, retaining a majority of the party in power, after a revision of the tariff, is unprecedented. Once before it happened, in 1897, after the passage of the Dingley Tariff Act when the Republican majority was reduced from 47 to 10. We are not in the least bit disturbed by the situation. We have for the first time elected Democratic Congressmen from the states of Utah, Washington, South Dakota and North Dakota.

With best wishes, I am,

Cordially and sincerely yours,

J. P. TUMULTY,

Secretary to the President.

COLONEL GEORGE HARVEY,

Hotel Chamberlain,

Old Point Comfort, Virginia.

While the Democratic Convention was in session at St. Louis the President remained in the White House, keeping in close touch by direct telephonic communication with affairs there.

What at first appeared to be an ordinary and rather spiritless convention was quickly turned into a most enthusiastic and fervent one by the notable speeches of Governor Glynn, of New York, the temporary chairman of the Convention, and Senator Ollie M. James, of Kentucky, the permanent chairman.

The key-note speech delivered by Governor Glynn,

contained this ringing defense of the President's policy of neutrality:

"This policy may not satisfy those who revel in destruction and find pleasure in despair. It may not satisfy the fire-eater or the swashbuckler but it does satisfy those who worship at the altar of the god of peace. It does satisfy the mothers of the land at whose hearth and fireside no jingoistic war has placed an empty chair. It does satisfy the daughters of the land from whom bluster and brag have sent no loving brother to the dissolution of the grave. It does satisfy the fathers of this land and the sons of this land who will fight for our flag, and die for our flag when Reason primes the rifle, when Honor draws the sword, when Justice breathes a blessing on the standards they uphold."

And Senator James in a masterly oration paid this splendid tribute to Woodrow Wilson:

"Four years ago they sneeringly called Woodrow Wilson the school-teacher; then his classes were assembled within the narrow walls of Princeton College. They were the young men of America. To-day he is the world teacher, his class is made up of kings, kaisers, czars, princes, and potentates. The confines of the schoolroom circle the world. His subject is the protection of American life and American rights under international law. The saving of neutral life, the freedom of the seas, and without orphaning a single American child, without widowing a single American mother, without firing a single gun, without the shedding of a single drop of blood, he has wrung from the most militant spirit that ever brooded above a battlefield an acknowledgment of American rights and an agreement to American demands."

These eloquent utterances prepared the way for the great slogan of the 1916 campaign: "*He kept us out of war.*"

The President himself never used that slogan, however. From the first declaration of hostilities in Europe he realized the precarious position of the United States and the possibility that, whether we would or not, we might be swept into the conflict. As early as August, 1914, he expressed his anxious apprehension that "something might occur on the high seas which would make our neutrality impossible." He emphatically believed at that time that America's neutrality would best serve the interests of the world; he respected the American tradition of non-interference in European quarrels; with his almost mystic ability to assess and understand the opinion of the people of the country at large he knew that the American people did not want war; in his comparative seclusion he read the mind of America clearer than did the "mixers" of the Pullman smoking compartments who mistook the clamour for intervention among certain classes along the north Atlantic seaboard for the voice of America at large; while the German rape of Belgium stirred his passionate indignation, he knew that there was no practical means by which the United States could stop it, that we could not immediately transport armies to the theatre of war, and that public opinion, especially in the West and South, was not prepared for active intervention; and in addition to all this he was genuinely, not merely professedly, a passionate lover of peace. But with all this he, realizing the magnitude of the war, had already glimpsed its wider significance, which caused him to say later that "this is the last war of its kind, or of any kind that involves the world, that the United States can keep out of. The business of neutrality is over." He saw that if the war should continue long, as it promised to do, our participation might be inevitable and the American tradition of isolation for ever destroyed by circumstances beyond human control. With patience mingled with firmness, he trod his difficult path, doing all he could to keep us from getting involved without sacrificing fundamental principles of

CORNISH, N. H.,
August 6, 1915

Dear Tumulty:

Thank you for sending me the edi-
torials from the World and from Life. You
don't need to have me tell you that I say
Amen to everything that Life says in the
article "Tumulty and Rome." The attitude
of some people about this irritates me more
than I can say. It is not only preposterous,
but outrageous, and of course you know it
never makes the slighest impression on me.

Always

Affectionately yours,

Woodrow Wilson

Hon. Joseph P. Tumulty,

Secretary to the President.

Showing the President's confidence in and loyalty toward
his secretary

human and national rights, but he neither believed nor pretended to believe that he could give guaranties for the future. Nor did any of those who were closest to him make rash promises. For instance, the Cabinet officers who actively participated in the campaign were careful to say in their speeches that he had done all that a president could honourably do to keep us out of war and that he could be depended upon to continue in the future the same course so long as it should prove humanly possible, for "peace" was not merely a word on his lips but a passion in his heart, but that neither he nor any other mortal could "look into the seeds of time" and say what would be and what would not be. The event was on the knees of the gods. Those who spoke with responsibility adhered strictly to the tense of the verb, the past tense: "kept." None rashly used, explicitly or by implication, the future tense: "will keep." In strictest truth they recited what had been, and, from their knowledge of the President's character and convictions, said that he would not be driven into war by the clamour of his critics, that he would refrain from hostility so long as it was humanly and honourably possible to refrain.

The President had sent Secretary of War Baker to the Convention to represent him before the various committees and to collaborate with the Committee on Resolutions in the preparation of a suitable platform.

Shortly after Mr. Baker's arrival in St. Louis the question of the attitude of the Convention and the party toward the "hyphen" vote came up for consideration, and there were indications that certain members of the Committee on Resolutions were inclined to ignore the matter of the hyphen and to remain silent on this grave issue.

While the Committee on Resolutions was meeting at
St. Louis, it was reported to me by Mr. Henry C. Campbell, one of the editors of the Milwaukee *Journal*, and
a devoted friend, that the Democratic party, through its
representatives on the Committee on Resolutions, was
engaged in "pussyfooting" on the hyphen issue and that
this would result in bitter disappointment to the country.
At the time of the receipt of this telephone message from
St. Louis the President was away from town for a day and
I called his attention to it in the following letter:

THE WHITE HOUSE,
WASHINGTON
June 13, 1916.

DEAR GOVERNOR:

It is clear, as the editorial appearing in this morning's New York
World says, that the "hyphenate vote is a definite factor that cannot
be discredited"; and that from the activities of the German-American
Alliance every effort, as their own supporters declare, should be made
to elect Justice Hughes. That there is abundant proof of this is
clear, so that he who runs may read. This is evident from the attitude of the German-American press, and from the statements of
professional German agitators, and from the campaign that has been
carried on against you from the very beginning.

I have not read the platform to be proposed by you. The only
part that I have any knowledge of is that which you read to me over
the telephone some nights ago; that had to do with the question of
Americanism.

Frankly, your mention of Americanism is on all fours with the
declarations found in the Bull Moose and regular Republican platforms. The characteristic of all these references to Americanism is
vagueness and uncertainty as to what is really meant. I believe that
the time has come when the Democratic party should set forth its
position on this vital matter in no uncertain terms. Efforts will soon
be made, from stories now appearing in the newspapers, by professional German-Americans, to dominate our Convention, either in
an effort to discredit you or to have embodied in the platform some

reference to the embargo question, or a prohibition against the sale of munitions of war. We ought to meet these things in a manly, aggressive and militant fashion. It is for that reason that I suggest an open letter to the chairman of the Committee on Resolutions, setting forth your position in this matter so that the Convention may know before it nominates you the things for which you stand. Mr. Baker at the Convention will doubtless know when the representatives of the German-American Alliance make their appearance, asking for consideration at the hands of the Committee of their resolutions. As soon as they do, it appears to me to be the time for you to strike.

I discussed this matter over the telephone yesterday with Mr. Henry C. Campbell, one of our devoted friends, and editor of the Milwaukee *Journal*. Mr. Frank Polk, Counsellor of the State Department, who was at the Convention, tells me that he was discussing this matter with Mr. Nieman, of the Milwaukee *Journal*, and that Mr. Nieman made the statement that both parties were "pussyfooting" and that he would not support the Democratic party unless its attitude in this matter was unequivocal. When Mr. Campbell discussed this matter with me over the telephone, I told him to send me a telegram, setting forth what he thought ought to find lodgment in the platform, by way of expressing our attitude in the matter. This morning I received the attached telegram from Senator Husting, expressing Mr. Campbell's and Mr. Nieman's views. The part I have underlined I think should be expressed in less emphatic language.

The purpose of this letter, therefore, is to urge you as strongly as I can to address at once an open letter to the chairman of the Committee on Resolutions, expressing fully your views in the matter.

TUMULTY.

As a result of the Husting telegram, the President wired Secretary Baker, insisting upon a definite and unequivocal repudiation of the hyphen vote. The President's "fighting" telegram to Baker which contained the substance of Husting's telegram resulted in the insertion in the platform of the following plank:

Whoever, actuated by the purpose to promote the interest of a foreign power, in disregard of our own country's welfare or to injure this Government in its foreign relations or cripple or destroy its industries at home, and whoever by arousing prejudices of a racial, religious or other nature creates discord and strife among our people so as to obstruct the wholesome processes of unification, is faithless to the trust which the privileges of citizenship repose in him and is disloyal to his country. We, therefore, condemn as subversive of this nation's unity and integrity, and as destructive of its welfare, the activities and designs of every group or organization, political or otherwise, that has for its object the advancement of the interest of a foreign power, whether such object is promoted by intimidating the Government, a political party, or representatives of the people, or which is calculated and tends to divide our people into antagonistic groups and thus to destroy that complete agreement and solidarity of the people and that unity of sentiment and purpose so essential to the perpetuity of the nation and its free institutions. We condemn all alliances and combinations of individuals in this country of whatever nationality or descent, who agree and conspire together for the purpose of embarrassing or weakening the Government or of improperly influencing or coercing our public representatives in dealing or negotiating with any foreign power. We charge that such conspiracies among a limited number exist and have been instigated for the purpose of advancing the interests of foreign countries to the prejudice and detriment of our own country. We condemn any political party which in view of the activity of such conspirators, surrenders its integrity or modifies its policy.

There is no doubt that for a while after the Convention at Chicago which nominated Mr. Hughes there was deep depression in the ranks of our party throughout the country, the opinion being that the former Supreme Court Justice was an invincible foe. I had engaged in sharp controversies with many of my friends, expressing the view that Mr. Hughes would not only be a sad disappointment to the Republican managers, but that in his campaigning methods he would fall far short of the expectations of his many Republican friends.

Previous to the nomination of Mr. Hughes the Presi-

dent was his cordial admirer and often spoke to me in
warm and generous terms of the work of Mr. Hughes as
Governor of New York, which he admired because of its
progressive, liberal character. Previous to the Republican Convention, he and I had often discussed the possible
nominee of the Republican Convention. The President,
for some reason, could not be persuaded that Mr. Justice
Hughes was a serious contender for the nomination and
often expressed the opinion that the idea of a nomination
for the Presidency was not even remotely in the thoughts
of the then Justice of the Supreme Court. I did not share
this view. Although the newspaper men who conferred
with Justice Hughes from day to day at his home in Washington informed me of the Judge's feelings toward the
nomination for the Presidency, I was always strongly of
the opinion that the Justice was in no way indifferent to
the nomination and that he was not inclined to go out of
his way publicly to resent the efforts that his friends were
making to land it for him. When I expressed the opinion
to the President, that as a matter of fact Mr. Justice
Hughes was a candidate and was doing nothing outwardly
to express his disapproval of the efforts being made by his
friends, the President resented my statements.

There was a warm feeling of friendship on the part of
all the members of the President's family toward Mr.
Justice Hughes, and at the Sayre wedding, held in the
White House, one of Justice Hughes' sons had played a
prominent part. Owing to the personal feelings of
friendship of the whole Wilson family for Mr. Hughes, the
curt character of the Justice's letter of resignation to the
President deeply wounded the President and the members
of his family who had been Mr. Hughes' stout defenders
and supporters.

I recall that on the day Mr. Hughes was nominated, and after the news of his nomination was published throughout the country, there came to the Executive offices a coloured messenger, bearing the following abrupt note to the President:

SUPREME COURT OF THE UNITED STATES,
WASHINGTON, D. C.
June 10, 1916.

TO THE PRESIDENT:
I hereby resign the office of Associate Justice of the Supreme Court of the United States.

I am, Sir,
Respectfully yours,
CHARLES E. HUGHES.

When I brought this letter of resignation to the White House the President was in conference with that sturdy Democrat from Kentucky, Senator Ollie M. James. When the President read the letter and observed its rather harsh character he was deeply wounded and disappointed. When he showed it to Senator James, the Senator read it and advised that by reason of its character the President ought not to dignify it by any acknowledgment. The President turned quickly to the Kentucky statesman and said: "No, my dear Senator, the President of the United States must always do the gentlemanly thing."

The President replied to Mr. Hughes in the following note:

THE WHITE HOUSE,
WASHINGTON
June 10, 1916.

DEAR MR. JUSTICE HUGHES:
I am in receipt of your letter of resignation and feel constrained to yield to your desire. I, therefore, accept your resignation as

Justice of the Supreme Court of the United States to take effect at once.

Sincerely yours,
WOODROW WILSON.

HON. CHARLES E. HUGHES,
Washington, D. C.

On the first of August, 1916, I prepared the following memorandum which explained my feelings regarding the campaign of 1916 and what appeared to me to be the weakness of the Republican party and the strength of our own candidacy:

One of the principal arguments upon which the Republican managers lay great stress in favour of Hughes' candidacy is his strength as a campaigner as evidenced in his Youngstown speech delivered years ago in a campaign in which Mr. Bryan was the leader of the Democratic hosts. The strength of that speech lies in its cool analysis of the attitude of a great emotional orator [Bryan] on public questions at a time when the Democracy was advocating economic principles of doubtful strength and virtue. In other words, the position of Justice Hughes in that campaign was that of attacking an economic principle which had cut the Democratic party in two.

The position of Hughes as a candidate in this the [1916] campaign will be radically different for he will have to face a candidate representing a united party; one whose power of analysis is as great as Hughes', and to this will be added this feature of strength in the Democratic candidate—the power of appeal to the emotional or imaginative side of the American people. Added to this will be the strength of conviction in urging his cause that comes to a man who has passed through a world crisis amid great dangers and who has brought to consummation substantial (not visionary) achievements unparalleled in the political history of the country. He will not speak to the country as the representative of a party divided in its counsels or as a dreamer or doctrinaire, but rather will he stand before the country as the practical idealist, defending, not apologizing for, every achievement of his administration.

In his Youngstown speech, Justice Hughes found no difficulty in attacking the economic theories of Bryan. In this attack he not only had the sympathy of his own party but there came to him the support of many Democrats, In this campaign he will have to attack achievements and not principles of doubtful virtue. *I predict that the trip of Hughes to the West will be a disastrous failure.*

When Justice Hughes' Western trip was announced, there was consternation in the ranks of the Democratic party, especially those Democrats with whom I came in contact in Washington. They declared that he would make a tremendous impression on the West and that he would destroy that great salient, and make it impossible for the Democrats to make any gains there.

In a letter which I addressed to Mr. Raymond T. Baker, Director of the Mint, I expressed the opinion that Mr. Hughes' Western trip would prove as distinct a disappointment to his friends as had his speech of acceptance. The letter is as follows:

THE WHITE HOUSE,
WASHINGTON
August 4, 1916.

DEAR RAY:

You have rightly sensed the feelings of the East as to the Hughes speech of acceptance, and I was indeed glad to know from your telegram, which came as welcome news from you, that the sentiment that the speech was a hit-and-miss affair was well nigh universal throughout the West.

There is no apparent slump that I can find here in Democratic ranks; the same buoyancy and optimisn which pervaded the whole Washington atmosphere while you were here still predominate. *My belief is that Hughes' trip to the West will prove another distinct disappointment to his friends.* A candidate following the path of expediency as exemplified by Hughes will find himself in an unenviable position in the West, merely criticizing, finding fault, and setting forth no policy of a constructive character.

As I told you and the boys some weeks ago, Mr. Hughes is going to prove a distinct disappointment as a candidate. He is so eager for the office that he will follow any path that may lead to it, even though it may be the rough path of expediency. We face the foe unafraid, and will soon have our big guns trained upon the frowning fortresses of the enemy. They look formidable at this time, but as we approach them it is my belief that they will be found to be made of cardboard and will fall at the touch of the President's logic and the record of his great achievements.

Sincerely yours,

TUMULTY.

MR. RAYMOND T. BAKER,
  Oakland, California.

CHAPTER XXIV

THE ADAMSON LAW

BETWEEN the Democratic Convention and the time of his departure for his summer home at Long Branch, New Jersey, the President was engaged in Washington in completing the most important items of his legislative programme, including the Income Tax, Child Labour Law, and the Adamson Eight-Hour Law.

A disastrous strike, involving the whole system of railroad transportation, now seemed imminent. At this critical juncture the President intervened. On August 13th he invited the disputants, before reaching any final decision, to confer with him personally at Washington. His intervention evoked general expressions of relief and approval.

At these conferences the railway men stood firm for an eight-hour day. The railway managers refused these demands. How to meet this grave situation, which if not checked might have resulted in giving Germany a victory, was one of the pressing problems that confronted the President that critical summer. Not only were American business interests involved in this matter, but the Allied governments of western Europe, then in the throes of the great war, were no less anxious, for a railroad strike would have meant a cutting off of the supplies to the Allied forces that were so much needed at this important juncture.

The President sent for the Brotherhood representatives and for the managers, to confer with him at the White House, and suggested arbitration by way of settling the controversy. The labour leaders, conscious of their strength, refused to arbitrate. The railroad managers were equally obdurate. I well remember the patience of the President at these conferences day after day. He would first hold conferences with the Brotherhood representatives and then with the railroad managers; but his efforts were unavailing. It is regrettable that the men on both sides were indifferent to the President's appeal and apparently unmindful of the consequences to the country that would inevitably follow a nation-wide strike.

I remember what he said to me as he left the Green Room at the conclusion of his final conference with the heads of the Brotherhoods. Shaking his head in a despairing way, he said: "I was not able to make the slightest impression upon those men. They feel so strongly the justice of their cause that they are blind to all the consequences of their action in declaring and prosecuting a strike. I was shocked to find a peculiar stiffness and hardness about these men. When I pictured to them the distress of our people in case this strike became a reality, they sat unmoved and apparently indifferent to the seriousness of the whole bad business. I am at the end of my tether, and I do not know what further to do."

His conferences with the managers were equally unproductive of result. Gathered about him in a semi-circle in his office, they were grim and determined men, some of them even resentful of the President's attempt to suggest a settlement of any kind to prevent the strike. I shall never forget his last appeal to them. I sat in a little room off the Cabinet room and could hear what went on. Seated about him were the heads of all the important railroads in the country. Looking straight at them, he said: "I have not summoned you to Washington as President of the United States to confer with me on this matter, for I have no power to do so. I have invited you merely as a fellow-citizen to discuss this great and critical situation. Frankly, I say to you that if I had the power as President I would say to you that this strike is unthinkable and must not be permitted to happen. What I want you to see, if you will, is the whole picture that presents itself to me and visualize the terrible consequences to the country and its people of a nation-wide strike at this time, both as affecting our own people and in its effect upon the Allied forces across the sea. For a moment I wish you to forget that I am President, and let us as fellow-citizens consider the consequences of such action. A nation-wide strike at this time would mean absolute famine and starvation for the people of America. You gentlemen must understand just what this means. Will your interests be served by the passions and hatreds that will flow from such an unhappy condition in the country? If this strike should occur, forces will be released that may threaten the security of everything we hold dear. Think of its effect upon the people of this country who must have bread to eat and coal to keep them warm. They will not quietly submit to a strike that will keep these things of life away from them. The rich will not suffer in case these great arteries of trade and commerce are temporarily abandoned, for they can provide themselves against the horror of famine and the distress of this critical situation. It is the poor unfortunate men, and their wives and children, who will suffer and die. I cannot speak to you without a show of emotion, for, my friends, beneath the surface in America there is a baneful seething which may express itself in radical action, the consequences of which no man can foresee. In asking your coöperation to settle this dispute I am but striving, as we stand in the shadow of a great war, to keep these forces in check and under control."

Getting closer to the men, and lowering his voice, he said: "The Allies are fighting our battle, the battle of civilization, across the way. They cannot 'carry on' without supplies and means of sustenance which the railroads of America bring to them. I am probably asking you to make a sacrifice at this time, but is not the sacrifice worth while because of the things involved? Only last night I was thinking about this war and its far-reaching effects. No man can foresee its extent or its evil effects upon the world itself. It is a world cataclysm, and before it ends it may unsettle everything fine and wholesome in America. We of America, although we are cut off from its terrible sweep, cannot be unmindful of these consequences, for we stand in the midst of it all. We must keep our own house in order so that we shall be prepared to act when action becomes necessary. Who knows, gentlemen, but by to-morrow a situation will arise where it shall be found necessary for us to get into the midst of this bloody thing? You can see, therefore, that we must go to the very limit to prevent a strike that would bring about a paralysis of these arteries of trade and commerce. If you will agree with me in this matter, I will address Congress and frankly ask for an increase of rates and do everything I can to make up for the loss you may sustain. I know that the things I ask you to do may be disagreeable and inconvenient, but I am not asking you to make a bloody sacrifice. Our boys may be called upon any minute to make that sacrifice for us."

On August 29, 1916, the President appeared before a joint session of the Congress and recommended immediate legislation to avert the impending strike. Following this, the chairman of the Interstate Commerce Commission of the House, Mr. Adamson, of Georgia, brought in a bill, now known as the Adamson Eight-Hour Law, which, after several unsuccessful attempts by members of the House and Senate to amend it, was signed by the President on September 5th.

CHAPTER XXV

EARLY in January, 1916, German sympathizers throughout the country began a drive on both Houses of Congress for the passage of a resolution warning or forbidding Americans to travel on passenger ships belonging to citizens or subjects of the belligerent nations. Petitions of various kinds, demanding vigorous action in this matter, began to pour in upon us at the White House from various parts of the country. While these petitions were signed by many devoted, patriotic Americans, it was clear to those of us who were on the inside of affairs that there lay back of this movement a sinister purpose on the part of German sympathizers in this country to give Germany full sway upon the high seas, in order that she might be permitted to carry on her unlawful and inhuman submarine warfare. This movement became so intense that leading Democratic and Republican senators and representatives soon became its ardent advocates, until it looked as if the resolution might pass with only a small minority found in opposition to it. Those of us who were in the Executive offices, and intimately associated with the President, kept in close touch with the situation on Capitol Hill and were advised that the movement for the resolution was in full swing and that it could not be checked. A resolution was finally introduced by Representative McLemore, of Texas, and quickly received the support of Senator Gore of Oklahoma, and Senator Stone of Missouri, chairman of the Committee on Foreign Relations. What the attitude of the President should be toward it was the subject of discussion between the President, two of his Cabinet officers, and myself, after a session of the Cabinet early in February, 1916.

The President was advised by the Cabinet officers with whom he conferred regarding the matter that it would be a hopeless task on his part to attempt to stem the tide that was now running in favour of the passage of the McLemore resolution, and that were he to attempt to prevent its passage it might result in a disastrous defeat of his leadership, that would seriously embarrass him on Capitol Hill and throughout the nation.

At the conclusion of this conference the President asked me whether my information about affairs on Capitol Hill and the attitude of the members of the House and Senate toward the McLemore resolution was in accord with the information he had just received from his Cabinet officers. I told him that it was, but that so far as I was concerned I did not share the opinion of the Cabinet officers and did not agree with the advice which they had volunteered, to the effect that it would be useless for him to throw down the gage of battle to those who sought to pass the Mc-Lemore resolution. I informed him that regardless of what the attitude of those on Capitol Hill was toward the resolution, he could not afford to allow the matter to pass without a protest from him, and that, indeed, he could afford to be defeated in making a fight to maintain American rights upon the high seas. The discussion between the President, the Cabinet officers, and myself became heated. They were reluctant to have the President go into the fight, while I was most anxious to have him do so.

Evidently, what I said made an impression upon the President and he asked me, as our conference was concluded, to let him have as soon as possible a memorandum containing my views upon the subject.

Shortly after the conference, Senator Stone, chairman of the Committee on Foreign Relations of the Senate, asked for an appointment with the President, to confer with him on the next morning, February 25th, regarding the McLemore resolution. I suggested to the President that inasmuch as Senator Stone was to see him in the morning it would be wise and prudent if, in answer to his letter asking for an appointment, the President should frankly state his views with reference to the proposed resolution. The President acted upon this suggestion and the letter was immediately dispatched to Senator Stone.

My letter to the President, advising him of the situation, was as follows:

THE WHITE HOUSE,
WASHINGTON
February 24, 1916.

DEAR GOVERNOR:

What I have heard since leaving you this morning confirms me in my belief that now is the time (before the night passes) to set forth your position to the country on the McLemore resolution in terms that no one can misunderstand. In the last hour I have talked with Speaker Clark, Senator Pittman, and Mr. Sims of Tennessee, and have received impressions from them which lead me to conclude: first, that the consideration of this resolution cannot much longer be postponed, as Speaker Clark so informed me, although Congressman Doremus and Senator Pittman say the situation on the hill is quieting down. I am more than convinced that underlying this resolution is a purpose to discredit your leadership, for the forces that are lined up for this fight against you are the anti-preparedness crowd, the Bryan-Kitchen-Clark group, and some of the anti-British

Senators like Hoke Smith and Gore. Therefore, I cannot urge you too strongly at once to send an identic letter to both Representative Flood, chairman of the Foreign Relations Committee of the House, and Senator Stone, chairman of the Foreign Relations Committee of the Senate. The letter, in my opinion, should embody the following ideas:

First, explain in the frankest fashion just what Secretary Lansing attempted to obtain when he suggested to the Entente nations an agreement on the arming of merchantmen, how this government was informed by Germany of her intention to destroy armed merchantmen without giving the passengers a moment of warning, and how, in order to stave off such a contingency, we tried as the friend and in the interest of humanity to get an agreement between both sides that would bring submarine warfare within the bounds of international law.

Second, explain that a possible adjustment of this matter is in process of negotiation right now, and that, of course, while we cannot change international law upon our own initiative, we are still of the hope that some general agreement among the belligerents may eventually be obtained. Explain how embarrassing such a resolution as the McLemore one will be to negotiations now being threshed out between the executive branches of the Government charged with the conduct of foreign relations, and foreign governments.

Third, then say that in the absence of any general agreement, the United States cannot yield one inch of her rights without destroying the whole fabric of international law, for in the last analysis this is what is involved. To yield one right to-day means another to-morrow. We cannot know where this process of yielding on the ground of convenience or expediency may lead us. These laws are the product of centuries. Our forefathers fought to establish their validity, and we cannot afford for the sake of convenience when our very life is threatened, to adandon them on any ground of convenience or expediency.

Fourth, to pass such a resolution at this time would seriously embarrass the Department of State and the Executive in the conduct of these most delicate matters at a time when everything is being done to bring about a peaceful solution of these problems.

Fifth, might you not diplomatically suggest, in your letter to

Senator Stone, that to pass favorably upon a resolution of this kind at this time would be showing lack of confidence in the Government, and particularly in its Chief Executive?

The morning papers have outlined the details of the opposition among the Democrats. The afternoon papers are repeating the same thing with emphasis on the fact that Joe Cannon, Jim Mann, and Lodge are going to support you. I would suggest that you insert the following in your letter to Senator Stone:

"I think that not only would such a vote on this resolution be construed as a lack of confidence in the executive branch of the Government in this most delicate matter but if the division continues as I am informed within the ranks of the Democratic party, it will be difficult for me to consider that the majority party speaks the will of the nation in these circumstances and as between any faction in my party and the interests of the nation, I must always choose the latter, irrespective of what the effect will be on me or my personal fortunes. What we are contending for in this matter is of the very essence of the things that have made America a sovereign nation. She cannot yield them without admitting and conceding her own impotency as a nation and the surrender of her independent position among the nations of the world."

Sincerely,

TUMULTY.

The letter of the President to Senator Stone was published in the morning papers of February 25, 1916, and is as follows:

THE WHITE HOUSE,
WASHINGTON
February 25, 1916.

MY DEAR SENATOR:

I very warmly appreciate your kind and frank letter of to-day, and feel that it calls for an equally frank reply.

You are right in assuming that I shall do everything in my power to keep the United States out of war. I think the country will feel no uneasiness about my course in that respect. Through many anxious months I have striven for that object, amid difficulties more manifold than can have been apparent upon the surface, and so far

I have succeeded. I do not doubt that I shall continue to succeed. The course which the central European powers have announced their intention of following in the future with regard to undersea warfare seems for the moment to threaten insuperable obstacles, but its apparent meaning is so manifestly inconsistent with explicit assurances recently given us by those powers with regard to their treatment of merchant vessels on the high seas that I must believe that explanations will presently ensue which will put a different aspect upon it. We have had no reason to question their good faith or their fidelity to their promises in the past, and I for one feel confident that we shall have none in the future.

But in any event our duty is clear. No nation, no group of nations, has the right, while war is in progress, to alter or disregard the principles which all nations have agreed upon in mitigation of the horrors and sufferings of war; and if the clear rights of American citizens should very unhappily be abridged or denied by any such action we should, it seems to me, have in honour no choice as to what our own course should be.

For my own part I cannot consent to any abridgment of the rights of American citizens in any respect. The honour and self-respect of the nation is involved. We covet peace, and shall preserve it at any cost but the loss of honor. To forbid our people to exercise their rights for fear we might be called upon to vindicate them would be a deep humiliation, indeed. It would be an implicit, all but an explicit, acquiescence in the violation of the rights of mankind everywhere and of whatever nation or allegiance. It would be a deliberate abdication of our hitherto proud position as spokesmen, even amid the turmoil of war, for the law and the right. It would make everything this government has attempted and everything that it has accomplished during this terrible struggle of nations meaningless and futile.

It is important to reflect that if in this instance we allowed expediency to take the place of principle the door would inevitably be opened to still further concessions. Once accept a single abatement of right, and many other humiliations would follow, and the whole fine fabric of international law might crumble under our hands piece by piece. What we are contending for in this matter is of the very essence of the things that have made America a sovereign nation. She cannot yield them without conceding her own impotency as a nation and making virtual surrender of her independent position among the nations of the world.

I am speaking, my dear Senator, in deep solemnity, without heat, with a clear consciousness of the high responsibilities of my office and as your sincere and devoted friend. If we should unhappily differ, we shall differ as friends, but where issues so momentous as these are involved we must, just because we are friends, speak our minds without reservation.

Faithfully yours,
WOODROW WILSON.

SENATOR WILLIAM J. STONE,
United States Senate.

The publication of the letter of the President to Senator Stone worked a complete reversal of opinion on the Hill.

Quickly the effect of the President's letter was seen, and the McLemore resolution was overwhelmingly defeated.

Early in August, 1916, the President took up his residence at Shadow Lawn, New Jersey, and began the preparation of his speech of acceptance. He forwarded me a draft of this speech which brought from me the following comment upon it:

THE WHITE HOUSE,
WASHINGTON

August 22, 1916.

DEAR GOVERNOR:

I think the failure to bring out the hyphen question in your speech of acceptance will be vigorously criticized even by our loyal friends. Mr. Hughes will soon be compelled to speak out on this question. Roosevelt's speeches in the main will force him to do this.

You might open the subject in that part of your speech in which you discuss neutrality, showing the embarrassments under which you have laboured in trying to keep the Nation at peace. After discussing these embarrassments, consisting of plots against our industries, etc., could you not introduce a sentence like this?: "While I am the candidate of the Democratic party, I am above all else an American citizen. I neither seek the favour nor fear the wrath of any alien element in America which puts loyalty to any foreign power first."

As to Huerta: I believe your reference to him could be strengthened. I think you ought to bring out the fact that the work of assassination shall never receive the endorsement, so far as you are concerned, of this American Republic. I suggest the following: "The United States will refuse, so long as that power remains with me, to extend the hand of welcome to one who gains power in a republic through treachery and bloodshed." (This is not only sound statesmanship but good morals.) "No permanency in the affairs of our sister republics can be attained by a title based upon intrigue and assassination."

Respectfully,

TUMULTY.

The President, always welcoming advice, approved and embodied some of these suggestions in his speech of acceptance.

It has often been said by unfair critics that Mr. Wilson was so tenacious of his own opinion and views that he resented suggestions from the outside in any matter with which he was called upon to deal.

As an intimate associate of his for eleven years, I think I was in a position to find out and to know how unfair the basis of this criticism really was. In my contact with public men I never met a more open-minded man; nor one who was more willing to act upon any suggestion that had merit in it. I have seen him readily give up his own views and often yield to the influence of a better argument. I always felt free in every public matter that he discussed and in every attitude which he took on public questions frankly to express my own opinion and openly

Dear Tumulty

How is this expurgated stuff. Do atest you please write it.

W.W.

---

24 Nov., 1918.

Dear Tumulty,

Here is the message. I wish you would read it and give me your impression of it.

And please keep it very carefully from any eyes but your own. It is still in provisional shape only, and there are a number of points I am still keeping under advisement.

Faithfully,

W.W.

THE WHITE HOUSE,
WASHINGTON.

17 May, 1918.

Dear Tumulty,

Thank you for the memorandum about peace suggestions. I have read it very carefully and find my own thoughts travelling very much the same route. You may be sure I am doing a great deal of serious thinking about it all.

Faithfully,

W.W.

Some insights into day-to-day affairs at the White House

to disagree with him. In his speeches and public statements he had no pride of opinion, nor did he attempt to hold his friends off at arms' length when they had suggestions of any kind to make.

In these reminiscences I am including my letters to him, embodying suggestions of various kinds, many of which he acted upon and many of which he rejected, in order that proof may be given of the fact, that despite what his critics may say, he not only did not resent suggestions, but openly invited them.

CHAPTER XXVI

AFTER the delivery of the speech of acceptance on September 2nd quiet ruled over the Wilson camp at Shadow Lawn. This lull in the matter of politics was intensified by the President's absence from Shadow Lawn because of the death of his only sister, which called him away and for a while took his mind and his energies from the discussion of politics.

On September 11th, the state elections in Maine were carried by the Republicans. The total vote was the largest ever cast in Maine in a state election. The Republican majorities ranged from 9,000 to 14,000. There had been a vigorous contest in Maine by both parties and the Republicans were greatly heartened by the result in the hope that "as goes Maine so goes the Union."

There is no doubt that the result in Maine, which many Democrats were of the opinion was a forecast of the results throughout the nation in November, had a depressing effect. The Republicans accepted it as a harbinger of victory and the Democrats as an indication of defeat. On the night of the Maine elections I kept close to the telephone at the Executive offices and engaged in conferences with two or three practical politicians from New Jersey. It was interesting to watch the effects of the returns from Maine upon these men. When the returns, as complete as we could get them at twelve o'clock on the

night of September 11th, came in, James Nugent, one
of the leading politicians of Essex County, New Jersey,
who was in the room, took from my desk a copy of the
"World Almanac", and referring to the returns of previous
elections, said: "Of course, the Republicans will hail this
as a great victory, but if they will sit down and analyze
the gains they have made, they will find no comfort in
them, for to me they indicate a Democratic victory in
November. If the Democrats make proportionate gains
in other states, you can absolutely count upon a Democratic victory in 1916.

This prophecy was verified by the results of the election
of November 7th.

It was difficult and almost impossible between the date
of the speech of acceptance and the first of October to
revive interest in the Democratic campaign and to bring
about a renewal of hope of success that had almost been
destroyed by the psychological results of the Maine
election.

Frequent demands were made upon us at the Executive
offices at Asbury Park to get busy and to do something.
"Wilson was not on the front page and Hughes was busily
engaged in campaigning throughout the West."   But the
President in his uncanny way knew better than we the
psychological moment to strike.   He went about his work
at the Executive offices and gave to us who were closely
associated with him the impression that nothing unusual
was afoot and that no Presidential campaign was impending.   I made frequent suggestions to him that he be up
and doing.   He would only smile and calmly say: "The
moment is not here.   Let them use up their ammunition
and then we will turn our guns upon them."

The psychological moment came, and the President

took full advantage of it. One afternoon in September the President telephoned me at the Executive offices at Asbury Park to have the newspaper men present for a conference that afternoon; that he would give out a reply to a telegram he had received. With the newspaper group, I attended this conference. It appeared that an Irish agitator named Jeremiah O'Leary, who had been organizing and speaking against the President and trying to array the Irish vote against him, wrote an offensive letter to the President, calling attention to the results of the Maine elections and to the New Jersey primaries, and to his anticipated defeat in November. The President handed to the newspaper men the following reply to O'Leary:

I would feel deeply mortified to have you or anybody like you vote for me. Since you have access to many disloyal Americans and I have not, I will ask you to convey this message to them.

This sharp and timely rebuke to the unpatriotic spirit to which O'Leary gave expression won the hearty and unanimous approval of the country to the President. Nothing like this bold defiance came from Hughes until a few days before the election.

The Democratic campaign, within twenty-four hours after the publication of the O'Leary telegram, was on again in full swing.

At this same newspaper conference the President, who had not seen the newspaper group since his arrival at Long Branch, discussed the campaign, so that they might have what he called the "inside of his mind." His criticism of the campaign that Justice Hughes was conducting contained bitter irony and sarcasm. Evidently, the petty things to which Mr. Hughes had adverted in his campaign speeches by way of criticizing the President and his administration had cut the President to the quick. One of the newspaper men asked him what he thought of Mr. Hughes' campaign, and he laughingly replied: "If you will give that gentleman rope enough he will hang himself. He has forgotten many things since he closeted himself on the bench, and he will soon find himself out of touch with the spirit of the nation. His speeches are nothing more or less than blank cartridges and the country, unless I mistake the people very much, will place a true assessment upon them."

The newspaper men left this conference heartened by the reply he had made to O'Leary and with the firm conviction that the Democratic candidate was just "playing" with Hughes and would pounce upon him at the psychological moment.

In the delivery of the campaign speeches at Shadow Lawn each Saturday afternoon President Wilson took full advantage of the swing toward the Democratic side which was manifest after the publication of the famous O'Leary telegram. While the Republican candidate was busily engaged in invading the West in his swing around the circle, the Democratic candidate each week from his porch at Shadow Lawn was delivering sledge-hammer blows at the Republican breastworks. As the Republican candidate in an effort to win the West was heaping maledictions upon Dr. E. Lester Jones, the head of the Geodetic Survey, a Wilson appointee, the President calmly moved on, ripping to pieces and tearing to shreds the poor front behind which the Republican managers were seeking to win the fight.

Mr. Hughes campaigned like a lawyer, Mr. Wilson like a statesman. Mr. Hughes was hunting small game with bird shot, Mr. Wilson trained heavy artillery on the enemies' central position. The essential difference between the two men and the operations of their minds was made clear in the campaign. No one would wish to minimize the unusual abilities of Mr. Hughes, but they are the abilities of an adroit lawyer. He makes "points." He pleases those minds which like cleverness and finesse. He deals with international affairs like an astute lawyer drawing a brief. But has he ever quickened the nation's pulse or stirred its heart by a single utterance? Did he ever make any one feel that behind the formalities of law, civil or international, he detected the heartbeats of humanity whom law is supposedly designed to serve? Mr. Wilson was not thinking of Mr. Hughes, but perhaps he was thinking of the type of which Mr. Hughes is an eminent example when he said in Paris: "This is not to be a lawyers' peace."

Every speech of President Wilson's was, to use a baseball phrase, a home run for the Democratic side. They were delivered without much preparation and were purely extemporaneous in character. The Republican opposition soon began to wince under the smashing blows delivered by the Democratic candidate, and outward proof was soon given of the fear and despair that were now gathering in the Republican ranks. With a few short trips to the West, and his final speech at Long Branch, President Wilson closed his campaign, with Democratic hopes on the rise.

The happenings of Election Day, 1916, will long linger in my memory. I was in charge of the Executive offices located at Asbury Park, while the President remained at Shadow Lawn, awaiting the news of the first returns from the country. The first scattered returns that filtered in

to the Executive offices came from a little fishing town
in Massachusetts early in the afternoon of Election Day,
which showed a slight gain for the President over the
election returns of 1912. Then followed early drifts from
Colorado and Kansas, which showed great Wilson gains.
Those of us who were interested in the President's cause
were made jubilant by these early returns. Every indication, though imperfect, up to seven o'clock on the
night of the election, forecasted the President's reëlection.

In the early afternoon the President telephoned the
Executive offices to inquire what news we had received
from the country and he was apprised of the results that
had come in up to that time. Then, quickly, the tide
turned against us in the most unusual way. Between
seven and nine o'clock the returns slowly came in from the
East and Middle West that undeniably showed a drift
away from us.

About nine-thirty o'clock in the evening I was seated
in my office, when a noise outside in the hallway attracted
my attention and gave me the impression that something
unusual was afoot. The door of my office opened and
there entered a galaxy of newspaper men connected with
the White House offices, led by a representative of the
New York *World*, who held in his hands a bulletin from
his office, carrying the news of Hughes' election. The
expression in the men's faces told me that a crisis was at
hand. The *World* man delivered his fateful message of
defeat for our forces, without explanation of any kind.
To me the blow was stunning, for the New York *World* had
been one of our staunchest supporters throughout the
whole campaign, and yet, I had faith to believe that the
news carried in the bulletin would be upset by subsequent
returns. Steadying myself behind my desk, I quickly

made up my mind as to what my reply should be to the
World bulletin and to the query of the newspaper men
whether we were ready to "throw up the sponge" and
concede Hughes' election. Concealing the emotion I felt,
I dictated the following statement, which was flashed
through the country:

> When Secretary Tumulty was shown the *World* bulletin, con-
> ceding Hughes' election, he authorized the following statement: "Wil-
> son will win. The West has not yet been heard from. Sufficient gains
> will be made in the West and along the Pacific slope to offset the losses
> in the East."

Shortly after the flash from the *World* bulletin was
delivered to me, conceding Hughes' election, the President
again telephoned me from Long Branch to find out the
latest news of the election. From what he said he had
already been apprised by Admiral Grayson of the bulletin
of the New York *World*. Every happening of that
memorable night is still fresh in my memory and I recall
distinctly just what the President said and how philosophi-
cally he received the news of his apparent defeat. Laughingly he said: "Well, Tumulty, it begins to look as if we
have been badly licked." As he discussed the matter
with me I could detect no note of sadness in his voice.
In fact, I could hear him chuckle over the 'phone. He
seemed to take an impersonal view of the whole thing and
talked like a man from whose shoulders a great load had
been lifted and now he was happy and rejoicing that he
was a free man again. When I informed him of the drifts
in our favour from other parts of the country and said that
it was too early to concede anything, he said: "Tumulty,
you are an optimist. It begins to look as if the defeat
might be overwhelming. The only thing I am sorry for,
and that cuts me to the quick, is that the people ap-

parently misunderstood us. But I have no regrets. We have tried to do our duty." So far as he was concerned, the issue of the election was disposed of, out of the way and a settled thing. That was the last telephone message between the President and myself until twenty-four hours later, when the tide turned again in our favour.

An unusual incident occurred about 8:30 o'clock in the evening, shortly after my talk with the President. I was called to the telephone and told that someone in New York wished to speak to me on a highly important matter. I went to the 'phone. At the other end in New York was an individual who refusing to give his name, described himself as a friend of our cause. I thought he was one of the varieties of crank, with whom I had been accustomed to deal at the White House on frequent occasions during my life there; but there was something about his talk that convinced me that he was in close touch with someone in authority at Republican headquarters. In his first talk with me, and in subsequent talks during the night of the election and on the following day, there was a warning to us, in no way, or by the slightest sign, to give up the fight, or to concede Hughes' election. He said: "Early returns will naturally run against Wilson in the East, particularly in Illinois and Iowa," and intimated to me that the plan at Republican headquarters would be to exaggerate these reports and to overwhelm us with news of Republican victories throughout the country. Continuing his talk he said: "The Wilson fight will be won in the West. I shall keep you advised of what is happening in Republican headquarters. I can only tell you that I will *know* what is happening and you may rely upon the information I shall give you."

All night long the loyal newspaper men and I kept vigil at the Executive offices. As I read over the bulletins that came to me, particularly those from Republican head-quarters in New York, I was quick to notice that although the Republican managers were blatantly proclaiming to the country that the fight was over, for some reason or other, the Republican candidate, Mr. Hughes, who was at his headquarters at the Hotel Astor, was silent.

Just about this time there was another message from the mysterious stranger in New York. The message, as I recall it, was as follows: "They [meaning the Republican managers] are trying to induce Hughes to claim the election, but he is unwilling to make an announcement and is asking for further returns. You boys stant pat. Returns that are now coming in are worrying them. Don't be swept off your feet by claims from Republican head-quarters. I know what is happening there."

Shortly after this telephone message came a bulletin from Republican headquarters, stating that the Re-publican managers were then in conference with Mr. Hughes and that a statement from Mr. Hughes would soon be forthcoming. This unusual coincidence convinced me that the man who was telephoning me either was on the inside of affairs at Republican headquarters, or had an uncanny way of knowing just what the managers were doing.

Up to eleven o'clock every bit of news ran against us. Finally, the Brooklyn *Eagle*, a supporter of the President, and then the New York *Times*, our last line of defense, gave way and conceded Hughes' election, but the unterrified Democrats at the Executive offices stood out against any admission of defeat.

The mysterious stranger was again on the wire, saying

that there was consternation in the Republican ranks; that George Perkins had just conferred with National Chairman Willcox and had left Willcox's room, shaking his head and saying to one of the attachés of headquarters, that "things were not looking well." A few minutes later a bulletin came from Republican headquarters confirming the story the mysterious stranger had just told over the 'phone.

All the while I was keeping in touch with our headquarters in New York City, and about 10:30 o'clock Robert W. Woolley, the publicity man of the Democratic National Committee, 'phoned me and advised me not to concede anything and assured me that the returns from the West, now coming in greater drifts, indicated Wilson's reëlection.

When I left the telephone booth, David Lawrence, the Washington correspondent of the New York *Evening Post*, who a few weeks before had predicted, in a remarkable article, the election of Wilson, and who was my friend and co-labourer during that night (in conjunction with Mr. L. Ames Brown, a noted newspaper man of Washington, connected with the Democratic National Committee) conferred with me, and from a table he had prepared showed me how the small states of the West, which the returns indicated were now coming into the Wilson column, would elect the Democratic candidate, and that under no circumstances must we, by any chance, in any statement, concede the election of Hughes.

All night long telephone messages, very brief, would come from the mysterious stranger in New York, and quickly there would follow bulletins from Republican headquarters confirming everything that he said. These messages came so rapidly that I was soon convinced that this individual, whoever he was, had the real inside of the Republican situation. So convinced was I that I followed up my statement of the early evening with additional statements, claiming the election for Mr. Wilson.

Just about the break of day on Wednesday morning, as David Lawrence, Ames Brown, and my son Joe, were seated in my office, a room which overlooked a wide expanse of the Atlantic Ocean, we were notified by Democratic headquarters of the first big drift toward Wilson. Ohio, which in the early evening had been claimed by the Republicans, had turned to Wilson by an approximate majority of sixty thousand; Kansas followed; Utah was leaning toward him; North Dakota and South Dakota inclining the same way. The Wilson tide began to rise appreciably from that time on, until state after state from the West came into the Wilson column. At five o'clock in the morning the New York *Times* and the New York *World* recanted and were now saying that the election of Mr. Hughes was doubtful.

Without sleep and without food, those of us at the Executive offices kept close to the telephone wire. We never left the job for a minute. The last message from the mysterious stranger came about one o'clock, the day following the election, when he 'phoned me that, "George Perkins is now at Republican headquarters and is telephoning Roosevelt and will soon leave to inform Roosevelt that, to use his own words, 'the jig is up,' and that Wilson is elected." Shortly after, from Republican headquarters came a bulletin saying: "George Perkins is on his way to confer with Mr. Roosevelt."

Some months after the election the mysterious stranger came to the White House offices, and without identifying

himself, informed me that he was the individual who
on the night of the election had kept me in touch with
Republican headquarters, and then astounded me by
telling me that in some mysterious way, which he did
not disclose, he had succeeded in breaking in on the Republican National Committee wire and had listened in
on every conversation that had passed between Willcox,
Hughes, George Perkins, Harvey, and Theodore Roosevelt himself during the night of the election and the day
following.

Mr. Wilson arose the morning after the election,
confident that he had been defeated. He went about his
tasks in the usual way. The first news that he received
that there had been a turn in the tide came from his daughter, Margaret, who knocked on the door of the bathroom
while the President was shaving and told him of the
"Extra" of the New York *Times*, saying that the election
was in doubt, with indications of a Wilson victory.
The President thought that his daughter was playing
a practical joke on him and told her to "tell that to the
Marines," and went on about his shaving.

When the President and I discussed the visit of his
daughter, Margaret, to notify him of his reëlection, he
informed me that he was just beginning to enjoy the
reaction of defeat when he was notified that the tide
had turned in his favour. This will seem unusual, but
those of us who were close to the man and who understood the trials and tribulations of the Presidency, knew
that he was in fact for the first time in four years enjoying
the freedom of private life.

Mr. Wilson's imperturbability on election night was
like that of sturdy Grover Cleveland, though tempera-
mentally the men were unlike. Mr. Cleveland used to

tell his friends how in 1884 he had gone to bed early not knowing who was elected, and how he learned the news of his election next morning from his valet, after having first made inquiries about the state of the weather. In 1892 Mr. Cleveland, his wife, and two friends played a quiet game of cards while the returns were coming in. In reciting these reminiscences, the old warrior used to say that he never could understand the excitement of candidates on election nights. "The fight is all over then," he would say, "and it is merely a matter of counting the ballots." Mr. Wilson preserved the same calmness, which appeared almost like indifference. In 1912 he sat in the sitting room of his little cottage in Cleveland Lane in Princeton quietly reading from one of his favourite authors and occasionally joining in the conversation of Mrs. Wilson and a few neighbours who had dropped in. In a rear room there was a telegraphic ticker, an operator, and some newspaper boys who at intervals would take an especially interesting bulletin in to Mr. Wilson, who would glance at it casually, make some brief comment, and then return to his book. One of the guests of the evening who read in a newspaper next day a rather melodramatic and entirely imaginative account of the scene, said: "The only dramatic thing about the evening was that there was nothing dramatic."

CHAPTER XXVII

WHILE President Wilson was giving his whole thought and effort to the solution of exacting domestic tasks, the European war broke upon him and thus turned his attention and study to the age-long and complicated political struggle between Germany, France, and England.

Fully conscious from the very beginning of the difficulties that lay in his path, he was aware of the eventualities the war now beginning might lead to. As a profound student of history he saw with a clear vision the necessity of neutrality and of America remaining disentangled in every way from the embroilments of Europe. To the people of the country it at first appeared that the war was one more in a long series of European quarrels and that we must play our part in the great conflict as mere spectators and strictly adhere to the American policy of traditional aloofness and isolation, which had been our immemorial custom and habit. Although we were bound to maintain a policy of isolation, Woodrow Wilson from the beginning foresaw its futility, and afterward gave expression to this conviction in a campaign speech in 1916, when he said:

This is the last war [meaning the World War] of its kind or of any kind that involves the world that the United States can keep out of. I say that because I believe that the business of neutrality is over; not because I want it to be over, but I mean this, that war now has such a scale that the position of neutrals sooner or later becomes intolerable.

He knew how difficult it would be to keep a people so variously constituted strictly neutral. No sooner was his proclamation of neutrality announced than the differences in points of view in racial stocks began to manifest themselves in language both intemperate and passionate, until his advice to his country "to be neutral in fact as well as in name" became a dead and spiritless thing.

I have often been asked if the policy of neutrality which the President announced, and which brought a fire of criticism upon him, represented his own personal feelings toward the European war, and whether if he had been a private citizen, he would have derided it as now his critics were engaged in doing.

As an intimate associate of Woodrow Wilson during the whole of the European war, and witnessing from day to day the play of his feelings, especially after the violation of the neutrality of Belgium, I am certain that had he been free to do so he would have yielded to the impulse of championing a cause that in his heart of hearts he felt involved the civilization of the world. But it was his devotion to the idea of trusteeship that held him in check, and the consciousness that in carrying out that trusteeship he had no right to permit his own passionate feelings to govern his public acts.

It would have been a dramatic adventure to accept Germany's assault on Belgium as a challenge to the humane interest of America, but the acceptance would have been only a gesture, for we were unable to transport armies to the theatre of war in time to check the outrage. Such action would have pleased some people in the East, but the President knew that this quixotic knight errantry would not appeal to the country at large, particularly the West, still strongly grounded in the Washingtonian tradition of non-interference in European quarrels.

Colonel Roosevelt himself, who subsequently attacked so strongly the "pusillanimity" of the Administration's course, said on September 23, 1914:

A deputation of Belgians has arrived in this country to invoke our assistance in the time of their dreadful need. What action our government can or will take I know not. It has been announced that no action can be taken that will interfere with our entire neutrality. It is certainly eminently desirable that we should remain entirely neutral and nothing but urgent need would warrant breaking our neutrality and taking sides one way or the other.

It was not the policy of a weakling or a timid man. It was the policy of a prudent leader and statesman, who was feeling his way amid dangers and who as an historian himself knew the difficulties of an imprudent or incautious move.

I recall the day he prepared his neutrality proclamation. At the end of one of the most strenuous days of his life in Washington, he left the Executive offices where he was engaged in meeting and conferring with senators and congressmen, and I found him comfortably seated under an elm tree, serenely engaged with pad and pencil in preparing his neutrality proclamation, which was soon to loose a fierce storm of opposition and ridicule upon him. He and I had often discussed the war and its effect upon our own country, and one day in August, 1914, just after the Great War had begun, he said to me: "We are going through deep waters in the days to come. The passions now lying dormant will soon be aroused and my motives and purposes at every turn will soon be challenged until there will be left but few friends to justify my course. It does not seem clear now, but as this war grows in intensity it will soon resolve itself into a war between autocracy and democracy. Various racial groups in America will seek to lead us now one way and then another. We must sit steady in the boat and bow our heads to meet the storm."

Bound as he was by the responsibilities of trusteeship to adhere to a policy of neutrality, personally he saw that the inevitable results would be only bitter disappointment. "We cannot remain isolated in this war," he said, "for soon the contagion of it will spread until it reaches our own shores. On the one side Mr. Bryan will censure the Administration for being too militaristic, and on the other we will find Mr. Roosevelt criticizing us because we are too pacifist in our tendencies."

Dr. William E. Dodd, in his book "Woodrow Wilson and His Work," has sensed the complicated situation in which the President found himself: "The British blockade, becoming more effective every day, barred the way of American goods to Germany and even neutral countries. Hoke Smith and a score of southern senators and representatives urged him to protest against the blockade. Representatives of the packers of Chicago and the farmers of the Northwest urged him to open the way to hungry markets for their goods. He made his fight during the autumn of 1914 and 1915 against all the more drastic phases of the British blockade, against British interference with our cargoes for neutral ports." Every artificial device for increasing our trade with neutral countries was suggested by those who sought his aid and counsel in the matter. Cotton of all the commodities

was the hardest hit. When a friend from Georgia urged
action by the President to help in the matter of cotton,
the President tried to impress upon him that, with the
World War in progress, the law of supply and demand
was deeply affected and that the sales of cotton were
necessarily restricted by reason of the closure of certain
markets to our goods. This friend, in urging his views
upon the President, said: "But you, Mr. President, can
suspend the law of supply and demand." The President
responded by saying: "If I did, Judge, and you ran
your head up against it, you might get hurt."

Every sympathizer with Germany pursued the President relentlessly with insistent demand that England
should be brought to book for the unreasonable character
of the blockade which she was carrying on against our
commerce on the high seas. The President in every
diplomatic way possible pressed America's claims against
England, but these demands did not satisfy the German
sympathizers throughout the country who covertly
sought to bring about a real breach between the two
countries. Even I felt that we should go further in our
demands upon England than the President seemed
willing to go.

The pressure upon us at the White House for satisfaction at the hands of England grew more intense
with each day. I recall a conversation I had with the
President shortly before the Congressional elections
when the President's political enemies were decrying his
kind treatment of England and excoriating him for the
stern manner in which he was holding Germany to strict
accountability for her actions. This conversation was
held while we were on board the President's train on our
way to the West. After dinner one evening I tactfully

broached the subject of the British blockade and laid
before the President the use our enemies were making of
his patient action toward England. My frank criticism
deeply aroused him. Replying to me he pitilessly attacked those who were criticizing him for "letting up
on Great Britain." Looking across the table at me he
said: "I am aware of the demands that are daily being
made upon me by my friends for more vigorous action
against England in the matter of the blockade; I am
aware also of the sinister political purpose that lies back
of many of these demands. Many senators and congressmen who urge radical action against England are
thinking only of German votes in their districts and are
not thinking of the world crisis that would inevitably
occur should there be an actual breach at this time between England and America over the blockade." Then
looking squarely at me, he said: "I have gone to the very
limit in pressing our claims upon England and in urging
the British Foreign Office to modify the blockade. Walter Page, our Ambassador to England, has placed every
emphasis upon our insistence that something be done,
and something will be done, but England, now in the
throes of a great war crisis, must at least be given a
chance to adjust these matters. Only a few days ago
Mr. Page wrote me a most interesting letter, describ-
ing the details of a conference he had had with Sir
Edward Grey, the British Foreign Secretary, to discuss our protests against the British blockade. Mr.
Page described the room in which the conference was
held, on the wall of which was hung as a memorial the
fifteen-million-dollar check with which Great Britain
paid the *Alabama* claims in the Civil War. Mr. Page
pointed to this *Alabama* check and said: 'If you don't

stop these seizures, Sir Edward, some day you will have
your entire room papered with things like that.' Sir
Edward replied: 'That may be so, but we will pay every
cent. Of course, many of the restrictions we have laid
down and which seriously interfere with your trade
are unreasonable. But America must remember that
we are fighting her fight, as well as our own, to save the
civilization of the world. You dare not press us too far!'"
Turning to me, the President said: "He was right. England is fighting our fight and you may well understand
that I shall not, in the present state of the world's affairs,
place obstacles in her way. Many of our critics suggest
war with England in order to force reparation in these
matters. War with England would result in a German
triumph. No matter what may happen to me personally
in the next election, I will not take any action to embarrass England when she is fighting for her life and the
life of the world. Let those who clamour for radical action against England understand this!"

While the critics of the President were busily engaged
in embarrassing and "hazing" him at every point and
insisting upon a "show-down" with Great Britain over
the blockade, the world was startled on May 7, 1915,
by the news of the sinking of the *Lusitania*, off the coast
of Ireland, resulting in the loss of many American lives.
A few days later came the news that the German people
were rejoicing at the fine stroke of the submarine commander in consummating this horrible tragedy.

The President's critics who, a few days before, were
assailing him for his supposed surrender to England, were
now demanding an immediate declaration of war against
Germany, but not for a moment did the President
waver before these clamorous demands. To such an

extent did he carry this attitude of calmness and steadiness of purpose that on "the outside" the people felt that there was in him a heartlessness and an indifference to the deep tragedy of the *Lusitania*. At my first meeting with him I tried to call to his attention many of the tragic details of the sinking of the great ship in an effort to force his hands, so to speak, but he quickly checked what appeared to be my youthful impetuosity and said: "Tumulty, it would be much wiser for us not to dwell too much upon these matters." When he uttered this admonition there was no suggestion of coldness about him. In fact, he seemed to be deeply moved as I adverted to some of the facts surrounding this regrettable and tragic affair. At times tears stood in his eyes, and turning to me he said: "If I pondered over those tragic items that daily appear in the newspapers about the *Lusitania*, I should see red in everything, and I am afraid that when I am called upon to act with reference to this situation I could not be just to any one. I dare not act unjustly and cannot indulge my own passionate feelings."

Evidently he saw that his turning away from the topic in this apparently indifferent way did not sit well with me. Quickly he understood my dissatisfaction and said: "I suppose you think I am cold and indifferent and little less than human, but, my dear fellow, you are mistaken, for I have spent many sleepless hours thinking about this tragedy. It has hung over me like a terrible nightmare. In God's name, how could any nation calling itself civilized purpose so horrible a thing?"

At the time we were discussing this grave matter we were seated in the President's study in the White House. I had never seen him more serious or careworn. I was aware that he was suffering under the criticism that had been heaped upon him for his apparent inaction in the matter of the *Lusitania*. Turning to me he said: "Let me try to make my attitude in this matter plain to you, so that you at least will try to understand what lies in my thoughts. I am bound to consider in the most careful and cautious way the first step I shall take, because once having taken it I cannot withdraw from it. I am bound to consider beforehand all the facts and circumstances surrounding the sinking of the *Lusitania* and to calculate the effect upon the country of every incautious or unwise move. I am keenly aware that the feeling of the country is now at fever heat and that it is ready to move with me in any direction I shall suggest, but I am bound to weigh carefully the effect of radical action now based upon the present emotionalism of the people. I am not sure whether the present emotionalism of the country would last long enough to sustain any action I would suggest to Congress, and thus in case of failure we should be left without that fine backing and support so necessary to maintain a great cause. I could go to Congress to-morrow and advocate war with Germany and I feel certain that Congress would support me, but what would the country say when war was declared, and finally came, and we were witnessing all of its horrors and bloody aftermath. As the people pored over the casualty lists, would they not say: 'Why did Wilson move so fast in this matter? Why didn't he try peaceably to settle this question with Germany? Why could he not have waited a little longer? Why was he so anxious to go to war with Germany, yet at the same time why was he so tender of the feelings of Great Britain in the matter of the blockade?' Were I to advise radical action now, we should have nothing, I am afraid, but regrets and heartbreaks. The vastness

of this country; its variegated elements; the conflicting
cross-currents of national feelings bid us wait and withhold ourselves from hasty or precipitate action. When
we move against Germany we must be certain that the
whole country not only moves with us but is willing to
go forward to the end with enthusiasm. I know that
we shall be condemned for waiting, but in the last analysis
I am the trustee of this nation, and the cost of it all
must be considered in the reckoning before we go forward."

Then leaning closer to me, he said: "It will not do
for me to act as if I had been hurried into precipitate
action against Germany. I must answer for the consequences of my action. What is the picture that lies
before me? All the great nations of Europe at war,
engaged in a death grapple that may involve civilization. My earnest hope and fervent prayer has been
that America could withhold herself and remain out
of this terrible mess and steer clear of European embroilments, and at the right time offer herself as the
only mediating influence to bring about peace. We are
the only great nation now free to do this. If we should
go in, then the whole civilized world will become involved. What a pretty mess it would be! America, the
only nation disconnected from this thing and now she is
surrendering the leadership she occupies and becomes
involved as other nations have. Think of the tragedy!
I am not afraid to go to war. No man fit to be President of this nation, knowing the way its people would
respond to any demand that might be made upon them,
need have fears or doubts as to what stand it would
finally take. But what I fear more than anything else is
the possibility of world bankruptcy that will inevitably

follow our getting into this thing, Not only world
chaos and bankruptcy, but all of the distempers, social,
moral, and industrial, that will flow from this world
cataclysm. No sane man, therefore, who knows the
dangerous elements that are abroad in the world would,
without feeling out every move, seek to lead his people
without counting the cost and dispassionately deliberat-
ing upon every move."

In a speech delivered at Helena, Montana, he frankly
spoke of the "break down" of neutrality in these words:

In the Providence of God, the leadership of this nation was in-
trusted to me during those early years of the war when we were not
in it. I was aware through many subtle channels of the movements
of opinion in this country, and I know that the thing that this country
chiefly desired, the thing that you men out here in the West chiefly
desired and the thing that of course every loving woman had at her
heart, was that we should keep out of the war, and we tried to persuade ourselves that the European business was not our business.
We tried to convince ourselves that no matter what happened on the
other side of the sea, no obligation of duty rested upon us, and finally
we found the currents of humanity too strong for us. We found that
a great consciousness was welling up in us that this was not a local
cause, that this was not a struggle which was to be confined to
Europe, or confined to Asia, to which it had spread, but that it was
something that involved the very fate of civilization; and there was
one great nation in the world that could not afford to stay out of it.
There are gentlemen opposing the ratification of this treaty who at
that time taunted the Administration of the United States that it had
lost touch with its international conscience. They were eager to go in,
and now that they have got in, and are caught in the whole network
of human conscience, they want to break out and stay out. We were
caught in this thing by the action of a nation utterly unlike ourselves.
What I mean to say is that the German nation, the German people,
had no choice whatever as to whether it was to go into that war or
not, did not know that it was going into it until its men were summoned
to the colours. I remember, not once, but often, that while sitting at the

Cabinet table in Washington I asked my colleagues what their impression was of the opinion of the country before we went into the war, and I remember one day one of my colleagues said to me: "Mr. President, I think the people of the country would take your advice and do what you suggested." "Why," I said, "that is not what I am waiting for; that is not enough. If they cannot go in with a whoop, there is no use of their going in at all. I do not want them to wait on me. I am waiting on them. I want to know what the conscience of this country is speaking. I want to know what purpose is arising in the minds of the people of this country with regard to this world situation." When I thought I heard that voice, it was then that I proposed to the Congress of the United States that we should include ourselves in the challenge that Germany was giving to mankind.

On May 10, 1915, he made a speech in Philadelphia, which contained the regrettable and much-criticized phrase, "Too proud to fight." Unfortunately, the headlines of the papers carried only the phrase, "Too proud to fight," and little or no attention was paid to the context of the speech in which the phrase was lodged. As a matter of fact, there was nothing unusual about the character of this speech. The phrase, "Too proud to fight," was simply expressive of the President's policy since the outbreak of the war. It was not a new thought with him. Some weeks before he had said the same thing, only in different words, in a speech delivered at a banquet of the Associated Press in New York: "My interest in the neutrality of the United States is not a petty desire to keep out of trouble. I am interested in neutrality because there is something so much greater to do than fight. There is a distinction awaiting this nation that no nation has ever yet got. That is the distinction of absolute self-control and mastery." The phrase, "Too proud to fight," was simply expressive of the idea that was close to his heart: a reliance upon means of settling our difficulties with Germany other than a resort to war.

On our way to Philadelphia on the day of the delivery of this speech I read a copy of it which the President handed to me, and when I ran across the phrase, "Too proud to fight," I scented the political danger in it and warned him, but he declined to be admonished because he was confident in the moral strength of his position, namely, that self-mastery is sometimes more heroic than fighting, or as the Bible states it, "He that ruleth his own spirit is greater than he that taketh a city," and trusted the people to understand his full meaning. The President himself was so above the petty tricks by which politicians wrest words from their context and force upon them unfavourable meaning that he sometimes incautiously played into the hands of this type of foe. Nor did he fully realize that his gift for making striking and quotable phrases added to the danger. It was an unfortunate phrase, "Too proud to fight," but none who thoughtfully read the context with unprejudiced mind could fail to see the moral grandeur of the President's position.

CHAPTER XXVIII

THE feelings of the people throughout the country began to be aroused as they witnessed the outlawry of Germany in ruthlessly attacking and wantonly interfering with American commerce on the high seas. The agitation for preparedness to meet a critical world situation was on in full swing. Congress and the President were harassed by conflicting demands from every side immediately to "put our house in order" and to set America safely on the road to national preparedness. Theodore Roosevelt was clamorously demanding universal compulsory military service and was ably aided by General Wood and Admiral Peary, who urged the adoption of conscription. Secretary of War Garrison and Senator Chamberlain, of Oregon, were converted to this radical movement and unwittingly became part and parcel of the Roosevelt-Wood preparedness propaganda. These gentlemen could see only the direct route to the accomplishment of the purpose they had in mind and were alike unmindful of the difficulties and obstacles that lay in the President's path. To them it appeared that all it was necessary for the President to do was boldly to announce his programme of preparedness and serenely to await its approval at the hands of Congress. They were unmindful of the difficulties of the situation and of the consummate tact that would be required on the part of the President to induce Congress to turn away from the old volunteer system and

238

to put into effect at once a system that overnight would transform America into an armed camp. The President was bound to consider the stern actualities of the situation and to withhold himself as far as possible from a too vigorous insistence on any programme of preparedness that was not traditionally, fundamentally American. It was a case of honest men seeing the same thing in the same way but differing as to the practicable means of accomplishing it. The President early realized that the volunteer system was unsuited to our present needs and that it could not be quickly turned into an active force to answer emergencies, but he was certain, also, that the people of the country must be convinced of this before they would agree to cut themselves away from the volunteer system under which previous American wars had been fought to a successful conclusion. The President felt that the old volunteer system was antiquated and not to be considered, but the duty lay upon him to convince the leaders of the Senate and House and the people that this was a fact. This was no easy task to accomplish. Haste or impetuous action on his part in advocating conscription could only, in his opinion, delay matters and embarrass the very purpose that lay in his mind.

While Roosevelt and Garrison were criticizing Congressional inaction, the President's mind was "open and to let" on the question of what constituted the best means of putting America in a state of actual and aggressive preparedness. As President, he was bound to take cognizance of the deep-seated antagonism on the part of the American people to any system of military preparedness that had a compulsory feature as its basic element. It was the President's opinion that the people of a country so big and varied as America had to be convinced by alternative methods as to what, in the last analysis, was the best means of preparing the country against aggression.

While he was convinced that we had to be prepared and ready to meet any emergency, he was not to be rushed in the matter and was keeping his mind open to find the best and most practical method of accomplishing what he thought the average opinion of the country demanded in the way of preparedness.

I had often discussed the matter with the President and, watching the agitation for preparedness from the side-lines, had stated my views in letters reading in part as follows:

DEAR GOVERNOR:

In my opinion, there is left to the Republican party but two available issues for the campaign of 1916,—the tariff and the question of national defense. How we are to meet the enemy on these questions is a subject which we ought thoroughly to consider and discuss in the coming months.

As to National Defense: In this matter we must have a sane, reasonable and workable programme. That programme must have in it, the ingredients that will call forth the hearty support of, first, the whole Cabinet (and particularly the Secretary of War); second, the leaders of the party in the Senate and House; third, the rank and file of Democrats in both Houses; fourth, the Army and the Navy; and last but not least, the great body of the American people.

Successfully to carry through this programme will tax your leadership in the party to the last degree. On the eve of the campaign of 1916, your attitude and accomplishment in this matter will be accepted by the country as the final test of your leadership and will be of incalculable psychological importance to the party; and, therefore, in the carrying out of this programme we cannot afford to hesitate or to blunder, because as election day approaches trivial mistakes will be magnified and exaggerated by the opposition, to the hurt and injury of our party and your prestige as leader.

TUMULTY.

THE PRESIDENT,
Cornish, New Hampshire.

MY DEAR GOVERNOR:

I cannot impress upon you too forcibly the importance of an appeal to the country at this time on the question of preparedness. No matter what the character of the information is that you are receiving, I have it from all sources that there is no enthusiasm on the "hill" for preparedness, and that the country itself is indifferent because of its apparent inability to grasp the importance and full significance of this question. This indifference arises out of two things: first, the attitude of the pacifists whose feelings have been nurtured by the preachings of Mr. Bryan; second, the attitude of those in the country who believe in preparedness and who are frightened because of the big talk of Roosevelt and others on their plan for military conscription.

There is no doubt how the body of the American people feel on this question of preparedness. You can, therefore, with much greater reason, address them on this question and with greater force and earnestness. I am afraid if you delay in this matter, it will be too late to act, because our enemies are already busy and active.

If some unfortunate thing should arise in international affairs or in Mexico within the next few weeks and announcement came then that you were to make an appeal to the country, it would appear as an anti-climax and an attempt upon your part to retrieve yourself. Now is the psychological moment to make your plea for national defense and incidentally to discuss Mexico and our foreign relations. In other words, you must ask the country to accept your leadership or the leadership of others who can't lead. Your voice is the only responsible voice in America that can speak with certainty, authority, and calmness as to the need for preparedness. There is no doubt of the will of a large majority of our people, but it lacks articulate expression. I am sure they will not fail to respond.

TUMULTY.

Upon conferring with the President in the matter of preparedness, I found that he had been slowly and patiently revolving the whole matter in his own mind and was then considering the advisability of taking a direct message to the people concerning the situation and was only awaiting the psychological moment to strike.

On January 27, 1916, the President commenced his tour of the North and Middle West, assuming the leadership of the movement for preparedness that had been started by his opponents, and called the attention of the country to the critical world situation and to the necessity that America "put her house in order." In St. Louis he declared that America must have comparably the greatest navy in the world. It was noticeable in his speeches that he never employed the term "universal military service" and that he was careful to explain that there was to be no militarism in the country.

When the President returned from his preparedness tour, he found himself at the centre of conflicting views as to method; on the one hand, Representative Hay of the Military Affairs Committee, advocated the use of the National Guard as the new army; on the other hand, Secretary Garrison advocated an increase of the Regular Army to 142,000 men and a new "continental army" of 400,000 men, with reserves of state militia. It was the recurrent conflict between the Army and Congress, between the military department's desire for a strong force and Congress' fear of "militarism." The Garrison plan met with decided opposition in the House, and upon the President's refusal to lend support to his Secretary of War in the programme he had outlined in his report of 1915, Mr. Garrison resigned. Immediately all the enemies of the President centred about the retiring

Secretary and proclaimed him a very much abused official. The letter which the President addressed to Secretary Garrison is as follows:

THE WHITE HOUSE,
WASHINGTON

January 17, 1916.

MY DEAR MR. SECRETARY:

I am very much obliged to you for your letters of January twelfth and January fourteenth. They make your views with regard to adequate measures of preparation for national defence sharply clear. I am sure that I already understood just what your views were, but I am glad to have them restated in this succinct and striking way. You believe, as I do, that the chief thing necessary is, that we should have a trained citizen reserve and that the training, organization, and control of that reserve should be under immediate federal direction.

But apparently I have not succeeded in making my own position equally clear to you, though I feel sure that I have made it perfectly clear to Mr. Hay. It is that I am not irrevocably or dogmatically committed to any one plan of providing the nation with such a reserve and am cordially willing to discuss alternative proposals.

Any other position on my part would indicate an attitude towards the Committee on Military Affairs of the House of Representatives which I should in no circumstances feel at liberty to assume. It woud never be proper or possible for me to say to any committee of the House of Representatives that so far as my participation in legislation was concerned they would have to take my plan or none.

I do not share your opinion that the members of the House who are charged with the duty of dealing with military affairs are ignorant of them or of the military necessities of the nation. On the contrary, I have found them well informed and actuated with a most intelligent appreciation of the grave responsibilities imposed upon them. I am sure that Mr. Hay and his colleagues are ready to act with a full sense of all that is involved in this great matter both for the country and for the national parties which they represent.

My own duty toward them is perfectly plain. I must welcome a frank interchange of views and a patient and thorough comparison of all the methods proposed for obtaining the objects we all have in view. So far as my own participation in final legislative action is concerned, no one will expect me to acquiesce in any proposal that I regard as inadequate or illusory. If, as the outcome of a free interchange of views, my own judgment and that of the Committee should prove to be irreconcilably different and a bill should be presented to me which I could not accept as accomplishing the essential things sought, it would manifestly be my duty to veto it and go to the country on the merits. But there is no reason to anticipate or fear such a result, unless we should ourselves take at the outset the position that only the plans of the Department are to be considered; and that position, it seems to me, would be wholly unjustifiable. The Committee and the Congress will expect me to be as frank with them as I hope they will be with me, and will of course hold me justified in fighting for my own matured opinion.

I have had a delightfully frank conference with Mr. Hay. I have said to him that I was perfectly willing to consider any plan that would give us a national reserve under unmistakable national control, and would support any scheme if convinced of its adequacy and wise policy. More he has not asked or desired.

Sincerely yours,
WOODROW WILSON.

HON. LINDLEY M. GARRISON,
  Secretary of War.

It was clear from the President's letter and the attitude of Secretary Garrison that there was to be no meeting of minds between the President and his Secretary of War on the matter of preparedness. Their views could not be reconciled, and when the President refused to support Garrison's programme, hook, line, and sinker, the Secretary tendered his resignation, which the President under the circumstances readily accepted. Immediately the friends of Garrison declared that the Administration had lost its strongest man and that it was now on the way to destruction. Neither the President nor his many friends, however, were disturbed by these direful predictions of disaster; and as the people pondered the President's letter of acceptance of Mr. Garrison's resignation, wherein he showed his own mind was open to the best method of preparing the country and that Mr. Garrison showed. petulance and impatience in handling the matter—the sober, second thought of the country readily and quickly came to the President's support in the belief that the dogmatic attitude of the Secretary of War, instead of helping, was embarrassing national preparedness.

Garrison had rendered distinguished service to the Administration and had won many friends, especially the newspaper group of Washington, by his open, frank method of dealing with public questions; but unfortunately for him he was swept off his feet by the unstinted praise that came to him from Republican journals throughout the country whenever it appeared that he was taking an attitude—especially in the two questions of major importance, preparedness and Mexico—that seemed to be at variance with the Administration's point of view.

When the President's letter to Garrison was read and the contents fully understood it showed Garrison autocratic and unyielding, and the President open-minded and willing to adopt any plan for preparedness that seemed to be workable. The gentle rebuke of Mr. Garrison contained in the President's statement that he did not share Mr. Garrison's opinion that the members of the House charged with the duty of dealing with military affairs "are ignorant of them or of the military necessities of the nation," completely won to the President the support of the members of that committee and put the President in the position of asking for and obtaining their hearty coöperation and support. Garrison's resignation, which at first blush appeared to be disastrous to the Administration, was soon turned to its advantage, with the result that a national defence act was passed during the summer. It was a compromise measure but it added very greatly to the military power of the country. In addition, it gave great powers to the President over the railroads in the event of war and authorized the establishment of a council of national defence.

Of course, the enemies of the President interpreted the episode as another example of his inability to coöperate with "strong men" and continued in the next breath to repeat their accusations that he was autocratic in his dealings with Congress, ignoring their own inconsistency. It was precisely because the President respected the constitutional prerogatives of the Congress, and Mr. Garrison did not, that the break came.

Every method of propaganda was resorted to to force the hand of the President in the matter of preparedness and to induce him to advocate and support a programme for universal military service put forth by the National Security League, whose backers and supporters throughout the country were mainly Republicans. Publicity on a grand scale, public meetings and great parades throughout the country were part of this propaganda. While many sincere, patriotic men and women, without realizing the politics that lay behind it, aided in this movement, it was easy to see that back of it was a sinister political purpose to embarrass and, if possible, to force the hand of the President. One of the leaders of this movement was General Wood, who established, with the permission of the War Department, the famous Plattsburg Camp. It will be recalled that this was the stage from which Mr. Roosevelt, on an occasion, freely gave expression to his views of bitter antagonism to the President for his seemingly slothful attitude in urging his views on Congress with reference to the preparedness programme. One of the favourite methods of rousing the people, to which the National Security League resorted, was demonstrations throughout the country in the form of preparedness parades. It was clear to us at the White House that these parades were part of an organized movement to "agitate" in favour of a radical programme of preparedness. The President and I had often discussed these demonstrations. One day I asked him if they were embarrassing him in any way and he said that they were not, but that they might affect opinion throughout the country in such a way as unreasonably to influence Congress for legislation so radical in its character as to be unnecessary and burdensome to the taxpayers of the country.

Our Republican opponents on the outside were claiming great political results from these demonstrations and felt sure they were a mighty force in embarrassing and weakening the President. It was finally suggested to the President that he ought to embrace the first opportunity presented to him of leading in one of the parades himself. Shortly after, the District of Columbia parade took place, and the President, upon my initiative, was invited to lead it. The effect of the President's personal participation in this parade and in the New York parade held subsequently was quickly evident. As soon as the moving pictures throughout the country began to feature the President leading the demonstrations, these parades became less frequent and finally obsolete. By getting into the "front line" the President had cleverly outwitted his enemies and took command of the forces in the country demanding preparedness.

CHAPTER XXIX

IN OCTOBER, 1916, during the Presidential campaign, while the President was at Shadow Lawn, New Jersey, Ambassador Gerard, at the President's invitation, paid a visit to him and reported in detail the general situation in Germany as to the submarine warfare. He said that the restrictions as to submarines imposed by Germany's acceptance of the President's ultimatum after the *Sussex* affair, were growing burdensome and intolerable to the military and naval masters of Germany and that they were bringing all kinds of pressure to bear upon the leaders of the Civil Government, notably Von Bethmann-Hollweg and Foreign Minister Von Jagow, to repudiate the undertaking. From the critical situation in Germany, arising out of the controversy over the question of unrestricted submarine warfare, which Ambassador Gerard laid before him, the President was convinced that we were now approaching a real crisis in our relations with Germany and that unless peace could be quickly obtained, the European struggle would soon enter upon a phase more terrible than any in the preceding two years, with consequences highly dangerous to the interests of our country. The passionate wish and deep desire of the President from the beginning was that we could keep aloof and by conserving our energies and remaining neutral, hold ourselves in reserve as the only mediating influence for peace; but with each passing week some untoward event brought about by the ruthlessness of Germany made the prospect for the interposition of America's influence daily more unlikely.

The following memorandum prepared by me on January 4, 1916, of a conversation between the President and myself, shortly after the sinking of the *Persia* by a submarine, imperfectly sets forth his idea with reference to war with Germany:

About ten minutes to ten o'clock this morning I had a very interesting conversation with the President at the White House, my purpose being to bring to him the atmosphere of Washington and the country as far as I could ascertain with reference to the sinking of the *Persia* by a submarine. The other purpose of my visit was to warn him that Senator Stone might induce him to make some admission with reference to his attitude which might embarrass the President in the future.

The President looked very well after his trip and seemed to be in a fine mood, although it was plainly evident that the *Persia* affair rested heavily upon him. My attitude toward this matter was for action, and action all along the line. This did not seem to meet with a very hearty response from the President. He informed me that it would not be the thing for us to take action against any government without our government being in possession of all the facts. I replied that that was my attitude, but I thought there should be action and vigorous action as soon as all the facts were ascertained. He agreed with me in this. When I began to tell him about the attitude of the country and the feeling in the country that there was a lack of leadership, he stiffened up in his chair and said: "Tumulty, you may as well understand my position right now. If my reëlection as President depends upon my getting into war, I don't want to be President. I have been away, and I have had lots of time to think about this war and the effect of our country getting into it, and I have made up my mind that I am more interested in the opinion that the country will have of me ten years from now than the opinion it may be willing to express to-day. Of course, I understand that the country wants action, and I intend to stand by the record I have made in all these cases, and take whatever action may be necessary, but I will not be rushed into war, no matter if every last Congressman and Senator stands up on his hind legs and proclaims me a coward." He continued, speaking of the severance of diplomatic relations,— "You must know that when I consider this matter, I can only consider it as the forerunner of war. I believe that the sober-minded people of this country will applaud any efforts I may make without the loss of our honour to keep this country out of war." He said that if we took any precipitate action right now, it might prevent Austria from coming across in generous fashion.

The President, ten months later, was re-elected, on the slogan, *"He kept us out of War."* If it was possible to continue at peace on terms that would protect and conserve our national honour, he was determined to do so.

I recall how passionately he laid before Senator Tillman of South Carolina, chairman of the Committee on Naval Affairs, his desire to keep the nation out of war. At the conclusion of the talk with the Senator, he said: "But, Senator, it rests with Germany to say whether we shall remain at peace." Turning to the President, Senator Tillman said: "You are right, Mr. President, we must not go around with a chip on our shoulder. I am for peace, but I am not for peace at any damn price." This was really expressive of the President's attitude. He earnestly desired peace, but he was not willing to remain at peace at the price of the nation's honour.

Early in May, 1916, the President and I had conferred regarding the European situation and had discussed the possibility of our suggesting to both sides that they consider the United States as a mediating influence to bring about a settlement. Early in May, 1916, I had addressed the following letter to the President with reference to the matter:

THE WHITE HOUSE,
WASHINGTON

May 16, 1916.

MY DEAR GOVERNOR:

As I have discussed with you on frequent occasions, it seems to me that the time is now at hand for you to act in the matter of *Peace*. The mere process of peace negotiations may extend over a period of months. Why should we wait until the moment of exhaustion before ever beginning a discussion? Everybody admits that the resources of the nations involved cannot last through another year without suffering of an untold character. It is now May. Let us assume that everybody accepts your offer. It would be physically impossible to get commissioners from various parts of the world, including Japan, in less than two months. Then the discussion would perhaps last until the fall, no matter what conclusion might be reached. Therefore, allowing for the time that might be consumed in persuading all the parties that the time is now ripe, the whole business will require almost a year in itself, during which time the hostilities would be continuing and certainly the chance of getting a truce would be better after the discussion had been in progress for some time. Similarly, as the time for the winter campaign approached, the inducement to agree on a truce on any terms would become more powerful each day.

Let us look at it from the point of view of postponement. If we waited until the fall and the negotiations stretched out through the winter, the temptation for making new drives in the spring, with the preparations made throughout the winter, would incline the militaristic element in the various countries involved to block peace negotiations. *It seems, therefore, that the time to act is now when these drives are spending their force.*

As to the Procedure:

It seems that no belligerent should be put in the position by your note of weakening or of suing for peace, for we must keep in mind the pride and sensibilities of all. The initiative must be ours—to all nations, on equal terms. One way to do this would be to send a note, saying that from the German note and from statesmen representing the Entente powers the Government of the United States assumes that the belligerent powers are willing at least to discuss suggestions for peace, each only reserving to itself liberty of action. The United States can, therefore, announce that it is willing to meet at The Hague a commission sent by the respective governments to discuss means for making peace, *and for establishing a world court or international tribunal to safeguard the peace of the world after the close of the war.*

In the latter, namely, *world peace*, the United States has a direct interest. The United States can in the note assume that commissioners will meet with it and hopes to be advised if there is any feeling to the contrary.

My idea is to go ahead with the plan on the theory that all the belligerents are in accord with the idea, so that in answering our note they will not have accepted anything but our proposals to discuss, first, the suggestion of peace, and, secondly, the idea of a world court.

The President should say, in order to elicit the sympathy of the world and mankind in general, that the note of the United States suggesting a meeting between the powers will be made public within a few days and after its receipt by the respective powers. This will give each government not only its own public opinion to reckon with, but the public opinion of the civilized world. The nation that objects to a discussion of peace will by no means be in an enviable position.

I hope you will read the article I am sending you by Mr. Strunsky, "Post Impressions," especially that part I have indicated in the margin. It is from this article that I got the idea of suggesting the alternative proposition of a world court. Your note setting forth your position in this matter should be an appeal to the heart and to the conscience of the world.

TUMULTY.

Evidently the President seriously had been considering this very matter as was shown by the following reply to my note:

THE WHITE HOUSE
WASHINGTON

DEAR TUMULTY:

Thank you for the memorandum about peace suggestions. I have read it very carefully and find my own thoughts travelling very much the same route. You may be sure I am doing a great deal of serious thinking about it all.

Faithfully,

W. W.

The President, through the State Department and various instrumentalities to which he had access for information, was keeping in touch with the German situation and understood from the beginning what the German game was with reference to peace, and to the various offers which he was making. He knew that the German peace offers were merely an attempt on the part of the civil government of Germany to avert a resumption of ruthlessness at sea; that they were mere gestures on the part of the German Government made to bolster up the morale of the German people and that these German offers did not indicate the real desire for peace on equitable terms, as subsequent events showed, but that they were the terms of peace of a nation which thought itself the victor, and, therefore, in a position ruthlessly to dictate a final settlement.

Many of the advisers of the President suggested that he should ignore these offers. But the President was wiser than those around him in accepting the German bid at its face value, and he finally called upon Germany to state the practical terms upon which she was willing to consider a settlement for peace. There was another reason for the President's patience. Foreseeing an inevitable crisis with Germany over the frequent sinking of our ships, he was fully conscious that he could not draw the whole country with him in aggressive action if before he took the step leading to war he had not tried out every means of peace. While his enemies denounced his meekness and apparent subservience to German diplomacy, and while some went so far as to characterize his conduct as cowardly, he serenely moved on and forced Germany to a show-down. He not only asked Germany to state her terms, but he frankly asked the Allies to give to the world their statement of what they considered the basis of peace.

One of the phrases in his note to the Allies which caused great irritation was that "neither side had stated the object for which the war had been started." While he was criticized for this at the time, it did just what he intended it to do. It forced Germany openly to avow what she believed to be the basis of peace, and gave the Allies their chance, as if they were being forced to do it by the American President, to say what they thought would be a just settlement.

In the latter part of January Germany announced to the United States that she was going to begin, on February first, unrestricted submarine warfare in the zone around the British Isles, and undertook to specify the route which a restricted number of American ships might take through this zone.

I vividly recall the day the Associated Press bulletin reached the White House. I took it immediately to the President who was at his desk in his private office. As I entered, he looked up from his writing, casual inquiry in his eyes. Without comment I laid the fateful slip of paper on his desk, and silently watched him as he read and then re-read it. I seemed to read his mind in the expressions that raced across his strong features: first, blank amazement; then incredulity that even Germany could be guilty of such perfidy; then gravity and sternness, a sudden grayness of colour, a compression of the lips and the familiar locking of the jaw which always characterized him in moments of supreme resolution. Handing the paper back to me, he said in quiet tones: "This means war. The break that we have tried so hard to prevent now seems inevitable."

On February 4th, he addressed Congress, announcing the severance of diplomatic relations with Germany, and stating his hope that Germany would pause before it was too late. On February 26th, the steamship *Ancona*, with Americans on board, was sunk, and on the next day the President addressed Congress, suggesting the proclamation of armed neutrality as a final effort to apply pressure to the Government of Germany, to show that the United States was in earnest and would protect its rights against lawless attacks at sea; but these measures failed. Germany seemed bent upon a break with us, and on April 6, 1917, in response to a memorable address delivered by the President on April second, the Congress of the United States declared solemnly that a state of war existed between the United States and the Imperial German Government.

In concluding his war message, the President said:

It is a fearful thing to lead this great, peaceful people into war, into the most terrible and disastrous of all wars, civilization itself seeming to be in the balance. But the right is more precious than peace, and we shall fight for the things which we have always carried nearest our hearts, for democracy, for the right of those who submit to authority to have a voice in their own governments, for the rights and liberties of small nations, for a universal dominion of right by such a concert of free peoples as shall bring peace and safety to all nations and make the world itself at last free. To such a task we can dedicate our lives and our fortunes, everything that we are and everything that we have, with the pride of those who know that the day has come when America is privileged to spend her blood and her might for the principles that gave her birth and happiness and the peace which she has treasured. God helping her, she can do no other.

I accompanied the President to Capitol Hill on the day of the delivery of his war message, and on that fateful day I rode with him from the Capitol back to the White House, the echo of applause still ringing in my ears.

For a while he sat silent and pale in the Cabinet Room. At last he said: "Think what it was they were applauding" [he was speaking of the people who were lined along the streets on his way to the Capitol]. "My message to-day was a message of death for our young men. How strange it seems to applaud that."

That simple remark is one key to an understanding of Woodrow Wilson. All politicians pretend to hate and to dread war, but Woodrow Wilson really hates and dreads it in all the fibres of his human soul; hates it and dreads it because he has an imagination and a heart; an imagination which shows his sensitive perception the anguish and the dying which war entails; a heart which yearns and aches over every dying soldier and bleeds afresh with each new-made wound.

I shall never forget that scene in the Cabinet Room between the President and myself. He appeared like a man who had thrown off old burdens only to add new ones.

It was apparent in his talk with me that he felt deeply wounded at the criticism that for months had been heaped upon him for his seeming unwillingness to go to war with Germany. As he discussed the step he had just taken, it was evident to me that he keenly felt the full solemnity and tragedy of it all. Turning to me, he said: "Tumulty, from the very beginning I saw the end of this horrible thing; but I could not move faster than the great mass of our people would permit. Very few understood the difficult and trying position I have been placed in during the years through which we have just passed. In the policy of patience and forbearance I pursued I tried to make every part of America and the varied elements of our population understand that we were willing to go any length rather than resort to war with Germany. As I told you months ago, it would have been foolish for us to have been rushed off our feet and to have gone to war over an isolated affair like the *Lusitania*. But now we are certain that there will be no regrets or looking back on the part of our people. There is but one course now left open to us. Our consciences are clear, and we must prepare for the inevitable—a fight to the end. Germany must be made to understand that we have rights that she must respect. There were few who understood this policy of patience. I do not mean to say this in a spirit of criticism. Indeed, many of the leading journals of the country were unmindful of the complexities of the situation which confronted us."

The President then took out of his pocket an old and worn newspaper clipping, saying: "I wish to read you an analysis of my position and my policy by a special writer for the *Manchester Guardian*, who seemed, without consulting me or ever conferring with me, to know just what I am driving at."

This special writer, commenting upon the Wilson policy, had said:

Mr. Wilson's patience, now derided and criticized, will inevitably be the means by which he will lead his people by easy stages to the side of the Allies. By his methods of patience and apparent sub-

servience to Germany, he will convince the whole American people
that no other course save war is possible. This policy of Wilson's,
now determined on, will work a complete transformation in his people.
It will not evidence itself quickly or overnight. The moral preach-
ment of Wilson before and after war will be the cause that will finally
bring his people to the side of the Allies.

Again turning to me, the President said: "Our course
from this time on is clear. The whole business of
war that we are now engaged upon is fraught with the
gravest difficulties. There will be great enthusiasm in
the country from this day. I trust it will not slacken or
weaken as the horrors of the war and its tragedies are
disclosed. Of course our motives will be misconstrued,
our purposes misunderstood; some of our best friends will
misinterpret what we seek to do. In carrying on the
war we will be obliged to do certain unusual things,
things that will interfere with the lives and habits of our
people, which will bring down upon us a storm of criticism
and ridicule. Our life, therefore, until this thing is over,
and God only knows when it will be over, will be full of
tragedy and heartaches."

As he spoke, he was no longer Woodrow Wilson, the
protagonist of peace, but Woodrow Wilson, the stern
warrior, now grimly determined to pursue the great cause
of America to the end.

The President continued talking to me. He said: "It
has not been easy to carry these burdens in these trying
times. From the beginning I saw the utter futility of
neutrality, the disappointment and heartaches that would
flow from its announcement, but we had to stand by our
traditional policy of steering clear of European embroilments. While I have appeared to be indifferent to the
criticism which has been my portion during these critical

days, a few have tried to understand my purpose and have sympathized throughout with what I sought to do."

Then, as he lowered his voice, he said: "There is a fine chap in Springfield, Massachusetts, editor of a great paper there, who understood my position from the beginning and who has sympathized with me throughout this whole business." For a moment he paused, and then went on: "I want to read you the letter I received from this fine man." As he read, the emotion he felt at the tender sympathy which the words conveyed gripped him. The letter is as follows:

> Springfield, Massachusetts,
> March 28, 1917.

MY DEAR MR. PRESIDENT:

In acknowledging your very kind and appreciative note of March 22nd, I must say at once that the note has given me the greatest possible pleasure. I prize this word from you all the more because after the political experience and conflicts of the past few years, I am conscious of a very real yet peculiar feeling of having summered and wintered with you, in spite of the immeasurable and rather awful distance that separates our respective places in the life and work of our time. Your note, for the moment, suddenly annihilates the distance and brings to me what I recognize as a very human touch.

There is summering and wintering to come,—with more wintering perhaps than we shall enjoy;—even so, I shall hope to be of timely service, as opportunity favours me.

I have the honour to be your admirer and friend,

> Most sincerely,
> (Signed) WALDO L. COOK.

"That man understood me and sympathized." As he said this, the President drew his handkerchief from his pocket, wiped away great tears that stood in his eyes, and then laying his head on the Cabinet table, sobbed as if he had been a child.

CHAPTER XXX

CARRYING ON

THE critics of the President will ask the question: "What was the President doing to prepare the country for war, which to him seemed inevitable?" From the inside, and without the blare of trumpets, he was quietly engaged in conferring with the heads of the Army and Navy departments. Indeed, from the minute the third *Lusitania* note was dispatched, actual preparations for war were begun. Immediately upon the dispatch of the note, the following statement was issued from the White House, under date of July 21, 1916.

THE WHITE HOUSE

WASHINGTON

July 21, 1916.

The President in association with the heads of departments, regardless of present-day conditions or controversies, has long been giving a great deal of consideration to the preparation of a reasonable and adequate naval programme, which he intends to propose to Congress at the proper time.

That is one of the things he is now considering in the quiet of Cornish. He feels, now that the note has been dispatched, that it is best, for the time being, to drop the discussion of it as far as he is concerned and is turning to questions of permanent national policy.

Of course, he realizes that he must have the best practical advice obtainable in this matter and is seeking for it from every available source. In fact, it is known that the best minds of the various departments of the Government, both of the Army and the Navy, are now and have been at work on these important matters for some time; that is, he is seeking advice from the men in those departments

who have been most directly in touch with the new conditions of
defence that have been evolved out of modern experience. He not
only wishes advice from those who have a knowledge of actual
modern conditions of warfare, but he is seeking light from those who
are able to understand and comprehend the altered conditions of
land and naval warfare. He wishes the Navy to stand upon an equality with the most efficient and serviceable.

As to the Army, it is known here that he is preparing to incorporate
in his next message to Congress a programme in regard to the development and equipment of the Army and a proper training of the
citizens of the United States to arms which, while in every way
consistent with American traditions and national policy, will be of
such a character as to commend itself to every patriotic and practical
mind. In this matter he is working with the Secretary of War and
his professional associates, who, it is understood, have reached some
very definite conclusions on these exceedingly important matters.
He is anxious to have a programme that will be definite and positive,
and wishes to have the information in hand before laying the matter
before the committees of the Senate and the House.

Contemporaneously with this statement was issued
the following, which was prepared by the President, but
issued over my name, the full significance of which was
not apparent at the time:

The note [Third *Lusitania* note] having been dispatched, the
President felt that it was best to drop further discussion of the matter
for the present, as far as he was concerned. He will be free now to
devote his time to a full consideration of a matter that the country
has for a long time been thoughtful of, that is a reasonable programme
of national defense. Of course, this programme will be considered regardless of present-day conditions.

It is known that the President has been considering this important
matter in all its aspects, and has been in touch with the Secretary of
War and the Secretary of the Navy regarding it. It is also known in
official circles here that the President had taken steps before leaving
for Cornish to instruct the Army and Navy departments to make
ready for his consideration a careful programme of national defense

in preparation for the presentation of his views to Congress at the proper time.

He desires to have the programme based on the most practicable lines obtainable from the departments and it is said that the best minds in the departments are at present at work on the subject. He hopes that the programme will express the best traditions of the country and not lose sight of modern experience. He is anxious to have a programme that will be definite and positive, and wishes to have the information in hand before laying the matter before the committees of the Senate and the House.

On July 21, 1915, he addressed the following letters to the Secretary of War and the Secretary of the Navy, respectively:

THE WHITE HOUSE
WASHINGTON

July 21, 1915.

MY DEAR MR. SECRETARY:

I have been giving scarcely less thought than you yourself have to the question of adequate preparation for national defense, and I am anxious, as you know, to incorporate in my next message to Congress a programme regarding the development and equipment of the Army and a proper training of our citizens to arms which, while in every way consistent with our traditions and our national policy, will be of such a character as to commend itself to every patriotic and practical mind.

I know that you have been much in conference with your professional associates in the department and that you have yourself come to some very definite conclusions on these exceedingly important matters. I shall be away from Washington for a few days, but I would be very much obliged if you would be kind enough to prepare for me a programme, with estimates, of what you and the best-informed soldiers in your counsels think the country ought to undertake to do. I should like to discuss this programme with you at as early a time as it can be made ready. Whether we can reasonably propose the whole of it to the Congress immediately or not we can determine when we have studied it. The important thing now is to know and know fully what we need. Congress will certainly welcome such advice and follow it to the limit of its opportunity.

Cordially and faithfully yours,
WOODROW WILSON.

HON. LINDLEY M. GARRISON,
Secretary of War.

THE WHITE HOUSE
WASHINGTON

July 21, 1915.

MY DEAR MR. SECRETARY:

I have been giving, as I am sure you have also, a great deal of thought to the matter of a wise and adequate naval programme to be proposed to the Congress at its next session, and I would like to discuss the whole subject with you at the earliest possible date.

But first we must have professional advice. I would be very much obliged to you if you would get the best minds in the department to work on the subject: I mean the men who have been most directly in contact with actual modern conditions, who have most thoroughly comprehended what the Navy must be in the future in order to stand upon an equality with the most efficient and most practically serviceable. I want their advice, a programme by them formulated in the most definite way. Whether we can reasonably propose the whole of it to the Congress immediately or not we can determine when we have studied it. The important thing now is to know fully what we need. Congress will certainly welcome such advice and follow it to the limit of its opportunity.

It should be a programme planned for a consistent and progressive development of this great defensive arm of the nation and should be of such a kind as to commend itself to every patriotic and practical man.

I shall return to Washington in a few days and shall be glad to take this important matter up with you at your early convenience.

Cordially and faithfully yours,
WOODROW WILSON.

HON. JOSEPHUS DANIELS,
Secretary of the Navy.

Immediately after the war message there arose an insistent demand for a coalition cabinet. It was the beginning of the Republican drive for what was called a bi-partisan government. Republicans chose to forget the experiences of England and France under their coalition cabinets, and when the President refused to act upon the suggestion, the impression was subtly conveyed to the unthinking that the President's refusal arose from his dislike of counsel and coöperation, and his unwillingness to share the responsibilities and glories of the war with people outside his own party.

As an historian, the President knew the troubles of Washington with a coalition cabinet, Lincoln's embarrassments from Cabinet members not of his own party, Mc-Kinley's sagacious refusal in 1898 to form a coalition cabinet. He also knew human nature; knew that with the best intentions, men sometimes find it difficult to work whole-heartedly with a leader of a political party not their own. He could not risk a chance of division in his own official family in the face of the common enemy.

The President looked upon the agitation for a coalition cabinet as a partisan effort to hamper and embarrass his administration, and so he coldly turned away from every suggestion that looked toward the establishment of a cabinet of the kind suggested by his too-solicitous Republican friends.

The following note which I addressed to the President, and his reply, bear upon the subject:

THE WHITE HOUSE
WASHINGTON

DEAR GOVERNOR:

The newspaper men asked me this morning what the attitude of the Administration was toward the proposed super-cabinet. I hedged as much as I could, but I asked if it was not the same proposition that came up some months ago, advocated by Senator Weeks,

in a new disguise—if it was not the same kind of a commission that
had harassed Mr. Lincoln.   I think we ought to let our attitude
be known unofficially for the guidance of men who wish to help us.
If we do nothing at this time to let it be known, it would seem that
our opposition to this kind of legislation had been silenced by the
furore over the fuel order.   In other words, we ought to show by
our attitude that the tantrums on the Hill are making no impression
on us whatever.

TUMULTY.

DEAR TUMULTY:
   Of course, I am opposed to the idea of a "super-cabinet," and regard
it as nothing more nor less than a renewal of the perpetual effort of
the Republicans to force representation in the Administration.
Republicans of the finest sort and of the finest capacity are working
for and with the Administration on all hands and there is no need
whatever for a change at the head of the administering departments.
I am utterly opposed to anything of the sort and will never consent
to it.   You will know how to create the impression on the minds of
the newspaper men that I regard it as merely a partisan effort to
hamper and embarrass the Administration.

THE PRESIDENT.

There were many misgivings in the minds of the people
when war was declared in April, 1917, and the nation embarked upon the most gigantic of all its wars, under the
leadership of a college professor, a doctrinaire, who did not
believe in war as a method of permanently solving international problems, and a Secretary of War who was an
avowed pacifist.   There was another matter which greatly
disturbed the peace of mind of the average American.
The political party that was conducting the struggle was
the Democratic party, the party of the plain folk, of the
average men and women of America.   Our Republican
friends had so cleverly "advertised" their conduct of the
Civil War and the Spanish-American War, that many

people in the country felt that the Republican party, because of its leading minds and the business genius of its masters, was the only political organization that could be depended upon successfully to carry on a great war.

Colonel Roosevelt's diary, first made public on September 28, 1921, throws interesting light on Republican claims of efficient management by Republicans of the Spanish-American War. Under date of May 7, 1898, the Colonel, then a lieutenant-colonel, recorded in his diary: "The delays and stupidity of the Ordnance Department surpass belief. The Quartermaster's Department is better, but bad. The Commissary Department is good. There is no management whatever in the War Department. Against a good nation we should be helpless," and these animadversions are reiterated in subsequent entries. Interesting comments from the greatest of contemporary Republicans on the divine right of the Republican party to conduct all American wars and transact all other American business of importance. But doubtless the Colonel had forgotten all this in 1917, and many other good Americans had also forgotten what was notorious in 1898 and the ineptitude of the Republican War Department, which, as Lieutenant-Colonel Roosevelt said under date of May 21, 1898, had "no head, no energy, no intelligence." But the old myth sedulously cultivated by Republicans continued in 1917, that only Republicans are fit to govern, no matter how badly they govern. Direful prophecies and predictions of disaster to the country by reason of the Democratic auspices under which the war was to be conducted were freely made.

It is an unpleasant fact that some of the leading Republicans in the Senate and the House harboured for the President a partisan and personal hatred which made the wish father to the thought. Yet the expected did not happen, to the amazement and chagrin of the Republican enemies of the President. No other war was attended with so little scandal and with greater expedition. The cause was plain. It was the magnificent and aggressive leadership of Woodrow Wilson exerting itself all along the line, and that leadership was based upon certain fundamental resolutions which had been taking form in the President's mind for many months previous to his appearance before Congress asking for the passage of a war declaration. They were as follows: (1) There was to be no "politics" in the conduct of the war; (2) no political generals would be selected; (3) every ounce of energy and force in the nation was to be put back of the heads of the Army and the Navy in a supreme effort to make our influence, moral and physical, quickly felt. Every effort was made to cut out scandal and to put an absolute embargo on the activities of army speculators, contractors, and profiteers.

Speaking to me one day about the conduct of the war, shortly after the delivery of his war message, he said: "We must not in our conduct of this war repeat the scandals of the Civil and the Spanish-American wars. The politics of generals and admirals must be tabooed. We must find the best trained minds that we can get and we must back them up at every turn. Our policy must be 'the best man for every job,' regardless of his political affiliations. This must be the only test, for, after all, we are the trustees of the boys whose lives will be spent in this enterprise of war."

This was not an easy policy to pursue. Every kind of harassing demand came from Democratic senators and representatives to induce the President to recognize

political considerations in the conduct of the war, the
argument being that after all the responsibility for its
conduct resting with the Democrats, the administration
of the war ought to be under Democratic tutelage throughout. But the President was firm—in his resolve to see
the war through to the end without political considerations. The political predilections of generals, admirals,
and war workers of every kind was ignored.

Mr. Creel by furnishing a list of Republicans appointed
by the President to conspicuous office has disproved the
charge against the President of niggard partisanship.
Although the President would not tolerate a coalition
cabinet, he gave to Republicans all manner of opportunities to share in the conduct and the credit of the war.
I quote from Mr. Creel:

> The search for "the best man for the place" was instituted without
> regard to party, faction, blood strain, or creed, and the result was a
> composite organization in which Democrats, Republicans, and In-
> dependents worked side by side, partisanship forgotten and service
> the one consideration.
>
> It stood recognized as a matter of course that the soldier selected
> to command our forces in France might well develop into a presiden-
> tial possibility, yet this high place was given without question to
> Gen. John J. Pershing, a life-long Republican and the son-in-law of
> Senator Warren, one of the masters of the Republican machine.
>
> Admiral William S. Sims, a vociferous Republican, was sent to
> English waters in high command, and while Secretary Daniels was
> warned at the time that Sims's partisanship was of the kind that would
> not recognize the obligations of loyalty or patriotism, he waved
> the objection aside out of his belief that Sims was "the best man for
> the job."
>
> For the head of the Aircraft Board, with its task of launching
> America's great aviation programme, Mr. Howard E. Coffin, a
> Republican, was selected and at his right hand Mr. Coffin placed
> Col. Edward A. Deeds, also a Republican of vigour and regularity.

It is to be remembered also that when failure and corruption were charged against the Aircraft Board, the man appointed by the President to conduct the highly important investigation was Charles E. Hughes.

Three Assistant Secretaries of War were appointed by Mr. Baker— Mr. Benedict Crowell, a Cleveland contractor; Doctor F. E. Keppel, dean of Columbia University, and Emmet J. Scott, formerly Booker Washington's secretary—and all three were Republicans. Mr. E. R. Stettinius of the J. P. Morgan firm and a Republican was made special assistant to the Secretary of War and placed in charge of supplies, a duty that he had been discharging for the Allies. Maj. Gen. George W. Goethals, after his unfortunate experience in shipbuilding, was given a second chance and put in the War Department as an assistant Chief of staff. The Chief of Staff himself, Gen. Peyton C. March, was a Republican no less definite and regular than General Goethals. Mr. Samuel McRoberts, president of the National City Bank and one of the pillars of the Republican party, was brought to Washington as chief of the procurement section in the Ordnance Section, with the rank of brigadier-general; Maj. Gen. E. H. Crowder was appointed Provost-Marshal-General, although his Republicanism was well known, and no objection of any kind was made when General Crowder put Charles B. Warren, the Republican National Committeeman from Michigan, in charge of appeal cases, a position of rare power.

The Emergency Fleet Corporation was virtually turned over to Republicans under Charles M. Schwab and Charles Piez. Mr. Vance McCormick, chairman of the Democratic National Committee, was made chairman of the War Trade Board, but of the eight members the following five were Republicans: Albert Strauss of New York, Alonzo E. Taylor of Pennsylvania, John Beaver White, of New York, Frank C. Munson of New York, and Clarence M. Woolley of Chicago.

The same conditions obtained in the Red Cross. A very eminent Republican, Mr. H. P. Davison, was put in supreme authority, and on the Red Cross War Council were placed ex-President Taft; Mr. Charles D. Norton, Mr. Taft's secretary while President; and Mr. Cornelius N. Bliss, former treasurer of the Republican National Committee. Not only was Mr. Taft thus honoured, but upon the creation of a National War Labour Board the ex-President was made its chairman and virtually empowered to act as the administration's representative in its contact with industry.

Mr. Frank A. Vanderlip, a Republican of iron regularity, was placed in charge of the War Savings Stamps Campaign, and when Mr. McAdoo had occasion to name Assistant Secretaries of the Treasury he selected Prof. L. S. Rowe of the University of Pennsylvania and Mr. H. C. Leffingwell of New York.

Harry A. Garfield, son of the Republican President, was made Fuel Administrator, and Mr. Herbert Hoover, now a candidate for President, on a platform of unadulterated Republicanism, was nominated as head of the Food Administration.

The Council of National Defense was an organization of high importance and one of tremendous influence from a partisan standpoint, yet its executive body was divided as follows: Republicans—Howard E. Coffin, Julius Rosenwald, Dr. Hollis Godfrey, Dr. Franklin Martin, Walter S. Gifford, Director; Democrats—Daniel Willard and Bernard M. Baruch; Independent—Samuel Gompers.

No sooner had the war begun than the preliminary war work of the President began to bear fruit.

Within a month from the declaration of war the traditional policy of the nation was reversed, by the enactment of the Selective Service Act. A vast machinery of registration was created that ran without a hitch, and on June 5th more than 10,000,000 men were registered quickly and efficiently.

Thirty-two encampments—virtual cities, since each had to house 40,000 men—were built in ninety days from the driving of the first nail, complete in every municipal detail, a feat declared impossible, and which will stand for all time as a building miracle.

In June, scarcely two months after the President's appearance before Congress, General Pershing and his staff reached France, and on July 3rd the last of four groups of transports landed American fighting men in the

home of La Fayette and Rochambeau.   On October 10th
our soldiers went on the firing-line.

Training camps for officers started in June, and in
August there were graduated 27,341 successful aspirants,
ready to assume the tasks of leadership.

In a notable speech, confidential in character, the
President on the 8th day of April, 1918, addressed the
foreign correspondents at the White House concerning
"our resolutions" and "actions in the war." The speech
was as follows:

I am very glad to have this opportunity to meet you. Some of
you I have met before, but not all. In what I am going to say I would
prefer that you take it in this way, as for the private information of
your minds and not for transmission to anybody, because I just want,
if I may, in a few words to create a background for you which may be
serviceable to you. I speak in confidence.

I was rendered a little uneasy by what Mr. Lloyd George was
quoted as having said the other day that the Americans have a great
surprise in store for Germany. I don't know in what sense he meant
that, but there is no surprise in store. I want you to know the se-
quence of resolves and of actions concerning our part in the war.
Some time ago it was proposed to us that we, if I may use the expression, feed our men into the French and English armies in any units
that might be ready—companies or regiments or brigades—and not
wait to train and coördinate the larger units of our armies before putting them into action. My instinctive judgment in the face of that
proposition was that the American people would feel a very much
more ardent interest in the war if their men were fighting under their
own flag and under their own general officers, but at that time, which
was some months ago, I instructed General Pershing that he had full
authority whenever any exigency that made such a thing necessary
should occur to put the men in any units or in any numbers or in any
way that was necessary—just as he is doing. What I wanted you to
know was that that was not a new action, that General Pershing was
fully instructed about that all along.

Then, similarly with regard to the impression that we are now going to rush troops to Europe. Of course, you cannot rush any faster than there is means of rushing and, what I have said recently is what I have said all along, that we are getting men over there just as fast as we can get them ready and as quickly as we can find the ships to transport them. We are doing that now and we have been doing it all along. Let me point out some of the circumstances: Our first programme was to send over ninety thousand men a month, but for several months we were sending over only thirty thousand—one third of the programme. Why? Not because we didn't have the men ready, not even because we didn't have the means of transportation, but because—and there is no criticism of the French Government involved in this—because the ports assigned to us for landing couldn't take care of the supplies we had to send over. We had to send materials and engineers, and workmen, even, over to build the docks and the piers that would be adequate to handle the number of men we sent over, because this was happening: We began with the ninety-thousand programme and the result was that cargo ships that we needed were lying in those ports for several weeks together without being unloaded, as there was no means of unloading them. It was bad economy and bad practice from every point of view to have those ships lying there during a period when they could have made two or three voyages. There is still this difficulty which I am afraid there is no means of overcoming rapidly, that the railroad communication between those ports and the front is inadequate to handle very large bodies of men. You may notice that General Pershing recommended that Christmas boxes should not be sent to the men. That sounded like a pretty hard piece of advice, but if you could go to those ports and see those Christmas boxes which are still there, you would know why he didn't want them sent. There was no means of getting them to the front. Vast accumulations of these gifts were piled up there with no means of storing them adequately even.

I just wanted to create for you this picture, that the channels have been inevitably choked. Now we believe that, inasmuch as the impediments on the other side are being largely removed, we can go ahead with the original programme and add to it in proportion as the British can spare us the tonnage, and they are going to spare us the tonnage for the purpose. And with the extra tonnage which the British are going to spare us we will send our men, not to France but to

Great Britain, and from there they will go to the front through the channel ports. You see that makes a new line where the means of handling them are already established and where they are more abundant than they are at the French ports. Now, I want to say again that none of this involves the least criticism of the French authorities, because I think they have done their very best in every respect, but they couldn't make ports out of hand, they couldn't build new facilities suddenly, and their man power was being drawn on in very much larger proportion than our man power. Therefore, it was perfectly proper that we should send men over there and send materials to make the means of handling the troops and the cargoes more expeditiously.

I want you gentlemen to realize that there was no wave-like motion in this thing so far as our purpose and preparation are concerned. We have met with delays, of course, in production, some of which might have been avoided and ought to have been avoided, and which are being slowly corrected, but apart from that the motive power has been back of this thing all the time. It has been the means of action that has oscillated, it has been sometimes greater and sometimes less than was necessary for the programme.

I for my own part don't like the idea of having surprises. I would like the people to be surprised if we didn't do our duty, but not surprised that we did do it. Of course, I don't mean that Mr. Lloyd George meant that we would surprise everybody by doing our duty, but I don't just know how to interpret his idea of it, because I have said the same thing to the British representatives all along as I informally expressed it to Lord Reading, that we had been and always would be doing our damnedest, and there could not be a more definite American expression of purpose than that.

As to another matter (I am just giving you things to think about and not things to say, if you will be kind enough to take it that way). That speech I made on Saturday I hope was correctly understood. We are fighting, as I understand it, for justice to everybody and are ready to stop just as soon as justice to everybody is everybody's programme. I have the same opinion privately about, I will not say the policy, but the methods of the German Government that some gentlemen have who see red all the time, but that is not a proper part of my thought. My thought is that if the German Government insist that the thing shall be settled unjustly, that is to say by force, then of course we accept that and will settle it by force. Whenever we see sincere symptoms of their desire to settle it by justice, we will not only accept their suggestions but we will be glad and eager to accept them, as I said in my speech. I would be ashamed to use the knock-down and drag-out language; that is not the language of liberty, that is the language of braggadocio. For my part, I have no desire to march triumphantly into Berlin. If they oblige us to march triumphantly into Berlin, then we will do it if it takes twenty years. But the world will come to its senses some day, no matter how mad some parts of it may be now, and this is my feeling, that we ought when the thing is over to be able to look back upon a course which had no element in it which we need be ashamed of. So it is so difficult in any kind of a speech, this kind or any other, to express two things that seem to be going in opposite directions that I wasn't sure that I had succeeded in expressing them on Saturday—the sincere willingness to discuss peace whenever the proposals are themselves sincere and yet at the same time the determination never to discuss it until the basis laid down for the discussion is justice. By that I mean justice to everybody. Nobody has the right to get anything out of this war, because we are fighting for peace if we mean what we say, for permanent peace. No injustice furnishes a basis for permanent peace. If you leave a rankling sense of injustice anywhere, it will not only produce a running sore presently which will result in trouble and probably war, but it ought to produce war somewhere. The sore ought to run. It is not susceptible to being healed except by remedying the injustice. Therefore, I for my part wouldn't want to see a peace which was based upon compelling any people, great or small, to live under conditions which it didn't willingly accept.

If I were just a sheer Machiavelli and didn't have any heart but had brains, I would say: "If you mean what you say and are fighting for permanent peace, then there is only one way to get it, whether you like justice or not." It is the only conceivable intellectual basis for it, because this is not like the time, years ago, of the Congress of Vienna. Peoples were then not willing, but so speechless and unorganized and without the means of self-expression, that the governments could sit on their necks indefinitely. They didn't know how to prevent it. But they are wide awake now and nobody is going to sit comfortably on the neck of any people, big or little, and the more uncomfortable he is who tries it, the more I am personally pleased. So that I am in the position in my mind of trying to work out a purely scientific proposition: "What will stay put?"

A peace is not going to be permanent until that principle is accepted by everybody, that, given a political unit, every people has the right to determine its own life. That, gentlemen, is all I have to say to you, but it is the real inside of my mind, and it is the real key to the present foreign policy of the United States which for the time being is in my keeping. I hope it will be useful to you, as it is welcome to me to have this occasion of telling you what I really think and what I understand we are really doing.

CHAPTER XXXI

THE PEN IS MIGHTIER THAN THE SWORD

DURING this time the President was constantly on guard at the Executive offices, never for a moment out of touch with the situation. He was the intimate associate of the men who were his co-labourers on the various boards that had been set up to prosecute the work of the war. He seemed to know what was going on in every phase. His evenings were given to examination of the long dispatches that came from diplomatic and consular representatives of America at the various capitals of Europe, apprising him of the developments of the great war.

One of the most effective measures for weakening the enemy was the method of attacking the Central Powers from within by propaganda designed to incite the masses to rebellion and to drive wedges between Germany and Austria. As George Creel says, "The projectile force of the President's idealism, its full military value may be measured by the fact that between April 6 and December 8, 1917, sixteen States, great and small, declared war against Germany, or severed diplomatic relations with her. From the very first the Allies accepted the President as their spokesman."

It was under the influence of Woodrow Wilson's clear vision and magic power of statement that the true significance of the war became clear. At first it had seemed a war of nations, and the belligerents had eagerly published official documents, Red Books, White Books, Yellow Books, and so forth, through all the colours of the spectrum, to show who had "started the war." The question of who began it became after a while quite secondary to the question of the fundamental principles at stake in the contest which was no longer a national conflict, but a world war, waged to the death between two irreconcilable views of the relationship of government to individuals, the autocratic view on the one hand, on the other the democratic. It was one man who brought the fundamental principle of the division into the clear light. A contemporary writer has said that the magical effect of Woodrow Wilson's utterances on all the Allies was due, not to his rhetoric but to his sublime gift of seeing and stating a profound truth after which others had been only groping. That is the prophet's power, to voice the latent, inarticulate aspirations of the multitude. Proof of the value of the President's method of attacking the Central Powers from within by propaganda was disclosed in General Ludendorff's and Von Tirpitz's revelations. In Ludendorff's opinion, the President's note to Germany had forced the Central Empires to yield to the President. Ludendorff says:

In his answer to our second note, Wilson gave us nothing; he did not even tell us whether the Entente took its stand on the Fourteen Points. He demanded, however, the suspension of the submarine campaign, stigmatized our conduct of the war in the west as a violation of international law, and once again sought to meddle with intimate questions of our domestic politics.

Speaking again of the answer to one of the Wilson notes, Ludendorff says:

The answer to Wilson was dispatched on the 20th of October. The submarine campaign was abandoned. This concession to Wilson was the deepest blow to the army, and especially to the navy. The injury to the morale of the fleet must have been immeasurable. The Cabinet had thrown up the sponge.

On October 23rd, President Wilson sent the following peremptory message to the Germans:

It is evident that the German people have no means of commanding the acquiescence of the military authorities of the Empire in the popular will; that the purpose of the King of Prussia to control the policy of the Empire is still unimpaired. If the United States must deal with the military masters and monarchical authorities now, or if it is likely to have to deal with them later in regard to international obligations of the German Empire, it must demand not peace negotiations but surrender. Nothing can be gained by leaving this essential thing unsaid.

In discussing this and the other Wilson notes, Ludendorff says that they had dealt a vital blow at the heart of militaristic Germans and finally loosed the grip they held on the German people. This entire situation is best expressed in Ludendorff's own words:

On October 23rd or 24th Wilson's answer arrived. It was a strong answer to our cowardly note. This time he had made it quite clear that the armistice conditions must be such as to make it impossible for Germany to resume hostilities, and to give the powers allied against her unlimited power to settle themselves the details of the peace accepted by Germany. In my view, there could no longer be doubt in any mind that we must continue the fight. I felt quite confident that the people were still to be won over to this course.

On the evening of the 24th, shortly after leaving Spa for Berlin, there was brought to me the following proclamation already signed by the Field Marshal, which expressed the views prevailing at G. H. Q. on the third Wilson note. It appeared essential that G. H. Q. in its dealings with Berlin should take up a definite stand to the note in order to eliminate its ill effects on the army. The telegram to the Army ran thus:

> "For the information of all troops: Wilson says in his answer that he is ready to propose to his allies that they should enter into armistice negotiations; but that the armistice must render Germany so defenseless that she cannot take up arms again. He will only negotiate with Germany for peace if she concedes all the demands of America's associates as to the internal constitutional arrangements of Germany; otherwise, there is no choice but unconditional surrender.
>
> "*Wilson's answer is a demand for unconditional surrender.* It is thus unacceptable to us soldiers. It proves that our enemies' desire for our destruction, which let loose the war in 1914, still exists undiminished. It proves, further, that our enemies use the phrase 'peace of justice' merely to deceive us and break our resistance. Wilson's answer can thus be nothing for us soldiers but a challenge to continue our resistance with all our strength.
>
> "When our enemies know that no sacrifices will achieve the rupture of the German front, then they will be ready for a peace which will make the future of our country safe for the broad masses of our people.
>
> "At the front, October 24th, 10 P. M."

This proclamation which was signed by Field Marshal Von Hindenburg was later signed by Ludendorff. It resulted in the Kaiser's immediate orders for a special conference at which both of these officials were dismissed from the Imperial German army.

Von Tirpitz in his Memoirs laid stress on the effect of the Wilson submarine notes. Ludendorff declares in his book that the "Wilson propaganda" that found root in Berlin and finally grew there eventually convinced the German people that it was not they themselves, but the Government and militarism that the United States was warring against. *This was the seed of dissension that ruined German morale at home.*

Tirpitz declared that the beginning of the end came when in answer to the President's Sussex note, "We showed the world that we were going down before America."

Probably the most enlightening chapter of either book is that containing Tirpitz's contention that the influence of the Wilson submarine notes resulted in Japan's stronger and more active alliance with the Allies. In this connection Von Tirpitz says:

Only the transmitting to Germany of the threatening notes of President Wilson, when he inveighed against my submarine campaign during the latter stages of the war, prevented Japan from coming to us in a great Germano-Japanese alliance, which would have ended the war at once.

The overtures of the Pope, in August, 1917, were rejected and again the attention of the world was arrested by the masterly leadership of the American President. On August 16, 1917, I addressed the following letter to the President with reference to the offers of peace made by His Holiness Pope Benedict XV:

The White House, Washington,
16 August, 1917.

DEAR GOVERNOR:

I do not believe that the proposals the Pope has submitted should lead us into a statement as to the terms of peace beyond that which the President has already given expression to in his address in the Senate and in his Russian note. In these two documents are discussed the fundamentals of international peace. Some of these fundamentals the Pope recognizes in his statement to the belligerents. To go beyond a discussion of these now might lead to a conflict of opinion even among our own allies (for instance, France hopes for the return of Alsace-Lorraine; Russia, for Constantinople, etc.).

When the President said in his address of April second, last, that we were not making war on the German people, I believe he set the stage for the abdication of the Kaiser. And I think our whole note in reply to the Pope should be so framed that this idea would always be kept in the forefront of our discussion so as to bring home to the people of Germany the distrust and utter contempt in which the ruling powers of Germany are held by the peoples of the world.

Our note in reply to the Pope should, I believe, embody the following ideas:

"First—More important now than the terms of peace are the spirit and character of the nations who wish to end the war.

"Second—How can any international agreement to bring an end to the conflict be discussed until those who brought it about can be made to realize the inviolability of treaty obligations?

"Third—Attack the good faith of the ruling powers of Germany, calling attention to the fact that Germany brought on the war; that Germany invaded Belgium; that Germany ravished France, sank the *Lusitania*, ravished the women and children of the conquered territories; that Germany decreed submarine warfare, and 'erected barbarism into a religion.'

"Fourth—And the democratic nations of the world are asked to confide their future and the future of the world to a nation that believes that force of arms should be substituted for the moral force of right. In other words, the ruling powers of Germany must purge themselves of contempt before they shall be given the hearing that the Pope feels they are entitled to."

This form of reply will, I am sure, rouse the people of Germany to a realization of the situation which confronts them, for there is abundant evidence that they are gradually arriving at the conclusion that the Kaiser no longer represents them or their ideals.

In other words, what I should like to see the President do is not to discuss in extenso our terms of peace but rather confine himself to a general attack upon the lack of good faith on the part of Germany in all of her dealings with us.

TUMULTY.

On August 27, 1917, the President, through his Secretary of State, addressed the following reply to the Pope:

To His HOLINESS BENEDICTUS XV, POPE:

In acknowledgment of the communication of Your Holiness to

the belligerent peoples, dated August 1, 1917, the President of the United States requests me to transmit the following reply:

Every heart that has not been blinded and hardened by this terrible war must be touched by this moving appeal of His Holiness the Pope, must feel the dignity and force of the humane and generous motives which prompted it, and must fervently wish that we might take the path of peace he so persuasively points out. But it would be folly to take it if it does not in fact lead to the goal he proposes. Our response must be based upon the stern facts and upon nothing else. It is not a mere cessation of arms he desires: it is a stable and enduring peace. This agony must not be gone through with again, and it must be a matter of very sober judgment what will insure us against it.

His Holiness in substance proposes that we return to the *status quo ante bellum*, and that then there be a general condonation, disarmament, and a concert of nations based upon an acceptance of the principle of arbitration; that by a similar concert freedom of the seas be established; and that the territorial claims of France and Italy, the perplexing problems of the Balkan States, and the restitution of Poland be left to such conciliatory adjustments as may be possible in the new temper of such a peace, due regard being paid to the aspirations of the peoples whose political fortunes and affiliations will be involved.

It is manifest that no part of this programme can be carried out successfully unless the restitution of the *status quo ante* furnishes a firm and satisfactory basis for it. The object of this war is to deliver the free peoples of the world from the menace and the actual power of a vast military establishment controlled by an irresponsible government which, having secretly planned to dominate the world, proceeded to carry the plan out without regard either to the sacred obligations of treaty or the long-established practices and long-cherished principles of international action and honour; which chose its own time for the war; delivered its blow fiercely and suddenly; stopped at no barrier either of law or mercy; swept a whole continent within the tide of blood—not the blood of soldiers only, but the blood of innocent women and children also and of the helpless poor; and now stands balked but not defeated, the enemy of four fifths of the world. This power is not the German people. It is the ruthless master of the

German people. It is no business of ours how that great people came under its control or submitted with temporary zest to the domination of its purpose: but it is our business to see to it that the history of the rest of the world is no longer left to its handling.

To deal with such a power by way of peace upon the plan proposed by His Holiness the Pope would, so far as we can see, involve a re-cuperation of its strength and a renewal of its policy; would make it necessary to create a permanent hostile combination of nations against the German people who are its instruments; and would result in abandoning the newborn Russia to intrigue, the manifold subtle interference, and the certain counter-revolution which would be at-tempted by all the malign influences to which the German Govern-ment has of late accustomed the world. Can peace be based upon a restitution of its power or upon any word of honour it could pledge in a treaty of settlement and accommodation?

Responsible statesmen must now everywhere see, if they never saw before, that no peace can rest securely upon political or economic restrictions meant to benefit some nations and cripple or embarrass others, upon vindictive action of any sort, or any kind of revenge or deliberate injury. The American people have suffered intolerable wrongs at the hands of the Imperial German Government, but they desire no reprisal upon the German people who have themselves suffered all things in this war which they did not choose. They believe that peace should rest upon the rights of peoples, not the rights of governments—the rights of peoples great or small, weak or powerful—their equal right to freedom and security and self-govern-ment and to a participation upon fair terms in the economic oppor-tunities of the world, the German people of course included if they will accept equality and not seek domination.

The test, therefore, of every plan of peace is this: Is it based upon the faith of all the peoples involved or merely upon the word of an ambitious and intriguing government on the one hand and of a group of free peoples on the other? This is a test which goes to the root of the matter; and it is the test which must be applied.

The purposes of the United States in this war are known to the whole world, to every people to whom the truth has been permitted to come. They do not need to be stated again. We seek no material advantage of any kind. We believe that the intolerable wrongs done in this war by the furious and brutal power of the Imperial German Government ought to be repaired, but not at the expense of the sovereignty of any people—rather a vindication of the sovereignty both of those that are weak and those that are strong. Punitive damages, the dismemberment of empires, the establishment of selfish and exclusive economic leagues, we deem inexpedient and in the end worse than futile, no proper basis for a peace of any kind, least of all for an enduring peace. That must be based upon justice and fairness and the common rights of mankind.

We cannot take the word of the present rulers of Germany as a guaranty of anything that is to endure, unless explicitly supported by such conclusive evidence of the will and purpose of the German people themselves as the other peoples of the world would be justified in accepting. Without such guaranties treaties of settlement, agreements for disarmament, covenants to set up arbitration in the place of force, territorial adjustments, reconstitutions of small nations, if made with the German Government, no man, no nation could now depend on. We must await some new evidence of the purposes of the great peoples of the Central Powers. God grant it may be given soon and in a way to restore the confidence of all peoples everywhere in the faith of nations and the possibility of a covenanted peace.

ROBERT LANSING,
Secretary of State of the United States.

CHAPTER XXXII

COLONEL ROOSEVELT AND GENERAL WOOD

IT WILL be recalled that early in the war Colonel Roosevelt called at the White House to confer with the President regarding his desire to lead a brigade to the other side. I recall distinctly every fact of that meeting. I was seated a few feet away in the Red Room of the White House at the time these two men were conferring. Nothing could have been pleasanter or more agreeable than this meeting. They had not met since they were political opponents in 1912, but prior to that they had had two or three friendly visits with each other. Mr. Wilson had once lunched with Colonel Roosevelt at Sagamore Hill, and when the Colonel was President, he and his party had been luncheon guests of President and Mrs. Wilson of Princeton University on the occasion of an Army and Navy game played on the Princeton gridiron.

They met in the White House in the most friendly fashion, told each other anecdotes, and seemed to enjoy together what the Colonel was accustomed to call a "bully time."

The object of the Colonel's call was discussed without heat or bitterness. The President placed before the Colonel his own ideas regarding Mr. Roosevelt's desire to serve, and the attitude of the General Staff toward the volunteer system, a system that would have to be recognized if the Colonel's ambition was to be realized. As a matter of fact, instead of being moved by any ill will toward the Colonel, the inclination of the President was to overrule the recommendation of the General Staff and urge that the Colonel be granted permission to go over seas. The salutations at the end of the conference were most friendly and the Colonel, on his way out, stopped in to see me. He slapped me on the back in the most friendly way, and said: "By Jove, Tumulty, you are a man after my own heart! Six children, eh? Well now, you get me across and I will put you on my staff, and you may tell Mrs. Tumulty that I will not allow them to place you at any point of danger."

Some weeks later, I received the following letter from Colonel Roosevelt:

Oyster Bay, Long Island, N. Y.
April 12, 1917.

MY DEAR MR. TUMULTY:

That was a fine speech of Williams. I shall write him and congratulate him.

Now, don't forget that it might be a very good thing to have you as one of my commissioned officers at Headquarters. You could do really important work there, and tell Mrs. Tumulty and the six children, that this particular service would probably not be dangerous. Come, sure!

Sincerely yours,
THEODORE ROOSEVELT.

MR. JOSEPH P. TUMULTY,
Secretary to the President,
Washington, D. C.

After the Colonel departed, the President in a boyish way said: "Well, and how did the Colonel impress you?" I told the President of the very favourable impression the Colonel had made upon me by his buoyancy, charm of manner, and his great good nature. The

April 12th, 1917.

My dear Mr. Tumulty:

That was a fine speech of Williams..   I shall
write him, and congratulate him.

Now, don't forget that it might be a very good
thing to have you as one of my commissioned officers at
Headquarters.   You could do really important work there,
and tell Mrs. Tumulty, and the six children, that this
particular service would probably not be dangerous. *Come, man!*

Sincerely yours,

Theodore Roosevelt

Mr. Joseph P. Tumulty,
Secretary to the President,
Washington, D.C.

Colonel Roosevelt sent this letter to Mr. Tumulty shortly after his one
and only call upon President Wilson at the White House

President replied by saying: "Yes, he is a great big boy. I was, as formerly, charmed by his personality. There is a sweetness about him that is very compelling. You can't resist the man. I can easily understand why his followers are so fond of him."

It was, therefore, with real pain that the President read the account of this interview as contained in John J. Leary's book entitled "Talks with T. R.," containing many slighting references made by the Colonel to the President. It appears that Mr. Leary accompanied the Colonel to the White House and immediately upon the conclusion of the conference was the recipient of a confidential statement of the Colonel's impression of the President. The account in Mr. Leary's book is as follows:

I found that, though I had written plainly enough, there was confusion in his [Wilson's] mind as to what I wanted to do. I explained everything to him. He seemed to take it well, but—remember I was talking to Mr. Wilson.

. . . .

"Tumulty, by way of a half joke, said he might go to France with me. I said: 'By Jove, you come right along! I'll have a place for you.' I would, too, but it wouldn't be the place he thinks. It is possible he might be sent along as sort of a watchdog to keep Mr. Wilson informed as to what was being done. He wouldn't be, though. He'd keep his distance from headquarters except when he was sent for.

. . . .

He [Wilson] has promised me nothing definitely, but as I have said, if any other man than he talked to me as he did, I would feel assured. If I talked to another man as he talked to me it would mean that that man was going to get permission to fight. But I was talking to Mr. Wilson. His words may mean much, they may mean little. He has, however, left the door open.

Of course, what ultimately happened is clear to everyone, civilian and soldier, who pauses a moment to reflect;
as plans for the conduct of the war matured, it became
continually clearer that it must be a professional war,
conducted by professionals with complete authority over
subordinates. There could be no experimenting with
volunteer commanders, no matter how great their valour,
how pure their motives, or how eminent their positions in
the nation. To make an exception of Colonel Roosevelt
would have been to strike at the heart of the whole
design. Military experts and the majority of Congressional opinion were at one in this matter, though
Congress put upon the President the responsibility of
making the final decision, together with whatever obloquy
this would entail. It was purely as a step in the interest of
waging the war with greatest effectiveness that the President announced the decision adverse to the Colonel's
wishes. Personally it would have been pleasanter for
the President to grant the Colonel's request, but President Wilson has never adopted "the easiest way."

A great deal of criticism was heaped upon the President
for what appeared to the outside as his refusal to send
General Leonard Wood to France. Although a fierce
storm of criticism beat upon him, the President displayed no resentment, nor, indeed, did he seem to notice
what his critics were saying.

As a matter of fact, the President played no part in the
movement to keep General Wood from realizing his ambition to lead his division to France. Mr. George Creel in
his book, "The War, The World and Wilson," has suc-
cinctly summarized this incident; has told how the
name of General Wood did not appear in any of the lists
of officers received from General Pershing; how the Presi-

dent took this as a plain indication that General Pershing
did not desire General Wood in France (the absence of so
eminent a name from the lists was certainly not an over-
sight on the part of the Commanding General in France);
how President Wilson was determined to support General
Pershing in every detail so long as General Pershing in
the President's opinion was meeting the requirements of
the great responsibility laid upon him; how the President
was insistent that General Pershing should not be embarrassed by political considerations of any kind in the
discharge of his great military duty; how the unfortunate
feature of the whole matter was that the recall of General Wood did not come until "after he had taken his
brigade to New York preparatory to sailing for the other
side"; how "General March treated the circumstance as
one of military routine entirely, utterly failing to realize
its political importance"; how "instead of informing
General Wood at once that he had not been chosen to go
to France, General March followed the established procedure and waited for the completion of the training
period before issuing orders to the division commanders";
how "General Wood left Camp Funston in advance of
his division and without waiting to receive his orders";
how General March sent these orders to New York; how
"in consequence there was an appearance of eleventh-
hour action, an effect of jerking General Wood from the
very deck of the transport"; how "General Wood carried
his complaint to the President and was told plainly that
the list would not be revised in the personal interest of any
soldier or politician."

I discussed the matter with General Wood immediately
upon the conclusion of his conference with the President.
Walking into my office after his interview, the General

informed me that his talk with the President was most
agreeable and satisfactory and that he was certain, although the President did not intimate it to him, that the
reason for his being held in America could not be attributed to the President. Turning to me, the General said:
"I know who is responsible for this. It is that man
Pershing." I assured the General that there was nothing
in the President's attitude toward him that was in the
least degree unfriendly, and reminded him how the President had retained him as Chief of Staff when he assumed
office in 1913. The General, very much to my surprise, intimated that back of Pershing's attitude toward
him was political consideration. I tried to reassure him
and, indeed, I resented this characterization of General
Pershing as an unjust and unwarranted imputation upon
the Commander of the American Expeditionary Forces.

I myself felt that General Wood was being unfairly
treated, although I did not admit this to him in our
interview. I took the liberty of saying this to the President over the telephone from my house that evening.
I tried to convince the President that there was a feeling
rapidly spreading throughout the country that Wood
was being unfairly treated and that it was not just that
the Administration, which I knew was blameless in the
matter, should be compelled to bear the responsibility
of the whole thing and pay what I was certain would be
a great price in the loss of popular esteem.

The President in his reply to my statement showed irritation at what I said in General Wood's behalf, and used
very emphatic language in conveying to me the idea
that he would not interfere in having the list, upon which
General Wood's name appeared, revised. I urged that
if General Wood was not to be sent to France, he should

be given a chance to go to Italy. Our conversation over the telephone in reference to the Wood matter was as follows:

"I trust, Governor, that you can see your way clear to send General Wood either to France or to Italy."

Without a moment's hesitation, the President said: "I am sorry, but it cannot be done."

Whereupon, I said: "It is not fair that the Administration should be carrying the burden of this whole affair. If General Pershing or the General Staff is responsible for holding General Wood in this country, surely they have good reason, and the public ought to be apprised of it, and thus remove the suspicion that we are playing politics."

The President quickly interrupted me and said: "I am not at all interested in any squabble or quarrel between General Pershing and General Wood. The only thing I am interested in is winning this war. I selected General Pershing for this task and I intend to back him up in every recommendation he makes."

When I tried to emphasize the feeling of dissatisfaction throughout the country over the Wood incident, he replied that the responsibility of winning the war was upon General Pershing and himself and not upon the critics who thought that General Wood was being badly treated. I then said: "But it is not fair to you to have it said that by reason of some feeling that you may have against Wood you are keeping him on this side."

The President replied: "I am sorry, but I do not care a damn for the criticism of the country. It would not be fair to Pershing if I tried to escape what appears to be my responsibility. I do not intend to embarrass General Pershing by forcing his hand. If Pershing does not make good, I will recall him, but it must not be said that I have failed to support him at every turn."

His attitude toward Wood and Roosevelt was consistently maintained, in supporting the General Staff and the War Department throughout the war. The only thing that seemed to interest him was how quickly and effectively to do the job and to find the man who could do it.

CHAPTER XXXIII

THE President had but one object: to throw all the nation's energy into the scale for the defeat of Germany. Because he did not bluster and voice daily hymns of hate against Germany, he was singularly misunderstood by some of his fellow-citizens, who, in their own boiling anger against the enemy, would sometimes peevishly inquire: "Does he really hate Germany?" The President was too much occupied with deeds to waste time in word-vapouring. By every honourable means he had sought to avoid the issue, but a truculent and fatuous foe had made war necessary, and into that war the peace-loving President went with the grim resolution of an iron warrior. In his attitude before and during the war his motto might have been the familiar words of Polonius:

> Beware of entrance to a quarrel; but being in,
> Bear't, that the opposed may beware of thee.

Occasionally, as at Baltimore, on April 6, 1918, the public heard from him brief, ringing speeches of warlike resolution:

Germany has once more said that force and force alone shall decide whether Justice and Peace shall reign in the affairs of men, whether Right as America conceives it or Dominion as she conceives it shall determine the destinies of mankind. There is therefore but one response possible from us. Force, Force to the utmost, Force without stint or limit, the righteous and triumphant Force which shall make Right the law of the world, and cast every selfish Dominion down in the dust.

Months after hostilities had ended, there appeared from time to time in the newspapers, without his or my knowledge of proposed publication, utterances of his to military men during the conflict which showed his warrior heart and his extraordinary ability to grasp a technical military problem such as his dispatch to Admiral Sims, his address to the officers of the Atlantic Fleet, and his interview with Marshal Joffre in the White House. Perhaps it is not generally known that Mr. Wilson, who has constantly read and loved the philosophic poetry of Wordsworth, has also been an intense admirer of Shakespeare's warrior-hero, Henry the Fifth, and has frequently read aloud to friends, with exclamations of admiration, the stirring speeches of Henry in the Shakespearean play. The cable message to Admiral Sims is as follows:

FROM THE PRESIDENT FOR ADMIRAL SIMS,
American Embassy, London, July 5, 1917.
Strictly confidential.
From the beginning of the war, I have been greatly surprised at the failure of the British Admiralty to use Great Britain's great naval superiority in an effective way. In the presence of the present submarine emergency they are helpless to the point of panic. Every plan we suggest they reject for some reason of prudence. In my view, this is not a time for prudence but for boldness even at the cost of great losses. In most of your dispatches you have quite properly advised us of the sort of aid and coöperation desired from us by the Admiralty. The trouble is that their plans and methods do not seem to us efficacious. I would be very much obliged to you if you would report to me, confidentially, of course, exactly what the Admiralty has been doing, and what they have accomplished, and

add to the report your own comments and suggestions, based upon independent thought of the whole situation, without regard to the judgments of any one on that side of the water. The Admiralty was very slow to adopt the protection or convoy and it is not now, I judge [protecting] convoys on adequate scale within the danger zone, seeming to keep small craft with the grand fleet. The absence of craft for convoy is even more apparent on the French coast than on the English coast and in the Channel. I do not see how the necessary military supplies and supplies of food and fuel oil are to be delivered at British ports in any other way within the next few months than under adequate convoy. There will presently not be ships or tankers enough and our shipbuilding plans may not begin to yield important results in less than eighteen months. I believe that you will keep these instructions absolutely and entirely to yourself, and that you will give me such advice as you would give if you were handling and if you were running a navy of your own.

(Signed) WOODROW WILSON.

For sheer audacity, there is not much that can be compared with his address to the officers of the Atlantic Fleet on August 11, 1917:

Now, the point that is constantly in my mind, gentlemen, is this: This is an unprecedented war and, therefore, it is a war in one sense for amateurs. Nobody ever before conducted a war like this and therefore nobody can pretend to be a professional in a war like this. Here are two great navies, not to speak of the others associated with us, our own and the British, outnumbering by a very great margin the navy to which we are opposed and yet casting about for a way in which to use our superiority and our strength, because of the novelty of the instruments used, because of the unprecedented character of the war, because, as I said just now, nobody ever before fought a war like this, in the way that this is being fought at sea, or on land either, for that matter. The experienced soldier—experienced in previous wars—is a back number so far as his experience is concerned; not so far as his intelligence is concerned. His experience does not count, because he never fought a war as this is being fought, and therefore he is an amateur along with the rest of us. Now, some-

body has got to think this war out. Somebody has got to think out
the way not only to fight the submarine, but to do something different from what we are doing.

We are hunting hornets all over the farm and letting the nest alone.
None of us know how to go to the nest and crush it; and yet I despair
of hunting for hornets all over the sea when I know where the nest
is and know that the nest is breeding hornets as fast as I can find
them. I am willing for my part, and I know you are willing because
I know the stuff you are made of—I am willing to sacrifice half the
navy Great Britain and we together have to crush out that nest, because if we crush it the war is won. I have come here to say that I do
not care where it comes from, I do not care whether it comes from
the youngest officer or the oldest, but I want the officers of this navy
to have the distinction of saying how this war is going to be won.
The Secretary of the Navy and I have just been talking over plans for
putting the planning machinery of the Navy at the disposal of the
brains of the Navy and not stopping to ask what rank those brains have,
because, as I have said before and want to repeat, so far as experience
in this kind of war is concerned we are all of the same rank. I am not
saying that I do not expect the admirals to tell us what to do, but I
am saying that I want the youngest and most modest youngster in
the service to tell us what we ought to do if he knows what it is.
Now I am willing to make any sacrifice for that. I mean any sacrifice of time or anything else. I am ready to put myself at the disposal of any officer in the Navy who thinks he knows how to run this
war. I will not undertake to tell you whether he does or not, because I know that I do not, but I will undertake to put him in communication with those who can find out whether his idea will work
or not. I have the authority to do that and I will do it with the
greatest pleasure.

.   .   .   .

We have got to throw tradition to the wind. Now, as I have said,
gentlemen, I take it for granted that nothing that I say here will be
repeated and therefore I am going to say this: Every time we have suggested anything to the British Admiralty the reply has come back
that virtually amounted to this, that it had never been done that way,
and I felt like saying: "Well, nothing was ever done so systematically
as nothing is being done now." Therefore, I should like to see some-

thing unusual happen, something that was never done before; and inasmuch as the things that are being done to you were never done before, don't you think it is worth while to try something that was never done before against those who are doing them to you. There is no other way to win, and the whole principle of this war is the kind of thing that ought to hearten and stimulate America. America has always boasted that she could find men to do anything. She is the prize amateur nation of the world. Germany is the prize professional nation of the world. Now when it comes to doing new things and doing them well, I will back the amateur against the professional every time, because the professional does it out of the book and the amateur does it with his eyes open upon a new world and with a new set of circumstances. He knows so little about it that he is fool enough to try to do the right thing. The men that do not know the danger are the rashest men, and I have several times ventured to make this suggestion to the men about me in both arms of the service. Please leave out of your vocabulary altogether the word "prudent." Do not stop to think about what is prudent for a moment. Do the thing that is audacious to the utmost point of risk and daring, because that is exactly the thing that the other side does not understand, and you will win by the audacity of method when you cannot win by circumspection and prudence. I think that there are willing ears to hear this in the American Navy and the American Army because that is the kind of folk we are. We get tired of the old ways and covet the new ones.

So, gentlemen, besides coming down here to give you my personal greeting and to say how absolutely I rely on you and believe in you, I have come down here to say also that I depend on you, depend on you for brains as well as training and courage and discipline.

When Marshal Joffre visited the President in the spring of 1917, he was surprised, as he afterward said to Secretary Daniels, "to find that President Wilson had such a perfect mastery of the military situation. He had expected to meet a scholar, a statesman, and an idealist; he had not expected to meet a practical strategist fully conversant with all the military movements.

In answer to my question as to whether it would be feasible to send in advance of his army the general who was to command American troops in France, the President said at once that it could be arranged."

The President and Marshal Joffre considered together a number of technical military problems. General Joffre gave the President his expert opinion as to what should be done in every instance and was surprised at the promptness with which in each case the President said: "It shall be done."

A little incident at the White House at the luncheon given by the President to the members of the Democratic National Committee throws light upon the fighting qualities of the man. He asked Mr. Angus W. McLean, a warm and devoted friend from North Carolina, who was seated near him at the table, what the Scots down in North Carolina were saying about the war. Mr. McLean replied he could best answer the question by repeating what a friend of the President's father and an ardent admirer of the President had said about the President's attitude a few days previous. "I am afraid our President is not a true Scot, he doesn't show the fighting spirit characteristic of the Scots." The President promptly replied: "You tell our Scotch friend, McLean, that he does not accurately interpret the real Scottish character. If he did, he would understand my attitude. The Scotsman is slow to begin to fight but when once he begins he never knows when to quit."

Two capital policies which contributed enormously to the winning of the war received their impulse from Woodrow Wilson—the unification of command of the Allied armies on the western front and the attack of submarines at their base in the North Sea. On November

18, 1918, Colonel House let it be known in London that
he had received a cable from President Wilson stating
emphatically that the United States Government considered unity of plan and control between the Allies and
the United States to be essential in order to win the war
and achieve a just and lasting peace.

It was Woodrow Wilson, a civilian, who advised, urged,
and insisted that a mine barrage be laid across the North
Sea to check German submarine activities at their source.
Naval experts pronounced the plan impossible: it would
take too long to lay the barrage, and, when laid, it would
not hold. A great storm would sweep it away. But the
President insisted that the thing could be done, and that
nothing else could check the submarine devastation
amounting by July, 1917, to 600,000 tons a month of
destroyed shipping. The President's audacity and persistence prevailed, and it is not too much to say that his
plan ended the submarine menace.

It will be recalled that European newspapers carried
a story of a farewell reception to Mr. Bonar Law, in which
he paid his compliments to his chief, Mr. Lloyd George,
saying, in substance, that he had seen Lloyd George discouraged only once. It was on the morning when the news
came of the great German offensive in March, 1918.
Mr. Lloyd George told Mr. Bonar Law that morning
that only a vast increase in American reinforcements
could save the Allies. A cable was immediately framed,
asking Mr. Wilson to send the number of reinforcements
necessary. Mr. Bonar Law stated in his speech that an
affirmative answer was received from Mr. Wilson the
same day.

A prominent Englishman, discussing the President's
work in connection with the war, while criticizing what

he characterized as the President's ignorance of European conditions, said: "I feel ashamed to be criticizing President Wilson for anything when I remember his practical services in prosecuting the war. No other man in any country gave such firm and instant support to every measure for making operations effective. His decisions were fearless and prompt and he stood by them like a rock. In sending troops promptly and in sending plenty of them, in coöperating in the naval effort, in insisting on the unity of command under Foch, in backing the high command in the field, and in every other practical detail Mr. Wilson had big, clear conceptions and the courage to carry them out."

Those who were critical of the President's conduct of the war forget the ringing statement that came from Lloyd George when the great offensive was on, when he said: "The race is now between Von Hindenburg and Wilson." And Wilson won.

The most important speech made by the President during the war was delivered at the Metropolitan Opera House, New York City, on September 27, 1918, opening the campaign for the Fourth Liberty Loan.

I recall a talk the President had with me on the way to New York on the afternoon of the delivery of this speech when he requested me to read the manuscript. As he gave it to me he said: "They [meaning the Allies] will not like this speech, for there are many things in it which will displease the Imperialists of Great Britain, France, and Italy. The world must be convinced that we are playing no favourites and that America has her own plan for a world settlement, a plan which does not contain the germs of another war. What I greatly fear, now that the end seems inevitable, is that we shall go

back to the old days of alliances and competing armaments and land grabbing. We must see to it, therefore,
that there is not another Alsace-Lorraine, and that when
peace finally comes, it shall be a permanent and a lasting
peace. We must now serve notice on everybody that
our aims and purposes are not selfish. In order to do
this and to make the right impressions, we must be bru-
tally frank with friends and foes alike."

As we discussed the subject matter of this momentous
speech, I gathered from the President's statements to
me that he clearly foresaw the end of the war and of the
possible proposal for a settlement that might be made
by the Allies. Therefore, he felt it incumbent upon him
frankly to discuss America's view of what a just and
lasting settlement should be. As one examines this
speech to-day, away from the excitement of that critical
hour in which it was delivered, he can easily find in it
statements and utterances that must have caused sharp
irritation in certain chancelleries of Europe. In nearly
every line of it there was a challenge to European Imperialism to come out in the open and avow its purposes as to
peace. Many of the Allied leaders had been addressing
their people on the matter of peace; now they were being
challenged by an American president to place their
cards face up on the table. An examination of the speech,
in the light of subsequent events, reëmphasizes the
President's pre-vision:

At every turn of the war we gain a fresh consciousness of what
·we mean to accomplish by it. When our hope and expectation are
most excited we think more definitely than before of the issues that
hang upon it and of the purposes which must be realized by means
of it. For it has positive and well-defined purposes which we did
not determine and which we cannot alter. No statesman or assem-

bly created them; no statesman or assembly can alter them. They have arisen out of the very nature and circumstances of the war. The most that statesmen or assemblies can do is to carry them out or be false to them. They were perhaps not clear at the outset; but they are clear now. The war has lasted more than four years and the whole world has been drawn into it. The common will of mankind has been substituted for the particular purposes of individual states. Individual statesmen may have started the conflict, but neither they nor their opponents can stop it as they please. It has become a peoples' war, and peoples of all sorts and races, of every degree of power and variety of fortune, are involved in its sweeping processes of change and settlement. We came into it when its character had become fully defined and it was plain that no nation could stand apart or be indifferent to its outcome. Its challenge drove to the heart of everything we cared for and lived for. The voice of the war had become clear and gripped our hearts. Our brothers from many lands, as well as our own murdered dead under the sea, were calling to us, and we responded, fiercely and of course.

The air was clear about us. We saw things in their full, convincing proportions as they were; and we have seen them with steady eyes and unchanging comprehension ever since. We accepted the issues of the war as facts, not as any group of men either here or elsewhere had defined them, and we can accept no outcome which does not squarely meet and settle them. Those issues are these:

Shall the military power of any nation or group of nations be suffered to determine the fortunes of peoples over whom they have no right to rule except the right of force?

Shall strong nations be free to wrong weak nations and make them subject to their purpose and interest?

Shall peoples be ruled and dominated, even in their own internal affairs, by arbitrary and irresponsible force or by their own will and choice?

Shall there be a common standard of right and privilege for all peoples and nations or shall the strong do as they will and the weak suffer without redress?

Shall the assertion of right be haphazard and by casual alliance or shall there be a common concert to oblige the observance of common rights?

No man, no group of men, chose these to be the issues of the struggle. They *are* issues of it; and they must be settled—by no arrangement or compromise or adjustment of interests, but definitely and once for all and with a full and unequivocal acceptance of the principle that the interest of the weakest is as sacred as the interest of the strongest.

That is what we mean when we speak of a permanent peace, if we speak sincerely, intelligently, and with a real knowledge and comprehension of the matter we deal with.

. . . .

As I have said, neither I nor any other man in governmental authority created or gave form to the issues of this war. I have simply responded to them with such vision as I could command. But I have responded gladly and with a resolution that has grown warmer and more confident as the issues have grown clearer and clearer. It is now plain that they are issues which no man can pervert unless it be wilfully. I am bound to fight for them, and happy to fight for . them as time and circumstance have revealed them to me as to all the world. Our enthusiasm for them grows more and more irresistible as they stand out in more and more vivid and unmistakable outline.

And the forces that fight for them draw into closer and closer array, organize their millions into more and more unconquerable might, as they become more and more distinct to the thought and purposes of the peoples engaged. It is the peculiarity of this great war that while statesmen have seemed to cast about for definitions of their purpose and have sometimes seemed to shift their ground and their point of view, the thought of the mass of men, whom statesmen are supposed to instruct and lead, has grown more and more unclouded, more and more certain of what it is that they are fighting for. National purposes have fallen more and more into the background and the common purpose of enlightened mankind has taken their place. The counsels of plain men have become on all hands more simple and straightforward and more unified than the counsels of sophisticated men of affairs, who still retain the impression that they are playing a game of power and playing for high stakes. That is why I have said that this is a peoples' war, not a statesmen's. Statesmen must follow the clarified common thought or be broken.

I take that to be the significance of the fact that assemblies and associations of many kinds made up of plain workaday people have demanded, almost every time they came together, and are still demanding, that the leaders of their governments declare to them plainly what it is, exactly what it is, that they were seeking in this war, and what they think the items of the final settlement should be. They are not yet satisfied with what they have been told. They still seem to fear that they are getting what they ask for only in statesmen's terms—only in the terms of territorial arrangements and divisions of power, and not in terms of broad-visioned justice and mercy and peace and the satisfaction of those deep-seated longings of oppressed and distracted men and women and enslaved peoples that seem to them the only things worth fighting a war for that engulfs the world. Perhaps statesmen have not always recognized this changed aspect of the whole world of policy and action. Perhaps they have not always spoken in direct reply to the questions asked because they did not know how searching those questions were and what sort of answers they demanded.

But I, for one, am glad to attempt the answer again and again, in the hope that I may make it clearer and clearer that my one thought is to satisfy those who struggle in the ranks and are, perhaps above all others, entitled to a reply whose meaning no one can have any excuse for misunderstanding, if he understands the language in which it is spoken or can get someone to translate it correctly into his own. And I believe that the leaders of the governments with which we are associated will speak, as they have occasion, as plainly as I have tried to speak. I hope that they will feel free to say whether they think I am in any degree mistaken in my interpretation of the issues involved or in my purpose with regard to the means by which a satisfactory settlement of those issues may be obtained. Unity of purpose and of counsel are as imperatively necessary as was unity of command in the battlefield, and with perfect unity of purpose and counsel will come assurance of complete victory. It can be had in no other way. "Peace drives" can be effectively neutralized and silenced only by showing that every victory of the nations associated against Germany brings the nations nearer the sort of peace which will bring security and reassurance to all peoples and make the recurrence of another such struggle of pitiless force and bloodshed for ever impossible, and that nothing else can. Germany is constantly intimating the "terms" she will accept; and always finds that the world does not want terms. It wishes the final triumph of justice and fair dealing.

When I had read the speech, I turned to the President and said: "This speech will bring Germany to terms and will convince her that we play no favourites and will compel the Allies openly to avow the terms upon which they will expect a war settlement to be reached. In my opinion, it means the end of the war." The President was surprised at the emphasis I laid upon the speech, but he was more surprised when I ventured the opinion that he would be in Paris within six months discussing the terms of the treaty.

The Washington *Post*, a critic of the President, characterized this speech, in an editorial on September 29, 1918, as "a marvellous intellectual performance, and a still more marvellous exhibition of moral courage."

CHAPTER XXXIV

GERMANY CAPITULATES

GERMANY had begun to weaken, and suddenly aware of the catastrophe that lay just ahead, changed her chancellor, and called upon the President for an armistice upon the basis of the Fourteen Points. The explanation of Germany's attitude in this matter was simply that she knew she was beaten and she recognized that Wilson was the only hope of a reasonable peace from the Berlin point of view. Germany professed to be a liberal and was asking Wilson for the "benefit of clergy."

On the 6th day of October, 1918, the following note from Prince Max of Baden was delivered to the President by the Secretary of State:

The German Government requests the President of the United States of America to take steps for the restoration of peace, to notify all belligerents of this request, and to invite them to delegate plenipotentiaries for the purpose of taking up negotiations. The German Government accepts, as a basis for the peace negotiations, the programme laid down by the President of the United States in his Message to Congress of January 8, 1918, and in his subsequent pronouncements particularly in his address of September 27, 1918. In order to avoid further bloodshed, the German Government requests the President of the United States of America to bring about the immediate conclusion of a general armistice on land, on water, and in the air.

(Signed) MAX, Prince of Baden,
Imperial Chancellor.

The President was not surprised when the offer of peace
came for on all sides there was abundant evidence of the
decline of Germany and of the weakening of her morale.
The President felt that Germany, being desperate, it
would be possible for him, when she proposed a settlement, like that proposed by Prince Max, to dictate our
own terms, and to insist that America would have nothing
to do with any settlement in which the Kaiser or his
brood should play a leading part. I stated to him that the
basis of our attitude toward Germany should be an insistence, in line with his speech of September 27, 1918,
wherein he said:

We are all agreed that there can be no peace obtained by any kind
of bargain or compromise with the governments of the Central Empires, because we have dealt with them already and have seen them
deal with other governments that were parties to this struggle, at
Brest-Litovsk and Bucharest. They have convinced us that they
were without honour and do not intend justice. They observe no
covenants, accept no principle but force and their own interest. We
cannot come to terms with them. They have made it impossible.
The German people must by this time be fully aware that we
cannot accept the word of those who forced this war upon us. We
do not think the same thoughts or speak the same language of agreement.

At the time of the receipt of Prince Max's note by
the State Department, on October 5, 1918, the President was in New York, staying at the Waldorf-Astoria,
preparatory to attending a concert given by the Royal
Italian Grenadiers. A message from the Army Intelligence Department, conveyed to me by General Churchill,
at the Knickerbocker Hotel, in New York, where I was
staying, was the first word we had of Germany's desire for
an armistice. General Churchill read me the German

proposal over the 'phone and I carried it to the President, who was in conference with Colonel House at the Waldorf. The offer of Germany was so frank and unequivocal in seeming to meet the terms of the President's formal proposals of peace, that when Colonel House read it to the President, he turned and said: "This means the end of the war." When I was interrogated as to my opinion, I replied that, while the German offer of peace seemed to be genuine, in my opinion no offer from Germany could be considered that bore the Hohenzollern-Hapsburg brand. For a moment this seemed to irritate the President, and he said: "But, at least, we are bound to consider in the most serious way any offer of Germany which is practically an acceptance of my proposals of peace." There our first discussion regarding the German peace offer ended.

At the conclusion of this talk I was invited to take dinner with the President and Colonel House and with the members of the President's family, but the matter of the note which we had just received weighed so heavily upon me that my digestive apparatus was not in good working order, and yet the President was seemingly unmindful of it, and refused to permit the evening to be interfered with because of the note, attending the concert and apparently enjoying every minute of the evening, and applauding the speeches that were made by the gentlemen who addressed us.

After the concert began, I left the Presidential box and, following a habit I had acquired since coming to the Executive offices, I conferred with the newspaper men in our party, endeavouring to obtain from them, without expressing any personal opinion of my own, just how they felt toward the terms proposed in the Max note. I then called up the State Department and discussed the note with Mr. Polk, expressing the same opinion to him that I had already expressed to the President, to the effect that we could not accept a German offer which came to us under the auspices of the Hohenzollerns.

Upon the conclusion of the concert, we left the Metropolitan Opera House, I accompanying the President to the Waldorf. As I took my place in the automobile, the President leaned over to Mrs. Wilson and whispered to her the news of the receipt of the German note. Then, turning to me, he said: "Have you had any new reaction on the note since I last talked with you?" I told him I had not, but that what I had learned since talking with him earlier in the evening had only confirmed me in the opinion that I had already expressed, that it would not be right or safe for us to accept the German proposals. When we arrived at the Waldorf it was 12:30 A. M. and the President asked me to his rooms, and there, for an hour and a half, we indulged in a long discussion of the German offer. As was usual with the President in all these important matters, his mind was, to use his own phrase, "open and to let."

I emphasized the idea that we could not consider a peace proposal in which the Kaiser and his brood played a part, and that the only proffer we could consider must come from the German people themselves; that in his Mexican policy he had proclaimed the doctrine that no ruler who came to power by murder or assassination would ever receive the recognition of the United States; that we must broaden the morality which underlay this policy, and by our attitude say to the European rulers who started this war, that guilt is personal and that until they had purged themselves from the responsibility of war, we could not consider any terms of peace that came through them.

The next day the President left for Cleveland Dodge's home on the Hudson, with Colonel House and Doctor Grayson. I remained in New York at the Knickerbocker Hotel, busily engaged in poring over the newspaper files to find out what the editorial attitude of the country was toward the German proposal of peace, and in preparing a brief on the whole matter for the President's consideration. Before Colonel House left, I again impressed upon him my view of the note and my conviction that it would be a disastrous blunder for us to accept it.

The President returned to Washington in the early afternoon, Colonel House accompanying him. I was eager and anxious to have another talk with him and was given an opportunity while in the President's compartment in the train on our way back to Washington. As I walked into the compartment, the President was conferring with Colonel House, and as I took a seat, the President asked me if I still felt that the German proposal should be rejected. I replied, that, if anything, I was stronger in the judgment I had already expressed. He said: "But it is not an easy matter to turn away from an offer like this. There is no doubt that the form of it may be open to objection, but substantially it represents the wishes of the German people, even though the medium through which it may be conveyed is an odious and hateful one, but I must make up my own mind on this and I must not be held off from an acceptance by any feeling of criticism that may come my way. The gentlemen in the Army who talk about going to Berlin and taking it by force are foolish. It would cost a million American lives to accomplish it; and what lies in my thoughts now is this: If we can accept this offer, the war will be at an end, for Germany cannot begin a new one, and thus we would save a great deal of bloodshed."

I remember, as I pointed out to him the disappointment of the people were he to accept the German offer, he said: "If I think it is right to accept it, I shall do so regardless of consequences. As for myself, I can go down in a cyclone cellar and write poetry the rest of my days, if necessary." He called my attention to the fact that John Jay, who negotiated the famous treaty with Great Britain, was burned in effigy and Alexander Hamilton was stoned while defending the Jay Treaty on the steps of the Treasury Building in New York City. I pointed out to him that there was no comparison between the two situations; that our case was already made up and that to retreat now and accept this proposal would be to leave intact the hateful dynasty that had brought on the war.

As was his custom and habit, he was considering all the facts and every viewpoint before he finally took the inevitable step.

Never before was the bigness of the President shown better than in this discussion; never was he more open-minded or more anxious to obtain all the facts in the grave situation with which he was called upon to deal. In the action upon which his mind was now at work he was not thinking of himself or of its effect upon his own political fortunes. All through the discussion one could easily see the passionate desire of the man to bring this bloody thing of war honourably to an end.

Mr. Edward N. Hurley furnishes me with a characteristic anecdote connected with a session of the War Conference Board, which Mr. Hurley calls "one of the most historic conferences ever held at the White House."

"The question," says Mr. Hurley, "was whether the President would be justified in agreeing to an armistice. Many people throughout the country were demanding an insistence upon unconditional surrender. Very little news was coming from abroad." Mr. Hurley says that the President met the Conference Board with the statement: "Gentlemen, I should like to get an expression from each man as to what he thinks we should or should not do regarding an unconditional surrender or an armistice." Mr. Hurley says that "every man at the meeting except one was in favour of an armistice." After the President had ascertained the opinion of each he said in a quiet way: "I have drawn up a tentative note to Germany which I should like to submit for your approval." After the paper had been passed around one member of the Board said: "Mr. President, I think it would be better politics if you were to change this paragraph"—indicating a particular paragraph in the document. The President replied, in what Mr. Hurley calls "a slow and deliberate manner": "I am not dealing in politics, I am dealing in human lives."

While the President was engaged in conference with Colonel House, I addressed a letter to him, as follows:

THE WHITE HOUSE
WASHINGTON

October 8, 1918.

DEAR GOVERNOR:

I do not know what your attitude is toward the late German and Austrian offers. The record you have made up to this time, however, is so plain that in my judgment there can be only one answer and that is an absolute and unqualified rejection of these proposals.

There is no safer counsellor in the country than the Springfield *Republican*. Speaking of the peace programme of the new German Chancellor, the *Republican* says:

"It [referring to the offer of Prince Max] does not meet the minimum requirements for the opening of negotiations. These have been variously stated, but in general may be reduced to restitution, reparation and guarantees. Under none of these heads has Germany yet come even measurably near meeting the plain requirements of the Allies, which have not been reduced in defeat and will not be increased with victory. Take, for example, the question of Belgium, now that Germany knows it cannot be kept, it makes a merit of giving it up, but beyond that Prince Maximilian is not authorized more than to say that 'an effort shall also be made to reach an understanding on the question of indemnity' . . . What is needed first of all from Germany is a clear, specific and binding pledge in regard to the essential preliminaries. It does not advance matters an inch for the Chancellor, like Baron Burian, to offer to take President Wilson's points as a 'basis' for negotiations. They will make a first-rate basis, but only when Germany has offered definite preliminary guarantees."

I beg to call your attention to another editorial in the Springfield *Republican*, entitled "Why Germany Must Surrender," hereto attached.

Speaking of Germany's promises, I mention still another editorial from the Springfield *Republican* which concludes by saying, "Even Mr. Wilson is not so simple-minded as the Kaiser may once have thought him to be."

It is the hand of Prussianism which offers this peace to America. As long ago as last June you exposed the hollowness of peace offered under such conditions as are now set forth by the German Chancellor. Referring to the German Government, you said: It wishes to close its bargain before it is too late and it has little left to offer for the pound of flesh it will demand."

In your speech of September 27th, you said:

"We are all agreed that there can be no peace obtained by any kind of bargain or compromise with the governments of the Central Empires, because we have dealt with them already and have seen them deal with other governments that were parties to this struggle, at Brest-Litovsk and Bucharest. They have convinced us that they were without honour and do not intend justice. They observe no covenants, accept no principle but force and their own interest. We cannot 'come to terms' with them, They have made it impossible. The German people must by this time be fully aware that we cannot accept the word of those who forced this war upon us. We do not think the same thoughts or speak the same language of agreement."

Certainly, the German people are not speaking through the German Chancellor. It is the Kaiser himself. He foresees the end and will not admit it. He is still able to dictate conditions, for, in the statement which appeared in the papers yesterday, he said: "It will only be an honourable peace for which we extend our hand."

The other day you said: "We cannot accept the word of those who forced this war upon us." If this were true then, how can we accept this offer now? Certainly nothing has happened since that speech that has changed the character of those in authority in Germany. Defeat has not chastened Germany in the least. The tale of their retreat is still a tale of savagery, for they have devastated the country and carried off the inhabitants; burned churches, looted homes, wreaking upon the advancing Allies every form of vengeance that cruelty can suggest.

In my opinion, your acceptance of this offer will be disastrous, for the Central Powers have made its acceptance impossible by their faithlessness.

TUMULTY.

While the President was conferring with Secretaries Lansing, Daniels, Baker, and Colonel House, I addressed the following letter to President Wilson and a practically identic letter to Colonel House:

THE WHITE HOUSE
WASHINGTON

7 October, 1918.

DEAR MR. PRESIDENT:

Since I returned, every bit of information that comes to me is along one line and that is, that an agreement in which the Kaiser is to play the smallest part will be looked upon with grave suspicion and I believe its results will be disastrous. In my opinion, it will result in the election of a Republican House and the weakening, if not impairing of your influence throughout the world. I am not on the inside and so I do not know, but I am certain that Lloyd George and Clemenceau will take full advantage of this opportunity in declaring that, so far as they are concerned, they are not going to sit down at the Council Table with William the Second, and you may be put in a position before the world, by your acceptance of these conditions, of seeming to be sympathetic with the Kaiser and his brood.

May not Germany be succeeding in splitting the Allies by this offer, just as Talleyrand succeeded, at the Congress of Vienna, in splitting the allies who had been victorious over Napoleon? You cannot blot out the record you have made in your speeches, which in every word and line showed a distrust of this particular autocracy, with which you are now asked to deal. Have you considered the possibility that as soon as Germany read your New York speech of September 27th, knowing, as they did, that it was neither palatable to the Allies nor in accordance with that which they had hitherto stood for, promptly accepted your attitude as a means of dividing the Entente at a critical moment and robbing her of the benefits of the military triumph? Did not Talleyrand do the very same thing to them, as the representative of defeated France, when he sided with Russia and Prussia as against England and thus made possible the return of Napoleon?

I realize the great responsibility that rests upon the President. In any other matter, not so vital as this, you could be wrong and time would correct it, but in a thing like this, when you are dealing with a question which goes to the very depths of international action and world progress, you are at the parting of the ways. If you wish to erect a great structure of peace, you must be sure and certain that every brick in it, that every ounce of cement that goes in it is solid and lasting, and above all, you must preserve your prestige for the bigger moments to come.

Sincerely,
TUMULTY.

Upon the conclusion of the conference, I had a talk with Colonel House and Secretaries Daniels, Lansing, and Baker, and again urged the necessity of a refusal on the part of the President to accept the German peace terms. Secretary Lansing informed me that the President had read my letter to the conference and then said: "We will all be satisfied with the action the President takes in this matter."

While at luncheon that afternoon, the President sent for me to come to the White House. I found him in conference with Secretary Lansing, Colonel House, and Mr. Polk. The German reply was discussed and I was happy when I found that it was a refusal on the part of the President to accept the German proposal.

The gist of the President's reply was a demand from him of evidence of a true conversion on the part of Germany, and an inquiry on the part of the President in these words:

"Does the Imperial Chancellor mean that the German Government accepts the Fourteen Points?" "Do the military men of Germany agree to withdraw all their armies from occupied territories?", and finally: "The President wishes to know whether the Chancellor speaks for the old group who have conducted the war, or does he speak for the liberated peoples of Germany?"

Commenting upon the receipt of the President's reply to the Germans, André Tardieu says:

It is a brief reply which throws the recipients into consternation they cannot conceal. No conversation is possible, declares the President, either on peace or on an armistice until preliminary guarantees shall have been furnished. These are the acceptation pure and simple of the bases of peace laid down on January 8, 1918, and in the President's subsequent addresses; the certainty that the Chancellor does not speak only in the names of the constituted authorities who so far have been responsible for the conduct of the war; the evacuation of all invaded territories. The President will transmit no communication to his associates before having received full satisfaction on these three points.

What must be the thought of those partisans in America who were crying out against the preliminary course of the President in dealing with Germany, who read this paragraph from Tardieu's book as to the impressions made in France and Germany by the notes which the President from week to week addressed to the Germans with reference to the Armistice?

Again Tardieu says:

Then comes the thunderbolt. President Wilson refuses to fall into the trap and, crossing swords in earnest, presses his attack to the utmost in the note of October 14. A mixed commission for evacuation? No! These are matters which like the Armistice itself "must be left to the judgment and advice of the military advisers of the Allied and Associated Governments." Besides no armistice is possible if it does not furnish "absolutely satisfactory safeguards and guarantees of the maintenance of the present military supremacy of the armies of the United States and of its allies." Besides, no armistice "so long as the armed forces of Germany continue the illegal and inhuman practices which they still persist in." Finally, no armistice so long as the German nation shall be in the hands of military power which has disturbed the peace of the world. As to Austria-Hungary, Germany has no interest therein and the President will reply directly. In a single page the whole poor scaffolding of the German Great General Staff is overthrown. The Armistice and peace are not to be the means of delaying a disaster and of preparing revenge. On the main question itself the reply must be Yes or No!

In the books of Ludendorff and Hindenburg we see the shattering effect of the President's answer upon the German military mind. Whatever misunderstanding and misrepresentation of the President's position there might be in his own country, whatever false rumours spread by party malice to the effect that he had entered into negotiations with Germany without the knowledge of the Allies and was imposing "soft" terms on Germany

to prevent a march to Berlin, the German commanders
were under no illusions. They knew that the President
meant capitulation and that in his demand he had the
sanction of his European associates.

Says Ludendorff:

This time he made it quite clear that the Armistice conditions must
be such as to make it impossible for Germany to resume hostilities
and to give the powers allied against her unlimited power to settle
themselves the details of the peace accepted by Germany. In my
view, there could no longer be doubt in any mind that we must continue the fight.

Said Hindenburg in an order "for the information of
all troops," an order never promulgated:

He [Wilson] will negotiate with Germany for peace only if she
concedes all the demands of America's allies as to the internal constitutional arrangements of Germany. . . . Wilson's answer is a
demand for unconditional surrender. It is thus unacceptable to us
soldiers.

In André Tardieu's book we read that from October 5th,
the day when Germany first asked for an armistice, President Wilson remained in daily contact with the European
governments, and that the American Government was in
favour of writing into the Armistice harsher terms than the
Allies thought it wise to propose to the Germans. It will
be recalled that the popular cry at the time was "On to Berlin!" and an urgent demand upon the part of the enemies
of the President on Capitol Hill that he should stand pat
for an unconditional surrender from Germany; that there
should be no soft peace or compromise with Germany, and
that we should send our soldiers to Berlin. At the time
we discussed this attitude of mind of certain men on the
Hill, the President said: "How utterly foolish this is!

Of course, some of our so-called military leaders, for propaganda purposes only, are saying that it would be more advantageous for us to decline the offer of Germany and to go to Berlin. They do not, however, give our people any estimate of the cost in blood and money to consummate this enterprise."

The story was also industriously circulated that Marshal Foch was demurring to any proposition for a settlement with Germany.

It appears now that in the negotiations for the Armistice Colonel House, representing the President's point of view in this vital matter, asked this fundamental question of Foch: "Will you tell us, Marshal, purely from a military point of view and without regard to any other condition, whether you would prefer the Germans to reject or sign the Armistice as outlined here?" Marshal Foch replied: "The only aim of war is to obtain results. If the Germans sign an armistice now upon the general lines we have just determined, we shall have obtained the results we asked. Our aims being accomplished, no one has the right to shed another drop of blood."

It was said at the time that the President was forcing settlement upon the military leaders of the Allies. General Foch disposed of this by saying, in answer to a question by Colonel House and Lloyd George: "The conditions laid down by your military leaders are the very conditions which we ought to and could impose after the success of our further operations, so that if the Germans accept them now, it is useless to go on fighting."

It was all over, and the protagonist of the grand climax of the huge drama was Woodrow Wilson, the accepted spokesman of the Allies, the Nemesis of the Central Powers, who by first isolating them through his moral appeal to the neutral world was now standing before them as the stern monitor, demanding that they settle not on their terms, but on his terms, which the Allies had accepted as their terms.

I shall never forget how happy he looked on the night of the Armistice when the throngs surged through Pennsylvania Avenue, in Washington, and he, unable to remain indoors, had come to the White House gates to look on, in his face a glow of satisfaction of one who realizes that he has fought for a principle and won.   In his countenance there was an expression not so much of triumph as of vindication.

As a light ending to a heavy matter, I may say here that when the Armistice terms were finally accepted, the President said: "Well, Tumulty, the war's over, and I feel like the Confederate soldier General John B. Gordon used to tell of, soliloquizing on a long, hard march, during the Civil War: 'I love my country and I am fightin' for my country, but if this war ever ends, I'll be dad-burned if I ever love another country.'"

CHAPTER XXXV

THE President's appeal to the country of October 24, 1918, asking for the election of a Democratic Congress, brought down upon him a storm of criticism and ridicule. Many leading Democrats who had strongly urged an appeal by the President as a necessary and proper thing in the usual war situation which confronted him, as the criticism directed toward it grew more bitter, turned away from it and criticized what they said was the ineptitude and lack of tact of the President in issuing it. As a matter of fact, opinion in the Democratic ranks as to the wisdom and necessity of a general appeal was unanimous prior to the issuance of the statement. What the President was seeking to do when he asked the support of the country through the election of a Democratic Congress was to prevent divided leadership at a moment when the President's undisputed control was a necessity because of the effect a repudiation of his administration would work upon the Central Powers. He realized that the defeat of his administration in the midst of the World War would give aid and comfort to the Central Powers, and that the Allied governments would themselves interpret it as a weakening of our war power and while the enemy would be strengthened, our associates would be distressed and disheartened.

He looked upon it, therefore, not as a partisan matter but as a matter involving the good faith of America.

At previous elections the White House had been inundated with requests from particular senators and congressmen, urging the President to write letters in their behalf, and this had resulted in so much embarrassment to the Chief Executive that as the critical days of the November elections of 1918 approached, the President was forced to consider a more general and, if possible, a more diplomatic method of handling this difficult situation. The gentlemen who criticized the appeal as outrageously partisan evidently forgot that for months Will Hays, chairman of the Republican National Committee, had been busily engaged in visiting various parts of the country and, with his coadjutors in the Republican National Committee, openly and blatantly demanding an emphatic repudiation of the Administration from the country.

The President and I discussed the situation in June, 1918, and I was asked by him to consider and work out what might be thought a tactful, effective plan by which the President, without arousing party rancour or bitterness, might make an appeal to the country, asking for its support. I considered the matter, and under date of June 18, 1918, I wrote him a letter, part of which was given over to a discussion of the way the matter might discreetly be handled:

THE WHITE HOUSE

WASHINGTON

June 18, 1918.

DEAR GOVERNOR:

I think the attitude of the leaders of the Republican party, as reflected in the speeches of Will Hays, National Chairman, and Senator Penrose, on Saturday last, will give you the opportunity at the psychological moment to strike and to define the issue in this campaign. I think for the present our policy should be one of silence and even a show of indifference to what the leaders on the other side, Messrs. Hay and Penrose, are saying and doing. This will, no doubt, embolden them to make rash statements and charges and by the time you are ready to make your general appeal, the whole country will realize how necessary it is for you frankly to ask for the reëlection of the Democratic Congress. In a speech on Friday night, delivered at Philadelphia, in urging the election of a Republican Congress, Will Hays said: "We will bring the Government back to the limitations and principles of the Constitution in time of peace and establish policies which will again bind up the wounds of war, renew our prosperity, administer the affairs of government with the greatest economy, enlarge our strength at home and abroad, etc. . . ."

Senator Penrose at the same time urging a Republican Congress said: "Let us keep up an efficient Republican organization in Pennsylvania and all through the United States, and make a successful Republican contest at every opportunity in every congressional district and at the next Presidential election, and endeavour to assure the election of Republican candidates."

I think these speeches will give you an opportunity some time in September or October frankly to state just what your attitude is toward the coming campaign, and thus lay before the country what the Republicans hope to gain by bringing about the election of a Republican Congress. I would suggest that some man of distinction in the country write you a letter, calling your attention to partisan speeches of this character, emphasizing the parts I have mentioned, and ask your opinion with reference to the plan of the Republican party to regain power. In other words, we ought to accept these speeches charging incompetency and inefficiency as a challenge, and call the attention of the country to the fact that the leadership of the Republican party is still reactionary and standpat, laying particular emphasis on what the effect in Europe would be of a divided leadership at this time. I think a letter along the lines of the Indiana platform which I suggested a few weeks ago would carry to the country just the impression we ought to make. This letter should be issued, in my opinion, some time in September or October.

While it would seem from a reading of my confidential letter to the President that we were engaged in preparing

In view of the unprecedented record of

this Congress, doesn't the President

wish to make some statement?

The Secretary.

C.L.S.

Do you think I could do this with the candour the country would expect without putting in a drop or two of acid about the Non-loyal & obstructionist member?

W.W.

Dear T.

to the President:

Please acknowledge this little with my thanks and say that I have read it attentively. (Some papers go out of their way to be unjust)

W.W.

Incidents in the daily routine at the White House

the way for an appeal, we were simply doing what other administrations had done.

Some time after this the President communicated with Colonel House, and when I next discussed the matter with the President, he informed me that he and Colonel House had finally agreed that the thing to do was frankly to come out without preliminaries of any kind and boldly ask for the election of a Democratic Congress. I told him that I thought the method I had proposed for bringing him into the discussion was one that would be most effective and would cause least resentment; but he was firm in his resolve to follow the course he finally pursued. He was of the opinion that this was the open and honourable way to ask for what he thought would be a vote of confidence in his administration.

It has often been stated that in this matter the President had acted upon the advice of Postmaster General Burleson, and many of those individuals throughout the country who criticized the President's appeal, pointed an accusing finger at General Burleson and held him responsible for what they said were the evil consequences of this ill-considered action. Simply by way of explanation, it can be truthfully said, in fairness to General Burleson, that he had nothing to do with the appeal and that he had never been consulted about it.

These facts are now related by me not by way of apology for what the President did, for in openly appealing to the country he had many honourable precedents, of which the gentlemen who criticized him were evidently ignorant. As Mr. George Creel, in his book, "The War, the World, and Wilson," says: "In various elections George Washington pleaded for 'united leadership,' and

Lincoln specifically urged upon the people the unwisdom of 'swapping horses in midstream.'"

In a paragraph in Herndon's "Life of Lincoln," I find the following appeal:

He did his duty as President, and rested secure in the belief that he would be reëlected whatever might be done for or against him. The importance of retaining Indiana in the column of Republican States was not to be overlooked. How the President viewed it, and how he proposed to secure the vote of the state is shown in the following letter written to General Sherman:

Executive Mansion,
Washington, September 19, 1864.
MAJOR GENERAL SHERMAN:
The State election of Indiana occurs on the 11th of October and the loss of it to the friends of the Government would go far toward losing the whole Union cause. The bad effect upon the November election, and especially the giving the State Government to those who will oppose the war in every possible way, are too much to risk if it can be avoided. The draft proceeds, notwithstanding its strong tendency to lose us the State. Indiana is the only important State voting in October whose soldiers cannot vote in the field. Anything you can safely do to let her soldiers or any part of them go home and vote at the State election will be greatly in point. They need not remain for the Presidential election, but may return to you at once. This is in no sense an order, but is merely intended to impress you with the importance to the army itself of your doing all you safely can, yourself being the judge of what you can safely do.
Yours truly,
A. LINCOLN.

Mr. Creel shows that the precedents established by Washington and Lincoln were followed by Presidents McKinley, Roosevelt, and Taft:

In a speech delivered at Boone, Iowa, October 11, 1898, President McKinley pleaded for a Republican Congress in these words:

This is no time for divided councils. If I would have you remember anything I have said in these desultory remarks, it would be to remember at this critical hour in the nation's history we must not be divided. The triumphs of the war are yet to be written in the articles of peace.

In the same year Theodore Roosevelt, argued for a Republican Congress as follows:

Remember that whether you will or not, your votes this year will be viewed by the nations of Europe from one standpoint only. They will draw no fine distinctions. A refusal to sustain the President this year will, in their eyes, be read as a refusal to sustain the war and to sustain the efforts of our peace commission to secure the fruit of war. Such a refusal may not inconceivably bring about a rupture of the peace negotiations. It will give heart to our defeated antagonists; it will make possible the interference of those doubtful neutral nations who in this struggle have wished us ill.

Ex-President Benjamin Harrison besought the people to "stand behind the President," saying:

If the word goes forth that the people of the United States are standing solidly behind the President, the task of the peace commissioners will be easy, but if there is a break in the ranks—if the Democrats score a telling victory, if Democratic Senators, Congressmen, and governors are elected—Spain will see in it a gleam of hope, she will take fresh hope, and a renewal of hostilities, more war, may be necessary to secure to us what we have already won.

When Colonel Roosevelt himself became President, he followed the usual precedent without even the excuse of a war emergency. In a letter dated August 18, 1906, to James E. Watson, he wrote:

If there were only partisan issues involved in this contest, I should hesitate to say anything publicly in reference thereto. But I do not feel that such is the case. On the contrary, I feel that all good citizens who have the welfare of America at heart should appreciate the immense amount that has been accomplished by the present Congress, organized as it is, and the urgent need of keeping this organization in power. To change the leadership and organization of the House at this time means to bring confusion to those who have been successfully engaged in the steady working out of a great and comprehensive scheme for the betterment of our social, industrial, and civic conditions. Such a change would substitute a purposeless confusion, a violent and hurtful oscillation between the positions of the extreme radical and the extreme reactionary for the present orderly progress along the lines of a carefully thought out policy.

Is it not clear in the light of the events that followed the repudiation of the President and his administration in 1918 that he was justified by reason of the unusual circumstances of a great world war, in asking for a "team" that would work in coöperation with him? Some of those who most indignantly criticized him for his partisan appeal attacked him and the measures which he recommended for the peace of the world with a partisanship without parallel in the history of party politics. Some who most bitterly condemned what he did gave the most emphatic proof that what he did was necessary. Nor can they honestly defend themselves by saying that their partisan attacks on the treaty were justifiable reprisal. Before he ever made his appeal they were doing all in their power to undermine his influence at home and abroad, and he knew it. The appeal was no reflection on Republicans as such, nor any minimization of the heroic service rendered in the war by Republicans and Democrats alike in the fighting and civilian services, but the President knew that Republicans organized in party opposition in Congress would not assist but obstruct the processes of peace-making under his leadership. And all the world now knows that his judgment was correct.

It will be interesting to read the President's appeal to the country, written by him on the typewriter:

My Fellow Countrymen: The Congressional elections are at hand. They occur in the most critical period our country has ever faced or is likely to face in our time. If you have approved of my leadership and wish me to continue to be your unembarrassed spokesman in affairs at home and abroad, I earnestly beg that you will express yourself unmistakably to that effect by returning a Democratic majority to both the Senate and the House of Representatives. I am your servant and will accept your judgment without cavil, but my power to administer the great trust assigned me by the Constitution would be seriously impaired should your judgment be adverse, and I must frankly tell you so because so many critical issues depend upon your verdict. No scruple of taste must in grim times like these be allowed to stand in the way of speaking the plain truth.

I have no thought of suggesting that any political party is paramount in matters of patriotism. I feel too keenly the sacrifices which have been made in this war by all our citizens, irrespective of party affiliations, to harbour such an idea. I mean only that the difficulties and delicacies of our present task are of a sort that makes it imperatively necessary that the nation should give its undivided support to the Government under a unified leadership, and that a Republican Congress would divide the leadership.

The leaders of the minority in the present Congress have unquestionably been pro-war, but they have been anti-Administration. At almost every turn, since we entered the war, they have sought to take the choice of policy and the conduct of the war out of my hands and put it under the control of instrumentalities of their own choosing. This is no time either for divided counsel or for divided leadership. Unity of command is as necessary now in civil action as it is upon the field of battle. If the control of the House and Senate should be taken away from the party now in power, an opposing majority could assume control of legislation and oblige all action to be taken amidst contest and obstruction.

My Fellow Countrymen: The Congressional elections are at hand. They occur in the most critical period our country has ever faced or is likely to face in our time. If you have approved of my leadership and wish me to continue to be your unembarrassed spokesman in affairs at home and abroad, I earnestly beg that you will express yourselves unmistakably to that effect by returning a Democratic majority to both the Senate and the House of Representatives. I am your servant and will accept your judgment without cavil, but my power to administer the great trust assigned me by the Constitution would be seriously impaired should your judgment be adverse, and I must frankly tell you so because so many critical issues depend upon your verdict. ~~No scruple of taste~~

~~the way of speaking the plain truth~~

~~let there~~ No scruple of taste must in grim times like these be allowed to stand in the way of speaking the plain truth.

I have no thought of suggesting that any political party is paramount in matters of patriotism. I feel too keenly the sacrifices which have been made in this war by all our citizens, irrespective of party affiliations, to harbour such an idea. I mean only that the difficulties and delicacies of our present task are of a sort that makes it imperatively necessary that the nation should give its undivided support to the govern-

The President's appeal for a Democratic Congress, as he wrote it on his typewriter and with his corrections

331

The return of a Republican majority to either House of the Congress would, moreover, certainly be interpreted on the other side of the water as a repudiation of my leadership. Spokesmen of the Republican party are urging you to elect a Republican Congress in order to back up and support the President, but even if they should in this way impose upon some credulous voters on this side of the water, they would impose on no one on the other side. It is well understood there as well as here that the Republican leaders desire not so much to support the President as to control him. The peoples of the Allied countries with whom we are associated against Germany are quite familiar with the significance of elections. They would find it very difficult to believe that the voters of the United States had chosen to support their President by electing to the Congress a majority controlled by those who are not in fact in sympathy with the attitude and action of the Administration.

I need not tell you, my fellow countrymen, that I am asking your support not for my own sake or for the sake of a political party, but for the sake of the nation itself, in order that its inward unity of purpose may be evident to all the world. In ordinary times I would not feel at liberty to make such an appeal to you. In ordinary times divided counsels can be endured without permanent hurt to the country. But these are not ordinary times. If in these critical days it is your wish to sustain me with undivided minds, I beg that you will say so in a way which it will not be possible to misunderstand either here at home or among our associates on the other side of the sea. I submit my difficulties and my hopes to you.

In an address at the White House to members of the Democratic National Committee, delivered February 28, 1919, which was never published, the President expressed his own feelings with reference to the defeat of the Democratic party at the Congressional elections a few months before. Discussing this defeat, he said:

Personally, I am not in the least discouraged by the results of the last Congressional election. Any party which carries out through a long series of years a great progressive and constructive programme is sure to bring about a reaction, because while in the main the reforms that we have accomplished have been sound reforms, they have necessarily in the process of being made touched a great many definite interests in a way that distressed them, in a way that was counter to what they deemed their best and legitimate interests. So that there has been a process of adaptation in the process of change. There is nothing apparently to which the human mind is less hospitable than change, and in the business world that is particularly true because if you get in the habit of doing your business a particular way and are compelled to do it in a different way, you think that somebody in Washington does not understand business, and, therefore, there has been a perfectly natural reaction against the changes we have made in the public policies of the United States. In many instances, as in the banking and currency reform, the country is entirely satisfied with the wisdom and permanency of the change, but even there a great many interests have been disappointed and many of their plans have been prevented from being consummated. So that, there is that natural explanation. And then I do not think that we ought to conceal from ourselves the fact that not the whole body of our partisans are as cordial in the support of some of the things that we have done as they ought to be.

You know that I heard a gentleman from one of the southern States say to his Senator (this gentleman was himself a member of the State Legislature)—he said to his Senator: "We have the advantage over you because we have no publication corresponding with the *Congressional Record* and all that is recorded in our state is the vote, and while you have always voted right we know what happened in the meantime because we read the *Congressional Record*." Now, with regard to a great many of our fellow partisans in Washington, the *Congressional Record* shows what happened between the beginning of the discussion and the final vote, and our opponents were very busy in advertising what the *Congressional Record* disclosed. And to be perfectly plain, there was not in the minds of the country sufficient satisfactory evidence that we had supported some of the great things that they were interested in any better than the other fellows. The voting record was all right and the balance in our favour; but they can show a great many things that discount the final record of the vote.

Now, I am in one sense an uncompromising partisan. Either a man must stand by his party or not. Either he has got to play the game or he has got to get out of the game, and I have no more sufferance for such a man than the country has. Not a bit. Some of them got exactly what was coming to them and I haven't any bowels of compassion for them. They did not support the things they pretended to support. And the country knew they didn't,—the country knew that the tone of the cloakroom and the tone of the voting were different tones. Now, I am perfectly willing to say that I think it is wise to judge of party loyalty by the cloakroom, and not by the vote and the cloakroom was not satisfactory. I am not meaning to imply that there was any kind of blameworthy insincerity in this. I am not assessing individuals. That is not fair. But in assessing the cause of our defeat we ought to be perfectly frank and admit that the country was not any more sure of us than it ought to be. So that we have got to convince it that the ranks have closed up and that the men who constitute those ranks are all on the war-path and mean the things they say and that the party professes. That is the main thing.

Now, I think that can be accomplished by many processes. Unfortunately, the members of Congress have to live in Washington, and Washington is not a part of the United States. It is the most extraordinary thing I have ever known. If you stay here long enough you forget what the people of your own district are thinking about. There is one reason on the face of things. The wrong opinion is generally better organized than the right opinion. If some special interest has an impression that it wants to make on Congress it can get up thousands of letters with which to bombard its Senators and Representatives, and they get the impression that that is the opinion at home and they do not hear from the other fellow; and the consequence is that the unspoken and uninsisted-on views of the country, which are the views of the great majority, are not heard at this distance. If such an arrangement were feasible I think there ought to be a Constitutional provision that Congressmen and Senators ought to spend every other week at home and come back here and talk and vote after a fresh bath in the atmosphere of their home districts and the opinions of their home folks.

CHAPTER XXXVI

THE GREAT ADVENTURE

A S WE conferred together for the last time before
the President left Washington for the other side,
I had never seen him look more weary or careworn. It was plain to me who had watched him from day
to day since the Armistice, that he felt most keenly the
heavy responsibility that now lay upon him of trying
to bring permanent peace to the world. He was not
unmindful of the criticism that had been heaped upon
him by his enemies on the Hill and throughout the
country. The only thing that distressed him, however,
was the feeling that a portion of the American people
were of the opinion that, perhaps, in making the trip
to Paris there lay back of it a desire for self-exploitation,
or, perhaps, the idea of garnering certain political advantages to himself and his party. If one who held this
ungenerous opinion could only have come in contact with
this greatly overworked man on the night of our final
talk and could understand the handsome, unselfish purpose that really lay behind his mission to France and could
know personally how he dreaded the whole business, he
would quickly free himself of this opinion. Discussing
the object of the trip with me in his usually intimate
way, he said: "Well, Tumulty, this trip will either be
the greatest success or the supremest tragedy in all history;
but I believe in a Divine Providence. If I did not have
faith, I should go crazy. If I thought that the direction

of the affairs of this disordered world depended upon
our finite intelligence, I should not know how to reason
my way to sanity; but it is my faith that no body of men
however they concert their power or their influence can
defeat this great world enterprise, which after all is the
enterprise of Divine mercy, peace and good will."

As he spoke these fateful words, he clearly foresaw the
difficulties and dangers and possible tragedy of reaction and
intrigue that would soon exert themselves in Paris, perhaps
to outwit him and if possible to prevent the consummation
of the idea that lay so close to his heart: that of setting
up a concert of powers that would make for ever impossible
a war such as we had just passed through. Indeed,
he was ready to risk everything—his own health, his own
political fortunes, his place in history, and his very life
itself—for the great enterprise of peace. "This intolerable thing must never happen again," he said.

No one more than Woodrow Wilson appreciated the
tragedy of disappointment that might eventually follow
out of his efforts for peace, but he was willing to make any
sacrifice to attain the end he had so close to his heart.

He realized better than any one the great expectations
of the American people. Discussing these expectations
with Mr. Creel, who was to accompany him, he said:
"It is to America that the whole world turns to-day,
not only with its wrongs but with its hopes and griev-
ances. The hungry expect us to feed them, the home-
less look to us for shelter, the sick of heart and body
depend upon us for cure. All of these expectations
have in them the quality of terrible urgency. There
must be no delay. It has been so always. People will
endure their tyrants for years, but they tear their de-
liverers to pieces if a millennium is not created immedi-

ately. Yet, you know and I know that these ancient wrongs, these present unhappinesses, are not to be remedied in a day or with a wave of the hand. What I seem to see—with all my heart I hope that I am wrong—is a tragedy of disappointment."

The President and I had often discussed the personnel of the Peace Commission before its announcement, and I had taken the liberty of suggesting to the President the name of ex-Secretary of State Elihu Root. The President appeared to be delighted with this suggestion and asked me to confer with Secretary Lansing in regard to the matter. I conferred with Mr. Lansing, to whom the suggestion, much to my surprise, met with hearty response. At this conference Mr. Lansing said that he and the President were attempting to induce some members of the Supreme Court—I think it was either Mr. Justice Day or Chief Justice White—to make the trip to Paris as one of the Commission; but that they were informed that Chief Justice White was opposed to the selection of a Supreme Court Judge to participate in any conference not connected with the usual judicial work of the Supreme Court.

After this conference I left for New York, there to remain with my father who lay seriously ill, and when I returned to the White House the President informed me that he and Mr. Lansing had had a further conference with reference to the Root suggestion and that it was about concluded that it would be inadvisable to make Mr. Root a member of the Commission. The President felt that it would be unwise to take Mr. Root, fearing that the reputation which Mr. Root had gained of being rather conservative, if not reactionary, would work a prejudice toward the Peace Commission at the outset.

Mr. Taft's name was considered, but it was finally decided not to include him among the commissions to accompany the President.

The personnel of the Commission, as finally constituted, has been much criticized, but the President had what were for him convincing reasons for each selection: he had formed a high opinion of Col. E. M. House's ability to judge clearly and dispassionately men and events; Mr. Robert Lansing as Secretary of State was a natural choice; Mr. Henry White, a Republican unembittered by partisanship, had had a life-long and honourable experience in diplomacy; General Tasker Bliss was eminently qualified to advise in military matters, and was quite divorced from the politics of either party. The President believed that these gentlemen would coöperate with him loyally in a difficult task.

I quote from Mr. Creel:

The truly important body—and this the President realized from the first—was the group of experts that went along with the Commission, the pick of the country's most famous specialists in finance, history, economics, international law, colonial questions, map-making, ethnic distinctions, and all those other matters that were to come up at the Peace Conference. They constituted the President's arsenal of facts, and even on board the *George Washington*, in the very first conference, he made clear his dependence upon them. "You are in truth, my advisers," he said, "for when I ask you for information I will have no way of checking it up, and must act upon it unquestioningly. We will be deluged with claims plausibly and convircingly presented. It will be your task to establish the truth or falsity of these claims out of your specialized knowledges, so that my positions may be taken fairly and intelligently."

It was this expert advice that he depended upon and it was a well of information that never failed him. At the head of the financiers and economists were such men as Bernard Baruch, Herbert Hoover,

Norman Davis, and Vance McCormick. As head of the War Industries Board, in many respects the most powerful of all the civil organizations called into being by the war, Mr. Baruch had won the respect and confidence of American business by his courage, honesty, and rare ability. At his side were such men as Frank W. Taussig, chairman of the Tariff Commission; Alex. Legg, general manager of the International Harvester Company; and Charles McDowell, manager of the Fertilizer and Chemical departments of Armour & Co.— both men familiar with business conditions and customs in every country in the world; Leland Summers, an international mechanical engineer and an expert in manufacturing, chemicals, and steel; James C. Pennie, the international patent lawyer; Frederick Neilson and Chandler Anderson, authorities on international law; and various others of equal calibre.

Mr. Hoover was aided and advised by the men who were his representatives in Europe throughout the war, and Mr. McCormick, head of the War Trade Board, gathered about him in Paris all of the men who had handled trade matters for him in the various countries of the world.

Mr. Davis, representing the Treasury Department, had as his associates Mr. Thomas W. Lamont, Mr. Albert Strauss, and Jeremiah Smith of Boston.

Dr. Sidney E. Mezes, president of the College of the City of New York, went with the President at the head of a brilliant group of specialists, all of whom had been working for a year and more on the problems that would be presented at the Peace Conference. Among the more important may be mentioned: Prof. Charles H. Haskins, dean of the Graduate School of Harvard University, specialist on Alsace-Lorraine and Belgium; Dr. Isaiah Bowman, director of the American Geographical Society, general territorial specialist; Prof. Allyn A. Young, head of the Department of Economics at Cornell; George Louis Beer, formerly of Columbia, and an authority on colonial possessions; Prof. W. L. Westermann, head of the History Department of the University of Wisconsin and specialist on Turkey; R. H. Lord, professor of History at Harvard, specialist on Russia and Poland; Roland B. Dixon, professor of Ethnography at Harvard; Prof. Clive Day, head of the Department of Economics at Yale, specialist on the Balkans; W. E. Lunt, professor of History at Haverford College, specialist on northern Italy; Charles Seymour, professor of History at Yale, specialist on Austria-Hungary; Mark Jefferson, professor of Geography at Michigan State Normal, and Prof. James T. Shotwell, professor of History at Columbia. These groups were the President's real counsellors and advisers and there was not a day throughout the Peace Conference that he did not call upon them and depend upon them.

No man ever faced a more difficult or trying job than the President, when he embarked upon the *George Washington* on his voyage to the other side. The adverse verdict rendered against the President in the Congressional elections was mighty dispiriting. The growing bitterness and hostility of the Republican leaders, and the hatred of the Germans throughout the country, added more difficulties to an already trying situation. America had seemed to do everything to weaken him at a time when united strength should have been behind him. Again I quote from Mr. Creel:

On November 27th, five days before the President's departure, Mr. Roosevelt had cried this message to Europe, plain intimation that the Republican majority in the Senate would support the Allies in any repudiation of the League of Nations and the Fourteen Points:

"Our allies and our enemies and Mr. Wilson himself should all understand that Mr. Wilson has no authority whatever to speak for the American people at this time. His leadership has just been emphatically repudiated by them. The newly elected Congress comes far nearer than Mr. Wilson to having a right to speak the purposes of the American people at this moment. Mr. Wilson and his Fourteen Points and his four supplementary points and his five complementary points and all his utterances every which way have ceased to have any shadow of right to be accepted as expressive of the will of the American people.

"He is President of the United States. He is a part of the treaty-making power; but he is only a part. If he acts in good faith to the American people, he will not claim on the other side of the water any representative capacity in himself to speak for the American people. He will say frankly that his personal leadership has been repudiated and that he now has merely the divided official leadership which he shares with the Senate."

What Mr. Roosevelt did, in words as plain as his pen could marshal, was to inform the Allies that they were at liberty to disregard the President, the League of Nations, and the Fourteen Points, and that the Republican party would stand as a unit for as hard a peace as Foch chose to dictate.

As the President left his office on the night of his departure for New York, preparatory to sailing for the other side, he turned to me and said: "Well, Tumulty, have you any suggestions before I leave?" "None, my dear Governor," I replied, "except to bid you Godspeed on the great journey." Then, coming closer to me, he said: "I shall rely upon you to keep me in touch with the situation on this side of the water. I know I can trust you to give me an exact size-up of the situation here. Remember, I shall be far away and what I will want is a frank estimate from you of the state of public opinion on this side of the water. That is what I will find myself most in need of. When you think I am putting my foot in it, please say so frankly. I am afraid I shall not be able to rely upon much of the advice and suggestions I will get from the other end."

Before the President left he had discussed with me the character of the Peace Conference, and after his departure I kept him apprised by cable of opinion in this country. Appendix "A", which contains this cabled correspondence shows how he welcomed imformation and suggestion.

As my duty held me in Washington, I am dependent upon others, especially Mr. Creel and Mr. Ray Stannard

The Secretary thinks the
President would like to
read this letter. *Thank you. What's his game?
W W.*

Dear Tumulty

*I have not sufficient
confidence in the man*

W. W.

Dear Tumulty:

      There is absolutely nothing new in
Root's speech and I do not see any necessity to
answer it. Certainly I would not be willing to
have so conspicuous a representative of the Administration as Mr. Colby take any notice of it.
Let me say again that I am not willing that
answers to Republican speakers or writers should
emanate from the White House or the Administration.

              The President.

                  C.L.S.

Some characteristic White House memoranda

Baker, a member of the President's official family, for a connected narrative of events in Europe.

Speaking of his attitude in the trials that confronted the President on the other side, Mr. Baker said:

No one who really saw the President in action in Paris, saw what he did in those grilling months of struggle, fired at in front, sniped at from behind—and no one who saw what he had to do after he came home from Europe in meeting the great new problems which grew out of the war—will for a moment belittle the immensity of his task, or underrate his extraordinary endurance, energy, and courage.

More than once, there in Paris, going up in the evening to see the President, I found him utterly worn out, exhausted, often one side of his face twitching with nervousness. No soldier ever went into battle with more enthusiasm, more aspiration, more devotion to a sacred cause than the President had when he came to Paris; but day after day in those months we saw him growing grayer and grayer, grimmer and grimmer, with the fighting lines deepening in his face.

Here was a man 63 years old—a man always delicate in health. When he came to the White House in 1913, he was far from being well. His digestion was poor and he had a serious and painful case of neuritis in his shoulder. It was even the opinion of so great a physician as Dr. Weir Mitchell, of Philadelphia, that he could probably not complete his term and retain his health. And yet such was the iron self-discipline of the man and such was the daily watchful care of Doctor Grayson, that instead of gradually going down under the tremendous tasks of the Presidency in the most crowded moments of our national history, he steadily gained strength and working capacity, until in those months in Paris he literally worked everybody at the Peace Conference to a stand-still.

It is so easy and cheap to judge people, even presidents, without knowing the problems they have to face. So much of the President's aloofness at Paris, so much of his unwillingness to expend energy upon unnecessary business, unnecessary conferences, unnecessary visiting—especially the visitors—was due directly to the determination to husband and expend his too limited energies upon tasks that seemed to him essential.

As I say, he worked everybody at the Peace Conference to a standstill. He worked not only the American delegates, but the way he drove the leisurely diplomats of Europe was often shameful to see. Sometimes he would actually have two meetings going on at the same time. Once I found a meeting of the Council of the Big Four going on in his study, and a meeting of the financial and economic experts—twenty or thirty of them—in full session upstairs in the drawing room—and the President oscillating between the two.

It was he who was always the driver, the initiator, at Paris: he worked longer hours, had more appointments, granted himself less recreation, than any other man, high or low, at the Peace Conference. For he was the central figure there. Everything headed up in him.

Practically all of the meetings of the Council of Four were held in his study in the Place des États-Unis. This was the true capitol of the Peace Conference; here all the important questions were decided. Everyone who came to Paris upon any mission whatsoever aimed first of all at seeing the President. Representatives of the little, downtrodden nationalities of the earth—from eastern Europe, Asia, and Africa—thought that if they could get at the President, explain their pathetic ambitions, confess their troubles to him, all would be well.

While the President was struggling in Europe, his friends in America had cause for indignation against the course adopted by the Republican obstructionists in the Senate, which course, they saw, must have a serious if not fatal effect upon developments overseas. Occurrences on both sides of the Atlantic became so closely interwoven that it is better not to separate the two narratives, and as Mr. Creel, upon whose history I have already drawn, tells the story with vigour and a true perception of the significance of events, I quote at length from him:

The early days of February, 1919, were bright with promise. The European press, seeming to accept the President's leadership as unshakable, was more amiable in its tone, the bitterness bred by the

decision as to the German colonies had abated. Fiume and the
Saar Basin had taken discreet places in the background with other
deferred questions, and the voice of French and English and Italian
liberalism was heard again. On February 14th the President reported
the first draft of the League constitution—a draft that expressed his
principles without change—and it was confirmed amid acclaim. It
was at this moment, unfortunately, that the President was compelled to return to the United States to sign certain bills, and for the
information of the Senate he carried with him the Covenant as agreed
upon by the Allies.

We come now to a singularly shameful chapter in American history.
At the time of the President's decision to go to Paris the chief point
of attack by the Republican Senators was that such a "desertion of
duty" would delay the work of government and hold back the entire
programme of reconstruction. Yet when the President returned for
the business of consideration and signature, the same Republican Senators united in a filibuster that permitted Congress to expire without
the passage of a single appropriation bill. This exhibition of sheer
malignance, entailing an ultimate of confusion and disaster, was not
only approved by the Republican press, but actually applauded.

The draft of the League Constitution was denounced even before
its contents were known or explained. The bare fact that the
document had proved acceptable to the British Empire aroused
the instant antagonism of the "professional" Irish-Americans,
the "professional" German-Americans, the "professional" Italian-
Americans, and all those others whose political fortunes depended
upon the persistence and accentuation of racial prejudices. Where
one hyphen was scourged the year before a score of hyphens was now
encouraged and approved. In Washington the President arranged
a conference with the Senators and Representatives in charge of foreign
relations, and laid the Covenant frankly before them for purposes of
discussion and criticism. The attitude of the Republican Senators
was one of sullenness and suspicion, Senator Lodge refusing to state
his objections or to make a single recommendation. Others, however,
pointed out that no express recognition was given to the Monroe
Doctrine; that it was not expressly provided that the League should
have no authority to act or express a judgment on matters of domestic
policy; that the right to withdraw from the League was not expressly

recognized; and that the constitutional right of the Congress to determine all questions of peace and war was not sufficiently safeguarded.

The President, in answer, gave it as his opinion that these points were already covered satisfactorily in the Covenant, but that he would be glad to make the language more explicit, and entered a promise to this effect. Mr. Root and Mr. Taft were also furnished with copies of the Covenant and asked for their views and criticism, and upon receipt of them the President again gave assurance that every proposed change and clarification would be made upon his return to Paris. On March 4th, immediately following these conferences, and the day before the sailing of the President, Senator Lodge rose in his place and led his Republican colleagues in a bold and open attack upon the League of Nations and the war aims of America. The following account of the proceedings is taken from the *Congressional Record:*

Mr. Lodge: Mr. President, I desire to take only a moment of the time of the Senate. I wish to offer the resolution which I hold in my hand, a very brief one:

Whereas under the Constitution it is a function of the Senate to advise and consent to, or dissent from, the ratification of any treaty of the United States, and no such treaty can become operative without the consent of the Senate expressed by the affirmative vote of two thirds of the Senators present; and

Whereas owing to the victory of the arms of the United States and of the nations with whom it is associated, a Peace Conference was convened and is now in session at Paris for the purpose of settling the terms of peace; and

Whereas a committee of the Conference has proposed a constitution for the League of Nations and the proposal is now before the Peace Conference for its consideration; Now, therefore, be it

Resolved by the Senate of the United States in the discharge of its constitutional duty of advice in regard to treaties, That it is the sense of the Senate that while it is their sincere desire that the nations of the world should unite to promote peace and general disarmament, the constitution of the League of Nations in the form now proposed to the Peace Conference should not be accepted by the United States; and be it

Resolved further, That it is the sense of the Senate that the negotiations on the part of the United States should immediately be directed to the utmost expedition of the urgent business of negotiating peace terms with Germany satisfactory to the United States and the nations with whom the United States is associated in the war against the German Government, and that the proposal for a League of Nations to insure the permanent peace of the world should be then taken up for careful and serious consideration.

I ask unanimous consent for the present consideration of this resolution.

Mr. Swanson: I object to the introduction of the resolution.

Mr. Lodge: Objection being made, of course I recognize the objection. I merely wish to add, by way of explanation, the following:

The undersigned Senators of the United States, Members and Members-Elect of the Sixty-sixth Congress, hereby declare that, if they had had the opportunity, they would have voted for the foregoing resolution:

Henry Cabot Lodge	James E. Watson
Philander C. Knox	Thomas Sterling
Lawrence Y. Sherman	J. S. Frelinghuysen
Harry S. New	W. G. Harding
George H. Moses	Frederick Hale
J. W. Wadsworth, Jr.	William E. Borah
Bert M. Fernald	Walter E. Edge
Albert B. Cummins	Reed Smoot
F. E. Warren	Asle J. Gronna
Frank B. Brandegee	Lawrence C. Phipps
William M. Calder	Selden P. Spencer
Henry W. Keyes	Hiram W. Johnson
Boies Penrose	Charles E. Townsend
Carroll S. Page	William P. Dillingham
George P. McLean	I. L. Lenroot
Joseph Irwin France	Miles Poindexter
Medill McCormick	Howard Sutherland
Charles Curtis	Truman H. Newberry

L. Heisler Ball

I ought to say in justice to three or four Senators who are absent at great distances from the city that we were not able to reach them;

but we expect to hear from them to-morrow, and if, as we expect, their answers are favourable their names will be added to the list.

A full report of this action was cabled to Europe, as a matter of course, and when the President arrived in Paris on March 14th, ten days later, he was quick to learn of the disastrous consequences. The Allies, eagerly accepting the orders of the Republican majority, had lost no time in repudiating the President and the solemn agreements that they had entered into with him. The League of Nations was not discarded and the plan adopted for a preliminary peace with Germany was based upon a frank division of the spoils, the reduction of Germany to a slave state, and the formation of a military alliance by the Allies for the purpose of guaranteeing the gains. Not only this, but an Allied army was to march at once to Russia to put down the Bolshevists and the Treaty itself was to be administered by the Allied high command, enforcing its orders by an army of occupation. The United States, as a rare favour, was to be permitted to pay the cost of the Russian expedition and such other incidental expenses as might arise in connection with the military dictatorship that was to rule Europe.

While primarily the plan of Foch and the other generals, it had the approval of statesmen, even those who were assumed to represent the liberal thought of England being neck-deep in the conspiracy. Not a single party to the cabal had any doubt as to its success. Was it not the case that the Republican Senators, now in the majority, spoke for America rather than the President? Had the Senators not stated formally that they did not want the League of Nations, and was the Republican party itself not on record with the belief that the Allies must have the right to impose peace terms of their own choosing, and that these terms should show no mercy to the "accursed Hun"? . . . The President allowed himself just twenty-four hours in which to grasp the plot in all its details, and then he acted, ordering the issuance of this statement:

"The President said to-day that the decision made at the Peace Conference in its Plenary Session, January 25, 1919, to the effect that the establishment of a League of Nations should be made an integral part of the Treaty of Peace, is of final force and that there is no basis whatever for the reports that a change in this decision was contemplated."

. . . On March 26th, it was announced, grudgingly enough, that there *would* be a league of nations as an integral part of the Peace Treaty. It was now the task of the President to take up the changes that had been suggested by his Republican enemies, and this was the straw that broke his back. There was not a single suggested change that had honesty back of it. The League was an association of sovereigns, and as a matter of course any sovereign possessed the right of withdrawal. The League, as an international advisory body, could not possibly deal with domestic questions under any construction of the Covenant. No power of Congress was abridged, and necessarily Congress would have to act before war could be declared or a single soldier sent out of the country. Instead of recognizing the Monroe Doctrine as an American policy, the League legitimized it as a world policy. The President, however, was bound to propose that these plain propositions be put in kindergarten language for the satisfaction of his enemies, and it was this proposal that gave Clemenceau, Lloyd George, and their associates a new chance for resistance.

All of the suggested changes were made without great demur until the question of the Monroe Dictrine was reached, and then French and English bitterness broke all restraints. Why were they expected to make every concession to American prejudice when the President would make none to European traditions? They had gone to the length of accepting the doctrine of Monroe for the whole of the earth, but now, because American pride demanded it, they must make public confession of America's right to give orders. No! A thousand times no! It was high time for the President to give a little consideration to French and English and Italian prejudices—time for him to realize that the lives of these governments were at stake as well as his own, and that Lloyd George, Clemenceau, and Sonnino had parliaments to deal with that were just as unreasonable as the Congress of the United States. If the President asked he must be willing to give.

As if at a given signal, France renewed her claim for the Rhine Valley and the Saar Basin; Italy clamoured anew for Fiume and the Dalmatian coast; and Japan, breaking a long silence, rushed to the fore with her demand for Shantung in fee simple and the right of her nationals to full equality in the United States.

Around this time the President fell suddenly ill and

took to his bed. That the illness was serious is evidenced by the following letter which Doctor Grayson wrote me:

Paris, 10 April 1919.

DEAR MR. TUMULTY:

While the contents of this letter may possibly be somewhat out of date by the time it reaches you, nevertheless you may find something in it of interest.

This has been one of the most complexing and trying weeks of my existence over here. The President was taken violently sick last Thursday. The attack was very sudden. At three o'clock he was apparently all right; at six he was seized with violent paroxysms of coughing, which were so severe and frequent that it interfered with his breathing. He had a fever of 103 and a profuse diarrhœa. I was at first suspicious that his food had been tampered with, but it turned out to be the beginning of an attack of influenza. That night was one of the worst through which I have ever passed. I was able to control the spasms of coughing but his condition looked very serious. Since that time he has been gradually improving every day so that he is now back at work—he went out for the first time yesterday. This disease is so treacherous, especially in this climate, that I am perhaps over-anxious for fear of a flare-back—and a flare-back in a case of this kind often results in pneumonia. I have been spending every minute of my time with him, not only as physician but as nurse. Mrs. Wilson was a perfect angel through it all.

Sincerely,

CARY T. GRAYSON.

Continuing the narrative Mr. Creel writes:

On April 7th, the President struggled to his feet and faced the Council in what everyone recognized as a final test of strength. There must be an end to this dreary, interminable business of making agreements only to break them. An agreement must be reached once for all. If a peace of justice, he would remain; if a peace of greed, then he would leave. He had been second to none in recognizing the wrongs of the Allies, the state of mind of their peoples, and he stood as firmly as any for a treaty that would bring guilt home to the Germans, but he could not, and would not, agree to the repudiation

of every war aim or to arrangements that would leave the world
worse off than before. The *George Washington* was in Brooklyn. By
wireless the President ordered it to come to Brest at once.

The gesture was conclusive as far as England and France were
concerned. Lloyd George swung over instantly to the President's
side, and on the following day *Le Temps* carried this significant
item:

"Contrary to the assertions spread by the German press and taken
up by other foreign newspapers, we believe that the Government has
no annexationist pretensions, openly or under cover, in regard to any
territory inhabited by a German population. This remark applies
peculiarly to the regions comprised between the frontier of 1871 and
the frontier of 1814."

Again, in the lock of wills, the President was the victor, and the
French and English press, exhausted by now, could only gasp their
condemnation of Clemenceau and Lloyd George.

The statement of Mr. David Hunter Miller, the legal
adviser of the American Peace Commission, with reference to the debate on the Monroe Doctrine, in which the
President played the leading part, is conclusive on this
point. Mr. Miller speaks of the President's devotion to
the Monroe Doctrine in these words:

But the matter was not at an end, for at the next meeting, the
last of all, the French sought by amendment to obtain some definition,
some description of the Monroe Doctrine that would limit the right
of the United States to insist upon its own interpretation of that
Doctrine in the future as in the past. The French delegates, hoping
for some advantage for their own proposals, urged such a definition:
and at that last meeting I thought for a moment, in despair, that
President Wilson would yield to the final French suggestion, which
contained only a few seemingly simple words: but he stood by his
position through the long discussion, and the meeting and the proceedings of the Commission ended early in the morning in an atmosphere of constraint and without any of the speeches of politeness
customary on such an occasion.

Of all the false reports about the President's attitude none was more erroneous than the combined statements that he was lukewarm about the Monroe Doctrine and that he declined to ask for or receive advice from eminent Americans outside of his own party.

In Appendix "B" there will be found a series of letters and cable messages, too long for insertion in the chapter, which will support the statement that he not only listened to but had incorporated in the Covenant of the League of Nations suggestions from Mr. Taft, including important reservations concerning the Monroe Doctrine, and suggestions from Mr. Root as to the establishment of an International Court of Justice.

Former-President Taft had intimated to me a desire to make certain suggestions to Mr. Wilson, and, upon my notification, Mr. Wilson cabled me that he would "appreciate Mr. Taft's offer of suggestions and would welcome them. The sooner they are sent the better." Whereupon, Mr. Taft's suggestions were cabled to the President together with Mr. Taft's statement that, "My impression is that if the one article already sent, on the Monroe Doctrine, be inserted in the Treaty, sufficient Republicans who signed the Round Robin would probably retreat from their position and vote for ratification so that it would carry. If the other suggestions were adopted, I feel confident that all but a few who oppose any league would be driven to accept them and to stand for the League."

Mr. Taft's recommendations were in substance incorporated in the Covenant of the League of Nations.

Emphasizing further the President's entire willingness to confer with leading Republicans, even those outside of official relationship, on March 27, 1919, Mr. Polk, Acting

Secretary of State, dispatched to Secretary of State Lansing, for the President, proposed amendments offered by Mr. Root to the constitution of the League of Nations, involving the establishment of a Court of Justice. Immediately upon receipt of Mr. Polk's cable, the President addressed to Colonel House, a member of the Peace Commission, the following letter, marked "Confidential."

Paris. March 30, 1919.

MY DEAR HOUSE:

Here is a dispatch somewhat belated in transmission stating Mr. Root's ideas as to amendments which should be made to the Covenant. I think you will find some of these very interesting. Perhaps you have already seen it.

In haste.

Affectionately yours,
WOODROW WILSON.

COLONEL E. M. HOUSE,
Hotel Crillon,
Paris.

A comparison of the suggestions presented by Mr. Taft and Mr. Root, which will be found in the Appendix, with the existing Covenant of the League of Nations, will readily convince any person desiring to reach the truth of the matter, that all the material amendments proposed by these eminent Republicans which had any essential bearing on the business in hand were embodied in the Covenant of the League of Nations as brought back by President Wilson.

CHAPTER XXXVII

WILSON—THE LONE HAND

IT HAS often been said by certain gentlemen who were associated with President Wilson on the other side that he was unyielding and dogmatic, that he insisted upon playing a "lone hand," that he was secretive and exclusive, and that he ignored the members of the Peace Commission and the experts who accompanied him to the Conference.

Contrary to this criticism, after an uninterrupted, continuous, and most intimate association with him for eleven years, an association which brought me into close contact with him in the most delicate crises through which his administration and the nation passed, a time which threw upon the Chief Executive of the nation a task unparalleled in the history of the world, I wish to say that there is no franker or more open-minded man, nor one less dogmatic in his opinion than Woodrow Wilson. In him the desire for information and guidance is a passion. Indeed, the only thing he resents is a lack of frankness upon the part of his friends, and no man is more ready courageously to act and to hold to his opinions after he has obtained the necessary information upon which he bases his position. It is his innate modesty and a certain kind of shyness that people mistake for coldness and aloofness. He is not a good fellow in the ordinary sense of that term. His friendship does not wear the cheap or tawdry trappings of the politician, but there is about it a depth of genuineness and sincerity, that while it does not overwhelm you, it wins you and holds you. But the permanent consideration upon which this friendship is based is sincerity and frankness.

No man ever worked under greater handicaps than did Woodrow Wilson at Paris. Repudiated by his own people in the Congressional elections; harassed on every side and at every turn by his political enemies, he still pursued the even tenor of his way and accomplished what he had in mind, against the greatest odds.

In the murky atmosphere of the Peace Conference, where every attitude of the President was grossly exaggerated, in order that his prestige might be lessened, it was not possible to judge him fairly, but it is now possible in a calmer day to review the situation from afar through the eyes of those who were actual participants with him in the great assembly, onlookers, as it were, who saw every move and witnessed every play of the Peace Conference from the side lines, and who have not allowed petty motives to warp their judgments.

This testimony, which forms part of "What Really Happened in Paris," edited by Edward M. House and Charles Seymour, comes from gentlemen who were his friends and co-labourers and who daily conferred with him upon the momentous questions that came up for consideration at the Peace Conference.

Mr. Thomas W. Lamont, a member of the great banking house of J. P. Morgan & Company, one of the representatives of the United States Treasury with the American Commission to Negotiate Peace, gives the lie to the unfair criticisms uttered about the President, to the effect that he was exclusive, secretive, and refused to confer with those associated with him. Mr. Lamont in speaking of the President's attitude throughout the Peace Conference said:

I am going to take this opportunity to say a word, in general, as to President Wilson's attitude at the Peace Conference. He is accused of having been unwilling to consult his colleagues. I never saw a man more ready and anxious to consult than he. He has been accused of having been desirous to gain credit for himself and ignore others. I never saw a man more considerate of those of his coadjutors who were working immediately with him, nor a man more ready to give them credit with the other chiefs of state. Again and again would he say to Mr. Lloyd George or Mr. Clemenceau: "My expert here, Mr. So-and-So, tells me such-and-such, and I believe he is right. You will have to argue with him if you want me to change my opinion." President Wilson undoubtedly had his disabilities. Perhaps, in a trade, some of the other chiefs of state could have "out-jockeyed" him; but it seldom reached such a situation, because President Wilson, by his manifest sincerity and open candour, always saying precisely what he thought, would early disarm his opponents in argument. President Wilson did not have a well-organized secretarial staff. He did far too much of the work himself, studying until late at night papers and documents that he should have largely delegated to some discreet aides. He was, by all odds, the hardest worked man at the Conference; but the failure to delegate more of his work was not due to any inherent distrust he had of men—and certainly not any desire to "run the whole show" himself—but simply to his lack of facility in knowing how to delegate work on a large scale. In execution, we all have a blind spot in some part of our eye. President Wilson's was in his inability to use men; and inability, mind you, not a refusal. On the contrary, when any one of us volunteered or insisted upon taking responsibility off his shoulders he was delighted. Throughout the Peace Conference, Mr. Wilson never played politics. I never witnessed an occasion when I saw him act from unworthy conception or motive. His ideals were of the highest, and he clung to them tenaciously and courageously. Many of the so-called "Liberals" in England have assailed Mr. Wilson bitterly because, as they declare, he yielded too much to their own Premier, Mr. Lloyd George, and to Mr. Clemenceau. But could

he have failed to defer to them on questions in which no vital principle was involved? I well remember his declaration on the question
whether the Allies should refuse, for a period of five years during the
time of France's recuperation, to promise Germany reciprocal tariff
provisions. What Mr. Wilson said to Mr. Lloyd George and Mr.
Clemenceau was this: "Gentlemen, my experts and I both regard the
principle involved as an unwise one. We believe it will come back
to plague you. But when I see how France has suffered, how she
has been devastated, her industries destroyed—who am I to refuse
to assent to this provision, designed, wisely or unwisely, to assist in
lifting France again to her feet."

The question has often been asked, whether the President freely consulted his experts on the other side, or
ignored them. The experience of the gentlemen who conferred with him is the best refutation of this insinuation
against the President. Charles Homer Haskins, Chief
of the Division of Western Europe, a member of the
American Peace Conference, answers this question in
these words:

The President was anxious to have the exact facts before him in
every situation. Doubtless, there were a number of occasions when
he could not consult with experts at a particular moment, but, in
general, the President sought such advice, although he naturally
had to use his own judgment whether that advice was to be adopted
in any particular case.

Answering this same question, Mr. Douglas Wilson
Johnson, Chief of the Division of Boundary Geography,
and a member of the Peace Commission, says:

Whenever we, in our capacity as specialists, thought we had found
something that the President ought to know about, and believed
we could not get it across effectively in any other manner, we could
ask for a personal conference with him. He was, of course, a very

busy man because, unlike the experts who usually had only one problem to consider, he had to do not only with all the territorial problems
but in addition with all the problems bearing on the League of Nations, the economic problems, and many other aspects of the peace.
Despite this fact I wish to state that while I repeatedly asked for
personal conferences with the President on this and certain other
problems, he never failed to respond immediately with an appointment. He had a private wire and on occasion he would call us at
the Crillon to make appointments on his own initiative or to secure
papers, maps, or other documents that he needed in his studies. I
will not forget that in one instance he called me on the telephone late
at night in my bedroom, asking for some papers which I had promised
to supply him, and which had not reached him with sufficient promptness. You can judge from this that he kept closely in touch with
the problems he was called upon to consider.

Another question that has been asked is: Did the
President have an intimate knowledge of the complicated
questions that came before him like the Adriatic problem,
for instance? That criticism was answered by Mr. Douglas
Wilson Johnson in these words:

> In answer to that question I will say that the President kept in
> constant touch with the experts on the Adriatic problem, not only
> through the memoranda furnished by the experts but in other ways.
> I can assure you that there was sent to him a voluminous quantity
> of material, and I want to say that when we had personal discussions
> with him upon the question it immediately became apparent that he
> had studied these memoranda most carefully. *It is only fair to say
> that of the details and intricacies of this most difficult problem the Presi-
> dent possessed a most astonishing command.*

It has also been said that the President in his attitude
toward Germany was ruthless, and yet we have the testimony of Mr. Isaiah Bowman, Chief Territorial Adviser
of the Peace Commission who, in answer to the direct

question: "Was there not a time when it looked as if the Peace Conference might break up because of the extreme policy of one of the Allies?" said: "Yes, there were a number of occasions when the Peace Conference might have broken up. Almost anything might have happened with so many nations represented, so many personalities and so many experts—perhaps half a thousand in all! Owing to the fact that President Wilson has been charged on the one hand with outrageous concessions to the Allies and on the other hand that he had always been soft with the Germans, particularly with Bulgaria, let us see just how soft he was! On a certain day three of us were asked to call at the President's house, and on the following morning at eleven o'clock we arrived. President Wilson welcomed us in a very cordial manner. I cannot understand how people get the idea that he is cold. He does not make a fuss over you, but when you leave you feel that you have met a very courteous gentleman. You have the feeling that he is frank and altogether sincere. He remarked: 'Gentlemen, I am in trouble and I have sent for you to help me out. The matter is this: the French want the whole left bank of the Rhine. I told M. Clemenceau that I could not consent to such a solution of the problem. He became very much excited and then demanded ownership of the Saar Basin. I told him I could not agree to that either because it would mean giving 300,000 Germans to France.' Whereupon President Wilson further said: 'I do not know whether I shall see M. Clemenceau again. I do not know whether he will return to the meeting this afternoon. In fact, I do not know whether the Peace Conference will continue. M. Clemenceau called me a pro-German and abruptly left the room. I want you to assist me in working out a solution true to the principles we are standing for and to do justice to France, and I can only hope that France will ultimately accept a reasonable solution. I want to be fair to M. Clemenceau and to France, but I cannot consent to the outright transfer to France of 300,000 Germans.' A solution was finally found—the one that stands in the Treaty to-day."

Among the unfair things said about the President during the last campaign and uttered by a senator of the United States, was that the President promised Premier Bratiano of Rumania to send United States troops to protect the new frontiers. Mr. Charles Seymour, a member of the American Peace Commission, answers this charge in the following way:

The evidence against it is overwhelming. The stenographic notes taken during the session indicate that nothing said by President Wilson could be construed into a promise to send United States troops abroad to protect frontiers. The allegation is based upon the report of the interpreter, Mantoux, and a book by a journalist, Dr. E. W. Dillon, called "The Inside Story of the Peace Conference," M. Mantoux, though a brilliant and cultivated interpreter, whose work enormously facilitated the progress of the Conference, did not take stenographic notes and his interpretations sometimes failed to give the exact meaning of the original. Doctor Dillon's evidence is subject to suspicion, since his book is based upon gossip, and replete with errors of fact. The stenographic report, on the other hand, is worthy of trust. I have heard the President on more than one occasion explain to M. Clemenceau and Lloyd George *that if troops were necessary to protect any troubled area, they must not look to the United States for assistance, for public opinion in this country would not permit the use of American forces.*

Even Mr. Lansing himself in his book testified to the open-mindedness and candour of the President in these words;

It had always been my practice as Secretary of State to speak to him with candour and to disagree with him whenever I thought he was reaching a wrong decision in regard to any matter pertaining to foreign affairs. There was a general belief that Mr. Wilson was not open-minded and that he was quick to resent any opposition however well founded. I had not found him so during the years we had been associated. Except in a few instances he listened with consideration to arguments and apparently endeavoured to value them correctly.

No men ever winced less under the criticism or bitter ridicule of his enemies than did Woodrow Wilson. Whether the criticism was directed at him or at some member of his Cabinet, or, mayhap, at a subordinate like myself, for some act, statement, or even an indiscretion, he bore up under the criticism like a true sportsman. I remember how manfully he met the storm of criticism that was poured upon him after the issuance of the famous Garfield Fuel Order. He courageously took the responsibility for the issuance of the order and stood by Doctor Garfield to the last.

It will be recalled what a tremendous impression and reaction the Garfield order caused when it was published throughout the country. Many about the President were greatly worried and afraid of the disastrous effect of it upon the country. Cabinet officers rushed in upon him and endeavoured to persuade him to recall it and even to repudiate Garfield for having issued the order without consulting the Cabinet, but their remonstrances fell unheeded upon the President's ears. I remember at the time that I wrote the President regarding the matter and called his attention to what appeared to me to be the calamitous results of the issuance of the Fuel Order.

My letter to the President is as follows:

THE WHITE HOUSE,
WASHINGTON

17 January, 1918.

DEAR GOVERNOR:

At twelve o'clock last night, Mr. Lincoln of the New York *World* called me out of bed by telephone to notify me that the Fuel Administration had issued a drastic order shutting down the factories of the country for five days, etc.

I do not know about the details of the order. I assume of course that it was necessary because of the tremendous shortage throughout the country. But what I am afraid of is that my own readiness to accept this assumption may not be shared by people outside. In other words, has the groundwork been laid for this radical step? Do the people know how much coal we have on hand and what the real shortage is? Have they not been led to believe that our chief ill was transportation and that by subjecting themselves to hardships by cutting down trains, etc., enough cars have been provided to carry coal?

In other words, I am afraid the country will want to be shown that the step just taken was absolutely necessary and if this cannot be proved, I greatly fear the consequences upon the morale of the people. I am so afraid that it will weaken their confidence in any action the Government may take hereafter which depends for its execution on the voluntary coöperation of the people. Again, it seems to me unjust that all industries are put on the same footing. It is a difficult thing I know to distinguish between the essential and non-essential industries, but I am sure the country will understand if such a distinction is made of, for instance, institutions that make pianos and talking machines and candy and articles that are not immediately necessary for our life, were cut down altogether and things necessary to our sustenance kept.

Sincerely yours,
TUMULTY.

THE PRESIDENT.

17 January 1918.

Dear Governor:

At twelve o'clock last night, Mr. Lincoln of the New York World called me out of bed by telephone to notify me that the Fuel Administration had issued a drastic order shutting down the factories of the country for five days, etc.

I do not know about the details of the order. I assume of course that it was necessary because of the tremendous shortage throughout the country. But what I am afraid is that my own readiness to accept this assumption may not be shared by people outside. In other words, has the ground-work been laid for this radical step? Do the people know how much coal we have on hand and what the real shortage is? Have they not been led to believe that our chief ill was transportation and that by subjecting themselves to hardships by cutting down trains, etc., enough cars have been provided to carry coal?

In other words I am afraid the country will want to be shown that the step just taken was absolutely necessary and if this cannot be proved, I greatly fear the consequences upon the morale of the people. I am so afraid that it will weaken their confidence in any action the Government may take hereafter which depends for its execution on the voluntary co-operation of the people. Again, it seems to me unjust that all industries are put on the same footing. It is a difficult thing I know to distinguish between essential and non-essential industries, but I am sure the country will understand if such a distinction is made if, for instance, institutions that make pianos and talking machines and candy and articles that are not immediately necessary for our life, were cut down altogether and things necessary to our sustenance kept.

Sincerely yours,

Tumulty

The President.

An inside view of a well-remembered national crisis

The President's reply, written on his own typewriter, is as follows:

DEAR TUMULTY:

Of course, this is a tremendous matter and has given me the deepest concern, but I really think this direct road is the road out of difficulties which never would have been entirely remedied if we had not taken some such action. We must just bow our heads and let the storm beat.

WOODROW WILSON.

Even to Mr. James M. Beck, a prominent Republican lawyer and one of his bitterest opponents and critics, he showed a tolerance and magnanimity that were worthy of the man himself. It appears that Mr. Beck was invited to confer at the White House on a matter having to do with the war, and the question was presented to the President by Mr. Creel as to whether the President considered Mr. Beck *persona non grata*. The President at once sent me the following note:

DEAR TUMULTY:

Mr. James M. Beck expressed some hesitation about coming with the committee which Creel has organized and which is coming to see me on Monday afternoon, because he was not sufficiently *persona grata* at the White House. I think his criticism and his whole atti- tude before we went into the war were abominable and inexcusable, but I "ain't harbouring no ill will" just now and I hope that you will have the intimation conveyed to him through Mr. Creel or other- wise that he will be welcomed.

WOODROW WILSON.

While the President was busily engaged in France in laying the foundation stones of peace, his partisan enemies were busily engaged in destroying the things he held so dear, and had industriously circulated the story that the mission to France was a mere political one, that the purpose back of it was personal exploitation, or an attempt on the part of the President to thrust himself into the councils of the Democratic party as an active and aggressive candidate for a third term. The President's attitude in this matter, his fear that talk of this kind would embarrass the League of Nations, is disclosed by the following correspondence:

Received at the White House,
June 2, 1919.

Paris.

TUMULTY,
White House, Washington.

Have just read the editorial in the Springfield *Republican*, discussing *"Wilson the Third Term and the Treaty,"* and would very much value your opinion with regard to the situation as it analyzes it. Please talk with Glass, Secretary Baker, Secretary Wilson, and Cummings and let me know what your opinion is and what theirs is. *We must let nothing stand in the way of the Treaty and the adoption of the League.* I will, of course, form no resolution until I reach home but wish to think the matter out in plenty of time.

WOODROW WILSON.

THE WHITE HOUSE,
WASHINGTON

2 June, 1919.

THE PRESIDENT OF THE UNITED STATES,
Paris.

Cummings on campaign trip covering Middle West and coast. Will be away six weeks. My own opinion is that it would be unwise at this time to act upon suggestion contained in Springfield *Republican* editorial. [The editorial suggested that the President withdraw his name from consideration in connection with a third term.] This is not the time to say anything about your attitude toward matter discussed in editorial because there is a depression in our ranks and a feeling that our prospects for 1920 are not bright. Republicans would say you had retreated under the threat of defeat and the cause of the League of Nations would be weakened instead of strengthened. The issue of the League of Nations is so clear-cut that your attitude toward a third term at present is not a real cause of embarrassment. In fact, I can see great advantage to be gained for the ratification of the League by giving the impression that you are seriously considering going to the country on the League of Nations. Am strongly of belief, as you know, that you should not under any circumstances consider or accept nomination for third term. In this matter I have very few supporters in our party. A trip I just made to Illinois and St. Louis over Decoration Day convinces me that a big drive will be made to induce you to allow your name to be used again. The Presidency for another four years would not add one whit to the honour that will be yours and the place of dignity that you will occupy in the hearts of our people when the League of Nations is consummated and your present term expires.

Upon your return to this country and with a clearer perception of what you are trying to do, there will come a turn of the tide in our favour. Many factors not now very clear are leading in that direction. The Republicans by the selection of Penrose have made the Republican party again the stand-pat party of America and their failure, which will become more evident as the days pass, to correct abuses that some months ago they called grave, will prove more and more the strength and value of Democratic policies.

Prosperity now sweeping in from coast and Middle West will soon be upon us. Even business which turned away from us in last campaign in the hope that Excess Profit Tax and other burdensome taxes would be reduced, will soon find out how fatuous and futile is the Republican policy. Many Progressive leaders will soon come to the front and will take up the work left undone by Roosevelt. My opinion, therefore, is that what action you take in this matter should await the turn of the tide so that as the hopes of Democracy rise and success for 1920 looks more promising than it does to-day, then that time in my opinion will offer the psychological moment for you to say what really is in your heart about a third term and thus help not only the party but the League of Nations. Therefore, until the psychological moment comes, the politic thing to do is to keep "mum" about this matter and await the happenings of the future.

TUMULTY.

A clear, inside view of the feeling of the man toward the Treaty, his deep heart interest in it, and his characterization of the opposition were disclosed in a speech delivered by him to the members of the Democratic National Committee at the White House on February 28, 1919. This speech is now published for the first time, and is as follows:

The real issue of the day, gentlemen, is the League of Nations, and I think we must be very careful to serve the country in the right way with regard to that issue. We ought not, as I know you already feel from the character of the action you have just taken—we ought not even to create the appearance of trying to make that a party issue. And I suggested this to Mr. Cummings and the others who sat by me: I think it would be wise if the several National Committeemen were to get in touch with their state organizations upon returning home and suggest this course of action—that the Democratic state organizations get into conference with the Republican state organizations and say to them: "Here is this great issue upon which the future peace of the world depends; it ought not to be made a party issue or to divide upon party lines; the country ought to support, it regardless of party (as you stated in your resolution); now we propose to you that you pass resolutions supporting it, as we intend to do, and we will not anticipate you in the matter if you agree to that policy; let us stand back of it and not make a party issue of it." Of course, if they decline, then it is perfectly legitimate, it seems to me, for the Democratic organization if it pleases to pass resolutions, framing these resolutions in as non-partisan language as is possible, but nevertheless doing what citizens ought to do in matters of this sort. But not without first making it a matter of party record that it has made these approaches to the Republican organizations and has proposed this similarity of action. In that way we accomplish a double object. We put it up to them to support the real opinion of their own people and we get instructed by the resolutions, and we find where the weak spots are and where the fighting has to be done for this great issue. Because, believe me, gentlemen, the civilized world cannot afford to have us lose this fight. I tried to state in Boston what it would mean to the people of the world if the United States did not support this great ideal with cordiality, but I was not able to speak when I tried fully to express my thoughts. I tell you, frankly, I choked up; I could not do it. The thing reaches the depth of tragedy. There is a sense in which I can see that the hope entertained by the people of the world with regard to us is a tragical hope—tragical in this sense, that it is so great, so far-reaching, it runs out to such depths that we cannot in the nature of things satisfy it. The world cannot go as fast in the direction of ideal· results as these people believe the United States can carry them, and that is what makes me choke up when I try to talk about it—the consciousness of what they want us to do and of our relative inadequacy. And yet there is a great deal that we can do, and the immediate thing that we can do is to have an overwhelming national endorsement of this great plan. If we have that we will have settled most of the immediate political difficulties in Europe. The present danger of the world—of course, I have to say this in the confidence of this company—but the present danger in this world is that the peoples of the world do not believe in their own governments. They believe these governments to be made up of the kind of men who have always run them, and who did not know how to keep them out of this war, did not know how to prepare them for war, and did not know how to settle international controversies in the past without making all sorts of compromising concessions. They do not believe in them, and therefore they have got to be buttressed by some outside power in which they do not believe. Perhaps it would not do for them to examine us too narrowly. We are by no means such ideal people as they believe us to be, but I can say that we are infinitely better than the others. We do purpose these things, we do purpose these great unselfish things; that is the glory of America, and if we can confirm that belief we have steadied the whole process of history in the immediate future; whereas if we do not confirm that belief I would not like to say what would happen in the way of utter dissolution of society.

The only thing that that ugly, poisonous thing called Bolshevism feeds on is the doubt of the man on the street of the essential integrity of the people he is depending on to do his governing. That is what it feeds on. No man in his senses would think that a lot of local soviets could really run a government, but some of them are in a temper to have anything rather than the kind of thing they have been having; and they say to themselves: "Well, this may be bad but it is at least better and more immediately in touch with us than the other, and we will try it and see whether we cannot work something out of it."

So that our immediate duty, not as Democrats, but as American citizens, is to concert the most powerful campaign that was ever concerted in this country in favour of supporting the League of Nations and to put it up to everybody—the Republican organizations and every other organization—to say where they stand, and to make a record and explain this thing to the people.

In one sense it does not make any difference what the Constitution of the League of Nations is. This present constitution in my judgment is a very conservative and sound document. There are some things in it which I would have phrased otherwise. I am modest enough to believe that the American draft was better than this, but it is the result of as honest work as I ever knew to be done. Here we sat around the table where there were representatives of fourteen nations. The five great powers, so-called, gave themselves two delegates apiece and they allowed the other nine one delegate apiece. But it did not count by members—it counted by purpose.

For example, among the rest was a man whom I have come to admire so much that I have come to have a personal affection for him, and that is Mr. Venizelos, Prime Minister of Greece, as genuine a friend of man as ever lived and as able a friend honest people ever had, and a man on whose face a glow comes when you state a great principle, and yet who is intensely practical and who was there to insist that nothing was to be done which would put the small nations of the world at the disposal of the big nations. So that he was the most influential spokesman of what may be called the small powers as contrasted with the great. But I merely single him out for the pleasure of paying him this tribute, and not because the others were less earnest in pursuing their purpose. They were a body of men who all felt this. Indeed, several of them said this to us: "The world expects not only, but demands of us that we shall do this thing successfully, and we cannot go away without doing it." There is not a statesman in that conference who would dare to go home saying that he had merely signed a treaty of peace no matter how excellent the terms of that treaty are, because he has received if not an official at least an influential mandate to see to it that something is done in addition which will make the thing stand after it is done; and he dare not go home without doing that. So that all around that table there was coöperation—generous coöperation of mind to make that document as good as we could make it. And I believe it is a thoroughly sound document. There is only one misleading sentence in it—only one sentence that conveys a wrong impression. That can, I dare say, be altered, though it is going to be extremely difficult to set up that fourteen-nation process again as will have to be done if any alteration is made.

The particular and most important thing to which every nation that joins the League agrees is this: That it won't fight on any question at all until it has done one of two things. If it is about a question that it considers suitable for arbitration it will submit it to arbitration. You know, Mr. Taft and other serious advocates of this general idea have tried to distinguish between justiciable and nonjusticiable subjects, and while they have had more or less success with it, the success has not been satisfactory. You cannot define expressly the questions which nations would be willing to submit to arbitration. Some question of national pride may come in to upset the definition. So we said we would make them promise to submit every question that they considered suitable to arbitration and to abide by the result. If they do not regard it as suitable for arbitration they bind themselves to submit it to the consideration of the Executive Council for a period not exceeding six months, but they are not bound by the decision. It is an opinion, not a decision. But if a decision, a unanimous decision, is made, and one of the parties to the dispute accepts the decision, the other party does bind itself not to attack the party that accepts the opinion. Now in discussing that we saw this difficulty. Suppose that Power B is in possession of a piece of territory which Power A claims, and Power A wins its claim so far as the opinion of the Executive Council is concerned. And suppose that the power in possession of the territory accepts the decision but then simply stands pat and does nothing. It has got the territory. The other party, inasmuch as the party that has lost has accepted the decision, has bound itself not to attack it and cannot go by force of arms and take possession of the country. In order to cure that quandary we used a sentence which said that in case—I have forgotten the phraseology but it means this—in case any power refuses to carry out the decision the Executive Council was to consider the means by which it could be enforced. Now that apparently applies to both parties but was intended to apply to the non-active party which refuses to carry it out. And that sentence is open to a misconstruction. The Commission did not see that until after the report was made and I explained this to the General Conference. I made an explanation which was substantially the same as I have made to you, and that this should be of record may be sufficient to interpret that phrase, but probably not. It is not part of the Covenant and possibly an attempt ought to be made to alter it.

But I am wandering from my real point. My point is that this is a workable beginning of a thing that the world insists on. There is no foundation for it except the good faith of the parties, but there could not be any other foundation for an arrangement between nations.

The other night after dinner Senator Thomas, of Colorado, said: "Then after all it is not a guarantee of peace." Certainly not. Who said that it was? If you can invent an actual guarantee of peace you will be a benefactor of mankind, but no such guarantee has been found. But this comes as near being a guarantee of peace as you can get.

I had this interesting experience when the Covenant was framed. I found that I was the only member of the Committee who did not take it for granted that the members of the League would have the right to secede. I found there was a universal feeling that this treaty could be denounced in the usual way and that a state could withdraw. I demurred from that opinion and found myself in a minority of one, and I could not help saying to them that this would be very interesting on the other side of the water, that the only Southerner on this conference should deny the right of secession. But nevertheless it is instructive and interesting to learn that this is taken for granted; that it is not a covenant that you would have to continue to adhere to. I suppose that is a necessary assumption among sovereign states, but it would not be a very handsome thing to withdraw after we had entered upon it. The point is that it does rest upon the good faith of all the nations. Now the historic significance of it is this:

We are setting up right in the path that German ambition expected to tread a number of new states that, chiefly because of their newness, will for a long time be weak states. We are carving a piece of Poland out of Germany's side; we are creating an independent Bohemia below that, an independent Hungary below that, and enlarging Rumania, and we are rearranging the territorial divisions of the Balkan States. We are practically dissolving the Empire of Turkey and setting up under mandatories of the League of Nations a number of states in Asia Minor and Arabia which, except for the power of the mandatories, would be almost helpless against any invading or agressive force, and that is exactly the old Berlin-to-Bagdad route. So that when you remember that there is at present a strong desire on the part of Austria to unite with Germany, you have the prospect of an industrial nation with seventy or eighty millions of people right in the heart of Europe, and to the southeast of it nothing but weakness, unless it is supported by the combined power of the world.

Unless you expect this structure built at Paris to be a house of cards, you have got to put into it the structural iron which will be afforded by the League of Nations. Take the history of the war that we have just been through. It is agreed by everybody that has expressed an opinion that if Germany had known that England would go in, she never would have started. What do you suppose she would have done if she had known that everybody else would have gone in? Of course she would never have started. If she had known that the world would have been against her, this war would not have occurred; and the League of Nations gives notice that if anything of that sort is tried again, the world will be against the nation that tries it, and with that assurance given that such a nation will have to fight the world, you may be sure that whatever illicit ambitions a nation may have, it cannot and will not attempt to realize them. But if they have not that assurance and can in the meantime set up an infinite network of intrigue such as we now know ran like a honeycomb through the world, then any arrangement will be broken down. This is the place where intrigue did accomplish the disintegration which made the realization of Germany's purposes almost possible.

So that those people will have to make friends with their powerful neighbour Germany unless they have already made friends with all the rest of the world. So that we must have the League of Nations or else a repetition of the catastrophe we have just gone through.

Now if you put that case before the people of the United States and show them that without the League of Nations it is not worth while completing the treaty we are making in Paris, then you have got an argument which even an unidealistic people would respond to, and ours is not an unidealistic people but the most idealistic people in the world. Just let them catch the meaning which really underlies this and there won't be any doubt as to what the response will be from the hearts and from the judgments of the people of the United States.

I would hope, therefore, that forgetting elections for the time being we should devote our thought and our energies and our plans to this great business, to concert bi-partisan and non-partisan action, and by whatever sort of action, to concert every effort in support of this thing. I cannot imagine an orator being afforded a better theme, so trot out your orators and turn them loose, because they will have an inspiration in this that they have never had before, and I would like a guarantee that the best vocabulary they can mobilize won't be equal to the job. It surpasses past experience in the world and seems like a prospect of realizing what once seemed a remote hope of international morale. And you notice the basis of this thing. It guarantees the members of the League, guarantees to each their territorial integrity and political independence as against external aggression.

I found that all the other men around the conference table had a great respect for the right of revolution. We do not guarantee any state against what may happen inside itself, but we do guarantee against aggression from the outside, so that the family can be as lively as it pleases, and we know what generally happens to an interloper if you interfere in a family quarrel. There was a very interesting respect for the right of revolution; it may be because many of them thought it was nearer at hand than they had supposed and this immediate possibility breathed a respect in their minds. But whatever the reason was, they had a very great respect for it. I read the Virginia Bill of Rights very literally but not very elegantly to mean that any people is entitled to any kind of government it pleases and that it is none of our business to suggest or to influence the kind that it is going to have. Sometimes it will have a very riotous form of government, but that is none of our business. And I find that that is accepted, even with regard to Russia. Even conservative men like the representatives of Great Britain say it is not our business to dictate what kind of government Russia shall have. The only thing to do is to see if we can help them by conference and suggestion and recognition of the right elements to get together and not leave the country in a state of chaos.

It was for that reasonable purpose that we tried to have the Conference at a place I had never heard of before—a place called Prinkipos. I understand it is a place on the Bosphorus with fine summer hotels, etc., and I was abashed to admit that I had never heard of it —but having plenty of house room, we thought that we could get the several Russian elements together there and see if we could not get them to sit down in one room together and tell us what it was all about and what they intended to do. The Bolshevists had accepted, but had accepted in a way that was studiously insulting. They said they would come, and were perfectly ready to say beforehand that they were ready to pay the foreign debt and ready to make concessions in economic matters, and that they were even ready to make territorial readjustments, which meant, "we are dealing with perjured governments whose only interest is in striking a bargain, and if that is the price of European recognition and coöperation, we are ready to pay it."

I never saw anybody more angered than Mr. Lloyd George, who said: "We cannot let that insult go by. We are not after their money or their concessions or their territory. That is not the point. We are their friends who want to help them and must tell them so." We did not tell them so because to some of the people we had to deal with the payment of the foreign debt was a more interesting and important matter, but that will be made clear to them in conference, if they will believe it. But the Bolshevists, so far as we could get any taste of their flavour, are the most consummate sneaks in the world. I suppose because they know they have no high motives themselves, they do not believe that anybody else has. And Trotsky, having lived a few months in New York,

was able to testify that the United States is in the hands of capitalists and does not serve anybody else's interests but the capitalists'.
And the worst of it is, I think he honestly believes it. It would not
have much effect if he didn't. Having received six dollars a week
to write for a socialistic and anarchistic paper which believed that
and printed it, and knowing how difficult it is to live on nothing but
the wages of sin, he believes that the only wages paid here are the
wages of sin.

But we cannot rescue Russia without having a united Europe.
One of my colleagues in Paris said: "We could not go home and say
we had made peace if we left half of Europe and half of Asia at war—
because Russia constitutes half of Europe and Siberia constitutes
half of Asia." And yet we may have to go home without composing
these great territories, but if we go home with a League of Nations,
there will be some power to solve this most perplexing problem.

And so from every point of view, it is obvious to the men in Paris,
obvious to those who in their own hearts are most indifferent to
the League of Nations, that we have to tie in the provisions of the
Treaty with the League of Nations because the League of Nations
is the heart of the Treaty. It is the only machinery. It is the only
solid basis of masonry that is in the Treaty, and in saying that I know
that I am expressing the opinion of all those with whom I have been
conferring. I cannot imagine any greater historic glory for the party
than to have it said that for the time being it is thinking not of
elections, but of the salvation of the plain people of the world, and
the plain people of the world are looking to us who call ourselves
Democrats to prove to the utmost point of sacrifice that we are indeed
Democrats, with a small d as well as a large D, that we are ready
to put the whole power and influence of America at the disposal
of free men everywhere in the world no matter what the sacrifice
involved, no matter what the danger to the cause.

And I would like, if I am not tiresome, to leave this additional
thought in your mind. I was one of the first advocates of the mandatory. I do not at all believe in handing over any more territory
than has already been handed over to any sovereign. I do not believe in putting the people of the German territories at the disposition,
unsubordinated disposition, of any great power, and therefore I
was a warm advocate of the idea of General Smuts—who, by the way,

is an extraordinary person—who propounded the theory that the pieces of the Austro-Hungarian Empire and the pieces of the Turkish Empire and the German colonies were all political units or territorial units which ought to be accepted in trust by the family of nations, and not turned over to any member of the family, and that therefore the League of Nations would have as one of its chief functions to act as trustee for these great areas of dismembered empires. And yet the embarrassing moment came when they asked if the United States would be willing to accept a mandatory. I had to say off-hand that it would not be willing. I have got to say off-hand that in the present state of American opinion, at any rate, it wants to observe what I may call without offense Pharisaical cleanliness and not take anything out of the pile. It is its point of pride that it does not want to seem to take anything even by way of superintendence. And of course they said: "That is very disappointing, for this reason" (The reason they stated in as complimentary terms as I could have stated it myself): "You would be the most acceptable mandatory to any one of these peoples, and very few of us, if any, would be acceptable." They said that in so many words, and it would greatly advance the peace of the world and the peace of mind of Europe if the United States would accept mandatories. I said: "I am perfectly willing to go home and stump the country and see if they will do it," but I could not truthfully say off-hand that they would, because I did not know.

Now what I wanted to suggest is this: Personally, and just within the limits of this room, I can say very frankly that I think we ought to. I think there is a very promising beginning in regard to countries like Armenia. The whole heart of America has been engaged for Armenia. They know more about Armenia and its sufferings than they know about any other European area; we have colleges out there; we have great missionary enterprises, just as we have had Robert College in Constantinople. That is a part of the world where already American influence extends, a saving influence and an educating and an uplifting influence. Colleges like Beirut in Syria have spread their influence very much beyond the limits of Syria, all through the Arabian country and Mesopotamia and in the distant parts of Asia Minor, and I am not without hope that the people of the United States would find it acceptable to go in and be the trustee of the interests of the Armenian people and see to it that the unspeakable Turk and the almost equally difficult Kurd had their necks sat on long enough to teach them manners and give the industrious and earnest people of Armenia time to develop a country which is naturally rich with possibilities.

Now the place where they all want us to accept a mandate most is at Constantinople. I may say that it seems to be rather the consensus of opinion there that Constantinople ought to be internationalized. So that the present idea apparently is to delimit the territory around Constantinople to include the Straits and set up a mandate for that territory which will make those Straits open to the nations of the world without any conditions and make Constantinople truly international—an internationalized free city and a free port—and America is the only nation in the world that can undertake that mandate and have the rest of the world believe that it is undertaken in good faith that we do not mean to stay there and set up our own sovereignty. So that it would be a very serious matter for the confidence of the world in this treaty if the United States did not accept a mandate for Constantinople.

What I have to suggest is that questions of that sort ought to be ventilated very thoroughly. This will appeal to the people of the United States: Are you going to take advantage of this and not any of the burden? Are you going to put the burden on the bankrupt states of Europe? For almost all of them are bankrupt in the sense that they cannot undertake any new things. I think that will appeal to the American people: that they ought to take the burdens—for they are burdens. Nobody is going to get anything out of a mandatory of Constantinople or Armenia. It is a work of disinterested philanthropy. And if you first present that idea and then make tentative expositions of where we might go in as a mandatory, I think that the people will respond. If we went in at Constantinople, for example, I think it is true that almost all the influential men who are prominent in the affairs of Bulgaria and were graduates of Robert College would be immediately susceptible to American interests. They would take American guidance when they would not take any other guidance.

But I wish I could stay home and tackle this job with you. There is nothing I would like to do so much as really to say in parliamentary language what I think of the people that are opposing it. I would reserve the right in private to say in unparliamentary language what I think of them, but in public I would try to stick to parliamentary language. Because of all the blind and little, provincial people, they are the littlest and most contemptible. It is not their character so much that I have a contempt for, though that contempt is thorough-going, but their minds. They have not got even good working imitations of minds. They remind me of a man with a head that is not a head but is just a knot providentially put there to keep him from ravelling out, but why the Lord should not have been willing to let them ravel out I do not know, because they are of no use, and if I could really say what I think about them, it would be picturesque. But the beauty of it is that their ignorance and their provincialism can be made so perfectly visible. They have horizons that do not go beyond their parish; they do not even reach to the edges of the parish, because the other people know more than they do. The whole impulse of the modern time is against them. They are going to have the most conspicuously contemptible names in history. The gibbets that they are going to be executed on by future histori-ans will scrape the heavens, they will be so high. They won't be turned in the direction of heaven at all, but they will be very tall, and I do not know any fate more terrible than to be exhibited in that future catalogue of the men who are utterly condemned by the whole spirit of humanity. If I did not despise them, I would be sorry for them.

Now I have sometimes a very cheering thought. On the fifth of March, 1921, I am going to begin to be an historian again instead of an active public man, and I am going to have the privilege of writ-ing about these gentlemen without any restraints of propriety. The President, if my experience is a standard, is liable some day to burst by merely containing restrained gases. Anybody in the Senate or House can say any abusive thing he pleases about the President, but it shocks the sense of propriety of the whole country if the President says what he thinks about them. And that makes it very fortunate that the term of the President is limited, because no president could stand it for a number of years. But when the lid is off, I am going to resume my study of the dictionary to find adequate terms in which to describe the fatuity of these gentlemen with their poor little minds that never get anywhere but run around in a circle and think they are going somewhere.   I cannot express my contempt for their intelligence, but because I think I know the people of the United States, I can predict their future with absolute certainty.   I am not concerned as to the ultimate outcome of this thing at all, not for a moment, but I am concerned that the outcome should be brought about immediately, just as promptly as possible.   So my hope is that we will all put on our war paint, not as Democrats but as Americans, get the true American pattern of war paint and a real hatchet and go out on the war path and get a collection of scalps that has never been excelled in the history of American warfare.

CHAPTER XXXVIII

JAPAN—SHANTUNG

ONE of the settlements embodied in the Versailles Treaty upon which the enemies of the President in this country concentrated their fires of wrath and hatred against the President was the so-called Shantung settlement. The partisan enemies of the President, realizing the irreconcilable antagonism of certain of our people to the Japanese, did everything they could to intensify this antagonism, picturing the President as one who had conceded something to Japan at the expense of helpless China.

Not love of China, but hatred of Woodrow Wilson led partisan Republicans, without careful investigation of the actual situation, to seize on the Shantung affair as an opportunity to embarrass the President. The ignorances and prejudices of many of our people on the subject of China played into the hands of those Republicans, whose main object was to injure the President and defeat the Treaty. Very few sought to understand the settlement or to ascertain the facts that formed the historic background of it.

These facts were clearly set forth by the President himself in a speech delivered at Los Angeles, California, on September 20, 1919. The President said:

Let me recall some circumstances which probably most of you have forgotten. I have to go back to the year 1898, for it was in March of that year that these cessions which formerly belonged to Germany were transferred to her by the Government of China. What had happened was that two German missionaries in China had been murdered. The Central Government at Peking had done everything that was in its power to do to quiet the local disturbances, to allay the local prejudice against foreigners which led to the murders, but had been unable to do so, and the German Government held them responsible, nevertheless, for the murder of the missionaries. It was not the missionaries that the German Government was interested in. That was a pretext. Germany insisted that, because this thing had happened for which the Peking Government could not really with justice be held responsible, a very large and important part of one of the richest provinces of China should be ceded to her for sovereign control, for a period of 99 years, that she should have the right to penetrate the interior of that province with a railway, and that she should have the right to exploit any ores that lay within 30 miles either side of that railway. She forced the Peking Government to say that they did it in gratitude to the German Government for certain services which she was supposed to have rendered but never did render. That was the beginning. I do not know whether any of the gentlemen who are criticizing the present Shantung settlement were in public affairs at that time or not, but I will tell you what happened, so far as this Government was concerned.

One of the most enlightened and humane presidents we have ever had was at the head of the Government—William McKinley, a man who loved his fellow men and believed in justice—and associated with him was one of our ablest secretaries of state—Mr. John Hay. The state of international law was such then that they did not feel at liberty to make even a protest against these concessions to Germany. Neither did they make any protest when, immediately following that, similar concessions were made to Russia, to Great Britain, and to France. It was almost immediately after that that China granted to Russia the right of the possession and control of Port Arthur and a portion of the region of Talienwan. Then England, not wishing to be outdone, although she had similar rights elsewhere in China, insisted upon a similar concession and got Weihaiwei. Then France insisted that she must have a port, and got it for 99 years. Not against one of those did the Government of the United States make any protest whatever. They only insisted that the door should not be shut in any of these regions against the trade of the United States. You have heard of Mr. Hay's policy of the open door. That was his policy of the open door—not the open door to the rights of China, but the open door to the goods of America. I want you to understand, my fellow countrymen, I am not criticizing this because, until we adopt the Covenant of the League of Nations, it is an unfriendly act for any government to interfere in the affairs of any other unless its own interests are immediately concerned. The only thing Mr. McKinley and Mr. Hay were at liberty to do was to call attention to the fact that the trade of the United States might be unfavourably affected and insist that in no circumstances it should be. They got from all of these powers the promise that it should not be a promise which was more or less kept. Following that came the war between Russia and Japan, and at the close of that war Japan got Port Arthur and all the rights which Russia enjoyed in China, just as she is now getting Shantung and the rights her recently defeated enemy had in China—an exactly similar operation. That peace that gave her Port Arthur was concluded, as you know, on the territory of the United States—at Portsmouth, N. H. Nobody dreamed of protesting against that. Japan had beaten Russia. Port Arthur did not at that time belong to China; it belonged for the period of the lease to Russia, and Japan was ceded what Japan had taken by the well-recognized processes of war.

Very well, at the opening of this war, Japan went and took Kiau-chow and supplanted Germany in Shantung Province. The whole process is repeated, but repeated with a new sanction. In the meantime, after this present war began, England and France, not at the same time, but successively, feeling that it was essential that they should have the assistance of Japan on the Pacific, agreed that if Japan would go into this war and take whatever Germany had in the Pacific she should retain everything north of the equator which had belonged to Germany. That treaty now stands. That treaty absolutely binds Great Britain and France. Great Britain and France can not in honour, having offered Japan this inducement to enter the war and continue her operations, consent to an elimination of the Shantung provision from the present treaty. Very well, let us put these gentlemen who are objecting to the Shantung settlement to the test. Are they ready to fight Great Britain and France and Japan, who will have to stand together, in order to get this province back for China? I know they are not, and their interest in China is not the interest of assisting China, but of defeating the Treaty. They know beforehand that a modification of the Treaty in that respect cannot be obtained, and they are insisting upon what they know is impossible; but if they ratify the Treaty and accept the Covenant of the League of Nations they do put themselves in a position to assist China. They put themselves in that position for the very first time in the history of international engagements. They change the whole faith of international affairs, because after you have read the much-debated Article 10 of the Covenant, I advise you to read Article 11. Article 11 says that it shall be the friendly right of any member of the League to call attention at any time to anything, anywhere, that threatens to disturb the peace of the world or the good understanding between nations upon which the peace of the world depends. That in itself constitutes a revolution in international relationships. Anything that affects the peace of any part of the world is the business of every nation. It does not have simply to insist that its trade shall not be interfered with; it has the right to insist that the rights of mankind shall not be interfered with. Not only that, but back of this provision with regard to Shantung lies, as everybody knows or ought to know, a very honourable promise which was made by the Government of Japan in my presence in Paris, namely, that just as soon as possible after the ratification of this treaty they will return to China all sovereign rights in the Province of Shantung. Great Britain has not promised to return Weihaiwei; France has not promised to return her part. Japan has promised to relinquish all the sovereign rights which were acquired by Germany for the remaining 78 of the 99 years of the lease, and to retain only what other governments have in many other parts of China, namely, the right to build and operate the railway under a corporation and to exploit the mines in the immediate neighbourhood of that railway. In other words, she retains only the rights of economic concessionaries. Personally, I am frank to say that I think all of these nations have invaded some of the essential rights of China by going too far in the concessions which they have demanded, but that is an old story now, and we are beginning a new story. In the new story we all have the right to balk about what they have been doing and to convince them, by the pressure of the public opinion of the world, that a different course of action would be just and right. I am for helping China and not turning away from the only way in which I can help her. Those are the facts about Shantung.

Of all the important decisions of the Peace Conference, none worried the President so much as that relating to the Shantung settlement, and in a speech at Des Moines, on September 6, 1919, he expressed his dissatisfaction in the following words:

There is the settlement, which you have heard so much discussed, about that rich and ancient province of Shantung in China. I do not like that settlement any better than you do, but these were the circumstances: In order to induce Japan to coöperate in the war and clear the Pacific of the German power, England, and subsequently France, bound themselves without any qualifications to see to it that Japan got anything in China that Germany had and that Japan would take it away from her, upon the strength of which promise Japan proceeded to take away Kiauchow and occupy the portions of Shantung Province which had been ceded by China for a term of years to Germany. The most that could be got out of it was that in view of the fact that America had nothing to do with it, the Japanese were ready to promise that they would give up every item of sovereignty which Germany would otherwise have enjoyed in Shantung Province and return it without restriction to China, and that they would retain in the province only the economic concessions such as other nations already had elsewhere in China—though you do not hear anything about that—concessions in the railway and the mines which had become attached to the railway for operative purposes. But suppose that you say that is not enough. Very well, then, stay out of the Treaty, and how will that accomplish anything? England and France are bound and cannot escape their obligation. Are you going to institute a war against Japan and France and England to get Shantung back for China? That is an operation which does not commend itself to the present generation.

Mr. Ray Stannard Baker, in his book "What Wilson Did in Paris," says:

Of all the important decisions at the Peace Conference none worried the President so much as that relating to the disposition of the Shantung peninsula—and none, finally, satisfied him less. Not one of the problems he had to meet at Paris, serious as they all were, did he take more personally to heart than this. He told me on one occasion that he.had been unable to sleep on the previous night for thinking of it.

Those last days before the Treaty was finished were among the hardest of the entire Conference. As I have said before, the most difficult and dangerous problems had inevitably been left to the last, and had all to be finally settled in those crowded days of late April.

Consider, for a moment, the exact situation at Paris on April 29th, when the Japanese-Chinese crises reached the explosive point.

It was on that very day that the German delegates were coming morosely into Versailles, ready for a treaty that was not yet finished. The Three—for Orlando had then withdrawn from the Conference— had been gradually lengthening their sessions, the discussions were longer and more acrimonious. They were tired out. Only six days before, on April 23rd, the High Council had been hopelessly deadlocked on the Italian question. The President had issued his bold message to the world regarding the disposition of Fiume and the Italian delegation departed from Paris with the expectation that their withdrawal would either force the hands of the Conference, or break it up.

While this crisis was at its height the Belgian delegation, which had long been restive over the non-settlement of Belgian claims for reparations, became insistent. They had no place in the Supreme Council and they were worried lest the French and British—neither of whom could begin to get enough money out of Germany to pay for its losses—would take the lion's share and leave Belgium unrestored. The little nations were always worried at Paris lest the big ones take everything and leave them nothing! Very little appeared in the news at the time concerning the Belgian demands, but they reached practically an ultimatum: if Belgium were not satisfied she also would withdraw from the Conference and refuse to sign the Treaty.

It was at this critical moment that the Chinese-Japanese question had to be settled. It had to be settled because the disposition of German rights in China (unlike Italian claims in the Adriatic) had to go into the German Treaty before it was presented to Brockdorff Rantzau and his delegates at Versailles; and because the Japanese would not sign the Treaty unless it was settled. The defection of Japan, added to that of Italy and the possible withdrawal of Belgium, would have made the situation desperate.

The two principal things that Japan wanted at the Peace Conference were: first, a recognition in the Covenant of the League of Nations of the "equality of the nations and the just treatment of their nationals"; and, second, the recognition of certain rights over the former German concessions in China (Shantung.)

After a struggle lasting all through the Conference, Japan had finally lost out, in the meeting of the League of Nations Commission on April 11th, in her first great contention. She was refused the recognition of racial or even national equality which she demanded although a majority of the nations represented on the League of Nations Commission agreed with her that her desire for such recognition was just and should find a place in the Covenant. . . .

Few people realize how sharply the Japanese felt this hurt to their pride: and few people realize the meaning of this struggle, as a forerunner of one of the great coming struggles of civilization—the race struggle. . . .

Having lost out in their first great contention the Japanese came to the settlement of their second demand with a feeling of irritation but with added determination. The Japanese delegates were the least expressive of any at the Conference: they said the least: but they were the firmest of any in hewing to the line of their interests and their agreements. It must not be forgotten also, in all fairness, that the Japanese delegates, not less than the British, French, and American, had their own domestic political problems, and opposition, and that there was a powerful demand in Japan that, while all the other nations were securing some return for their losses and sacrifices in the war, Japan should also get some return.

At the same time Japan was in a stronger position than any other of the Allied and Associated Powers except the United States. She had been little hurt, and much strengthened by the war. She was far distant from danger; she did not need the League of Nations as much as did the countries of Europe; and, more than anything else, she occupied a strong legal status, for her claims were supported by treaties both with China and the Allies; and she was, moreover, in a position, if she were rendered desperate, to take by force what she considered to be her rights if the Allies refused to accord them.

At a dark moment of the war, the spring of 1917, the British and French, in order to sharpen Japanese support of the allied cause, made private agreements to sustain the claims of Japan at the Peace Conference to German rights in Shantung. It thus happened, in the Council of Three, for Orlando had then gone home, that two of the powers, Great Britain and France, were bound by their pledged word to Japan. Indeed, the British argued that they felt themselves indebted to the Japanese not only as a long-friendly ally but for helping to keep the Pacific free of the enemy while Australian troops were being transported to Europe and thus relieving a great burden for the British fleet. It must not be forgotten that China was also bound by the Treaty and Notes of 1915 and the Notes of 1918 with Japan— although China vigorously asserted that all of these agreements were entered into upon her part under coercion by Japan. In fact, one of the Chinese delegates at Paris had actually signed one of the agreements which he was now asking the Conference to overthrow.

It was not only this wire entanglement of treaties which Mr. Wilson found in his advance, but it must be said, in all frankness, that, in opposing Japan's demands for economic privileges and a "sphere of influence" in China, he was also opposing a principle which every other strong nation at the Conference believed in and acted upon, if not in China, then elsewhere in the world. Japan asserted that she was only asking for the rights already conceded to other nations. Japan was thus in a very strong position in insisting upon her claims, and China in a very weak position.

In this crisis Mr. Wilson was face to face with difficult alternatives. If he stood stiffly for immediate justice to China, he would have to force Great Britain and France to break their pledged word with Japan. Even if he succeeded in doing this, he still would have had to face the probability, practically the certainty, that Japan would withdraw from the Conference and go home. This would not only keep Japan out of the League, but it would go far toward eventually disrupting the Peace Conference, already shaken by the withdrawal of Italy and the dangerous defection of Belgium. Such a weakening of the Peace Conference and of the Alliance of the Great Powers would have the immediate effect of encouraging the Germans not to sign the Treaty and of holding off in the hope that the forces of industrial unrest then spreading all over Europe might overwhelm France or Italy. It would also have a highly irritating effect upon all the bolshevist elements in Europe—increasing uncertainty, and the spread of anarchical conditions. With Japan out of the association of western nations there was also the possibility, voiced just at this time in both French and British newspapers, that she would begin building up alliances of her own in the East—possibly with Germany and Russia. Indeed, if the truth were told, this was probably the most important consideration of all in shaping the final decision. It was the plain issue between the recrudescence, in a new and more dangerous form, of the old system of military alliances and balances of power, and the new system of world organization in a league of nations. It was the militaristic Prussian idea against the American Wilsonian idea.

No statesman probably ever had a more difficult problem presented to him than did Mr. Wilson upon the momentous 29th of April, 1919. At that moment three things seemed of extreme importance if anything was to be saved out of the wreckage of the world. The first was a speedy peace, so that men everywhere might return to the work of production and reconstruction and the avenues of trade everywhere be opened. Peace and work! The second was of supreme importance—keeping the great Allies firmly welded together to steady a world which was threatened with anarchy. It was absolutely necessary to keep a going concern in the world! The third was to perpetuate this world organization in a league of nations: this the most important of all, for it had reference to the avalanche of new problems which were just ahead.

If the Conference were broken up, or even if Italy remained out, and Japan went out, these things would be impossible. On the other hand, if the Allies could be kept firmly together, peace established, and a league of nations brought into being, there was a chance of going forward with world reconstruction on the broadest lines, and of the full realization of the principles of justice laid down in the

Armistice terms and accepted by all nations. The Treaty, after all, is no final settlement; it is only one step in the great process of world reconstruction.

It was with all these considerations in view that the Shantung settlement was made by the Council of Three sitting in the President's house in the Place des États-Unis—with the Japanese in full agreement.

This settlement was in two parts, the first set forth in the Treaty itself, and the second a special agreement of the three Great Powers with Japan. I find that this fact is not clear to many people, who look for the entire settlement in the Treaty itself.

Under sections 156, 157, and 158 of the Treaty all the rights at Kiauchow and in Shantung Province formerly belonging to Germany are transferred without reservation to Japan. This conforms broadly with the various treaties, and gives a proud nation what it considered its full rights.

On the other hand, the Japanese delegates at the Conference, on behalf of their government, made a voluntary agreement "to hand back the Shantung peninsula in full sovereignty to China, retaining only the economic privileges granted to Germany and the right to establish a settlement under the usual conditions at Tsingtao.

Under this agreement, by which Japan makes an unqualified recession of the sovereign rights in Shantung to China, she also agrees to remove all Japanese troops remaining on the peninsula "at the earliest possible time."

Japan thus gets only such rights as an economic concessionaire as are already possessed by one or two great powers and the whole future relationship between the two countries falls at once under the guarantee of the League of Nations, by the provisions of which the territorial integrity and political independence of China will be insured.

If the President had risked everything in standing for the immediate and complete realization of the Chinese demands, and had broken up the Conference upon that issue, it would not have put Japan either politically or economically out of China. Neither our people nor the British would go to war with Japan solely to keep her out of Shantung. The only hope of China in the future—and Wilson looks not only to the removal of the sphere of influence which Japan controls but to the removal of all other spheres of foreign influence in China—is through a firm world organization, a league of nations in which these problems can be brought up for peaceful settlement. . . . "The settlement, of course, was a compromise: a balance of considerations. It was the problem of the President, all through the Conference, when to 'accommodate' and when to use decided policies. 'The wisdom of the statesman,' said Cavour (quoted by Thayer in his admirable 'Life'), 'consists in discerning when the time has come for the one or the other.'"

"The Shantung decision is about as good a settlement as could be had out of a dirty past."

Even I felt bitterly critical of what seemed to me to be the President's surrender to Japan in the matter of Shantung. But when he returned and told me the whole story and explained the complicated and delicate world situation which confronted him, I agreed with him that he had obtained out of a bad mess the best possible settlement.

In addition to the various cabled messages which passed between the President and myself, which will be found in Appendix "C," was the following:

Received at The White House, Washington,
April 30, 1919.

Paris
TUMULTY, White House,
Washington.

The Japanese-Chinese matter has been settled in a way which seems to me as satisfactory as could be got out of the tangle of treaties in which China herself was involved, and it is important that ·the exact facts should be known. I therefore send you the following for public use at such time as the matter may come under public discussion. In the Treaty all the rights at Kiao-Chau and in Shantung Province belonging to Germany are to be transferred without opposition to Japan, but Japan voluntarily engages, in answer to the questions put in Conference, that it will be her immediate policy to *Quote* hand back the surveyed peninsula in full sovereignty to China, retaining only the economic privileges granted to Germany and the right to establish a settlement under the usual conditions at Tsingtau. Owners of the railway will use special police only to insure security for traffic. They will be used for no other purpose. The police force will be composed of Chinese and such Japanese instructors as the directors of the railway may select will be appointed by the Chinese government *End quote*.

It was understood in addition that inasmuch as the sovereign rights receded to China were to be unqualified, all Japanese troops remaining on the peninsula should be withdrawn at the earliest possible time. Japan thus gets only such rights as an economic concessionaire as are possessed by one or two other great powers and are only too common in China, and the future relationship between the two countries falls at once under the guarantee of the League of Nations of territorial integrity and political independence. I find a general disposition to look with favour upon the proposal that at an early date throughout the mediation of the League of Nations all extraordinary foreign rights in China and all spheres of influence should be abrogated by the common consent of all the nations concerned. I regard the assurances given by Japan as very satisfactory in view of the complicated circumstances. Please do not give out any of the above as a quotation from me, but use it in some other form for public information at the right time.

WOODROW WILSON.

CHAPTER XXXIX

IRELAND

TO ONE standing on the side-lines in the capital of the nation and witnessing the play of the ardent passions of the people of the Irish race, demanding that some affirmative action be taken by our government to bring about the realization of the right of self-determination for Ireland, it seemed as if the American President, Woodrow Wilson, who first gave utterance to the ideal of self-determination for all the oppressed peoples of the world, was woefully unmindful of the age-long struggle that Irishmen had been making to free their own beloved land from British domination. But to those, like myself, who were on the inside of affairs, it was evident that in every proper and legitimate way the American President was cautiously searching for efficient means to advance the cause of self-government in Ireland and to bring about a definite and satisfactory solution of this complicated problem.

Embarrassed as he was by a delicate diplomatic situation, which to a great extent governed his conduct, he was not free openly to espouse the cause of Ireland. To have done so would have been to add difficulties to an already chaotic world situation. He was compelled in what he was seeking to do for Ireland to move quietly and by informal conferences impressively to lay the case of Ireland before those who sought his counsel in the matter. Unfortunately, these quiet methods of helpful-

ness which he brought to the task were the things that
drew the fire of criticism and even distrust of many men of
the Irish race in America, who in their passionate devotion
to the cause which lay so close to their hearts could see
only a direct route to accomplishing what they had in
mind.

Long before the European war the President and I had
often discussed the Irish cause and how to make his
influence felt in a way that would bring results without
becoming involved in diplomatic snarls with Great Britain.
He was of the opinion that the Irish problem could not be
settled by force, for the spirit of Ireland, which for
centuries had been demanding justice, was unconquerable.
He pointed out to me on many occasions when we discussed this delicate matter, that the policy of force and
reprisal which the English Government had for centuries
practised in had but strengthened the tenacious purpose
of the Irish people and had only succeeded in keeping
under the surface the seething dissatisfaction of that indomitable race.

I recall that at the conclusion of one of our talks after
a Cabinet meeting, shaking his head as if he despaired of a
settlement, the President said: "European statesmen can
never learn that humanity can be welded together only
by love, by sympathy, and by justice, and not by jealousy
and hatred." He was certain that the failure of England
to find an adjustment was intensifying feeling not only in
our own country, but throughout the world, and that the
agitation for a settlement would spread like a contagion
and would inevitably result in a great national crisis.

An interesting comment on the President's attitude
toward the Irish question appears in an article in the
Atlantic Monthly for October, 1921. The article is by

Joseph Fort Newton, in his series, "Preaching in London." The comment is as follows:

To-day a distinguished London minister told me a story about the President, for which he vouches. He had it from the late Sylvester Horne—Member of Parliament and minister of Whitefield's Chapel—who had known the President for years before he was elevated to his high office. Horne happened to be in America—where he was always a welcome guest—before the war, shortly after the President was inaugurated, and he called at the White House to pay his respects. In the course of the talk, he expressed satisfaction that the relations between England and America would be in safe hands while the President was in office. The President said nothing, and Horne wondered at it. Finally he forced the issue, putting it as a question point-blank. The President said, addressing him in the familiar language of religious fellowship: "Brother Horne, one of the greatest calamities that has befallen mankind will come during my term of office. It will come from Germany. Go home and settle the Irish question, and there will be no doubt as to where America will stand.

In discussing the matter with me, he said: "The whole policy of Great Britain in its treatment of the Irish question has unfortunately been based upon a policy of fear and not a policy of trusting the Irish people. How magnificently the policy of trust and faith worked out in the case of the Boers. Unfortunately, the people of Ireland now believe that the basis of England's policy toward them is revenge, malice, and destruction. You remember, Tumulty, how the haters of the South in the days of reconstruction sought to poison Lincoln's mind by instilling into it everything that might lead him in his treatment of the South toward a policy of reprisal, but he contemptuously turned away from every suggestion as a base and ignoble thing. Faith on the part of Great Britain in the deep humanity and inherent generosity of the Irish people is the only force that will ever lead to a

settlement of this question. English statesmen must realize that in the last analysis force never permanently settles
anything. It only produces hatreds and resentments that
make a solution of any question difficult and almost impossible. I have tried to impress upon the Englishmen
with whom I have discussed this matter that there never
can be a real comradeship between America and England
until this issue is definitely settled and out of the way."

Many times in informal discussions with British representatives that came to the White House the President
sought to impress upon them the necessity for a solution,
pointing out to them how their failure was embarrassing
our relations with Great Britain at every point. I am
sure that if he could with propriety have done so, Woodrow Wilson would long ago have directly suggested to
Great Britain a settlement of the Irish question, but,
unfortunately, serious diplomatic obstacles lay in the
way of an open espousal of the Irish cause. He was
sadly aware that under international law no nation has
the right to interest itself in anything that directly concerns the affairs of another friendly nation, for by the
traditions of diplomacy such "interference" puts in
jeopardy the cordial relations of the nations involved in
such controversy.

Long before he became president, Woodrow Wilson had
eloquently declared his attitude with reference to self-
government for Ireland and had openly espoused the
cause of Irish freedom. In a speech delivered at New
Brunswick, New Jersey, on October 26, 1910, he said:

Have you read the papers recently attentively enough to notice
the rumours that are coming across the waters? What are the
rumours? The rumours are that the English programme includes,
not only self-government for Ireland, but self-government for Scot-

land, and the drawing together in London or somewhere else of a parliament which will represent the British Empire in a great confederated state upon the model, no doubt, of the United States of America, and having its power to the end of the world. What is at the bottom of that programme? At the bottom of it is the idea that no little group of men like the English people have the right to govern men in all parts of the world without drawing them into real substantial partnership, where their voice will count with equal weight with the voice of other parts of the country.

This voice that has been crying in Ireland, this voice for home rule, is a voice which is now supported by the opinion of the world; this impulse is a spirit which ought to be respected and recognized in the British Constitution. It means not mere vague talk of men's rights, men's emotions, and men's inveterate and traditional principles, but it means the embodiment of these things in something that is going to be done, that will look with hope to the programme that may come out of these conferences.

If those who conduct the Government of Great Britain are not careful the restlessness will spread with rapid agitation until the whole country is aflame, and then there will be revolution and a change of government.

In this speech he plainly indicated that his plan for the settlement of the Irish question was the establishment of some forum to which the cause of Ireland might be brought, where the full force of the public opinion of the world, including the United States, could be brought to play in a vigorous and whole-hearted insistence upon a solution of this world-disturbing question.

As we read the daily papers, containing accounts of the disturbances in Ireland, what a prophetic vision underlay the declaration contained in the speech of Woodrow Wilson in 1910!

If those who conduct the Government of Great Britain are not careful the restlessness will spread with rapid agitation until the whole country is aflame, and then there will be revolution and a change of government.

I recall his passionate resentment of the attitude and threats of Sir Edward Carson, leader of the Unionist forces in the British Parliament, when he read the following statement of Carson carried in the American Press, after the passage of Home Rule through the House of Lords: "In the event of this proposed parliament being thrust upon us, we solemnly and mutually pledge ourselves not to recognize its authority. I do not care two pence whether this is treason or not."

Discussing Carson's utterance the President said: "I would like to be in Mr. Asquith's place. I would show this rebel whether he would recognize the authority of the Government or flaunt it. He ought to be hanged for treason. If Asquith does not call this gentleman's bluff, the contagion of unrest and rebellion in Ireland will spread until only a major operation will save the Empire. Dallying with gentlemen of this kind who openly advocate revolution will only add to the difficulties. If those in authority in England will only act firmly now, their difficulties will be lessened. A little of the firmness and courage of Andrew Jackson would force a settlement of the Irish question right now."

The President did not agree with the friends of Irish freedom in America that coercive methods put upon England through the instrumentality of the United States could accomplish anything. When he left for the other side to take part in the Peace Conference, the future of Ireland was much in his thoughts, but his solution of the problem lay in the establishment of a forum under the League of Nations before which not only the cause of Ireland but the cause of any oppressed people might be brought to the judgment of mankind.

Ireland's affairs were always in the background of the

President's thoughts and he welcomed conversations with those who were in a position to offer helpful suggestions. I append a correspondence, intimate in character and now for the first time "exposed to the public view," between the President, Mr. Sidney Brooks, a noted English writer, and myself:

Friday, April 20, 1917.

DEAR MR. PRESIDENT:

After several months in America I am now returning to England, returning, I need not say, in a very happy mood and with the consciousness that the relations between our two countries are at length set fair. There is nothing nearer to my heart than improving them, and I believe I see how they could be improved and particularly how the last great obstacle to their betterment—I mean, of course, Ireland—could be lessened, if not removed. I should very greatly value an opportunity of setting before you some views I have formed on the matter, if an opportunity could be found before the arrival of the British Commission.

I leave Washington on Sunday and sail for England on the following Saturday, but not, I trust, without being able to pay you my respects and say my adieux in person.

Believe me, dear Mr. President,

Yours very sincerely,
SIDNEY BROOKS.

The President,
The White House.

In forwarding this letter to the President, I accompanied it by the following note:

THE WHITE HOUSE
WASHINGTON

April 20, 1917.

DEAR GOVERNOR:

I just had a little talk with Sidney Brooks who says he has been in correspondence with Lloyd George and Lord Northcliffe with reference to the Home Rule question. He believes that just a little push by you in your private talk with Mr. Balfour would put over home rule. He says if you could bring home to Balfour the amount of American public sentiment which favours it and how a denial of it is working to the disadvantage of England in this country, it would make a great impression. He says after the war there will of course be a great and generous coöperation between England and this country; but that there will never be genuine coöperation between the people of America and the people of England until the Irish question is settled.

Sincerely yours,
TUMULTY.

The President replied to me in the following note:

DEAR TUMULTY:
Confidentially (for I beg that you will be careful not to speak of or intimate this), I have been doing a number of things about this which I hope may bear fruit.

THE PRESIDENT.

Mr. John D. Crimmins, a leading Irish sympathizer, addressed the following letter to the President:

Washington, D. C., April 28, 1917.

MY DEAR MR. PRESIDENT:
The press this morning leads to the impression that at some timely hour, in your own manner, you will have a word on the Irish problem that at this moment appears to be near solution.

It would be most timely and would have the heartfelt gratitude of millions of people in this and other lands who have long hoped, and many prayed, for Ireland as a small nation to have autonomy, thereby establishing peace with England and among English-speaking people. Then if an emergency should arise there would be all for one and one for all. Mr. President, you have gone a long step in that direction in declaring the rights of small nations—another step may be the means of reaching the goal for the Irish people.

Faithfully yours,
JOHN D. CRIMMINS.

His Excellency,
Woodrow Wilson.

The President read this letter with a great deal of interest and sent me the following note, evidencing his sincere
interest in all that Mr. Crimmins had said:

DEAR TUMULTY:
You are right about Mr. Crimmins having been a good friend,
but I don't like to write any letters on this subject at present. I
would appreciate it very much if you would assure him of my interest
and of your knowledge of the fact that I am showing in every way
I possibly can my sympathy with the claim of Ireland for home rule.
                                        THE PRESIDENT.

On December 3, 1919, Bishop Shahan, of the Catholic
University, addressed a letter to the President in behalf
of the rector and faculties of the Catholic University of
America with reference to the question of Home Rule, to
which the President replied:

THE WHITE HOUSE
WASHINGTON

3 December, 1919.
MY DEAR BISHOP SHAHAN:
Allow me to acknowledge your letter of November 30th written
in behalf of the rector and faculties of the Catholic University
of America, and to say that it will be my endeavour in regard to
every question which arises before the Peace Conference to do my
utmost to bring about the realization of the principles to which your
letter refers. The difficulties and delicacy of the task are very great,
and I cannot confidently forecast what I can do. I can only say
that I shall be watchful of every opportunity to insist upon the
principles I have enunciated.
                        Cordially and sincerely yours,
                            WOODROW WILSON.
The Rt. Rev. Thomas J. Shahan, Rector,
  Catholic University of America,
  Washington, D. C.

On December 3, 1918, he addressed a letter to Senator
Thomas J. Walsh, of Montana, as follows:

THE WHITE HOUSE
WASHINGTON
3 December, 1919.

MY DEAR SENATOR:
I appreciate the importance of a proper solution of the Irish question and thank you for the suggestions of your letter of yesterday.
Until I get on the other side and find my footing in delicate matters
of this sort I cannot forecast with any degree of confidence what
influence I can exercise, but you may be sure that I shall keep this
important interest in mind and shall use my influence at every opportunity to bring about a just and satisfactory solution.

I greatly value the expressions of your confidence and feel very
much strengthened by them.
                    With the best wishes,
                            Cordially and sincerely yours,
                                    WOODROW WILSON.
Hon. Thomas J. Walsh,
    United States Senate.

While the President was in Paris, I constantly kept
him in touch with the situation in this country, and that
he was interested in bringing to the attention of the Peace
Conference the cause of Ireland is made clear by the
following cables that were exchanged between us.

On June 7, 1919, I cabled Admiral Grayson, for the
President as follows:

The White House, Washington,
7 June, 1919.

You cannot overestimate real intensity of feeling behind Irish
question here. It is growing every day and is not at all confined
to Irishmen. The passage of resolution of sympathy with almost
unanimous vote in Senate last night is but a slight evidence of interest here. I wish the President could do just a little for I fear

reaction here upon League of Nations. If this situation could be straightened out, it would help a great deal.

TUMULTY.

The President himself replied to this cable, showing the depth of his interest in the matter:

Paris, 8 June, 1919.

I have tried to help in the Irish matter, but the extraordinary indiscretion of the American delegation over here has almost completely blocked everything.

WOODROW WILSON.

On June 9, 1919, I received a further cable from the President, as follows:

Paris, 9 June, 1919.

The American Committee of Irishmen have made it exceedingly difficult, if not impossible, to render the assistance we were diligently trying to render in the matter of bringing the Irish aspirations to the attention of the Peace Conference. By our unofficial activity in the matter we had practically cleared the way for the coming of the Irish Representatives to Paris when the American Commission went to Ireland and behaved in a way which so inflamed British opinion that the situation has got quite out of hand, and we are utterly at a loss how to act in the matter without involving the Government of the United States with the Government of Great Britain in a way which might create an actual breach between the two. I made an effort day before yesterday in this matter which shows, I am afraid, the utter futility of further efforts. I am distressed that the American Commission should have acted with such extreme indiscretion and lack of sense, and can at the moment see nothing further to do.

WOODROW WILSON.

To this cable I replied as follows:

The White House, Washington,
9 June, 1919.

Thanks for message about Ireland, Hope you will not allow indiscretions of American Commission to influence your judgment against Ireland. Lloyd George's mistakes in handling this will be his undoing, for it has in it the elements of a revolution. It is our own political situation here and the fate of the Treaty itself that concern me. In this country the Irish are united in this matter and in every large city and town are carrying on a propaganda, asking that Ireland be given the right of self-determination. George Creel, in a powerful article yesterday in the newspapers, said: Quote The question of Ireland cannot be ignored, either in honour or decency End quote. I trust you can say a word. Could you not ask that Irish delegates be give a chance to present their case to the Conference?

TUMULTY.

On June 25, 1919, I sent the following cable to the President:

General Maurice, in wonderful article in New York *Times* on League of Nations, says about Ireland: *Quote* One obvious need to complete the process of bringing all nations together is that we should show that we know what America did in the war, but there is another obvious need, which presents greater difficulties. We must have a policy in regard to Ireland, which we can explain to the American people. At present Ireland threatens to reopen all the rifts which comradeship in the war is closing *End quote*.

The New York *Evening Post* of last night prints the following editorial:

Quote Self-Government for the Irish people, short of independence, is a right and a necessity, and it is a satisfaction that once more a movement is under way for the establishment of Ireland on the basis which logic and history have determined—a dominion on an equal footing with the other dominions under the British crown *End quote*.

Frankly, this represents the opinion of the average man in America, without regard to race or religion. The arrival of De Valera in America is going to intensify the feeling and the Republicans will take full advantage of it. Now that the League of Nations is on its feet, we should take the lead in this matter. It would do more toward bringing about a real comradeship between England and America than anything that could happen. I think that the situation in Africa, India, and the seriousness of the situation in Canada, will inevitably force England to consider these matters. It is in anticipation of this that I am anxious to have you play a leading part in this situation. It would do much to make the League of Nations a living, vital force in the affairs of the world. There are no boundary lines between free peoples any more.

TUMULTY.

TUMULTY,
    White House, Washington.   Paris, June 27, 1919.
    I entirely agree with the general tenor of your cable of the twenty-fifth about the Irish question and I firmly believe when the League of Nations is once organized it will afford a forum not now available for bringing the opinion of the world and of the United States in particular to bear on just such problems.

WOODROW WILSON.

Of course, the thing which lay close to Woodrow Wilson's heart was the setting up of the League of Nations. Unless England and France should consent to the establishment of a league as part of a world settlement, any solution of the Irish question through the influence of world opinion was not in the reckoning. The wise, prudent thing, therefore, to do was first to establish a world court before which the cause of any oppressed peoples might be brought. This is just what he had in mind and what he succeeded in doing. To have thrust a settlement of Ireland's affairs into the foreground of the Peace Conference and to have made it a *sine qua non* would have been futile and foolish and might have resulted in disaster. Unfortunately, the friends of Irish freedom, deprecating and bitterly resenting well-considered methods like this, were desirous of having the matter thrust into the early conferences at Paris. The President knew that England would never consent to this and would resent any attempt on his part to carry out this idea. If the President had done so, England would undoubtedly have withdrawn from the Conference and thus the great cause of the League of Nations, which formed the foundation stone upon which the Armistice was based, would have gone by the board. The President was looking far beyond a mere recognition of the Irish Republic. He was seeking to accomplish its security and guarantee its permanency through the instrumentality of a world court like the League of Nations. What would it have availed Ireland to have been granted Dominion government or independence unless contemporaneously with the grant there was set up an instrumentality that would guarantee and protect it? The only thing upon which the Peace Conference functioned was the settlement of the affairs of those nations affected by the war.

Why didn't Wilson bring Ireland's cause to the attention of the Peace Conference? was the query which frequently reached us at the White House. The President in his Western speeches discussed this matter in the following way:

"It was not within the privilege of the Conference of peace to act upon the right of self-determination of any peoples except those which had been included in the territories of the defeated empires—that is to say, it was not then within their power—but the moment the Covenant of the League of Nations is adopted it becomes their right. If the desire for self-determination of any people in the world is likely to affect the peace of the world or the good understanding between nations it becomes the business of the League; it becomes the right of any member of the League to call attention to it; it becomes the function of the League to bring the whole process of the opinion of the world to bear upon that very matter.

"Article XI is the favourite article in the Treaty so far as I am concerned. It says that every matter which is likely to affect the peace of the world is everybody's business; that it shall be the friendly right of any nation to call attention of the League to anything that is likely to affect the peace of the world or the good understanding between nations, upon which the peace of the world depends, whether that matter immediately concerns the nation drawing attention to it or not. In other words, at present we have to mind our own business, under the rules of diplomacy and established custom. Under the covenant of the League of Nations we can mind other people's business, and anything that affects the peace of the world, whether we are parties to it or not, can by our delegates be brought to the attention of mankind. We can force a nation on the other side of the globe to bring to that bar of mankind any wrong that is afoot in that part of the world which is likely to affect the good understanding between nations, and we can oblige them to show cause why it should not be remedied. There is not an oppressed people in the world which cannot henceforth get a hearing at that forum, and you know what a hearing will mean if the cause of those people is just. The one thing that those doing injustice have most reason to dread is publicity and discussion. At present what is the state of international law and understanding? No nation has the right to call attention to anything that does not directly affect its own affairs. If it does, it cannot only be told to mind its own business, but it risks the cordial relationship between itself and the nation whose affairs it draws under discussion; whereas, under Article XI, which I had the honour of advocating, the very sensible provision is made that the peace of the world

transcends all the susceptibilities of nations and governments, and that they are obliged to consent to discuss and
explain anything which does affect the good understanding
between nations.''

Sir Frederick Pollock, in his valuable work on the
League of Nations, comments pointedly on this privilege:

Various Irish writers, including some who deserve serious attention, have raised the question whether the standing problem of Irish
autonomy can come before the League of Nations. There is only
one way in which this could happen—namely, that the Government
of the United States should declare Irish-American sympathy with
unsatisfied nationalist claims in Ireland to be capable of disturbing
good understanding between Great Britain and the United States.
That is a possible event if a solution is not reached within a reasonable time, but it is more likely that a confidential intimation from the
United States would not only precede a formal reference to the Council, but avoid the necessity for it.

The friends of Ireland in this country have often asked
me the question: "Would Woodrow Wilson have intervened in behalf of Ireland?"

I can answer this question only by saying that Ireland
has never had a truer friend than Woodrow Wilson.
From the day that we went to war it has been his steadfast purpose to induce the Government of England to
settle the Irish question justly and permanently. His
statesmanlike approach to a settlement of the problem is
the only one that holds hope of success.

As I completed this chapter, an article appeared in a
Washington newspaper apparently confirmatory of the
President's foresight, showing that by September, 1921,
Mr. De Valera had arrived at the same view. The article
seems to show Mr. De Valera as insisting that the British

Government grant Ireland membership in the League of Nations as one of the guarantees of autonomy.

As for myself, I believe that Ireland is going to be free in company with the rest of the world and in accordance with a new world order which shall function through the machinery for justice and liberty which is provided for in the Covenant of the League of Nations, and is provided for nowhere else.

CHAPTER XL

ONE of the things for which the Wilson Administration was held to "strict accountability" was the passage of the Eighteenth Amendment to the Federal Constitution, establishing nation-wide prohibition.

Unfair critics of the President, in their foolish attempt to charge the Administration with every unusual happening in the eight years of Democratic control, had stated that the President was the real motive force that lay back of the movement to establish the Eighteenth Amendment as part of the fundamental law of the country. As a matter of fact, during the discussion of this amendment in the Senate and House, the President maintained toward it an attitude of absolute neutrality. While he was an ardent advocate of temperance, he felt that Congress in enforcing the amendment by the passage of the Volstead Act, so extreme and unreasonable in character, had gone a long way toward alienating the support of every temperance-loving citizen in the country, and that certain of its provisions had struck at the foundation of our government by its arbitrary interference with personal liberty and freedom. He felt that the practical unanimity with which the Eighteenth Amendment was supported arose from a nation-wide resentment against abuses by the American saloon and the economic evils that had grown out of the unorganized liquor traffic. He felt that it was unreasonable for Congress, in the Volstead Act, to declare any beverage containing an excess of one half of one per cent. of alcohol intoxicating and that to frame a law which arbitrarily places intoxicating and non-intoxicating beverages within the same classification was openly to invite mental resentment against it. He was of the opinion that it required no compromise or weakening of the Eighteenth Amendment in order to deal justly and fairly with the serious protests that followed the enactment into law of the Volstead Act. He was, therefore, in favour of permitting the manufacture and sale, under proper governmental regulations, of light wines and beers, which action in his opinion would make it much easier to enforce the amendment in its essential particulars and would help to end the illicit traffic in liquor which the Volstead Act fostered by its very severity. This would put back of the enforcement of the Eighteenth Amendment the public sentiment always necessary to the execution of laws. Satisfied with a reasonable recognition of their rights to personal liberty and control of their personal habits, he believed that the American people would be the readier to turn their attention to the grave issues of reconstruction and steadier in meeting these issues which would test to the utmost our capacity for progressive self-government.

Time and time again when we discussed the Volstead Act, he would say: "The wrong way of doing the right thing. You cannot regulate the morals and habits of a great cosmopolitan people by placing unreasonable restrictions upon their liberty and freedom. All such attempts can only end in failure and disappointment. In the last analysis, in these matters that seek to regulate personal habits and customs, public opinion is the great regulator."

In New Jersey, where he served as governor, the liquor question had been for many years a burning issue and had been thrust into every gubernatorial campaign up to the time when Woodrow Wilson as governor took hold of the situation. Many political futures had been wrecked and wasted by ambitious politicians who tried to "pussyfoot" on this issue. But there was no shying away from it by Woodrow Wilson. When the question was presented to him by the ardent advocates of the Anti-Saloon League early in his administration as governor, without evasion of any kind, he stated his views in the following letter addressed to the head of the Anti-Saloon League:

Executive Office,
Trenton, New Jersey.

I am in favour of local option. I am a thorough believer in local self-government and believe that every self-governing community which constitutes a social unit should have the right to control the matter of the regulation or the withholding of licenses.

But the questions involved are social and moral, not political, and are not susceptible of being made parts of a party programme. Whenever they have been made the subject matter of party contests, they have cut the lines of party organization and party action athwart, to the utter confusion of political action in every other field. They have thrown every other question, however important, into the background and have made constructive party action impossible for long years together.

So far as I am myself concerned, therefore, I can never consent to have the question of local option made an issue between political parties in this state. My judgment is very clear in this matter. I do not believe that party programmes of the highest consequence to the political life of the state and the nation ought to be thrust to one side and hopelessly embarrassed for long periods together by making a political issue of a great question that is essentially non-political, non-partisan, moral and social in its nature.

Holding these views, that the liquor question was one which was "essentially non-political, non-partisan, moral and social in its nature," the President refused by any act of his to influence public opinion when the Eighteenth Amendment was up for consideration in the Senate and House.

He deeply resented and strenuously opposed the passage of war-time prohibition as uncalled for and unnecessary. In his opinion, it was not a food-conservation measure, but an out-and-out attempt by the anti-saloon forces to use the war emergency to declare the country "dry" by Congressional action. There was another reason for his attitude of opposition to war-time prohibition. He believed with an embargo placed upon beer, the consumption of whiskey, of which there were large stocks in the country, would be stimulated and increased to a great extent. In this opinion he was supported by Mr Herbert Hoover, Food Administrator. In a letter ·of May 28, 1918, to Senator Sheppard, the leader of the prohibition forces in the Senate, he explained his opposition to war-time prohibition in these words:

THE WHITE HOUSE,
WASHINGTON
May 28, 1918.

HON. MORRIS SHEPPARD,
United States Senate.

MY DEAR SENATOR:
I was very much distressed by the action of the House. I do not think that it is wise or fair to attempt to put such compulsion on the Executive in a matter in which he has already acted almost to the limit of his authority. What is almost entirely overlooked is that there were, as I am informed, very large stocks of whiskey in this country, and it seems to me quite certain that if the brewing of beer were prevented entirely, along with all other drinks, many of them harmless, which are derived from food and food stuffs, the consumption of whiskey would be stimulated and increased to a very considerable extent.

My own judgment is that it is wise and statesmanlike to let the situation stand as it is for the present, until at any rate I shall be apprised by the Food Administration that it is necessary in the way suggested still further to conserve the supply of food and food stuffs. The Food Administration has not thought it necessary to go any further than we have in that matter already gone.

I thank you most cordially, Senator, for your kindness in consulting me in this matter, which is of very considerable importance, and has a very distinct bearing upon many collateral questions.

Cordially and sincerely yours,

WOODROW WILSON.

War-time prohibition was ingenuously made part of the Agricultural Appropriation Bill, which contained many items necessary for the effective prosecution of the war. So strongly did the President feel about the matter, that I am frank to say that if war-time prohibition had stood alone and was disconnected from any other bill, I believe it would have been vetoed.

After the Armistice, agitation at once began, inspired by the "dry" advocates throughout the country, to prolong war-time prohibition, but the President felt that the object and purpose of war-time prohibition, if any ever existed, having been served, it was only right, proper, and fair that there should be an immediate repeal of it, and that only resentment and restlessness throughout the country would follow the attempt to prolong war-time prohibition beyond the time provided in the statute which created it.

It was unfortunate that the "dry" advocates did not see the thing through the eyes of the President. Apparently not fully satisfied with the victory they had won through the adoption of the Eighteenth Amendment, they sought to push the advantage thus gained still further, and through war-time prohibition to establish their policy of restriction as a permanent policy of the country. Realizing that prohibition as a permanent policy and by constitutional amendment had been definitely established in a constitutional way, the President was reluctant to take a stand that would even in spirit be a violation of this, but he also felt that the "dry" advocates were simply using a war crisis ruthlessly to press forward their views and to cajole vacillating congressmen into supporting it because it was known as a "dry" measure. In a letter which I addressed to the President on September 7, 1918, I strongly urged the veto of the Agricultural Appropriation Bill containing war-time prohibition:

THE WHITE HOUSE
WASHINGTON
September 7, 1918.

MY DEAR GOVERNOR:

In the discussion we had a few days ago with reference to the pending "dry" legislation, I tried to emphasize the fact that under the Food Control Law you had the power to do what Congress is now seeking to do in a way that will cause great irritation. Your action of yesterday fixing December first as the day on which the prohibition of the manufacture of beer is to take place, I believe, strengthens what I said. Your action and the action of the Senate a day or two ago in giving you the right to establish zones about shipyards and munitions plants again shows the unnecessary character of this legislation. You are, therefore, now in a strong position to veto this legislation as unnecessary and unwarranted.

In view of all of this, I wish to emphasize the dangers, both of a political and industrial character, that confront us should we agree to go forward with those who favour legislation of this radical and restricted character. Even the most ardent prohibitionists fear the reactionary effect of this legislation upon the pending constitutional amendment. I am afraid of its effects upon the voters of our party in the large centres of population throughout the country, and of the deep resentment from all classes that is bound to follow.

In matters of legislation that seek to regulate the morals and

habits of the people, the average American feels the only safe course
to follow is the method set forth in the Constitution for the regulation of these vital matters. The proponents of this measure agree
that it is not a conservation measure, but that it is an out-and-out
attempt to declare the country "dry." In my opinion, it is mob
legislation, pure and simple.

The danger of submitting quietly to any class legislation that
has its basis in intolerance, especially at a time like this where the
emotions of people can be whipped into a fury, is obvious. Your
strength in the country comes from the feeling on the part of the
people that under no circumstances can you be "hazed" by any class.
If you yield in this instance, similar demands from other sources
will rise to harass and embarrass you.

The viewpoint of the gentlemen on the Hill in charge of this bill
is provincial. They have no idea of the readjustments that will
have to come in the finances of our largest cities and municipalities
through the country. Tax rates are bound to go up. Increased
taxation in large cities, coming at a time when federal taxes are
growing more burdensome, is bound to play a large part in the opinion
of the people, and we cannot escape our responsibility if we seem to
be afraid to oppose legislation of this kind. Our policy in every
matter at this time should be one based upon magnanimity and
tolerance toward every class and interest in the country.

Under date of May 9, 1919, I sent the following cable
to the President who was then in Paris:

I sincerely hope you will consider the advisability of raising the
embargo on beer. The most violent reaction has taken place
throughout the country since the enactment of this law, especially
in the larger cities. It is not, I assure you, the result of brewery
propaganda. It comes from many of the humbler sort who resent
this kind of federal interference with their rights. We are being
blamed for all this restrictive legislation because you insist upon
closing down all breweries and thus making prohibition effective
July first. The country would be more ready to accept prohibition
brought about by Constitutional amendment than have it made
effective by Presidential ukase. The psychological effect of raising
this embargo would be of incalculable benefit to America in every

way at this time. The Springfield *Republican* says, *Quote* The establishment of national prohibition by Federal statute, through the mere
act of Congress, does not appeal to one as so desirable as the establishment of national prohibition by the direct action of three fourths of the
states *End Quote*. The war-time Prohibition Law, according to the text
of the Act, was enacted for the purpose of conserving the man-power
of the nation and to increase the efficiency in the production of arms,
munitions, ships, and for the Army and Navy.

The New York *World*, in an editorial, says: *Quote* This war-time prohibition act is breeding social, industrial, and economic discontent
every day. What makes it still more infamous is that under its
provisions the rich man, because he has money, can accumulate
for his personal consumption whatever stocks of wines and liquors
he pleases, but the workingman, because he cannot afford to lay
in a supply of anything, is deprived even of a glass of beer with
his evening meal. There has never been another such measure of
outrageous class and social discrimination on the statute books of
the United States. It should never have been enacted by Congress. It should never have been signed by the President. If it
is not repealed it is bound to cause more trouble than any other
piece of Federal legislation since the Fugitive Slave Act *End Quote*.

By taking vigorous action in this matter, you would do more for
the cause of real temperance and hearten those people who feel the
sting of the wave of intolerance which is now spreading over the
country than anything you could think of. I wish I could meet you
face to face and try to impress upon you the utter necessity for this
action. You will have to take action soon.

TUMULTY.

On May 12, 1919, I received the following cable from the
President:

Paris.
TUMULTY, White House,
　Washington.
　Please ask the Attorney General to advise me what action I can
take with regard to removing the ban from the manufacture of drink
and as to the form the action should take.

WOODROW WILSON.

On May 12, 1919, I replied to this cable as follows:

White House, Washington,
May 12, 1919.

THE PRESIDENT OF THE UNITED STATES,
Paris, France.

Have consulted Attorney General with regard to removing ban upon manufacture of alcoholic liquor. Am in receipt of a letter from him in which he says: *Quote* The only action you can take until demobilization may be determined and proclaimed, will be to issue a public statement or send a message to Congress declaring that since the purpose of the Act has been entirely satisfied, nothing prevents your lifting the ban on the manufacture and sale of beer, wine, or other intoxicating malt or vinous liquors except the limitations imposed by the Act which maintains it in force until demobilization is terminated after the conclusion of the war. *End Quote*

TUMULTY.

On May 20, 1919, in a message to Congress, the President made the following recommendation with reference to war-time prohibition:

The demobilization of the military forces of the country has progressed to such a point that it seems to me entirely safe now to remove the ban upon the manufacture and sale of wines and beers, but I am advised that without further legislation I have not the legal authority to remove the present restrictions. I therefore recommend that the Act approved November 21, 1918, entitled "an Act to enable the Secretary of Agriculture to carry out, during the fiscal year ending June 30, 1919, the purposes of the Act, entitled 'An Act to provide further for the national security and defense by stimulating agriculture and facilitating the distribution of agricultural products, and for other purposes,' be amended and repealed in so far as it applies to wines and beers."

Congress refused to act upon the President's recommendation.

Under date of June 27, 1919, I sent the following cable to the President:

There are only four days left until nation-wide prohibition becomes effective and the country will go on a whiskey basis unless you act to suspend it. Everything that has happened in the last few weeks confirms the views I expressed to you in May excepting that added force has been given to every argument made, especially by the action of the American Federation of Labour whose membership almost unanimously voted at its convention for lifting the ban. The action of Canada in lifting the ban is regarded by the country as significant. Workingmen and common people all over the country cannot understand why light wines and beer cannot be permitted until the Constitutional amendment becomes effective. Only this week the Pennsylvania Legislature voted to legalize two and three-quarters per cent. beer and light wines. Similar action will follow in other states. The consensus of opinion in the press is that if prohibition is to be effective, it might better be by action of three quarters of the states rather than by Presidential proclamation for which you alone and our party would bear the responsibility. The prohibitionists in Congress are fearful that the enforcement of wartime prohibition will cause a harmful reaction on real prohibition, and I believe that they are secretly in favour of your lifting the ban for this reason. Demobilization figures officially announced by the War Department show that the number of troops now remaining in service is practically only the number of troops in the Regular Army. Samuel Gompers, Mary Roberts Rinehart, Mrs. Douglass Robinson, sister of the late Theodore Roosevelt, Miss Gertrude Atherton, Frank J. Goodnow, president of Johns Hopkins University, and Cardinal Gibbons out in strong statement favouring retention of beer and light wines. If you do not intend to lift the ban on July first, you can announce your intention to suspend it as soon as the War Department notifies you demobilization is accomplished which, the best opinion says, will be August first. The feeling all over the country is one of harmful uncertainty and I strongly recommend that a definite announcement, of some nature which will clear the atmosphere, be made.

TUMULTY.

On June 28, 1919, I again cabled the President, as follows:

The White House, Washington,
28 June, 1919.

THE PRESIDENT OF THE UNITED STATES,
Paris.

Received your message saying that you do not intend to lift the ban. The Republicans have been industriously spreading the story throughout the country that you in fact have power under the Act of November 21, 1918, to lift the ban. I think it important, wise, and politic, therefore, for you to make a statement which we can issue from the White House along the following lines: *Quote* I am convinced that I have no legal power at this time in the matter of the ban of liquor. Under the Act of November 21, 1918, my power to take action is restricted. The Act provides that after June 30, 1919, until the conclusion of the present war and thereafter until the termination of demobilization, the date of which shall be determined and proclaimed by the President, it shall be unlawful, etc. This law does not specify that the ban shall be lifted with the signing of peace but with the termination of the demobilization of the troops, and I cannot say that that has been accomplished. My information from the War Department is that there are still a million men in the service under the emergency call. It is clear, therefore, that the failure of Congress to act upon the suggestion contained in my message of the 20th of May, 1919, asking for a repeal of the Act of November 21, 1918, so far as it applies to wines and beers, makes it impossible to act in this matter at this time. If course when demobilization is terminated, my power to act without congressional action will be exercised *End quote*.

TUMULTY.

The President replied to my cables as follows:

Paris, June 28, 1919.

TUMULTY,
White House, Washington.

Please issue following statement: I am convinced that the Attorney General is right in advising me that I have no legal power at this time in the matter of the ban on liquor. Under the act of November, 1918, my power to take action is restricted. The act provides that after June 30, 1919, until the conclusion of the present war and thereafter until the termination of demobilization, the date of which shall be determined and proclaimed by the President, it shall be unlawful, etc. This law does not specify that the ban shall be lifted with the signing of peace but with the termination of the demobilization of the troops and I cannot say that that has been accomplished. My information from the War Department is that there are still a million men in the service under the emergency call. It is clear therefore that the failure of Congress to act upon the suggestion contained in my message of the twentieth of May, 1919, asking for a repeal of the Act of November 21, 1918, so far as it applies to wines and beers makes it impossible to act in this matter at this time. When demobilization is terminated my power to act without congressional action will be exercised.

WOODROW WILSON.

When the Volstead Act reached the President, he found, upon examining it, that it in no way repealed war-time prohibition, and so he vetoed it.

In vetoing it, he admonished Congress, that "in all matters having to do with the personal habits and customs of large numbers of people, we must be certain that the established processes of legal change are followed. In no other way can the salutary object sought to be accomplished by great reforms of this character be made satisfactory and permanent."

The House of Representatives with its overwhelming "dry" majority passed the Volstead Act over the President's veto. The President clearly foresaw the inevitable reaction that would follow its passage and its enforcement throughout the country.

As the days of the San Francisco Convention approached, he felt that it was the duty of the Democratic party frankly to speak out regarding the matter and boldly avow its attitude toward the unreasonable features of the Volstead enforcement act. In his conferences with the Democratic leaders he took advantage of every opportunity to put before them the necessity for frank and courageous action. So deep were his convictions about this vital matter, that it was his intention, shortly after the passage of the Volstead Act over his veto, to send a special message to Congress regarding the matter, asking for the repeal of the Volstead Act and the passage of legislation permitting the manufacture and sale of light wines, or at least a modification of the Volstead Act, changing the alcoholic content of beer.

Upon further consideration of the matter it was agreed that it would be unwise to ask for any change at the hands of a congress that had so overwhelmingly expressed its opinion in opposition to any such modification. We, therefore, thought it wise to conserve our energies and to await the psychological moment at the Convention for putting forward the President's programme.

A few days before the Convention the President delivered to a trusted friend a copy of a proposed "wet" plank, and asked his friend to submit it to the Committee on Resolutions at the Convention in San Francisco. The tentative draft of the plank was as follows:

We recognize that the American saloon is opposed to all social, moral, and economic order, and we pledge ourselves to its absolute elimination by the passage of such laws as will finally and effectually exterminate it. But we favour the repeal of the Volstead Act and the substitution for it of a law permitting the manufacture and sale of light wines and beer.

Evidently, the trusted friend who had this matter in charge felt that the "dry" atmosphere of the Convention was unfavourable and so the President's plank, prepared by himself, was not even given a hearing before the Committee on Resolutions.

CHAPTER XLI

UPON his return home from Paris, the President immediately invited, in most cordial fashion, the members of the Senate Foreign Relations Committee to confer with him at the White House. Some of those who received the invitation immediately announced that as a condition precedent to their acceptance they would insist that the conference should not be secret in character and that what would happen there should be disclosed to the public. The President quickly accepted the conditions proposed by the Republican senators and made a statement from the White House that the conditions which the conferees named were highly acceptable to him and that he was willing and anxious to give to the public a stenographic report of everything that transpired.

In view of subsequent history, the conversation between the President and Senator Harding about the distinction between "legal" and "moral" obligations, which was interesting at the time, takes on an added interest. Said Senator Harding: "If there is nothing more than a moral obligation on the part of any member of the league, what avail articles X and XI?"

The President: Why, Senator, it is surprising that that question should be asked. If we undertake an obligation, we are bound in the most solemn way to carry it out.

Senator Harding: If you believe there is nothing more to this than a moral obligation, any nation will assume a moral obligation on its own account. Is it a moral obligation? The point I am trying to get at is: Suppose something arises affecting the peace of the world, and the council takes steps as provided here to conserve or preserve, and announces its decision, and every nation in the League takes advantage of the construction that you place upon these articles and says: "Well, this is only a moral obligation, and we assume that the nation involved does not deserve our participation or protection," and the whole thing amounts to nothing but an expression of the league council.

The President: There is a national good conscience in such a matter. I should think that was one of the most serious things that could possibly happen. When I speak of a legal obligation, I mean one that specifically binds you to do a particular thing under certain sanctions. That is a legal obligation, and, if I may say so, has a greater binding force; only there always remains in the moral obligation the right to exercise one's judgment as to whether it is indeed incumbent upon one in those circumstances to do that thing. In every moral obligation there is an element of judgment. In a legal obligation there is no element of judgment.

Never before did the President show himself more tactful or more brilliant in repartee. Surrounded by twenty or thirty men, headed by Senator Lodge, who hated him with a bitterness that was intense, the President, with quiet courtesy, parried every blow aimed at him.

No question, no matter how pointed it was, seemed to disturb his serenity. He acted like a lawyer who knew his case from top to bottom, and who had confidence in the great cause he was representing. His cards were frankly laid upon the table and he appeared like a fighting champion, ready to meet all comers. Indeed, this very attitude of frankness, openness, sincerity, and courtesy, one could see from the side-lines, was a cause of discomfort to

Senator Lodge and the Republicans grouped about him, and one could also see written upon the faces of the Democratic senators in that little room a look of pride that they had a leader who carried himself so gallantly and who so brilliantly met every onslaught of the enemy. The President anticipated an abrupt adjournment of the conference with a courteous invitation to luncheon. Senator Lodge had just turned to the President and said: "Mr. President, I do not wish to interfere in any way, but the conference has now lasted about three hours and a half, and it is half an hour after the lunch hour." Whereupon, the President said: "Will not you gentlemen take luncheon with me? It will be very delightful."

It was evident that this invitation, so cordially conveyed, broke the ice of formality which up to that time pervaded the meeting, and like boys out of school, forgetting the great affair in which they had all played prominent parts, they made their way to the dining room, the President walking by the side of Senator Lodge. Instead of fisticuffs, as some of the newspaper men had predicted, the lion and the lamb sat down together at the dining table, and for an hour or two the question of the ratification of the Treaty of Versailles was forgotten in the telling of pleasant stories and the play of repartee.

Although, at this conference of August 19, 1919, the President had frankly opened his mind and heart to the enemies of the Treaty, the opposition instead of moderating seemed to grow more intense and passionate. The President had done everything humanly possible to soften the opposition of the Republicans, but, alas, the information brought to him from the Hill by his Democratic friends only confirmed the opinion that the opposition to the Treaty was growing and could not be overcome by personal contact of any kind between the President and members of the Foreign Relations Committee.

It is plain now, and will become plainer as the years elapse, that the Republican opposition to the League was primarily partisan politics and a rooted personal dislike of the chief proponent of the League, Mr. Wilson. His reëlection in 1916, the first reëlection of an incumbent Democratic President since Andrew Jackson, had greatly disturbed the Republican leaders. The prestige of the Republican party was threatened by this Democratic leader. His reception in Europe added to their distress. For the sake of the sacred cause of Republicanism, this menace of Democratic leadership must be destroyed, even though in destroying it the leaders should swallow their own words and reverse their own former positions on world adjustment.

An attempt was made by enemies of the President to give the impression to the country that an association of nations was one of the "fool ideas" of Woodrow Wilson; that in making it part of his Fourteen Points, he was giving free rein to his idealism. As a matter of fact, the idea did not originate with Woodrow Wilson. If its American origin were traced, it would be found that the earliest supporters of the idea were Republicans.

I remember with what reluctance the President accepted the invitation of the League to Enforce Peace, tendered by Mr. Taft, to deliver an address on May 27, 1916, at the New Willard Hotel, Washington, a meeting at which one of the principal speakers was no less a personage than Senator Henry Cabot Lodge, with Mr. Taft presiding. For many months the President had been revolving this idea in his mind and for a long time he was reluctant to accept any invitation that would seem to give approval to the idea. He patiently waited to make a complete survey of the whole world situation, to be convinced that the permanent participation of the United States in world affairs was a necessity if peace was to be secured.

It was not an easy thing to draw the President away from the traditional policy of aloofness and isolation which had characterized the attitude of the United States in all international affairs. But the invitation to discuss universal peace, urged upon the President by ex-President William H. Taft, was finally accepted.

In that speech he said: "We are participants, whether we would or not, in the life of the world, and the interests of all nations are our own; henceforth, there must be a common agreement for a common object, and at the heart of that common object must lie the inviolable rights of peoples and of mankind. We believe these fundamental things: First, that every people has a right to choose the sovereignty under which they shall live. Second, that the small states of the world have a right to enjoy the same respect for their sovereignty and for their territorial integrity that great and powerful nations expect and insist upon. [This idea was substantially embodied in Article X]; and third, that the world has a right to be free from every disturbance of its peace that has its origin in aggression and disregard of the rights of peoples and nations."

These statements were uttered in the presence of Senator Lodge and applauded by Mr. Taft and his Republican associates gathered at the banquet.

The President, continuing his address, then gave expression to his views regarding the means to attain these ends. He was convinced that there should be an "uni-

versal association of the nations to maintain the inviolate
security of the highway of the seas for the common use of
all nations of the world, and to prevent any war begun
either contrary to treaty agreements or without warning
and full submission of the causes to the opinion of the
world—a virtual guarantee of territorial integrity and
political independence." And he ventured to assert, in
the presence of Senator Lodge, who afterward became the
leader of the opposition to these very ideas, "that the
United States is willing to become a partner in any feasible
association of nations formed in order to realize these
objects and make them secure against violation."

Woodrow Wilson believed that the League of Nations
was the first modern attempt to prevent war by discussion
in the open and not behind closed doors or "within the
cloistered retreats of European diplomacy." To him the
League of Nations was the essence of Christianity. Yet
when he took up the advocacy of the League of Nations,
Senator Lodge, the spokesman of the Republican party at
the dinner of the League to Enforce Peace, became the
leader in bitter opposition to it.

Senator Lodge at this very dinner on May 27, 1916,
delivered the following address:

I know, and no one, I think, can know better than one who has
served long in the Senate, which is charged with an important share of
the ratification and confirmation of all treaties; no one can, I think, feel
more deeply than I do the difficulties which confront us in the work
which this league—that is, the great association extending throughout
the country, known as the League to Enforce Peace—undertakes,
but the difficulties cannot be overcome unless we try to overcome
them. I believe much can be done. Probably it will be impossible
to stop all wars, but it certainly will be possible to stop some wars,
and thus diminish their number. The way in which this problem
must be worked out must be left to this league and to those who are

giving this great subject the study which it deserves. I know the obstacles. I know how quickly we shall be met with the statement that this is a dangerous question which you are putting into your argument, that no nation can submit to the judgment of other nations, and we must be careful at the beginning not to attempt too much. I know the difficulties which arise when we speak of anything which seems to involve an alliance, but I do not believe that when Washington warned us against entangling alliances he meant for one moment that we should not join with the other civilized nations of the world if a method could be found to diminish war and encourage peace.

It was a year ago in delivering the chancellor's address at Union College I made an argument on this theory, that if we were to promote international peace at the close of the present terrible war, if we were to restore international law as it must be restored, we must find some way in which the united forces of the nations could be put behind the cause of peace and law. I said then that my hearers might think that I was picturing a Utopia, but it is in the search of Utopias that great discoveries are made. Not failure, but low aim, is the crime. This league certainly has the highest of all aims for the benefits of humanity, and because the pathway is sown with difficulties is no reason that we should turn from it.

Theodore Roosevelt, in his Nobel Prize thesis, also expressed himself as follows, with reference to an association of nations:

The one permanent move for obtaining peace which has yet been suggested with any reasonable chance of obtaining its object is by an agreement among the great powers, in which each should pledge itself not only to abide by the decisions of a common tribunal, but to back with force the decision of that common tribunal. The great civilized nations of the world which do not possess force, actual or immediately potential, should combine by solemn agreement in a great world league for the peace of righteousness.

Upon the President taking up the League of Nations fight, Senator Lodge drew away from it as if in fear and trembling and began discussing our responsibilities abroad,

evidencing a complete change of heart. He no longer
asked Americans to be generous and fearless, but said:

> The hearts of the vast majority of mankind would beat on strongly
> without any quickening if the League were to perish altogether.

The first objection to the League of Nations, urged by
Senator Lodge, was that it involved the surrender of our
sovereignty. There is a striking analogy between the
argument of Senator Lodge and those put forth by gentlemen in Washington's day who feared that the proposed
Constitution which was designed to establish a federal
union would mean danger, oppression, and disaster.

Mr. Singletary of Massachusetts, Mr. Lowndes of
South Carolina, Mr. Grayson of Virginia, even Patrick
Henry himself, foresaw the virtual subjugation of the
States through a Constitution which at that time was
often called the Treaty between the Thirteen States.

As Senator Brandegee and others contended that the
Covenant of the League of Nations was a "muddy, murky,
and muddled document," so Mr. Williams of New York,
in 1788, charged "ambiguity" against the proposed Constitution, saying that it was "absolutely impossible to
know what we give up and what we retain."

Mandates and similar bogies had their counterpart in
Washington's day. George Mason, fearful like Senator
Sherman of Illinois in a later day, "apprehended the
possibility of Congress calling in the militia of Georgia to
quell disturbances in New Hampshire."

The attitude of George Washington in his day was very
similar to that of Woodrow Wilson. Writing to Knox,
on August 19, 1797, he said: "I am fully persuaded it
[meaning the Federal Constitution] is the best that can
be obtained at this time. And, as a constitutional door

is open for amendment hereafter, our adoption of it, under the present circumstances of the union, is in my opinion desirable." And of the opponents of the proposed Constitution he said, "The major part of them will, it is to be feared, be governed by sinister and self-important motives."

The storm centre of the whole fight against the League was the opposition personally conducted by Senator Lodge and others of the Republican party against the now famous Article X. The basis of the whole Republican opposition was their fear that America would have to bear some responsibility in the affairs of the world, while the strength of Woodrow Wilson's position was his faith that out of the war, with all its blood and tears, would come this great consummation.

It was the President's idea that we should go into the League and bear our responsibilities; that we should enter it as gentlemen, scorning privilege. He did not wish us to sneak in and enjoy its advantages and shirk its responsibilities, but he wanted America to enter boldly and not as a hypocrite.

With reference to the argument made by Senator Lodge against our going into the League, saying that it would be a surrender of American sovereignty and a loss of her freedom, the President often asked the question on his Western trip: How can a nation preserve its freedom except through concerted action? We surrender part of our freedom in order to save the rest of it. Discussing this matter one day, he said: "One cannot have an omelet without breaking eggs. By joining the League of Nations, a nation loses, not its individual freedom, but its selfish isolation. The only freedom it loses is the freedom to do wrong. Robinson Crusoe was free to shoot in any direction on his island until Friday came. Then there was one direction in which he could not shoot. His freedom ended where Friday's rights began."

There would have been no Federal Union to-day if the individual states that went to make up the Federal Union were not willing to surrender the powers they exercised, to surrender their freedom as it were.

Opponents of the League tried to convey the impression that under Article X we should be obliged to send our boys across the sea and that in that event America's voice would not be the determining voice.

Lloyd George answered this argument in a crushing way, when he said:

We cannot, unless we abandon the whole basis of the League of Nations, disinterest ourselves in an attack upon the existence of a nation which is a member of that league and whose life is in jeopardy. That covenant, as I understand it, does not contemplate, necessarily, military action in support of the imperilled nation. It contemplates economic pressure; it contemplates support for the struggling people; and when it is said that if you give any support at all to Poland it involves a great war, with conscription and with all the mechanism of war with which we have been so familiar in the last few years, that is inconsistent with the whole theory of the covenant into which we have entered. We contemplated other methods of bringing pressure to bear upon the recalcitrant nation that is guilty of acts of aggression against other nations and endangering their independence.

The Republicans who attacked the President on Article X had evidently forgotten what Theodore Roosevelt said about the one effective move for obtaining peace, when he urged: "The nations should agree on certain rights that should not be questioned, such as territorial integrity, their rights to deal with their domestic affairs, and with such matters as whom they should admit to citizenship." They had, also, evidently forgotten that Mr. Taft said: "The arguments against Article X which have been most pressed are those directed to showing that under its obligations the United States can be forced into many wars and to burdensome expeditionary forces to protect countries in which it has no legitimate interest. This objection will not bear examination."

Mr. Taft answered the question of one of the Republican critics if Article X would not involve us in war, in the following statement:

How much will it involve us in war? Little, if any. In the first place, the universal boycott, first to be applied, will impose upon most nations such a withering isolation and starvation that in most cases it will be effective. In the second place, we'll not be drawn into any war in which it will not be reasonable and convenient for us to render efficient aid, because the plan of the Council must be approved by our representatives, as already explained. In the third place, the threat of the universal boycott and the union of overwhelming forces of the members of the League, if need be, will hold every nation from violating Article X, and Articles XII, XIII, and XV, unless there is a world conspiracy, as in this war, in which case the earliest we get into the war, the better.

Evidently Mr. Taft did not look upon Article X as the bugaboo that Mr. Lodge pretended it was, for he said:

Article X covers the Monroe Doctrine *and extends it to the world.* The League is not a super-sovereign, but a partnership intended to secure to us and all nations only the sovereignty we can properly have, i. e., sovereignty regulated by the international law and morality consistent with the same sovereignty of other nations. The United States is not under this constitution to be forced into actual war against its will. This League is to be regarded in conflict with the advice of Washington only from a narrow and reactionary viewpoint.

Mr. Herbert Hoover, now a member of Mr. Harding's Cabinet, in a speech delivered on October 3, 1919, answering the argument that America would be compelled to send her boys to the other side, said:

We hear the cry that the League obligates that our sons be sent to fight in foreign lands. Yet the very intent and structure of the League is to prevent wars. There is no obligation for the United States to engage in military operations or to allow any interference with our internal affairs without the full consent of our representatives in the League.

And further discussing the revision of the Treaty, Mr. Hoover said:

I am confident that if we attempt now to revise the Treaty we shall tread on a road through European chaos. Even if we managed to keep our soldiers out of it we will not escape fearful economic losses. If the League is to break down we must at once prepare to fight. Few people seem to realize the desperation to which Europe has been reduced.

CHAPTER XLII

TENTATIVE plans for a Western trip began to be formed in the White House because of the urgent insistence from Democratic friends on the Hill that nothing could win the fight for the League of Nations except a direct appeal to the country by the President in person.

Admiral Grayson, the President's physician and consistent friend, who knew his condition and the various physical crises through which he had passed here and on the other side, from some of which he had not yet recovered, stood firm in his resolve that the President should not go West, even intimating to me that the President's life might pay the forfeit if his advice were disregarded. Indeed, it needed not the trained eye of a physician to see that the man whom the senators were now advising to make a "swing around the circle" was on the verge of a nervous breakdown. More than once since his return from the Peace Conference I had urged him to take a needed rest; to get away from the turmoil of Washington and recuperate; but he spurned this advice and resolved to go through to the end.

No argument of ours could draw him away from his duties, which now involved not only the fight for the ratification of the Treaty, but the threatened railway strike, with its attendant evils to the country, and added administrative burdens growing out of the partisanship

fight which was being waged in Congress for the ostensible
purpose of reducing the high cost of living.

One day, after Democratic senators had been urging
the Western trip, I took leave to say to the President that,
in his condition, disastrous consequences might result if
he should follow their advice. But he dismissed my
solicitude, saying in a weary way: "I know that I am at
the end of my tether, but my friends on the Hill say that
the trip is necessary to save the Treaty, and I am willing to
make whatever personal sacrifice is required, for if the
Treaty should be defeated, God only knows what would
happen to the world as a result of it. In the presence
of the great tragedy which now faces the world, no decent
man can count his own personal fortunes in the reckoning.
Even though, in my condition, it might mean the giving
up of my life, I will gladly make the sacrifice to save the
Treaty."

He spoke like a soldier who was ready to make the
supreme sacrifice to save the cause that lay closest to his
heart.

As I looked at the President while he was talking, in my
imagination I made a comparison between the man,
Woodrow Wilson, who now stood before me and the man
I had met many years before in New Jersey. In those
days he was a vigorous, agile, slender man, active and
alert, his hair but slightly streaked with gray. Now, as he
stood before me discussing the necessity for the Western
trip, he was an old man, grown grayer and grayer, but
grimmer and grimmer in his determination, like an old
warrior, to fight to the end.

There was another whose heroism was no less than his,
Mrs. Wilson. She has since referred to the Western trip
as "one long nightmare," though in the smiling face which

she turned upon the crowds from Columbus to San Diego and back to Pueblo none could have detected a trace of the anxiety that was haunting her. She met the shouting throngs with the same reposeful dignity and radiant, friendly smile with which she had captivated the people of England, France, Italy, and Belgium.

At home and abroad she has always had a peculiar power to attract the populace, though she herself has never craved the spotlight. Like her husband, she finds home more congenial, and, like him, she prefers not to be written about.

In her husband's career she has played a notable rôle, the more noble because self-effacing. She has consistently disavowed intention to participate actively in public affairs, and yet in many a crisis she, out of her strong intelligence and sagacity, has been able to offer timely, wise suggestion. No public man ever had a more devoted helpmeet, and no wife a husband more dependent upon her sympathetic understanding of his problems. The devotion between these two has not been strengthened, for that would be impossible, but deepened by the President's long illness. Mrs. Wilson's strong physical constitution, combined with strength of character and purpose, has sustained her under a strain which must have wrecked most women. When the strong man broke, she nursed him as tenderly as a mother nurses a child.

Mrs. Wilson must have left the White House for that ill-omened journey with a sinking heart, for she knew, none better, that her husband was suffering from accumulated fatigue, and that he should be starting on a long vacation instead of a fighting tour that would tax the strength of an athlete in the pink of condition. For seven practically vacationless years he had borne burdens too great for any constitution; he had conducted his country through the greatest of all wars; he had contended, at times single-handed, in Paris with the world's most adroit politicians; he had there been prostrated with influenza, that treacherous disease which usually maims for a time those whom it does not kill, and he had not given himself a chance to recuperate; he had returned to America to engage in the most desperate conflict of his career with the leaders of the opposition party; and now, when it was clear even to his men friends, and much clearer to the intuition of a devoted wife, that nature was crying out for rest, he was setting out on one of the most arduous programmes of public speaking known even in our country, which is familiar with these strenuous undertakings. Mrs. Wilson's anxieties must have increased with each successive day of the journey, but not even to we of the immediate party did she betray her fears. Her resolution was as great as his.

When the great illness came she had to stand between him and the peril of exhaustion from official cares, yet she could not, like the more fortunately obscure, withdraw her husband from business altogether and take him away to some quiet place for restoration. As head of the nation he must be kept in touch with affairs, and during the early months of his illness she was the chief agent in keeping him informed of public business. Her high intelligence and her extraordinary memory enabled her to report to him daily, in lucid detail, weighty matters of state brought to her by officials for transmission to him. At the proper time, when he was least in pain and least exhausted, she would present a clear, oral résumé of each case and lay the documents before him in orderly arrangement.

As woman and wife, the first thought of her mind and

the first care of her heart must be for his health. Once at an acute period of his illness certain officials insisted that they must see him because they carried information which it was "absolutely necessary that the President of the United States should have," and she quietly replied: "I am not interested in the President of the United States. I am interested in my husband and his health."

With loving courage she met her difficult dilemma of shielding him as much as possible and at the same time keeping him acquainted with things he must know. When it became possible for him to see people she, in counsel with Admiral Grayson, would arrange for conferences and carefully watch her husband to see that they who talked with him did not trespass too long upon his limited energy.

When it became evident that the tide of public opinion was setting against the League, the President finally decided upon the Western trip as the only means of bringing home to the people the unparalleled world situation.

At the Executive offices we at once set in motion preparations for the Western trip. One itinerary after another was prepared, but upon examining it the President would find that it was not extensive enough and would suspect that it was made by those of us—like Grayson and myself—who were solicitious for his health, and he would cast them aside. All the itineraries provided for a week of rest in the Grand Canyon of the Colorado, but when a brief vacation was intimated to him, he was obdurate in his refusal to include even a day of relaxation, saying to me, that "the people would never forgive me if I took a rest on a trip such as the one I contemplate taking. This is a business trip, pure and simple, and the itinerary must not include rest of any kind." He insisted that there be no suggestion of a pleasure trip attaching to a journey which he regarded as a mission.

As I now look back upon this journey and its disastrous effects upon the President's health, I believe that if he had only consented to include a rest period in our arrangements, he might not have broken down at Pueblo.

Never have I seen the President look so weary as on the night we left Washington for our swing into the West. When we were about to board our special train, the President turned to me and said: "I am in a nice fix. I am scheduled between now and the 28th of September to make in the neighbourhood of a hundred speeches to various bodies, stretching all the way from Ohio to the coast, and yet the pressure of other affairs upon me at the White House has been so great that I have not had a single minute to prepare my speeches. I do not know how I shall get the time, for during the past few weeks I have been suffering from daily headaches; but perhaps to-night's rest will make me fit for the work of to-morrow."

No weariness or brain-fag, however, was apparent in the speech at Columbus, Ohio. To those of us who sat on the platform, including the newspaper group who accompanied the President, this speech with its beautiful phrasing and its effective delivery seemed to have been carefully prepared.

Day after day, for nearly a month, there were speeches of a similar kind, growing more intense in their emotion with each day. Shortly after we left Tacoma, Washington, the fatigue of the trip began to write itself in the President's face. He suffered from violent headaches each day, but his speeches never betrayed his illness.

In those troublous days and until the very end of our Western trip the President would not permit the slightest variation from our daily programme. Nor did he ever permit the constant headaches, which would have put an ordinary man out of sorts, to work unkindly upon the members of his immediate party, which included Mrs. Wilson, Doctor Grayson, and myself. He would appear regularly at each meal, partaking of it only slightly, always gracious, always good-natured and smiling, responding to every call from the outside for speeches—calls that came from early morning until late at night—from the plain people grouped about every station and watering place through which we passed. Even under the most adverse physical conditions he was always kind, gentle, and considerate to those about him.

I have often wished, as the criticisms of the Pullman smoking car, the cloak room, and the counting house were carried to me, picturing the President's coldness, his aloofness and exclusiveness, that the critics could for a moment have seen the heart and great good-nature of the man giving expression to themselves on this critical journey. If they could have peeped through the curtain of our dining room, at one of the evening meals, for instance, they would have been ashamed of their misrepresentations of this kind, patient, considerate, human-hearted man.

When he was "half fit," an expression he often used, he was the best fellow in the little group on our train— good-natured, smiling, full of anecdotes and repartee, and always thinking of the comforts and pleasure of the men gathered about him. The illness of a newspaper man, or of one of the messengers or conductors, or attachés of the train was a call to service to him, and one could find the President in one of the little compartments of the train, seated at the bed of a newspaper man or some attaché who had been taken ill on the trip. There

is in the President a sincere human sympathy, which is
better than the cheap good-fellowship which many public
men carefully cultivate.

It was on the Western trip, about September 12th,
while the President, with every ounce of his energy, was
attempting to put across the League of Nations, that
Mr. William C. Bullitt was disclosing to the Committee
on Foreign Relations at a public hearing the facts of a
conference between Secretary Lansing and himself, in
which Mr. Bullitt declared that Mr. Lansing had severely
criticized the League of Nations.

The press representatives aboard the train called Mr.
Bullitt's testimony to the President's attention. He made
no comment, but it was plain from his attitude that
he was incensed and distressed beyond measure. Here
he was in the heart of the West, advancing the cause
so dear to his heart, steadily making gains against what
appeared to be insurmountable odds, and now his intimate associate, Mr. Lansing, was engaged in sniping and
attacking him from behind.

On September 16th, Mr. Lansing telegraphed the following message to the President:

On May 17th, Bullitt resigned by letter giving his reasons with
which you are familiar. I replied by letter on the 18th without any
comment on his reasons. Bullitt on the 19th asked to see me to say
good-bye and I saw him. He elaborated on the reasons for his resignation and said that he could not conscientiously give countenance
to a treaty which was based on injustice. I told him that I would
say nothing against his resigning since he put it on conscientious
grounds, and that I recognized that certain features of the Treaty
were bad, as I presumed most everyone did, but that was probably
unavoidable in view of conflicting claims and that nothing ought to
be done to prevent the speedy restoration of peace by signing the
Treaty. Bullitt then discussed the numerous European commissions

provided for by the Treaty on which the United States was to be represented. I told him that I was disturbed by this fact because I was afraid the Senate and possibly the people, if they understood this, would refuse ratification, and that anything which was an obstacle to ratification was unfortunate because we ought to have peace as soon as possible.

When the President received this explanation from Mr. Lansing, he sent for me to visit with him in his compartment. At the time I arrived he was seated in his little study, engaged in preparing his speech for the night's meeting. Turning to me, with a deep show of feeling, he said: "Read that, and tell me what you think of a man who was my associate on the other side and who confidentially expressed himself to an outsider in such a fashion? Were I in Washington I would at once demand his resignation! That kind of disloyalty must not be permitted to go unchallenged for a single minute. The testimony of Bullitt is a confirmation of the suspicions I have had with reference to this individual. I found the same attitude of mind on the part of Lansing on the other side. I could find his trail everywhere I went, but they were only suspicions and it would not be fair for me to act upon them. But here in his own statement is a verification at last of everything I have suspected. Think of it! This from a man whom I raised from the level of a subordinate to the great office of Secretary of State of the United States. My God! I did not think it was possible for Lansing to act in this way. When we were in Paris I found that Lansing and others were constantly giving out statements that did not agree with my viewpoint. When I had arranged a settlement, there would appear from some source I could not locate unofficial statements telling the correspondents not to take things too seriously; that a compromise would be made, and this news, or rather news of this kind, was harmful to the settlement I had already obtained and quite naturally gave the Conference the impression that Lansing and his kind were speaking for me, and then the French would say that I was bluffing."

I am convinced that only the President's illness a few days later prevented an immediate demand on his part for the resignation of Mr. Lansing.

That there was no real devotion on the part of Mr. Lansing for the President is shown by the following incident.

A few days after the President returned from the West and lay seriously ill at the White House, with physicians and nurses gathered about his bed, Mr. Lansing sought a private audience with me in the Cabinet Room. He informed me that he had called diplomatically to suggest that in view of the incapacity of the President we should arrange to call in the Vice-President to act in his stead as soon as possible, reading to me from a book which he had brought from the State Department, which I afterward learned was "Jefferson's Manual," the following clause of the United States Constitution:

In case of the removal of the President from office, or his death, resignation, or inability to discharge the powers and duties of the said office, the same shall devolve upon the Vice-President.

Upon reading this, I coldly turned to Mr. Lansing and said: "Mr. Lansing, the Constitution is not a dead letter with the White House. I have read the Constitution and do not find myself in need of any tutoring at your hands of the provision you have just read." When I asked Mr. Lansing the question as to who should certify

to the disability of the President, he intimated that that
would be a job for either Doctor Grayson or myself. I
immediately grasped the full significance of what he intimated and said: "You may rest assured that while
Woodrow Wilson is lying in the White House on the broad
of his back I will not be a party to ousting him. He
has been too kind, too loyal, and too wonderful to me to
receive such treatment at my hands." Just as I uttered
this statement Doctor Grayson appeared in the Cabinet
Room and I turned to him and said: "And I am sure that
Doctor Grayson will never certify to his disability. Will
you, Grayson?" Doctor Grayson left no doubt in Mr.
Lansing's mind that he would not do as Mr. Lansing suggested. I then notified Mr. Lansing that if anybody
outside of the White House circle attempted to certify
to the President's disability, that Grayson and I would
stand together and repudiate it. I added that if the
President were in a condition to know of this episode
he would, in my opinion, take decisive measures. That
ended the interview.

It is unnecessary to say that no further attempt was
made by Mr. Lansing to institute ouster proceedings
against his chief.

I never attempted to ascertain what finally influenced
the action of the President peremptorily to demand the
resignation of Mr. Lansing. My own judgment is that
the demand came as the culmination of repeated acts
of what the President considered disloyalty on Mr.
Lansing's part while in Paris, and that the situation was
aggravated by Mr. Lansing's notes to Mexico during
the President's illness.

When I received from the President's stenographer
the letter to Mr. Lansing, intimating that his resignation

would not be a disagreeable thing to the President, I conferred with the President at once and argued with him that in the present state of public opinion it was the wrong time to do the right thing. At the time the President was seated in his invalid chair on the White House portico. Although physically weak, he was mentally active and alert. Quickly he took hold of my phrase and said, with a show of the old fire that I had seen on so many occasions: "Tumulty, it is never the wrong time to spike disloyalty. When Lansing sought to oust me, I was upon my back. I am on my feet now and I will not have disloyalty about me."

When the announcement of Lansing's resignation was made, the flood-gates of fury broke about the President; but he was serene throughout it all. When I called at the White House on the following Sunday, I found him calmly seated in his bathroom with his coloured valet engaged in the not arduous task of cutting his hair. Looking at me with a smile in his eye, he said: "Well, Tumulty, have I any friends left?" "Very few, Governor," I said. Whereupon he replied: "Of course, it will be another two days' wonder. But in a few days what the country considers an indiscretion on my part in getting rid of Lansing will be forgotten, but when the sober, second thought of the country begins to assert itself, what will stand out will be the disloyalty of Lansing to me. Just think of it! Raised and exalted to the office of Secretary of State, made a member of the Peace Commission, participating in all the conferences and affixing his signature to a solemn treaty, and then hurrying to America and appearing before the Foreign Relations Committee of the Senate to repudiate the very thing to which he had given his assent."

During the illness of the President his political enemies sought to convey the impression that he was incapacitated for the duties of his office. As one who came in daily contact with him I knew how baseless were these insinuations. As a matter of fact, there was not a whole week during his entire illness that he was not in touch with every matter upon which he was called to act and upon which he was asked to render judgment. The White House files contain numerous memoranda showing his interest in all matters to which department heads felt it incumbent to call his attention during his illness. One of the most critical things upon which he passed was the question of the miners' strike, which resulted in the beginning from an injunction suit by the Attorney General, Mr. Palmer, to restrain the miners from carrying out their purpose to strike. This was one of the most critical situations that arose during his illness and with which he daily kept in touch.

Uncomplainingly the President applied himself to the difficult tasks of the Western trip. While the first meeting at Columbus was a disappointment as to attendance, as we approached the West the crowds grew in numbers and the enthusiasm became boundless. The idea of the League spread and spread as we neared the coast. Contrary to the impression in the East, the President's trip West was a veritable triumph for him and was so successful that we had planned, upon the completion of the Western trip, to invade the enemy's country, Senator Lodge's own territory, the New England States, and particularly Massachusetts. This was our plan, fully developed and arranged, when about four o'clock in the morning of September 26, 1919, Doctor Grayson knocked at the door of my sleeping compartment and told me to dress quickly, that the President was seriously ill. As we walked toward the President's car, the Doctor told me in a few words of the President's trouble and said that he greatly feared it might end fatally if we should attempt to continue the trip and that it was his duty to inform the President that by all means the trip must be cancelled; but that he did not feel free to suggest it to the President without having my coöperation and support. When we arrived at the President's drawing room I found him fully dressed and seated in his chair. With great difficulty he was able to articulate. His face was pale and wan. One side of it had fallen, and his condition was indeed pitiful to behold. Quickly I reached the same conclusion as that of Doctor Grayson, as to the necessity for the immediate cancellation of the trip, for to continue it, in my opinion, meant death to the President. Looking at me, with great tears running down his face, he said: "My dear boy, this has never happened to me before. I felt it coming on yesterday. I do not know what to do." He then pleaded with us not to cut short the trip. Turning to both of us, he said: "Don't you see that if you cancel this trip, Senator Lodge and his friends will say that I am a quitter and that the Western trip was a failure, and the Treaty will be lost." Reaching over to him, I took both of his hands and said: "What difference, my dear Governor, does it make what they say? Nobody in the world believes you are a quitter, but it is your life that we must now consider. We must cancel the trip, and I am sure that when the people learn of your condition there will be no misunderstanding." He then tried to move over nearer to me to continue his argument against the cancellation of the trip; but he found he was unable to do so. His left arm and leg refused to function.

I then realized that the President's whole left side was paralyzed. Looking at me he said: "I want to show them that I can still fight and that I am not afraid. Just postpone the trip for twenty-four hours and I will be all right."

But Doctor Grayson and I resolved not to take any risk, and an immediate statement was made to the inquiring newspaper men that the Western trip was off.

Never was the President more gentle or tender than on that morning. Suffering the greatest pain, paralyzed on his left side, he was still fighting desperately for the thing that was so close to his heart—a vindication of the things for which he had so gallantly fought on the other side. Grim old warrior that he was, he was ready to fight to the death for the League of Nations.

In the dispatches carried to the country, prepared by the fine newspaper men who accompanied us on the trip, it was stated that evidences of a breakdown on the part of the President were plainly visible in the speech he delivered at Pueblo.

I had talked to him only a few minutes before the delivery of that speech, and the only apparent evidence that he was approaching a breakdown was in his remark to me that he had a splitting headache, and that he would have to cut his speech short. As a matter of fact, this last speech he made, at Pueblo, on September 25, 1919, was one of the longest speeches delivered on the Western trip and, if I may say so, was one of the best and most passionate appeals he made for the League of Nations.

Many things in connection with the Pueblo meeting impressed themselves upon me. In the peroration of the speech he drew a picture of his visit on Decoration Day, 1919, to what he called a beautiful hillside near

Paris, where was located the cemetery of Suresnes, a cemetery given over to the burial of the American dead. As he spoke of the purposes for which those departed American soldiers had given their lives, a great wave of emotion, such as I have never witnessed at a public meeting, swept through the whole amphitheatre. As he continued his speech, I looked at Mrs. Wilson and saw tears in her eyes. I then turned to see the effect upon some of the "hard-boiled" newspaper men, to whom great speeches were ordinary things, and they were alike deeply moved. Down in the amphitheatre I saw men sneak their handkerchiefs out of their pockets and wipe the tears from their eyes. The President was like a great organist playing upon the heart emotions of the thousands of people who were held spell-bound by what he said.

It is possible, I pray God it may not be so, that the speech at Pueblo was the last public speech that Woodrow Wilson will ever make, and I, therefore, take the liberty of introducing into this story the concluding words of it:

What of our pledges to the men that lie dead in France? We said that they went over there not to prove the prowess of America or her readiness for another war but to see to it that there never was such a war again. It always seems to make it difficult for me to say anything, my fellow ctiizens, when I think of my clients in this case. My clients are the children; my clients are the next generation. They do not know what promises and bonds I undertook when I ordered the armies of the United States to the soil of France, but I know, and I intend to redeem my pledges to the children; they shall not be sent upon a similar errand.

Again, and again, my fellow citizens, mothers who lost their sons in France have come to me and, taking my hand, have shed tears upon it not only, but they have added: "God bless you, Mr. President!" Why, my fellow citizens, should they pray God to bless me?

I advised the Congress of the United States to create the situation that led to the death of their sons. I ordered their sons overseas. I consented to their sons being put in the most difficult parts of the battle line, where death was certain, as in the impenetrable difficulties of the forest of Argonne. Why should they weep upon my hand and call down the blessings of God upon me? Because they believe that their boys died for something that vastly transcends any of the immediate and palpable objects of the war. They believe, and they rightly believe, that their sons saved the liberty of the world. They believe that wrapped up with the liberty of the world is the continuous protection of that liberty by the concerted powers of all the civilized world. They believe that this sacrifice was made in order that other sons should not be called upon for a similar gift—the gift of life, the gift of all that died—and if we did not see this thing through, if we fulfilled the dearest present wish of Germany and now dissociated ourselves from those alongside whom we fought in the war, would not something of the halo go away from the gun over the mantelpiece, or the sword? Would not the old uniform lose something if its significance? These men were crusaders. They were going forth to prove the might of justice and right, and all the world accepted them as crusaders, and their transcendent achievement has made all the world believe in America as it believes in no other nation organized in the modern world. There seems to me to stand between us and the rejection or qualification of this treaty the serried ranks of those boys in khaki, not only those boys who came home, but those dear ghosts that still deploy upon the fields of France.

My friends, on last Decoration Day I went to a beautiful hillside near Paris, where was located the cemetery of Suresnes, a cemetery given over to the burial of the American dead. Behind me on the slopes was rank upon rank of living American soldiers, and lying before me on the levels of the plain was rank upon rank of departed American soldiers. Right by the side of the stand where I spoke there was a little group of French women who had adopted those graves, had made themselves mothers of those dear ghosts by putting flowers every day upon those graves, taking them as their own sons, their own beloved, because they had died in the same cause—France was free and the world was free because America had come! I wish some men in public life who are now opposing the settlement for which these men died could visit such a spot as that. I wish that the thought that comes out of those graves could penetrate their consciousness. I wish that they could feel the moral obligation that rests upon us not to go back on those boys, but to see the thing through, to see it through to the end and make good their redemption of the world. For nothing less depends upon this decision, nothing less than the liberation and salvation of the world.

Now that the mists of this great question have cleared away, I believe that men will see the trust, eye to eye and face to face. There is one thing that the American people always rise to and extend their hand to, and that is the truth of justice and of liberty and of peace. We have accepted that truth and we are going to be led by it, and it is going to lead us, and through us the world, out into pastures of quietness and peace such as the world never dreamed of before.

CHAPTER XLIII

O N JUNE 25, 1919, I received from President Wilson the following cabled message:

My clear conviction is that the adoption of the treaty by the Senate with reservations will put the United States as clearly out of the concert of nations as a rejection. We ought either to go in or stay out. To stay out would be fatal to the influence and even to the commercial prospects of the United States, and to go in would give her a leading place in the affairs of the world. Reservations would either mean nothing or postpone the conclusion of peace, so far as America is concerned, until every other principal nation concerned in the treaty had found out by negotiation what the reservations practically meant and whether they could associate themselves with the United States on the terms of the reservations or not.

WOODROW WILSON.

The President consistently held to the principle involved in this statement. To his mind the reservations offered by Senator Lodge constituted a virtual nullification on the part of the United States of a treaty which was a contract, and which should be amended through free discussion among all the contracting parties. He did not argue or assume that the Covenant was a perfected document, but he believed that, like our American Constitution, it should be adopted and subsequently submitted to necessary amendment through the constitutional processes of debate. He was unalterably opposed to having the United States put in the position of seeking exemptions and special

privileges under an agreement which he believed was in
the interest of the entire world, including our own country.
Furthermore, he believed that the advocacy for reservations in the Senate proceeded from partisan motives
and that in so far as there was a strong popular opinion
in the country in favour of reservations it proceeded from
the same sources from which had come the pro-German
propaganda. Before the war pro-German agitation had
sought to keep us out of the conflict, and after the war it
sought to separate us in interest and purpose from other
governments with which we were associated.

By his opposition to reservations the President was
seeking to prevent Germany from taking through diplomacy what she had been unable to get by her armies.

The President was so confident of the essential rightness
of the League and the Covenant and of the inherent right-
mindedness of the American people, that he could not
believe that the people would sanction either rejection or
emasculation of the Treaty if they could be made to see the
issue in all the sincerity of its motives and purposes, if
partisan attack could be met with plain truth-speaking.
It was to present the case of the people in what he considered its true light that he undertook the Western tour,
and it was while thus engaged that his health broke.
Had he kept well and been able to lead in person the
struggle for ratification, he might have won, as he had
previously by his determination and conviction broken
down stubborn opposition to the Federal Reserve system.

So strong was his faith in his cause and the people that
even after he fell ill he could not believe that ratification
would fail. What his enemies called stubbornness was his
firm faith in the righteousness of the treaty and in the
reasonableness of the proposition that the time to make

amendments was not prior to the adoption of the Treaty and by one nation, but after all the nations had agreed and had met together for sober, unpartisan consideration of alterations in the interest of all the contracting parties and the peace and welfare of the world.

Even when he lay seriously ill, he insisted upon being taken in his invalid chair along the White House portico to the window of my outer office each day during the controversy in the Senate over the Treaty. There day after day in the coldest possible weather I conferred with him and discussed every phase of the fight on the Hill. He would sit in his chair, wrapped in blankets, and though hardly able, because of his physical condition, to discuss these matters with me, he evidenced in every way a tremendous interest in everything that was happening in the Capitol that had to do with the Treaty. Although I was warned by Doctor Grayson and Mrs. Wilson not to alarm him unduly by bringing pessimistic reports, I sought, in the most delicate and tactful way I could, to bring the atmosphere of the Hill to him. Whenever there was an indication of the slightest rise in the tide for the League of Nations a smile would pass over the President's face, and weak and broken though he was, he evidenced his great pleasure at the news. Time and time again during the critical days of the Treaty fight the President would appear outside my office, seated in the old wheel chair, and make inquiry regarding the progress of the Treaty fight on Capitol Hill.

One of the peculiar things about the illness from which the President suffered was the deep emotion which would stir him when word was brought to him that this senator or that senator on the Hill had said some kind thing about him or had gone to his defense when some political enemy was engaged in bitterly assailing his attitude in the Treaty fight. Never would there come from him any censure or bitter criticism of those who were opposing him in the fight. For Senator Borah, the leader of the opposition, he had high respect, and felt that he was actuated only by sincere motives.

I recall how deeply depressed he was when word was carried to him that the defeat of the Treaty was inevitable. On this day he was looking more weary than at any time during his illness. After I had read to him a memorandum that I had prepared, containing a report on the situation in the Senate, I drew away from his wheel chair and said to him: "Governor, you are looking very well to-day." He shook his head in a pathetic way and said: "I am very well for a man who awaits disaster," and bowing his head he gave way to the deep emotion he felt.

A few days later I called to notify him of the defeat of the Treaty. His only comment was, "They have shamed us in the eyes of the world." Endeavouring to keep my good-nature steady in the midst of a trying situation, I smiled and said: "But, Governor, only the Senate has defeated you. The People will vindicate your course. You may rely upon that." "Ah, but our enemies have poisoned the wells of public opinion," he said. "They have made the people believe that the League of Nations is a great Juggernaut, the object of which is to bring war and not peace to the world. If I only could have remained well long enough to have convinced the people that the League of Nations was their real hope, their last chance, perhaps, to save civilization!"

I said, by way of trying to strengthen and encourage him at this, one of the critical moments of his life—a moment that I knew was one of despair for him—"Governor,

I want to read a chapter from the third volume of your 'History of the American People,' if it will not tire you." He graciously gave his assent and I took from under my arm the volume containing an account of the famous John Jay treaty, in the defense of which Alexander Hamilton was stoned while he stood defending it on the steps of the New York City Hall. There was, indeed, a remarkable similarity between the fight over the John Jay treaty and the Versailles Treaty. I read an entire chapter of Woodrow Wilson's "History of the American People," including the passage:

Slowly the storm blew off. The country had obviously gained more than it had conceded, and tardily saw the debt it owed Mr. Jay and to the administration, whose firmness and prudence had made his mission possible. But in the meantime things had been said which could not be forgotten. Washington had been assailed with unbridled license, as an enemy and a traitor to the country; had even been charged with embezzling public moneys during the Revolution; was madly threatened with impeachment, and even with assassination; and had cried amidst the bitterness of it all that "he would rather be in his grave than in the presidency."

The country knew its real mind about him once again when the end of his term came and it was about to lose him. He refused to stand for another election. His farewell address, with its unmistakable tone of majesty and its solemn force of affection and admonition, seemed an epitome of the man's character and achievements, and every man's heart smote him to think that Washington was actually gone from the nation's counsels.

When I concluded reading this chapter, the President's comment was, "It is mighty generous of you to compare my disappointment over the Treaty with that of Washington's. *You have placed me in mighty good company.*"

CHAPTER XLIV

THERE is no one who wishes to feel the camaraderie of life, "the familiar touch," more than Woodrow Wilson; but it seems that it cannot be so, and the knowledge that it could not saddened him from the outset of his public career.

I remember a meeting between us at the Governor's Cottage at Sea Girt, New Jersey, a few hours after the news of his nomination for the Presidency had reached us from Baltimore in 1912. In this little talk he endeavoured in an intimate way to analyze himself for my benefit. "You know, Tumulty," he said, "there are two natures combined in me that every day fight for supremacy and control. On the one side, there is the Irish in me, quick, generous, impulsive, passionate, anxious always to help and to sympathize with those in distress." As he continued his description of himself, his voice took on an Irish brogue, "And like the Irishman at the Donnybrook Fair, always willin' to raise me shillalah and to hit any head which stands firninst me. Then, on the other side," he said, "there is the Scotch—canny, tenacious, cold, and perhaps a little exclusive. I tell you, my dear friend, that when these two fellows get to quarrelling among themselves, it is hard to act as umpire between them.".

For every day of my eleven years' association with Woodrow Wilson I have seen some part of these two

natures giving expression to itself. I have witnessed
the full play of the Irish passion for justice and sympathy
for the under-dog, the man whom he was pleased to call
the "average man," whose name never emerges to the
public view. I have seen the full tide of Irish passion
and human sympathies in him flow at some story of injustice which I had called to his attention; that Irish
sympathy in him expressed itself not dramatically, but
in some simple, modest way; an impulse to lift someone, to help an unfortunate person in distress. That
sympathy might be expressed in the presence of some
father, seeking pardon at the hands of the President in
behalf of a wayward son, or some mother pleading for the
release of a loved one, or it would show itself in full
sway, as it often did, when I called his attention to some
peculiar case that had evoked my sympathy and pity.
And again I saw the Scotch in him—strict, upstanding,
intractable, and unrelenting. I saw the Scotch rise in
him when an attempt would be made by personal friends
to influence his action where it was evident to him there
was at the base of it some hint of personal privilege, of
favouritism on grounds of friendship. I saw the full
sweep of that Scotch tenacity during the war, in the very
midst of that bloody thing, at a time when bitter ridicule
and jeers were his portion. Throughout it he was calm,
imperturbable, undisturbed by the frenzied passions of
the moment.

I saw him express the Irish sense of gratitude in a striking way in the White House, in my presence, as the
result of a conference, in which the participants were
the President and Senators Stone and Reed, both of
Missouri.

The incident arose out of Senator Reed's failure to

get the President to agree to appoint an intimate friend of Reed's postmaster of St. Louis. Charges, many of them unfounded, had been made to the Postmaster General's office against the Reed candidate and, although Reed had made many appeals to Postmaster General Burleson to send the appointment of his friend to the President for his approval, Burleson refused to ₍do so, and Reed thereupon brought his case to the President. I remember how generous and courteous the President was in his treatment of Reed and Stone on this occasion. Senator Stone, in his usual kindly way, walked over to the President and putting his hand on his shoulder, said: "Now, Mr. President, I want you to do this favour for my friend, Jim Reed. Jim is a damned good fellow." The President laughingly replied, "Why, Senator, you just know that there is nothing personal in my attitude in this matter. I have no desire to injure or humiliate Senator Reed, but the Postmaster General has refused to recommend the appointment of the Senator's friend for the St. Louis postmastership." The President then turned to Senator Reed and said, "Senator, I will tell you what I will do for you. I will allow you to name any other man, outside of the one whose name you have already suggested, and I will appoint him at once without making any inquiry or investigation whatever as to his qualifications. This I will do in order to convince you that I have no personal feeling whatever toward you in this matter." But Senator Reed continued to argue for the appointment of his friend. The President was adamant. Senator Stone and Senator Reed then turned away from the President and made their way to my office which was adjoining that of the President. It was plain that the two Senators were deeply disappointed and highly displeased with the President. As the President opened the door for the Senators to make their entrance into my room Senator Reed turned to the President again and in the most emphatic way, said, "Mr. President, Senator Stone told me before I came to see you that you were not a cold man and that you were a good fellow. It was upon that hypothesis that I took the liberty of appealing to you personally in behalf of my friend." Senator Reed then continued, and in the most eloquent short speech I have ever heard, said, "They tell me that before you became governor of New Jersey you had a fight at Princeton with the Trustees of that University. You better than any one else in this country know what it is to have a pack of enemies at your heels. This is what is happening in my friend's case. My enemies in Missouri have conspired to destroy this man because he has been my friend and has fought my battles for me. This man whom I have asked you to appoint has been my campaign manager. He has visited my home; we have been life-long friends, and I will stake my life upon his reputation and upon his standing. But because he has been my friend he is now to be punished and now by your action you will complete the conspiracy that is afoot to defeat and destroy him."

The President then said, "But, Senator, I have tried to convince you that there is nothing personal in my attitude and that I will appoint any other man you may name." Whereupon Senator Reed said, "If God Almighty himself asked me to surrender in this fight for my friend, I would not do it. I think I know you well enough to know that in the fight you had for your ideals and your friends at Princeton, you would not have surrendered to anybody. I am fighting now for the reputation and the character of my friend, and you ought not to ask me to surrender him to his executioners."

The President was standing with his arms folded while the Senator was addressing him and was evidently deeply touched by Reed's appeal. As Reed concluded his eloquent speech in behalf of his friend quickly the President reached out his hand to Reed and said, "Senator, don't surrender your friend; stick by him to the end and I will appoint him." Whereupon he turned from the Senators, walked over to the telephone which stood on my desk, called up the Postmaster General and directed him to send over to the White House at once the appointment of Senator Reed's friend for the postmastership at St. Louis. The Postmaster General protested but was overruled by the President. As the two Senators left my room, Senator Stone said to Senator Reed, "By God, Jim, I told you so. There is a great man and a true friend. I told you he was a regular fellow."

It has been said by the enemies of Woodrow Wilson that he was ungrateful, that he never appreciated the efforts of his friends in his behalf, and that when it came to the question of appointments he was unmindful of his obligations to them.

The following letter is so characteristic of the man that I beg leave to introduce it:

The White House,
Washington D. C.
April 14, 1916.

My dear Davies:

Thank you for having let me read this letter again.

There is one thing that distresses me. The implication of Mr. Alward's letter is (or would seem to one who did not know the circumstances to be) that I had not shown my gratitude for all the generous things he did in promoting my candidacy. Surely he does not feel that. Is it not true that I appointed him to the office he now holds? that I did so with the greatest pleasure as gratifying his own personal wish, and that the office itself has afforded him an opportunity of showing his real quality and mettle to the people of his state in the performance of duties for which he is eminently qualified? And have I not tried, my dear Davies, in every possible way to show my warm and sincere appreciation and my loyal friendship both to you and to him? It distresses me to find any other implication even latent between the lines, and the inference left to be. drawn is that if I should not appoint him to the Federal Bench, it would be virtually an act of ingratitude on my part. I am sure he cannot soberly mean that, for it is so far from just.

It seems to me my clear duty to do in this case as in all others, the thing which commends itself to my judgment after the most careful consideration as the wisest and best thing, both for the interests of the Bench and the interests of the party.

Always, with real affection,

Faithfully yours,
WOODROW WILSON.

Hon. Joseph E. Davies,
Federal Trade Commission.

On one of the most critical days of the war, when Lloyd George was crying out in stentorian tones from across the sea that the war was now a race between Von Hindenburg and Wilson, a fine old Southern gentleman appeared at my office at the White House, dressed in an old frock coat and wearing a frayed but tolerably respectable high hat. He was the essence of refinement and culture and seemed to bring with him to the White House a breath of the old Southland from which he had come. In the most courteous way he addressed me, saying, "Mr. Secretary, I am an old friend of the President's father, Doctor Wilson, and I want to see Woodrow. I have not seen the boy since the old days in Georgia, and I have come all the way up here to shake him by the hand."

So many requests of a similar nature came to my desk during the critical days of the war and at a time when the President was heavily burdened with weighty responsibilities that I was reluctant to grant the old man's request and was about to turn him away with the usual excuse as to the crowded condition of the President's calendar, etc., when the old man said, "I know Woodrow will see me for his father and I were old friends." He then told me a story that the President had often repeated to me about his father. It seems that the old gentleman who was addressing me was on a hot summer's day many years ago sitting in front of a store in the business street of Augusta, Georgia, where the President's father was pastor of the Presbyterian Church, when he sighted the parson, in an old alpaca coat, seated in his buggy driving a well-groomed gray mare, and called out to him, "Doctor, your horse looks better groomed than yourself." "Yes," replied Doctor Wilson dryly as he drove on, "I take care of my horse; my congregation takes care of me."

I knew that if I repeated this story to the President it would be the open sesame for the old man. I excused myself and quickly made my way to the Cabinet Room where the President was holding a conference with the Cabinet members. After making my excuses to the Cabinet for my interruption, I whispered into the President's ear that there was an old man in my office who knew his father very well in the old days in Georgia and that he wanted an opportunity to shake hands with him. I then said to the President, "He told me the old horse story, the one that you have often told me. I am sure that he is an old friend of your father's." This struck the President's most tender spot, for many times during the years of our association the President had regaled me with delightful stories of his father and of the tender, solicitous way in which his father had cared for him. One of the passions of President Wilson's life was his love for and recollection of that old father, himself a man of remarkable force of character and intellect. Turning to the members of the Cabinet, the President said, "Gentlemen, will you please excuse me for a few minutes?" When I told the fine old chap that the President would see him at once he almost collapsed. Then, fixing himself up, rearranging his old frock coat, taking his high hat in hand, striking a statesmanlike posture, he walked into the President's office. No words passed between the two men for a few seconds. The old man looked silently at the President, with pride and admiration plainly visible in his eyes, and then walked slowly toward the President and took both his hands. Releasing them, he put one of his arms around the President's shoulder and looking straight into the President's eyes, he said, "Woodrow, my boy, your old father was a great friend of mine and he was mighty proud of you. He often told me that some day you would be a great man and that you might even become President." While the old man was addressing him the President stood like a big bashful schoolboy, and I could see that the old man touched the mystic chord of memories that were very sweet and dear to the President. Removing his arm from about the President's shoulder, the old man said, "Well, well, Woodrow, what shall I say to you?" Then, answering his own question, he said, "I shall say to you what your dear old father would have said were he here: 'Be a good boy, my son, and may God bless you and take care of you!'"

The President said nothing, but I could see that his

lips were quivering. For a moment he stood still, in his eyes the expression of one who remembers things of long ago and sacred. Then he seemed, as with an effort, to summon himself, and his thoughts back to the present, and I saw him walk slowly toward the door of the Cabinet Room, place one hand on the knob, with the other brush his handkerchief across his eyes. I saw him throw back his shoulders and grow erect again as he opened the door, and I heard him say in quiet, steady tones, "I hope you will pardon the interruption, gentlemen."

The popular cry of the unthinking against Woodrow Wilson in the early days of his administration was that he was a pacifist and unwilling to fight. The gentlemen who uttered these unkind criticisms were evidently unmindful of the moral courage he manifested in the various fights in which he had participated in his career, both at Princeton University, where he served as president, and as governor of New Jersey, in challenging the "old guard" of both parties to mortal combat for the measures of reform which he finally brought to enactment. They also forgot the moral courage which he displayed in fighting the tariff barons and in procuring the enactment of the Underwood tariff, and of the fine courage he manifested in decentralizing the financial control of the country and bringing about the Federal Reserve Act, which now has the whole-hearted approval of the business world in America and elsewhere, but which was resisted in the making by powerful interests.

I do not wish to make an invidious comparison between Woodrow Wilson and his predecessors in the White House, but if one will examine the political history of this country, he will find that very few Presidents had ever succeeded, because of the powerful interests they were compelled to attack, in finally putting upon the statute books any legislation that could control the moneyed interests of the country. The reform of the tariff and the currency had been the rocks upon which many administrations had met disaster.

Nearly every adviser about Woodrow Wilson, even those who had had experience in the capital of the nation, warned him that he might, after a long fight, succeed in reforming the tariff, but that his efforts would fail if he attempted to pass a bill that would establish currency reform. But the President allowed nothing to stand in the way of the establishment of the Federal Reserve system without which the financing of the greatest war in the history of the world would have been impossible. It was his courage and his persistency that provided the first uniform and harmonious system of banking which the United States has ever had.

If Woodrow Wilson had accomplished nothing more than the passage of this Federal Reserve Act, he would have been entitled to the gratitude of the nation. This Act supplied the country with an elastic currency controlled by the American people. Panics—the recurring phenomena of disaster which the Republican party could neither control nor explain—are now but a memory. Under the Republican system there was an average of one bank failure every twenty-one days for a period of nearly forty years. After the passage of the Federal Reserve system there were, in 1915, four bank failures; in 1916 and 1917, three bank failures; in 1918, one bank failure; and in 1919, no bank failures at all.

Woodrow Wilson is not a showy fighter, but he is a tenacious and a courageous one.

A little story came to me at the White House, illustrat-

ing alike the calmness and the fighting quality of Woodrow
Wilson.   The incident happened while he was a student
at the University of Virginia.   It appears that some of
the University boys went to a circus and had got into
a fight with the circus men and been sadly worsted.
They called a meeting at "wash hall," as they termed it.
Many of the boys made ringing speeches, denouncing the
brutality and unfairness of the circus people and there
was much excitement.   It was then moved that all the
boys present should proceed to the circus and give proper
battle, to vindicate the honour of the college.   Just before
the motion was put a slim, black-haired, solemn youth
arose from his seat in the rear of the hall, and walking up
the aisle, requested a hearing.   He stated that perhaps
he was being forward, because he was a "first-year"
man, in asking to be heard; that he felt that the action
of the circus men deserved the severest condemnation;
that it was a natural impulse to want to punish cowardly
acts and to "clean up" the show; but that it was lawless-
ness they were about to engage in; that it would bring
disgrace on the college, as well as on the state and the
Southland; more than this, many of the showmen would
be armed with clubs, knives, and pistols, and if the boys
did go, some of them might not come back alive and others
might be maimed or crippled for life.   He then paused,
but resuming, said, "However, if my views do not meet
with your approval; if you decide to go as a body, or if a
single man wants to go to fight, I shall ask to go with
him."

Was not his attitude in this incident characteristic of
his dealing with Germany?   He was patient with Germany
and stood unmoved under the bitterest criticism and
ridicule; but when he found that patience was no longer a

virtue, he went into the war in the most ruthless way and punished Germany for her attempt to control the high seas.

I recall my own antagonism to him in New Jersey when I was engaged, as now certain of his enemies are engaged, in attacking him, and I recall how my opposition abated and altogether disappeared by the recital by one of his friends to me one day of the controversy among the Princeton Trustees that arose over the now-famous Proctor gift. I was discussing the Princeton professor with this old friend one day and I said to him that I suspected that Wall Street interests were back of his candidacy for the governorship. My friend said, "Tumulty, you are wrong. There is no unwholesome interest or influence back of Wilson. I tell you he is a fine fellow and if he is elected governor, he will be a free man." He then cited the instance of the Princeton fight over the Proctor gift. It will be recalled that Mr. Proctor bequeathed to Princeton University a large sum of money, but attached certain conditions to the gift that had to do with the policy or internal control of the University. The gift was made at a time when Princeton was in sore need of funds. President Wilson, in a prolonged fight, bitterly waged by some who had been his close personal friends, persuaded the Board of Trustees to vote, by a narrow margin, for rejection of the gift on the grounds that a great educational institution could not afford to have its internal policies dictated by purchase on the part of a rich man. By his position he alienated from his leadership many of the wealthy, influential Princeton alumni, especially in the larger Eastern cities, but he stood like a rock on the principle that the educational policy of a college must be made by those authorized to make it and not changed at the bidding of wealthy benefactors. This was a convincing answer to my attack upon the Princeton professor.

This same moral courage was given free play on many an occasion during our intimacy. It was made manifest in the famous Panama Tolls fight, at a time when he was warned that a fight made to rectify mistakes in the matter of Panama tolls would destroy his political future.

He was always a fair fighter and a gentleman throughout every contest he engaged in. Many unkind and untrue things were said about Woodrow Wilson from the time he entered politics, but there is one charge that has never been made against him and that is the charge of untruthfulness or "hitting below the belt." No one in the country during his eight years at the White House ever charged him with making an untrue statement. No politician or statesman ever said that Wilson had broken a promise, though many have complained that he would not make promises.

In the matter of promises I never met a man who was so reluctant to give a promise, especially in the matter of bestowing office upon willing candidates. I have known him on many occasions to make up his mind for months in advance to appoint a certain man and yet he would not say so to his most intimate friends who urged it. Speaking to me one day about the matter of promises, he said, "The thing to do is to keep your mind open until you are bound to act. Then you have freedom of action to change your mind without being charged with bad faith."

One reason for the charge made against him of coldness and "political ingratitude" was that he steadfastly refused to barter public offices for political support. He is by instinct, as well as by conviction, utterly opposed to the "spoils system." He considers government the people's business to be conducted as such and not as a matter of personal exchange of political favours. Nor can those who failed to get from him what they fancied their political services earned, complain truthfully that they were deceived by him into supposing that he shared their own opinion of their deserts. Frequently they had explicit warning to the contrary. There was the case of Jim Smith and the New Jersey machine, for instance. When those gentlemen paid the president of Princeton University an unsolicited call to suggest that he be candidate for the Democratic nomination for the governorship of New Jersey, Mr. Wilson, after thanking them for the compliment, with disconcerting directness asked, "Gentlemen, why do you want me as the candidate?" They replied, because they believed he could be elected and they wanted a Democratic governor. He asked why they believed he could be elected, he who had never held any public office. They answered that the people of New Jersey would have confidence in him. "Precisely," said Mr. Wilson; "they will have confidence in me because they will believe that I am free of the political entanglements which have brought distress to New Jersey, because they are tired of political bargain and sale, because they want their government delivered back into their hands. They want a government pledged to nobody but themselves. Now, don't you see, gentlemen, that if I should consider your flattering suggestion, I must be what the people think I am. I must be free to consider nothing but their interests. There must be no strings tied to your proposal. I cannot consider it an obligation of returned personal favours to any individual. We must clearly understand that we are acting in the interest of the people of New

Jersey and in the interest of nobody else." If the self-constituted committee thought this merely handsome talk without specific meaning, they had only themselves to thank for their subsequent predicament. They found he meant exactly what he said.

There has never been a public man in America with a profounder faith in popular government, or a stronger conviction that the bane of free government is secret bargaining among those ambitious to trade public office for private benefits. Mr. Wilson could no more pay for political support from public offices than he could pay for it from the public treasury. He abhors all forms of political favoritism including nepotism. He not only would not appoint kinsmen to office; he would discountenance their appointment by others. He resisted the efforts of well-meaning friends to have his brother, Mr. Joseph R. Wilson, Jr., who had rendered a substantial service to the 1912 campaign by his effective work as a trained journalist, elected secretary of the United States Senate, saying that his brother in this position would inevitably be misunderstood, would be thought a spy on the Senate to report matters to the President. His son-in-law, Mr. Francis B. Sayre, is by profession a student of international law, a professor of the subject in Harvard University, and as such was employed by Colonel House on the research committee preparatory to the Paris Conference. Mr. Sayre assumed he was to go to Paris, but the President set his personal veto on this, saying that it would not do for the President's son-in-law to be on a list of those who were going abroad at the public expense. When Mr. Sayre asked if he could not go and pay his own expenses, the President replied, "No, because it would not be believed that you had really paid your own expenses." Mr. Sayre, respecting the President's views, did not press the claim.

If it has appeared that the President has sometimes "leaned backward" in these matters, it is because of his strong conviction that politicians have leaned too far forward in using public office for private rewards, a bad system toward which the President's attitude may be stated in Hamlet's impatient injunction to the players, "Oh, reform it altogether!"

My experiences with him, where one could witness the full play of the Scotch and Irish strains in him, came particularly in the matter of the numerous pardon cases and the applications for Executive Orders, placing this man or that woman under the classified civil service. The latter were only issued in rare instances and always over the protest of the Civil Service Commission. In many of these applications there was a great heartache or family tragedy back of them and to every one of them he gave the most sympathetic consideration.

I remember his remark to me one day when I was urging him to sign an Executive Order in behalf of a poor woman, the widow of an old soldier. After I had argued with him for a time he turned to me and said, "Every unfortunate person in distress seems to come to me for relief, but I must not let my sympathies get the best of me, it would not be right to do these things upon any basis of sympathy." Although I stood rebuked, the order was signed. It was a thing urged against him in the last campaign, that he held the record for the number of Executive Orders issued by him. His Scotch nature would also assert itself on many occasions. While I was living with the President at the White House one summer, on a night after dinner we engaged in the discussion of an article which appeared that month in one of the popular magazines of the country. In this article Woodrow Wilson was portrayed as a great intellectual machine. Turning to me, he said,"Tumulty, have you read that article? What do you think of it?" I said that I thought in many respects it was admirable. "I don't agree with you at all," he said. "It is no compliment to me to have it said that I am only a highly developed intellectual machine. Good God, there is more in me than that!" He then said, rather sadly, "Well, I want people to love me, but I suppose they never will." He then asked me this question, "Do you think I am cold and unfeeling?" I replied, "No, my dear Governor, I think you are one of the warmest hearted men I ever met."

And when I say this of Woodrow Wilson I mean it. I hope I have all of the generous tendencies of my race and that I know a great heart when I see its actions. I could not have been associated with him all these years, witnessing the great heart in action, without having full faith in what I now say. No man of all my acquaintance, with whom I have discussed life in all of its phases and tragedies, at least those tragedies that stalked in and out of the White House, was more responsive, more sympathetic, and more inclined to pity and help than Woodrow Wilson. His eyes would fill with tears at the tale of some unfortunate man or woman in distress. It was not a cheap kind of sympathy. It was quiet, sincere, but always from the heart. The President continued talking to me—and now he spoke as the canny Scot—"I am cold in a certain sense. Were I a judge and my own son should be convicted of murder, and I was the only judge privileged to pass judgment upon the case, I would do my duty even to the point of sentencing him to death. It would be a hard thing to do but it would be my solemn duty as a judge to do it, but I would do it, because the state cannot be maintained and its sovereignty vindicated or its integrity preserved unless the law is strictly enforced and without favour. It is the business of the judge to uphold it and he must do it to the point of every sacrifice. If he fails, justice fails, the state falls. That looks cold-blooded, doesn't it? But I would do it." Then his voice lowered and he said, "Then, after sentencing my own son to death, I would go out and die of a broken heart, for it would surely kill me."

That is one key to the character of the man that was revealed before my own eyes in the years of our intimacy.

It showed itself on many other occasions. It was his idea of the duty of the trustee, the judge, the guardian.

I remember a visit that two very warm friends from the Pacific Coast made to him, both of whom had worked night and day for his cause in the great state of the Golden West.

Their son had been convicted and was incarcerated in the Federal Prison. They had every personal reason for feeling that a mere appeal on their part on behalf of this son would be a winning one, for their friendship with the President was one of long standing and most affectionate in character. I can see him now, standing in the centre of the room, with the two old people grouped about him, shaking his head and saying, "I wish I could do it, but I must not allow personal consideration to influence me in the least. I know it is hard for you to believe that I will turn away from your request, but the only basis upon which you make it is our friendship. I would be doing an injustice to many a boy like yours who has similarly offended and for whom no one is able to speak or approach me in the intimate contact which is your privilege. Please do not think me cold-hearted, but I cannot do it."

I remember one of the last pardon cases we handled in the White House was that of an old man, charged with violating the banking laws and sentenced to imprisonment. I pleaded with the President to pardon the old man; the Attorney General had recommended it, and some of the warm-hearted members of the President's family had gone to him and sought to exert their influence in behalf of the old man. It seemed as if everything was moving smoothly and that the old man might be pardoned, until the family influence was brought to bear. It was the last pardon case I brought to his attention before the fall of the curtain on March fourth. I went to him, and said, "My dear Governor, I hope you will close your official career here by doing an act of mercy." He smiled at me and I thought I could see the prison gates open for the old man, but when I mentioned the name in the case, the President stiffened up, stopped smiling, and looking at me in the coldest way, said, "I will not pardon this man. Certain members of my family to whom I am deeply devoted, as you know, have sought to influence my judgment in this matter. They have no right to do it. I should be unworthy of my trust as President were I to permit family interference of any kind to affect my public actions, because very few people in the country can exert that kind of influence and it must not be tolerated." The case was closed; the pardon refused.

He often spoke to me in the frankest way of his personal appearance; how he looked and appeared and of the "old Scotch face," as he called it, which gave him the appearance of what Cæsar called a "lean and hungry look." Speaking at the annual banquet of the Motion Picture Board of Trade, he discussed his personal appearance in this way:

"I have sometimes been very much chagrined in seeing myself in a motion picture. I have wondered if I really was that kind of a 'guy.' The extraordinary rapidity with which I walked, for example, the instantaneous and apparently automatic nature of my motion, the way in which I produced uncommon grimaces, and altogether the extraordinary exhibition I made of myself sends me to bed very unhappy. And I often think to myself that, although all the world is a stage and men and women but actors upon it, after all, the external appearance of things are very superficial indeed."

He knew that his facial expression gave one the impression that he was a cold and canny Scot. In repose one would get that impression, but when that old Scotch face took on a winning smile it was most gracious and appealing. One of his favourite limericks was:

> For beauty I am not a star,
> There are others more handsome by far.
> But my face I don't mind it,
> For I am behind it,
> It's the people in front that I jar.

Behind the cold exterior and beneath the "gleam of the waters" there was a warm, generous heart. I have often thought of the character discussed by Israel Zangwill in his book "The Mantle of Elijah." These lines, in my opinion, draw a perfect picture of Woodrow Wilson as I knew him:

Speaking of Allegra's father Zangwill said:

"With him freedom was no nebulous figure, aureoled with shining rhetoric, blowing her own trumpet, but Free Trade, Free Speech, Free Education. He did not rail against the Church as the enemy, but he did not count on it as a friend.   His Millennium was earthly, human; his philosophy sunny, untroubled by Dantesque depths or shadows; his campaign unmartial, constitutional, a frank focussing of the new forces emergent from the slow dissolution of Feudalism and the rapid growth of a modern world.   Towards such a man the House of Commons had an uneasy hostility.   He did not play the game.   Whig and Tory, yellow and blue, the immemorial shuffling of Cabinet cards, the tricks and honours—he seemed to live outside them all.   He was no clubman in 'The best club in England.'   He did not debate for argument's sake or to upset Ministers.   He was not bounded by the walls of the Chamber nor ruler from the Speaker's chair; the House was resentfully conscious it had no final word over his reputation or his influence.   He stood for something outside it, something outside himself, something large, vague, turbulent, untried, unplumbed, unknown—the People."

A little incident illustrating the warmth of the heart of Woodrow Wilson and the sympathetic way he manifested his feeling came to me in a letter received at the White House in 1920 from a Red Cross nurse, who was stationed at the Red Cross Base Hospital at Neuilly, France.   An excerpt from it follows:

I might interest you to recite an incident within my own personal knowledge that proves the depths of his sympathy—his sincerity.   I was one of the unit of Red Cross Workers who went to France to help our soldiers blinded in battle.   I was at the time of this incident stationed at the Red Cross Base Hospital No. 1 at Neuilly.   After a a visit of the President and Mrs. Wilson to the hospital, one of my charges, a totally blind private to whom Mr. Wilson had spoken, said to me: "Miss Farrell, I guess the President must be very tired."   I said, "Why do you think that, Walter?"   "Well, because," replied the soldier, "he laughed and joked with all the other fellows but was so quiet when he talked with me and just said, 'Honourable wound, my boy,' so low I could hardly hear him. But say," continued Walter, "look at my hand please and see if it is all there, will you? The President sure has some hand and he used it when he shook hands, I'll say."

The fact was, Walter was the first blind soldier the President had met in France and knowing from experience the appeal the blind make to our emotions, I knew the President was so touched that he was overcome and couldn't joke further—he was scarcely able to manage the one remark and could not trust himself to venture another. 'Twas with tears in his eyes and a choking voice that he managed the one. Both he and Mrs. Wilson wept in that blind ward.

As a political fighter, he was gallant and square. No one ever heard him call an opponent a name or knew him unworthily to take advantage of an opponent.

Illustrative of the magnanimous attitude of the President toward his political enemies was the striking incident that occurred a few weeks before the close of the last Presidential campaign, 1920. Early one afternoon two Democratic friends called upon me at the Executive offices and informed me that they could procure certain documents that would go a long way toward discrediting the Republican campaign and that they could be procured for a money consideration. They explained the character of the documents to me and left it to me to say what I considered a fair price for them. They explained the serious nature of these documents, and it was certainly a delicate situation for me to handle and embarrassed me greatly. I was reluctant to offend these gentlemen, and yet I was certain from what they said that the documents, as they explained them to me, even though they might discredit the Republican campaign, were not of a character that any party of decent men ought to have anything to do with. When the gentlemen told me the name of the person who claimed to have these damaging papers in his possession, I at once recalled that we had in the files of the White House certain letters that could be used to discredit this very man who claimed to possess these incriminating documents. I thought it wise, therefore, to listen politely to these gentlemen until I could get a chance to confer with the President. I did this at once.

At this time the President was lying ill in his sick room at the White House. The nurse raised him up in the bed and I explained the whole situation to him, saying to him that it was my opinion that the Democratic party ought not to have anything to do with such a matter and that I thought we should at once apprise the Republican managers of the plan that was afoot to discredit by these unfair means the Republican candidate and campaign. When I told the President of the character of these documents that had been offered to me he was filled with indignation and said, "If we can't win this fight by fair means, we will not attempt to win it by unfair means. You have my authority to use whatever files we have against this party who would seek unfairly to attack the Republican nominee and you must at once notify the Republican managers of the plan proposed and explain the whole situation to them. Say to the Attorney General that he must place at the disposal of Mr. Harding and his friends every officer he has, if necessary, to disclose and overcome this plot. I am sure that Governor Cox will agree with me that this is the right and decent thing to do."

Acting upon the President's suggestion, I at once called upon a certain Republican senator from the West, now a member of President Harding's Cabinet, and told him of the proposed plot that was afoot to discredit the Republican campaign. I told him I was acting upon the express authority of the President. He expressed his high appreciation of the information I had brought him and informed me that he would place the matter in our hands with the utmost confidence in us to handle it honourably.

It ought to be said here that upon investigation, personally made by myself, I found that there was nothing in this whole matter that in the slightest degree reflected upon the honour or the integrity or high standing of President Harding.

One of the things for which President Wilson was unduly censured shortly after he took office was the recognition he gave to his political enemies in the Democratic party. The old-line politicians who had supported him in 1912 could not understand why the loaves and fishes were dealt out to these unworthy ones. Protests were made to the President by some of his close personal friends, but he took the position that as the leader of the party he was not going to cause resentment and antagonisms by seeming to classify Democrats; that as leader of his party he had to recognize all factions, and there quickly followed appointments of Clark men, Underwood men, Harmon men, all over the country. A case in point illustrates the bigness of the President in these matters—that of George Fred Williams as Minister to Greece. In the campaign of 1912 Mr. Williams had travelled up and down the state of Massachusetts making the bitterest sort of attacks upon Woodrow Wilson. I remember how I protested against this appointment. The President's only reply was that George Fred Williams was an eccentric fellow, but that he believed he was thoroughly honest. "I have no fault to find, Tumulty, with the men who disagree with me and I ought not to penalize them when they give expression to what they believe are honest opinions."

I have never seen him manifest any bitterness or resentment toward even his bitterest, most implacable enemies. Even toward William Randolph Hearst, whose papers throughout the country have been his most unrelenting foes, he never gave expression to any ill feeling or chagrin at the unfair attacks that were made upon him. I remember a little incident that shows the trend of his feelings in this regard, that occurred when we were discussing the critical Mexican situation. At this time the Hearst papers were engaged in a sensational propaganda in behalf of intervention in Mexico. The President said to me, "I heard of a delightful remark that that fine old lady, Mrs. Phoebe Hearst, made with reference to what she called her 'big boy Willie.' You know," he continued, "Mrs. Hearst does not favour intervention in Mexico and it was reported to me that she chided her son for his flaming headlines urging intervention, and told him that unless he behaved better she would have to take him over her knee and spank him."

The President has one great failing, inherent in the very character of the man himself, and this is his inborn, innate modesty—his unwillingness to dramatize the part he played in the great events of the war, so that the plain people of the country could see him and better understand him. There is no man living to-day who has a greater power of personal appeal or who is a greater master in the art of presenting ideals, facts, and arguments than Woodrow Wilson. As his secretary for nearly eleven years, I was often vexed because he did not, to use a newspaper phrase, "play up" better, but he was always averse to doing anything that seemed artificially contrived to win applause. Under my own eyes, seated in the White House offices, I have witnessed many a great story walk in and out but the President always admonished us that such things must not be pictured or capitalized in any way for political purposes; and thus every attempt we made to dramatize him, as Colonel Roosevelt's friends had played him up, was immediately placed under the Presidential embargo.

His unwillingness to allow us in the White House to "play him up" as the leading actor in this or that movement was illustrated in the following way: On July 1, 1919, a cable reached the White House from His Holiness, Pope Benedict, expressing the appreciation of His Holiness for the magnificent way in which the President had presented to the Peace Conference the demands of the Catholic Church regarding Catholic missions, and conveying to the President his thanks for the manner in which the President had supported those demands. The cable came at a time when certain leaders of my own church, the Roman Catholic Church, were criticizing and opposing the President for what they thought was his anti-Catholic attitude. I tried to induce the President to allow me to give publicity to the Pope's cable, but he was firm in his refusal. The cable from the Pope and the President's reply are as follows:

Rome, The Vatican.
1 July, 1919.

To His Excellency,
   Doctor Woodrow Wilson,
      President of the United States.
Excellency:

Monsignor Carretti, upon his return from Paris, hastened to inform us with what spirit of moderation Your Excellency examined the demands regarding the Catholic Missions which we presented to the Peace Conference, and with what zeal Your Excellency subsequently supported these demands. We desire to express to you our sincere gratitude and at the same time we urge Your Excellency to be good enough to employ your great influence, also, in order to prevent the action, which according to the Peace Treaty with Germany it is desired to bring against the Kaiser and the highly placed German commanders. This action could only render more bitter national hatred and postpone for a long time that pacification of souls for which all nations long. Furthermore, this trial, if the rules of justice are to be observed, would meet insurmountable difficulties as may be seen from the attached article from the *Osservatore Romano*, which deals exclusively with the trial of the Kaiser, the newspaper reserving right to treat in another article the question of the trial of the generals.

It pleases us to take advantage of this new occasion to renew to Your Excellency the wishes which we entertain for your prosperity and that of your family, as well as for the happiness of the inhabitants of the Confederation of the United States.

(signed) BENEDICTUS PP. XV.

The White House,
Washington, D. C.
15 August, 1919.

YOUR HOLINESS:

I have had the pleasure of receiving at the hands of Monsignor Cossio the recent letter you were kind enough to write me, which I now beg to acknowledge with sincere appreciation. Let me assure you that it was with the greatest pleasure that I lent my influence to safeguarding the missionary interests to which you so graciously refer, and I am happy to say that my colleagues in the Conference were all of the same mind in this wish to throw absolute safeguards around such missions and to keep them within the influences under which they had hitherto been conducted.

I have read with the gravest interest your suggestion about the treatment which should be accorded the ex-Kaiser of Germany and the military officers of high rank who were associated with him in the war, and beg to say that I realize the force of the considerations which you urge. I am obliged to you for setting them so clearly, and shall hope to keep them in mind in the difficult months to come.

With much respect and sincere good wishes for your welfare,

Respectfully and sincerely yours,
(signed) WOODROW WILSON.

His Holiness,
Pope Benedict XV.

TO HIS EXCELLENCY
DOCTOR WOODROW WILSON
PRESIDENT OF THE UNITED STATES.

Excellency,

Monsignor Cerretti, upon his return from Paris, hastened to inform Us with what spirit of moderation Your Excellency examined the demands regarding the Catholic Missions which We presented to the Peace Conference, and with what zeal Your Excellency subsequently supported these demands. We desire to express to you Our sincere gratitude and at the same time We urge Your Excellency to be good enough to employ your great influence, also, in order to prevent the action, which according to the Peace Treaty with Germany, it is desired to bring against the Kaiser and the highly placed German commanders. This action could only render more bitter national hatred and perpetuate for a long time that pacification of souls for which all nations long.

Furthermore, this trial, if the rules of justice are to be observed, would meet insurmountable difficulties as may be seen from the attached article from the Osservatore Romano, which deals exclusively with the trial of the Kaiser, the newspaper reserving right to treat is another article the question of the trial of the generals.

It pleases Us to take advantage of this new occasion to renew to Your Excellency the wishes which We entertain for your prosperity and that of your family, as well as for the happiness of the inhabitants of the Confederation of the United States.

Rome, The Vatican, 1 July, 1919.
(signed) BENEDICTUS PP. XV

White House,
15 August, 1919

Your Holiness:

I have had the pleasure of receiving at the hands of Monsignor Cerretti the recent letter you were kind enough to write me, which I now beg to acknowledge with sincere appreciation. Let me assure you that it was with the greatest pleasure that I lent my influence to safeguarding the missionary interests to which you so graciously refer, and I am happy to say that my colleagues in the Conference were all of the same mind in their wish to throw absolute safeguards around such missions and to keep them within the influences under which they had hitherto been conducted.

I have read with the gravest interest your suggestion about the mil-treatment which should be accorded the ex-Kaiser of Germany and the military officers of high rank who were associated with him in the war, and beg to say that I realize the force of the considerations which you urge. I am obliged to you for setting them so clearly, and shall hope to keep them in mind in the difficult months to come.

With much respect and sincere good wishes for your welfare,

Respectfully and sincerely yours,

Woodrow Wilson

His Holiness,
Pope Benedict XV.

Correspondence with the Pope

There was something too fine in his nature for the dramatics and the posturings of the political game, as it is usually played. He is a very shy man, too sincere to pose, too modest to make advances. He craves the love of his fellow-men with all his heart and soul. People see only his dignity, his reserve, but they cannot see his big heart yearning for the love of his fellow-men. Out of that loving heart of his has come the passion which controlled his whole public career—the passion for justice, for fair dealing, and democracy.

Never during the critical days of the war, when requests of all kinds poured in upon him for interviews of various sorts, did he lose his good-nature. Nor did he show that he was disturbed when various requests came from this or that man who claimed to have discovered some scientific means of ending the war.

The following letter to his old friend, Mr. Thomas D. Jones of Chicago, is characteristic of his feeling toward those who claimed to have made such a scientific discovery:

> The White House, Washington,
> 25 July 1917.

MY DEAR FRIEND:

It was generous of you to see Mr. Kenney and test his ideas. I hope you derived some amusement from it at least.

I am afraid I have grown soft-hearted and credulous in these latter days, credulous in respect to the scientific possibility of almost any marvel and soft-hearted because of the many evidences of simple-hearted purpose this war has revealed to me.

With warmest regard,

> Cordially and faithfully yours,
> (signed) WOODROW WILSON.

Nor did the little things of life escape him, as is shown by the following letter to Attorney General Gregory:

The White House, Washington,
1 October, 1918.

MY DEAR GREGORY:

The enclosed letter from his wife was handed to me this morning by a rather pitiful old German whom I see occasionally looking after the flowers around the club house at the Virginia Golf Course. I must say it appeals to me, and I am sending it to you to ask if there is any legitimate way in which the poor old fellow could be released from his present restrictions.

In haste,

Faithfully yours,
(signed) WOODROW WILSON.

I recall a day when he sat at his typewriter in the White House, preparing the speech he was to deliver at Hodgensville, Kentucky, in connection with the formal acceptance of the Lincoln Memorial, built over the log cabin birthplace of Lincoln. When he completed this speech, which I consider one of his most notable public addresses—perhaps in literary form, his best—he turned to me and asked me if I had any comment to make upon it. I read it very carefully. I then said to him, "Governor, there are certain lines in it that might be called a self-revelation of Woodrow Wilson." The lines that I had in mind were:

I have read many biographies of Lincoln; I have sought out with the greatest interest the many intimate stories that are told of him, the narratives of near-by friends, the sketches at close quarters, in which those who had the privilege of being associated with him have tried to depict for us the very man himself "in his habit as he lived"; but I have nowhere found a real intimate of Lincoln. I nowhere get the impression in my narrative or reminiscence that the writer had in fact penetrated to the heart of his mystery, or that any man could penetrate to the heart of it. That brooding spirit had no real familiars. I get the impression that it never spoke out in complete self-revelation, and that it could not reveal itself complete to any one. It was a very lonely spirit that looked out from underneath

THE WHITE HOUSE,
WASHINGTON,

1 October, 1918.

My dear Gregory:

The enclosed letter from his wife was handed to
me this morning by a rather pitiful old German whom
I see occasionally looking after the flowers around
the club house at the Virginia Golf Course.   I must
say it appeals to me, and I am sending it to you to
ask if there is any legitimate way in which the poor
old fellow could be released from his present restrictions.

In haste,

Faithfully yours,

WOODROW WILSON.

Hon. Thomas W. Gregory,
The Attorney General.

An evidence of the tender-heartedness which Mr. Tumulty claims for the President those shaggy brows, and comprehended men without fully communing with them, as if, in spite of all its genial efforts at comradeship, it dwelt apart, saw its visions of duty where no man looked on. There is a very holy and very terrible isolation for the conscience of every man who seeks to read the destiny in the affairs for others as well as for himself, for a nation as well as for individuals. That privacy no man can intrude upon. That lonely search of the spirit for the right perhaps no man can assist.

To Woodrow Wilson the business of government was a solemn thing, to which he gave every ounce of his energy and his great intellectual power. No President in the whole history of America ever carried weightier responsibilities than he. Night and day, with uncomplaining patience, he was at his post of duty, attending strictly to the pressing needs of the nation, punctiliously meeting every engagement, great or small. Indeed, no man that I ever met was more careless about himself or thought less of vacations for the purpose of rest and recuperation.

There are three interesting maps which show the mileage covered by Presidents Roosevelt, Taft, and Wilson. These maps show the states traversed by each of the Presidents. Great black smudges show the trail covered by President Roosevelt, which included every state in the Union, and equally large black marks show the territory covered by President Taft, but only a thin line shows the peregrinations and wanderings of President Wilson. The dynamic, forceful personality of Mr. Roosevelt, which radiated energy, charm, and good-nature, and the big, vigorous, lovable personality of Mr. Taft, put the staid, simple, modest, retiring personality of the New Jersey President, Mr. Wilson, at a tremendous disadvantage. Into the atmosphere created by these winning personalities of Mr. Roosevelt and Mr. Taft the personality of Mr. Wilson did not easily fit, and he realized it, when he said to me one day, "Tumulty, you must realize that I am not built for the dramatic things of politics. I do not want to be displayed before the public, and if I tried it, I should do it badly."

Without attempting to belittle the great achievements of former Presidents of the United States, particularly Roosevelt, it is only fair to say that, comparing the situations which confronted them with those that met President Wilson from the very beginning of his incumbency, their jobs were small. As a genial Irishman once said to me, "Hell broke loose when Wilson took hold." Every unusual thing, every extraordinary thing, seemed to break and break against us. From the happening of the Dayton flood, which occurred in the early days of the Wilson Administration, down to the moment when he laid down the reins of office, it seemed as if the world in which we lived was at the point of revolution. Unusual, unprecedented, and remarkable things began to happen, things that required all the patience, indomitable courage, and tenacity of the President to hold them steady. The Mexican situation, left on our door-step, was one of the great burdens that he carried during his administration. Then came the fight for the revision of the tariff, the establishment of the Federal Reserve System, all items that constituted the great programme of domestic reform which emanated from the brain of Woodrow Wilson, and then in the midst of it all came the European war, the necessity for neutrality, the criticism which was heaped upon the President for every unusual happening which his critics seemed to think called for intervention of the United States in this great cataclysm. It was not a time for the camaraderie and good-fellowship that had characterized the good old days in which Mr. Roosevelt served as President.

And yet no man was less exclusive in dealing with the members of the Senate and House. In preparing the Federal Reserve Act in collaboration with Senator Glass, he was constantly in touch with the members of the Senate Banking and Currency Committee, in an endeavour to make clear the road for the passage of this important piece of constructive legislation. Constant demands were made upon his time and he gave of his energy and of the small reserve of strength that he had uncomplainingly and without a protest. No rest, no recreation, no vacation intervened. Every measure that he sought to press to enactment was the challenge to a great fight, as, for instance, the tariff, the currency, the rural credits, and the Panama tolls acts.

I have often been asked whether anger or passion ever showed itself in the President, and I am reminded of a little incident that happened at the White House during one of those conferences with the newspaper men, which, before the days of the war, and for a long time afterward, took place in the Executive offices. At the time of this particular conference, the President's first wife lay seriously ill at the White House, and stories were carried in the various newspapers exaggerating the nature of her illness, some of them going so far as to say she was suffering from this or from that disease. At the very time these stories were appearing in the newspapers there were also articles that his daughter, Margaret, was engaged to marry this man or that man. The President came to the newspaper men's conference this morning fighting mad. It was plain that something serious was afoot. Taking hold of the back of the chair, as if to strengthen himself for what he had to say, he looked squarely at the newspaper men and said, "I hope that you gentlemen will pardon me for a personal word this morning. I have read the stories that have appeared in certain newspapers of the country, containing outrageous statements about the illness of my wife and the marriage of my daughter. I realize that as President of the United States you have a perfect right to say anything you damn please about me, for I am a man and I can defend myself. I know that while I am President it will be my portion to receive all kinds of unfair criticism, and I would be a poor sport if I could not stand up under it; but there are some things, gentlemen, that I will not tolerate. You must let my family alone, for they are not public property. I acquit every man in this room of responsibility for these stories. I know that you have had nothing to do with them; but you have feelings and I have feelings, even though I am President. My daughter has no brother to defend her, but she has me, and I want to say to you that if these stories ever appear again I will leave the White House and thrash the man who dares to utter them."

A little letter came to my notice in which the President replies to an old friend in Massachusetts who had asked him to attempt to interpret himself:

My dear Friend:
  You have placed an impossible task upon me—that of interpreting myself to you. All I can say in answer to your inquiry is that I have a sincere desire to serve, to be of some little assistance in improving the condition of the average man, to lift him up, and to make his life more tolerable, agreeable, and comfortable. In doing this I try hard to purge my heart of selfish motives. It will only be known when I am dead whether or not I have succeeded.

Sincerely your friend,
WOODROW WILSON.

CHAPTER XLV

DURING the winter of 1919-1920 President Wilson was the target of vicious assaults. Mrs. Wilson and Admiral Grayson with difficulty curbed his eagerness to take a leading hand in the fight over the Peace Treaty in the Senate, and to organize the Democratic party on a fighting basis. It was not until after the Chicago Convention had nominated Mr. Harding and enunciated a platform repudiating the solemn obligations of the United States to the rest of the world that the President broke his silence of many months. Because he had something he wanted to say to the country he asked me to send for Louis Seibold, a trusted friend and an experienced reporter, then connected with the New York *World*. When Mr. Seibold arrived in Washington on the Tuesday following Mr. Harding's nomination, the President talked unreservedly and at length with him, discussed the Republican Convention, characterized its platform as "the apotheosis of reaction," and declared that "it should have quoted Bismarck and Bernhardi rather than Washington and Lincoln." During the two days of Mr. Seibold's visit to the White House he had abundant opportunity to observe the President's condition of health which had been cruelly misrepresented by hostile newspapers. Mr. Seibold found him much more vigorous physically than the public had been given to understand and mentally as alert and aggressive as he had been before his illness. Mr. Seibold's article, which by the way was regarded as a journalistic classic and for which Columbia University awarded the author the Pulitzer prize for the best example of newspaper reporting of the year, exposed the absurd rumours about the President's condition and furnished complete evidence of his determination to fight for the principles to establish which he had struggled so valiantly and sacrificed so much.

As the days of the San Francisco Convention approached those of us who were intimately associated with the President at the White House were warned by him that in the Convention fight soon to take place we must play no favourites; that the Convention must be, so far as the White House was concerned, a free field and no favour, and that our attitude of "hands off" and strict neutrality must be maintained. Some weeks before the Convention met the President conferred with me regarding the nominations, and admonished me that the White House must keep hands off, saying that it had always been charged in the past that every administration sought to use its influence in the organization of the party to throw the nomination this way or that. Speaking to me of the matter, he said, "We must make it clear to everyone who consults us that our attitude is to be impartial in fact as well as in spirit. Other Presidents have sought to influence the naming of their successors. Their efforts have frequently brought about scandals and factional disputes that have split the party. This must not happen with us. We must not by any act seek to give the impression that we favour this or that man."

This attitude was in no way an evidence of the Presi-

dent's indifference to the nominee of the Convention,
or to what might happen at San Francisco. He was
passionately anxious that his party's standard bearer
should win at the election if for no other reason than to
see his own policies continued and the League of Nations
vindicated.

There was another and personal reason why he insisted
that no White House interference should be brought
into play for any particular nominee. His son-in-law,
Mr. William G. McAdoo, was highly thought of in connection with the nomination, and therefore the President
felt that he must be more than ordinarily strict in insisting
that we keep hands off, for anything that savoured of
nepotism was distasteful to him and, therefore, he "leaned
backward" in his efforts to maintain a neutral position
in the Presidential contest and to take no part directly
or indirectly that might seem to give aid and comfort
to the friends of his son-in-law. While Mr. McAdoo's
political enemies were busily engaged in opposing him
on the ground of his relationship to the President, as a
matter of fact, the President was making every effort
to disassociate himself and his administration from the
talk that was spreading in favour of McAdoo's candidacy.
While every effort was being made by Mr. McAdoo's
enemies to give the impression that the Federal machine
was being used to advance his candidacy, the President
was engaged wholly in ignoring Mr. McAdoo's candidacy.

Every family visit which Mr. McAdoo and his wife, the
President's daughter, paid the White House, was distorted in the newspaper reports carried to the country
into long and serious conferences between the President
and his son-in-law with reference to Mr. McAdoo's

THE SAN FRANCISCO CONVENTION 495

candidacy. I know from my own knowledge that the matter of the nomination was never discussed between the President and Mr. McAdoo. And Mr. McAdoo's real friends knew this and were greatly irritated at what they thought was the gross indifference on the part of the President to the political fortunes of his own son-in-law. So meticulously careful was the President that no one should be of the opinion that he was attempting to influence things in Mr. McAdoo's behalf, that there was never a discussion even between the President and myself regarding Mr. McAdoo's candidacy, although we had canvassed the availability of other Democratic candidates, as well as the availability of the Republican candidates.

I had often been asked what the President's attitude would be toward Mr. McAdoo's candidacy were he free to take part in the campaign. My only answer to these inquiries was that the President had a deep affection and an admiration for Mr. McAdoo as a great executive that grew stronger with each day's contact with him. He felt that Mr. McAdoo's sympathies, like his own, were on the side of the average man; and that Mr. McAdoo was a man with a high sense of public service.

And while the President kept silent with reference to Mr. McAdoo, the basis of his attitude was his conviction that to use his influence to advance the cause of his son-in-law was, in his opinion, an improper use of a public trust.

That he was strictly impartial in the matter of Presidential candidates was shown when Mr. Palmer, the Attorney General, requested me to convey a message to the President with reference to his [Palmer's] candidacy for the nomination, saying that he would be a candidate and would so announce it publicly if the President had no

objection; or that he would resign from the Cabinet if
the announcement would embarrass the President in any
way, and that he would support any man the President
saw fit to approve for this great office.

I conveyed this message to the President and he requested me to notify Mr. Palmer that he was free to do
as he pleased, that he had no personal choice and that the
Convention must be left entirely free to act as it thought
proper and right and that he would gladly support the
nominee of the Convention.

Mr. Homer S. Cummings, the permanent chairman
of the Convention, Senator Glass of Virginia, and Mr.
Colby, Secretary of State, called upon the President at
the White House previous to taking the train for San
Francisco to inquire if the President had any message
for the Convention or suggestion in the matter of candidates or platforms. He informed them that he had no
message to convey or suggestions to offer.

Thus, to the end, he maintained this attitude of neutrality. He never varied from this position from the opening
of the Convention to·its conclusion. There was no direct
wire between the White House and the San Francisco
Convention, although there were frequent long-distance
telephone calls from Colby, Cummings, and others to
me; never once did the President talk to any one at the
Convention. At each critical stage of the Convention
messages would come from someone, urging the President to say something, or send some message that would
break the deadlock, but no reply was forthcoming. He
remained silent.

There came a time when it looked as if things at the
Convention had reached an impasse and that only the
strong hand of the President could break the deadlock.

THE WHITE HOUSE
WASHINGTON

26 September 1920.

My dear Governor:

I think I have found a suitable way to begin our attack if you care to take part in this campaign. The whole country is filled with the poison spread by Lodge and his group and it has to do principally with the attacks made upon you for failing to commit anyone about possible changes in the Treaty and your reluctance toward suggesting to your associates on the other side changes of any kind.

George Creel and I have examined the cables that passed between you and Mr. Taft and we have prepared a statement which is attached to this letter. This statement, with the Taft cables will be a knockout, (I know that Mr. Taft is already preparing a book on the Treaty which will carry these cables) and will clear the air and show how contemptible our enemies have been in circulating stories. We have carefully gone over the Covenant and find that nearly every change suggested by Mr. Taft was made and in some cases you went further than he asked.

George Creel is of the opinion that the statement should come from the white House.

Sincerely,

[signature]

Dear Humily:

I have read your letter of September twenty-sixth with a sincere effort to keep an open mind about the suggestions you make, but I must say that it has not changed my mind at all. No answer to Harding of any kind will proceed from the White House with my consent.

It pleases me very much that you and Creel are in collaboration on material out of which smashing answers can be made, and I beg that you will press those materials on the attention of the Speakers' Bureau of the National Committee. It is their clear duty to supply those materials in turn to the speakers of the campaign. If they will not, I am sorry to say I know of no other course that we can pursue.

The President.

C.L.S.

An inside view of the Cox campaign

I was informed by long-distance telephone that the slightest intimation from the President would be all that was necessary to break the deadlock and that the Convention would nominate any one he designated.

I conveyed this information to the President. He shook his head. This told me that he would not act upon my suggestion and would in no way interfere with the Convention. To the end he steered clear of playing the part of dictator in the matter of the nomination. That he took advantage of every occasion to show that he was playing an impartial hand is shown by the documents which follow. The Associated Press had carried a story to the effect that Senator Glass had notified certain delegates that Governor Cox was persona non grata to the President. When Governor Cox's friends got me on the long-distance telephone and asked me if there was any foundation for such a story and after Governor Cox himself had talked with me over the 'phone from Columbus, I addressed the following note to the President:

4 July, 1920.

DEAR GOVERNOR:
Simply for your information:
Governor Cox just telephoned me from Columbus. He felt greatly aggrieved at the statement which it is claimed Glass gave out last night, and which he says prevented his nomination. He says that Glass made the statement that the President had said that "Governor Cox would not be acceptable to the Administration."
He says he has been a loyal supporter of the Administration and has asked no favours of it. He also says that Mr. Bryan has been attacking him in the most relentless way and that Mr. Bryan's antagonism toward him became particularly aggravated since the Jackson Day dinner, when the Governor went out of his way to disagree with Mr. Bryan in the matter of the Lodge reservations.
He thinks, whether he himself is nominated or not, this action

of Glass's has hurt the Democratic chances in Ohio. He says he does not ask for any statement from the Administration, but he would leave it to the President's sense of justice whether or not he has been treated in fairness.

Sincerely,

TUMULTY.

The President read my note and immediately authorized me to issue the following statement:

The White House, Washington,
4 July, 1920.

When a report was brought to Secretary Tumulty's attention of rumours being circulated in San Francisco that the President had expressed an opinion with reference to a particular candidate, he made the following statement:

"This is news to me. I had discussed all phases of this convention with the President and had been in intimate touch with him during its continuance, and I am positive that he has not expressed an opinion to any one with reference to a particular candidate for the Presidency. It has always been his policy to refrain from taking any stand that might be construed as dictation."

The proceedings of the Convention finally resulted in the nomination of Governor Cox. The President expressed his great pleasure at the nomination for Governor Cox had long been a devoted friend and admirer of his, and he was certain that he would not desert him on the issue so close to his heart—the League of Nations.

When Governor Cox visited the White House and conferred with the President, the Governor assured the President that he intended to stand by him. The President showed deep emotion and expressed his appreciation to Governor Cox. Governor Cox afterward told me that no experience of his life had ever touched him so deeply as that through which he had just passed at the White

House. He spoke of the modesty of the President, his simplicity and the great spiritual purpose that lay back of his advocacy of the League of Nations. Turning to me, he said, "No man could talk to President Wilson about the League of Nations and not become a crusader in its behalf." Governor Cox may have entered the White House that day as a politician. He left it as a crusader, ready to fight for the cause.

As the campaign progressed we attempted to induce the President to issue weekly statements from the White House, but after long consideration he concluded that in view of the Republican strategy of trying to make him personally, instead of Governor Cox and the League of Nations, the issue, it would be better tactics for him to remain silent. He broke his silence only once, a week before the election, in a message to the people insisting upon the League of Nations as the paramount issue of the campaign.

It was really touching when one conferred with him to find him so hopeful of the result. Time and time again he would turn to me and say, "I do not care what Republican propaganda may seek to do. I am sure that the hearts of the people are right on this great issue and that we can confidently look forward to triumph."

I did not share his enthusiasm, and yet I did not feel like sending reports to him that were in the least touched with pessimism because of the effect they might have upon his feelings.

Then came the news of Governor Cox's defeat and with it the news of the defeat of the solemn referendum on the League of Nations.

The loneliest place in the country on election night is the White House Office, especially when the tide of opinion throughout the country is running strongly against you. I have noticed the difference in the atmosphere of the place and in the crowds that come to congratulate and to rejoice when you are winning and the few loyal ones that remain with you throughout the night of defeat. It takes a stout heart to withstand the atmosphere of the White House on election night.

The first reports from the country were overwhelming, and there was no spot in the country where we could look for hope and consolation.   In the early hours of the evening I sent whatever few optimistic reports I could get to the President, so that at least he would not feel the full weight of the blow on election night.   His intimate friends had told me that they feared the effect of defeat upon his health; but these fears were groundless and never disturbed me in the least, for I had been with him in many a fight and I was sure that while he would feel the defeat deeply and that it would go to his heart, its effect would only be temporary.

My feeling in this regard was justified for in my talk with him the day after the election no bitterness was evident.   He said, "They have disgraced us in the eyes of the world.   The people of America have repudiated a fruitful leadership for a barren independence.   Of course, I am disappointed by the results of the election for I felt sure that a great programme that sought to bring peace to the world would arouse American idealism, and that the Nation's support would be given to it. It is a difficult thing, however, to lead a nation so variously constituted as ours quickly to accept a programme such as the League of Nations.   The enemies of this enterprise cleverly aroused every racial passion and prejudice, and by poisonous propaganda made it appear that the

League of Nations was a great Juggernaut which was intended to crush and destroy instead of saving and bringing peace to the world. The people will have to learn now by bitter experience just what they have lost. There will, of course, be a depression in business for the isolation which America covets will mean a loss of prestige which always in the end means a loss of business. The people will soon witness the tragedy of disappointment and then they will turn upon those who made that disappointment possible."

When I intimated to him that the Cox defeat might in the long run prove a blessing, he rebuked me at once by saying: "I am not thinking of the partisan side of this thing. It is the country and its future that I am thinking about. We had a chance to gain the leadership of the world. We have lost it, and soon we will be witnessing the tragedy of it all."

After this statement to me with reference to the result of the election, he read to me a letter from his old friend, John Sharp Williams, United States senator from Mississippi, a letter which did much to bolster and hearten him on this, one of the most trying days of his life in the White House. The letter follows:

DEAR MR. PRESIDENT:

God didn't create the world in one act. I never expected that we would win in the United States the first battle in the campaign for a league of nations to keep the peace of the world. Our people were too "set" by our past history and by the *apparent* voice of the Fathers in an opposite course, a course of isolation. This course was hitherto the best for accomplishing the very purpose we must now accomplish by a seemingly contrary course. We must now begin the war in earnest. We will win it. Never fear, the stars in their courses are fighting with us. The League is on its feet, learning to walk, Senate coteries willy-nilly.

20 October 1920.

My dear Governor:

Of course nothing will be done in the Root matter, according to your suggestion to me of this morning; but I feel it my duty to advise you that nearly all the reports from the men whose judgment and opinion are usually good are to the effect that unless you will intervene and take a more active interest in the campaign, the Administration will be repudiated at the election.

There is a slight drift towards Cox, but unless you take advantage of it and speed it up, there is very little hope.

Tumulty

The President.

503

Of course I will help.

I was under the impression that I was helping. But I will do it in my own way.

Tumulty and in my own way.

W. W.

Further light on the Cox campaign

As for the vials of envy and hatred which have been emptied on your head by all the un-American things, aided by demagogues who wanted their votes and got them, abetted by yellow journals, etc., these lines of Byron can console you:

> "There were two cats in Kilkenny
> They fit and fit until of cats there weren't any."

This is almost a prophecy of what will happen now between Borah, Johnson & Co. and Root, Taft & Co., with poor Lodge mewing "peace" when there is no peace—except a larger peace outside their horizon. They have been kept united by hatred of you, by certain foreign encouragements, and by fear of the Democratic party. With the necessity to act, to do something, the smouldering fire of differences will break forth into flame. Conserve your health. Cultivate a cynical patience. *Give them all the rope you can.* Now and then when they make too big fools of themselves, throw in a keynote veto —not often—never when you can give them the benefit of the doubt and with it responsibility. They have neither the coherence nor the brains to handle the situation. Events will work their further confusion, events in Europe. God still reigns. The people *can* learn, though not quickly.

With regards,

(signed) JOHN SHARP WILLIAMS.

One would think that after the election the President would show a slackening of interest in the affairs of the nation; that having been repudiated by a solemn referendum, he would grow indifferent and listless to the administrative affairs that came to his desk. On the contrary, so far as his interest in affairs was concerned, one coming in contact with him from day to day after the election until the very night of March 3rd would get the impression that nothing unusual had happened and that his term of office was to run on indefinitely.

One of the things to which he paid particular attention at this time was the matter of the pardon of Eugene

V. Debs. The day that the recommendation for pardon arrived at the White House, he looked it over and examined it carefully, and said: "I will never consent to the pardon of this man. I know that in certain quarters of the country there is a popular demand for the pardon of Debs, but it shall never be accomplished with my consent. Were I to consent to it, I should never be able to look into the faces of the mothers of this country who sent their boys to the other side. While the flower of American youth was pouring out its blood to vindicate the cause of civilization, this man, Debs, stood behind the lines, sniping, attacking, and denouncing them. Before the war he had a perfect right to exercise his freedom of speech and to express his own opinion, but once the Congress of the United States declared war, silence on his part would have been the proper course to pursue. I know there will be a great deal of denunciation of me for refusing this pardon. They will say I am cold-blooded and indifferent, but it will make no impression on me. This man was a traitor to his country and he will never be pardoned during my administration."

CHAPTER XLVI

THE LAST DAY

I WAS greatly concerned lest the President should be unable by reason of his physical condition to stand the strain of Inauguration Day. Indeed, members of his Cabinet and intimate friends like Grayson and myself had tried to persuade him not to take part, but he could not by any argument be drawn away from what he believed to be his duty—to join in the inauguration of his successor, President-elect Harding. The thought that the people of the country might misconstrue his attitude if he should remain away and his firm resolve to show every courtesy to his successor in office were the only considerations that led him to play his part to the end.

When I arrived at the White House early on the morning of the 4th of March, the day of the inauguration, I found him in his study, smiling and gracious as ever. He acted like a boy who was soon to be out of school and free of the burdens that had for eight years weighed him down to the breaking point. He expressed to me the feeling of relief that he was experiencing now that his term of office was really at an end. I recalled to him the little talk we had had on the same day, four years before, upon the conclusion of the ceremonies incident to his own inauguration in 1917. At the time we were seated in the Executive office. Turning away from his desk and gazing out of the window which overlooked the beautiful White House lawn and gardens, he said: "Well, how I wish this

were March 4, 1921. What a relief it will be to do what I
please and to say what I please; but more than that, to
write my own impressions of the things that have been
going on under my own eyes. I have felt constantly a
personal detachment from the Presidency. The one thing
I resent when I am not performing the duties of the office
is being reminded that I am President of the United States.
I feel toward this office as a man feels toward a great
function which in his working hours he is obliged to perform but which, out of working hours, he is glad to get
away from and resume the quiet course of his own thought.
I tell you, my friend, it will be great to be free again."

On this morning, March 4, 1921, he acted like a man
who was happy now that his dearest wish was to be
realized. As I looked at Woodrow Wilson, seated in his
study that morning, in his cutaway coat, awaiting word
of the arrival of President-elect Harding at the White
House, to me he was every inch the President, quiet,
dignified; ready to meet the duties of the trying day upon
which he was now to enter, in his countenance a calm
nobility. It was hard for me to realize as I beheld him,
seated behind his desk in his study, that here was the head
of the greatest nation in the world who in a few hours was
to step back into the uneventful life of a private citizen.

A few minutes and he was notified that the President-
elect was in the Blue Room awaiting his arrival. Alone,
unaided, grasping his old blackthorn stick, the faithful
companion of many months, his "third leg," as he play-
fully called it, slowly he made his way to the elevator and
in a few seconds he was standing in the Blue Room meeting
the President-elect and greeting him in the most gracious
way. No evidence of the trial of pain he was undergoing
in striving to play a modest part in the ceremonies was

apparent either in his bearing or attitude, as he greeted the President-elect and the members of the Congressional Inaugural Committee. He was an ill man but a sportsman, determined to see the thing through to the end. President-elect Harding met him in the most kindly fashion, showing him the keenest consideration and courtesy.

And now the final trip to the Capitol from the White House. The ride to the Capitol was uneventful. From the physical appearance of the two men seated beside each other in the automobile, it was plain to the casual observer who was the out-going and who the in-coming President. In the right sat President Wilson, gray, haggard, broken. He interpreted the cheering from the crowds that lined the Avenue as belonging to the President-elect and looked straight ahead. It was Mr. Harding's day, not his. On the left, Warren Gamaliel Harding, the rising star of the Republic, healthy, vigorous, great-chested, showing every evidence in his tanned face of that fine, sturdy health so necessary a possession in order to grapple with the problems of his country. One, the man on the right, a battle-scarred veteran, a casualty of the war, now weary and anxious to lay down the reins of office; the other, agile, vigorous, hopeful, and full of enthusiasm for the tasks that confronted him. Upon the face of the one were written in indelible lines the scars and tragedies of war; on that of the other, the lines of confidence, hope, and readiness for the fray.

The Presidential party arrived at the Capitol. Woodrow Wilson took possession of the President's room. Modestly the President-elect took a seat in the rear of the room while President Wilson conferred with senators and representatives who came to talk with him about bills in which they were interested, bills upon which he must act before the old clock standing in a corner of the room should strike the hour of twelve, noon, marking the end of the official relationship of Woodrow Wilson with the affairs of the Government of the United States. It was about eleven-thirty. Senators and congressmen of both parties poured into the office to say good-bye to the man seated at the table, and then made their way over to congratulate the President-elect.

It was a few minutes before twelve o'clock. The weary man at the table was still the President, still the ruler of a great people, the possessor for a little while longer, just a little while longer, of more power than any king in Christendom.

Presently there appeared at the door a gray-haired man of imperious manner. Addressing the President in a sharp, dry tone of voice, he said: "Mr. President, we have come as a committee of the Senate to notify you that the Senate and House are about to adjourn and await your pleasure." The spokesman for the committee was Henry Cabot Lodge, the distinguished senator from Massachusetts, the implacable political foe of the man he was addressing.

It was an interesting study to watch the face and manner of Woodrow Wilson as he met the gaze of Senator Lodge who by his attacks had destroyed the great thing of which the President had dreamed, the thing for which he had fought and for which he was ready to lay down his life. It appeared for a second as if Woodrow Wilson was about to give full sway to the passionate resentment he felt toward the man who, he believed, had unfairly treated him throughout the famous Treaty fight. But quickly the shadow of resentment passed. A ghost of a smile flitted across his firm mouth, and steadying himself in his chair, he said in a low voice: "Senator Lodge, I have no further communication to make. I thank you. Good morning."

Senator Lodge and the committee withdrew from the room. I looked at the clock in the corner. A few minutes more and all the power which the weary man at the table possessed would fall from his shoulders. All left the room except the President, Mrs. Wilson, Admiral Grayson, and myself.

The old clock in the corner of the room began to toll the hour of twelve. Mechanically I counted, under my breath, the strokes: "One, two, three," on through "twelve," and the silent room echoed with the low vibration of the last stroke.

Woodrow Wilson was no longer President. By the votes of the American people he had been returned to the ranks of his fellow countrymen. A great warrior had passed from the field, a leading actor had made his exit. The dearest wish of his political enemies had at last been realized. The prayers of his devoted friends that he would live to see the eight years of his administration through, had been answered. His own bearing and attitude did not indicate that anything unusual had happened.

Quickly Woodrow Wilson, now the private citizen, turned to make his way to the elevator, leaning on his cane, the ferrule striking sharply on the stone pavement as he walked; but his spirit was indomitable. A few minutes before all interest had been centred upon him. Now but a few loyal friends remained behind. Interest was transferred to the scene being enacted a few feet away in the Senate Chamber, the induction into office of Vice-President Coolidge. By the time we reached the elevator, the brief ceremony in the Senate Chamber had ended, and the multitude outside were cheering Mr. Harding as he appeared at the east front of the Capitol to deliver his inaugural address. We heard the United States Marine Band playing "Hail to the Chief." For a few seconds I looked toward the reviewing stand. The new President, Warren G. Harding, was taking his place on the stand amid the din and roar of applause. He was the focus of all eyes, the pivot around which all interest turned. Not one of the thousands turned to look at the lonely figure laboriously climbing into the automobile. The words of Ibsen flashed into my mind:

The strongest man in the world is he who stands most alone.

THE END

APPENDIX

APPENDIX "A"

Cablegram

The White House, Washington,
10 December, 1918.

THE PRESIDENT OF THE UNITED STATES,
Paris, France.

Stories that you have agreed to sinking of German ships have caused great deal of unfavourable comment here.

TUMULTY.

Cablegram

The White House, Washington,
16 December, 1918.

THE PRESIDENT OF THE UNITED STATES,
% American Embassy, Paris, France.

Most popular note in this country in your speech are the words *Quote* We must rebuke acts of terror and spoliation and make men everywhere aware that they cannot be ventured upon without certainty of just punishment *End Quote*.

TUMULTY.

Cablegram

The White House, Washington,
21 December, 1918.

THE PRESIDENT OF THE UNITED STATES,
Paris.

If it is America's intention to back up the Allies in sinking German ships, the idea is so vague in this country that there ought to be a great deal of elucidation if the President intends to take this stand. Hope the President will be more definite than he has been in speeches in reference to League of Nations and freedom of the seas. His enemies here and abroad hope that he will particularize so that they can attack him. People of the world are with him on general principles. They care little for details.

TUMULTY.

Cablegram

The White House, Washington,
22 December, 1918.

THE PRESIDENT OF THE UNITED STATES,
American Embassy, Paris.

Springfield *Republican* editorially gives expression to fear that President may be made captive by Allied Imperialism and says *Quote* The conditions and atmosphere which now envelop him may be calculated to fill his mind with doubts as to the wisdom of his previous views and to expose him to the peril of vacillation, compromise, and virtual surrender of vital principles *End Quote*. Country deeply pleased by impression Mrs. Wilson has made abroad.

TUMULTY.

Cablegram

The White House, Washington,
24 December, 1918

THE PRESIDENT OF THE UNITED STATES,
Care of American Embassy, Paris, France.

Stories appearing here stating in effect that you intend to appeal to people of Europe bound to do great deal of harm. My affectionate Christmas Greetings to Mrs. Wilson and you.

TUMULTY.

Cablegram

The White House, Washington,
31 December, 1918.

THE PRESIDENT OF THE UNITED STATES,
Paris, France.

Clemenceau's speech, wherein he advocated a world settlement based upon the old balance of power ideas, demonstrates necessity for and wisdom of your trip, and has set stage for final issue between balance of power and League of Nations. If America fails now, socialism rules the world and if international fair-play under democracy cannot curb nationalistic ambitions, there is nothing left but socialism upon which Russia and Germany have already embarked. You can do nothing more serviceable than without seeming to disagree with Clemenceau, drive home in your speeches differences between two ideals, one, the balance of power means continuance of war; other, concert of nations means universal peace. One has meant great standing armies with larger armaments and burdensome taxation, consequent unrest and bolshevism. If the statesmanship at Versailles cannot settle these things in the spirit of justice, bolshevism will settle them in a spirit of injustice. The world is ready for the issue. Clemenceau has given you great chance, this country and whole world will sustain you. Country ready to back you up when you ask for its support. Everything fine here.

TUMULTY.

Cablegram

The White House, Washington,
6 January, 1919.

THE PRESIDENT OF THE UNITED STATES,
Paris.

Hope you will consider the suggestion for your return trip. Your personal contact with peoples of Europe has done much to help your programme. Our people will be with your programme, but it (the programme) must be personally conducted. If you return here without reception or ovation, public opinion on other side liable to misunderstand. The time of your return (in my opinion) is the hour for you to strike in favour of League of Nations. Lodge and leading Republicans constantly attacking, excepting Taft, who is daily warning them of political dangers of their opposition to your programme. Could you not consider stopping upon your return at Port of Boston instead of New York. The announcement of your stopping at Boston would make ovation inevitable throughout New England and would centre attack on Lodge. You have not been to New England in six years. It would be a gracious act and would help much. It would strengthen League of Nations movement in House and Senate and encourage our friends in Senate and House and throughout country. Our people just as emotional as people of Europe. If you return without reception, Lodge and others will construe *it as weakness*. If the people of our country could have seen you as people of Europe, our situation would be much improved, especially result of last November would have been different. My suggestion would be speech at Faneuil Hall, Boston; speech in Providence, New Haven, New York and reception upon return to Washington, to be participated in by returning soldiers.

TUMULTY.

Cablegram

The White House, Washington,
6 January, 1919.

THE PRESIDENT OF THE UNITED STATES,
Paris.

The attitude of the whole country toward trip has changed. Feeling universal that you have carried yourself magnificently through critical situations, with prestige and influence greatly enhanced here and abroad. The criticisms of the cloak-room statesmen have lost their force. I realize difficulties still to be met, but have no doubt of result. Trip admitted here by everybody to be wonderful success. Last week with perils of visit to Vatican most critical. The whole psychology favours the success of your trip. The peoples of Europe and the United States with you for League of Nations and against settlements based upon balance of power. Opinion here is that cards are stacked against you. My own opinion your influence so great in Europe that European leaders cannot stand in your way. Now is the critical moment and there must be no wasting away of your influence in unnecessary delay of conference. Hearts of the peoples of the world for League of Nations and they are indifferent to its actual terms. They are against militarism and for any reasonable plan to effectuate peace.

TUMULTY.

Cablegram

The White House, Washington,
13 January 1919.

THE PRESIDENT,
Paris.

In past two weeks the trend of newspaper dispatches from Paris has indicated a misunderstanding of your general attitude towards problems pending at peace conference. One newspaper cablegram says today that France, Italy and Great Britain have agreed to subordinate your league of nations programme to the need for counteracting bolshevism and collecting damages from Germany. Another a few days ago reported that Clemenceau had made headway with his insistence upon maintenance of balance of power. Still another outlined victory of Great Britain in her opposition to freedom of seas, stating that you had abandoned your position in response to arguments of France, supporting Great Britain. Similar stories would give impression that you were yielding, although we are aware that some of the suggestions for compromise are probably your own. Situation could easily be remedied if you would occasionally call in the three press association correspondents who crossed on *George Washington* with you, merely giving them an understanding of the developments as they occur and asking them not to use information as coming from you, but merely for their own guidance. It would show wisdom of various compromises as well as circumstances of such compromises. Proposal of Lloyd George that the Russian Bolshevik be invited to send peace delegates to Paris produced very unfavourable impression everywhere. It is denounced here as amazing.

TUMULTY.

Cablegram

The White House, Washington,
16 January 1919.

REAR ADMIRAL CARY T. GRAYSON,
Care of President Wilson, Paris.

American newspapers filled with stories this morning of critical character about rule of secrecy adopted for Peace Conference, claiming that the first of the fourteen points has been violated. In my opinion, if President has consented to this, it will be fatal. The matter is so important to the people of the world that he could have afforded to go any length even to leaving the conference than to submit to this ruling. His attitude in this matter will lose a great deal of the confidence and support of the people of the world which he has had up to this time.

TUMULTY.

Cablegram—Paris.

Received at White House, Washington,
January 16, 1919.

TUMULTY, White House,
Washington.

Your cable about misunderstandings concerning my attitude toward problems created by the newspaper cablegrams concerns a matter which I admit I do not know how to handle. Every one of the things you mention is a fable. I have not only yielded nothing but have been asked to yield nothing. These manœuvres which the cablegram speaks of are purely imaginary. I cannot check them from this end because the men who sent them insist on having something to talk about whether they know what the facts are or not. I will do my best with the three press associations.

WOODROW WILSON.

Cablegram—Paris.

Received at White House, Washington,
January 17, 1919.

TUMULTY, White House,
Washington.

Distressed to hear of your illness. Beg that you will make it your chief duty to take care of yourself and get well. All unite in most affectionate messages. Everything going well here. Very few of the troubles spoken of by the newspapers are visible to me on the spot.

WOODROW WILSON.

Cablegram—Paris.

Received at White House, Washington,
January 21, 1919.

TUMULTY, White House,
Washington.

The issue of publicity is being obscured by the newspaper men and we have won for the press all that is possible or wise to win, namely, complete publicity for real conferences. Publicity for the conversations I am holding with the small group of the great powers will invariably break up the whole thing, whereas the prospects for agreement are now, I should say, very good indeed. Delighted that you are up and beg that you will not expose yourself or exert yourself too soon. Affectionate messages from us all.

WOODROW WILSON.

Cablegram

The White House, Washington,
29 January, 1919.

THE PRESIDENT OF THE UNITED STATES,
    Paris.

Notice in morning papers discussion with reference to disposition of German colonies. Call your attention to speech of British Premier delivered in January as follows: *Quote* with regard to German colonies, I have repeatedly declared that they are held at the disposal of a conference whose decision must have primary regard to the wishes of the native inhabitants. The general principle of national self-determination therefore is applicable in their cases as in those of the occupied European territories *End quote*. I believe that Balfour made a similar statement.

TUMULTY.

Cablegram—Paris.

Received at White House, Washington,
March 15, 1919.

President's Residence, Paris
TUMULTY, White House,
    Washington.

The Plenary Council has positively decided that the League of Nations is to be part of the Peace Treaty. There is absolutely no truth in report to the contrary.

WOODROW WILSON.

Cablegram

The White House, Washington,
16 March 1919.

PRESIDENT WILSON,
    Paris.

Believe your most critical time in setting forward America's position at conference has come. Opposition to League growing more intense from .day to day. Its bitterness and pettiness producing reaction. New polls throughout country indicate strong drift toward league. League of Nations and just peace inseparable. Neither half can stand alone. Know you will not be drawn away from announced programme to incorporate League covenant in treaty. You can afford to go any length in insisting upon this. There is no doubt of your success here and abroad. The real friends of a constructive peace have not begun to fight. Everything fine here.

TUMULTY.

Cablegram

The White House, Washington,
25 March, 1919.

THE PRESIDENT OF THE UNITED STATES,
  Paris.

  There is great danger to you in the present situation. I can see signs
that our enemies here and abroad would try to make it appear that you are
responsible for delay in peace settlement and that delay has increased mo-
mentum of bolshevism and anarchy in Hungary and Balkans. Can responsibility for delay be fixed by you in some way?

                                                               TUMULTY.

Cable From the Associated Press at Paris.
  Paris, March 27, 1919.

President Wilson to-day issued the following statement:

  Quote in view of the very surprising impression which seems to exist in some
quarters, that it is the discussions of the commission on the league of nations
that are delaying the final formulation of peace, I am very glad to take the
opportunity of reporting that the conclusions of this commission were the
first to be laid before the plenary conference.

  They were reported on February 14, and the world has had a full month
in which to discuss every feature of the draft covenant then submitted.

  During the last few days the commission has been engaged in an effort
to take advantage of the criticisms which the publication of the covenant
has fortunately drawn out. A committee of the commission has also had
the advantage of a conference with representatives of the neutral states,
who are evidencing a very deep interest and a practically unanimous desire
to align themselves with the league.

  The revised covenant is now practically finished. It is in the hands of a
committee for the final process of drafting, and will almost immediately be
presented a second time to the public.

  The conferences of the commission have invariably been held at times
when they could not interfere with the consultation of those who have undertaken to formulate the general conclusions of the conference with regard to
the many other complicated problems of peace, so that the members of the
commissions congratulate themselves on the fact that no part of their conferences has ever interposed any form of delay *End quote.*

Cablegram

The White House, Washington,
25 March, 1919.

THE PRESIDENT OF THE UNITED STATES,
  Paris.

  St. Louis *Republic* of Saturday reporting speech of Senator Reed referring to provision naming members of League says: *Quote* he told of what he

called a secret protocol and intimated that Germany is included in this secret protocol *End quote.* Advise whether or not there is any secret protocol such as Senator claims or of any character, attached to League Covenant.

TUMULTY.

Cablegram—Paris.

Received at White House, Washington,
March 27, 1919.

TUMULTY, White House,
Washington.

Statement that there is any sort of secret protocol connected with or suggested in connection with the League of Nations is absolutely false.

WOODROW WILSON.

Cablegram

The White House, Washington,
March 28, 1919.

PRESIDENT WILSON,
Paris.

Stories here this morning that amendment for Monroe Doctrine and racial discrimination to be excluded from covenant causing a great deal of uneasiness.

TUMULTY.

Cablegram

The White House, Washington,
March 30, 1919.

PRESIDENT WILSON,
Paris.

In an editorial entitled *Treat or Fight,* Springfield *Republican* says: *Quote* It is plain that the Allies dare not commit themselves to an avowed war on the soviets and that it is not possible for the Allies with the world in its present temper to take the position that the existence of the soviet form of government in any country constitutes a casus belli; that the world would recoil from the proposal to begin a new series of war with so dubious an object; that Russia should be left to manage her own affairs *End Quote.* Editorial disagrees with policy of French Government towards Russia and soviets. Calls attention to disastrous results of foreign intervention during French Revolution. Editorial further says: *Quote* Impossible to fight revolution in one place and be at peace elsewhere. If Allies mean to fight Hungary because it has set up a soviet form of government and allied itself to Russia they will have to fight

Russia. If they fight Russia they will have to fight the Ukraine. Such a war would mean the end of the League of Nations. It is plain that the Allies dare not commit themselves to an avowed war on the soviets *End Quote.*

TUMULTY.

Cablegram

The White House, Washington,
March 30, 1919.

PRESIDENT WILSON,
Paris.

Dispatches from Simonds and others prove stories of weeks ago were most optimistic now touched with deep pessimism. Simonds in article on Saturday says: *Quote* No common objective in council; no dominating influence; drifting, etc. *End Quote.* I fear your real position in council not understood here and that lack of publicity strengthening many false impressions. The responsibility attaching to those associated with you, including France and England, when they accepted Fourteen Points evidently lost sight of by them. Do not know what your real situation is, but it appears to me that Germany is not prepared to accept the kind of peace which is about to be offered. or if she does accept, with its burdensome conditions, it means the spread of bolshevism throughout Germany and central Europe. It seems to me that you ought in some way to reassert your leadership publicly. I know the danger, but you cannot escape responsibility unless you do so. Now is the moment in my opinion to strike for a settlement permanent and lasting.

TUMULTY.

Cablegram

The White House, Washington,
2 April, 1919.

PRESIDENT WILSON,
Paris.

The proposed recognition of Lenine has caused consternation here.

TUMULTY.

Cablegram—Paris.

Received at White House, Washington,
April 4, 1919.

TUMULTY, White House,
Washington.

Am still confident that President will win. Encountering difficulties; situation serious. President is the hope of the world more than ever, and with his courage, wisdom, and force he will lead the way. Have you any suggestions as to publicity or otherwise?

GRAYSON.

Cablegram—Paris.

Received at White House, Washington,
April 4, 1919.

TUMULTY, White House,
Washington.

The President took very severe cold last night; confined to bed. Do not worry; will keep you advised.

GRAYSON.

Cablegram—Paris.

Received at White House, Washington,
April 5, 1919.

TUMULTY, White House,
Washington.

We are naturally disappointed at progress being made but not discouraged. Hopeful everything will turn out all right. Will advise you if anything definite develops. The President is better this morning but confined to bed. No cause for worry.

GRAYSON.

Cablegram—Paris.

Received at White House, Washington,
April 5, 1919.

GRAYSON, % President Wilson,
Paris.

In my opinion the President must in some dramatic way clear the air of doubts and misunderstandings and despair which now pervade the whole world situation. He must take hold of the situation with both hands and shake it out of its present indecision, or political sabotage and scheming will triumph. Only a bold stroke by the President will save Europe and perhaps the world. That stroke must be made regardless of the cries and admonitions of his friendly advisers. He has tried to settle the issue in secret; only publicity of a dramatic kind now can save the situation. This occasion calls for that audacity which has helped him win in every fight.

TUMULTY.

Cablegram—Paris.

Received at White House, Washington,
April 6, 1919.

TUMULTY,
Washington.

The President says the situation here is extremely complex and intricate, but seems to be improving and he expects to have it in hand this week, but if necessary will act according to your suggestions. The President is confined to bed but steadily improving. Thanks for your telegram.

GRAYSON.

Cablegram—Paris.

Received at White House, Washington,
April 8, 1919.

TUMULTY,
Washington.

President attended conference in his study this afternoon. Situation shows some improvement. President has ordered *George Washington* to proceed here immediately.

GRAYSON.

Cablegram

The White House, Washington,
April 9, 1919.

GRAYSON,
Care President Wilson, Paris.

The ordering of the *George Washington* to return to France looked upon here as an act of impatience and petulance on the President's part and not accepted here in good grace by either friends or foes. It is considered as an evidence that the President intends to leave the Conference if his views are not accepted. I think this method of withdrawal most unwise and fraught with the most dangerous possibilities here and abroad, because it puts upon the President the responsibility of withdrawing when the President should by his own act place the responsibility for a break of the Conference where it properly belongs. The President should not put himself in the position of being the first to withdraw if his 14 points are not accepted. Rather he should put himself in the position of being the one who remained at the Conference until the very last, demanding the acceptance of his 14 principles. Nothing should be said about his leaving France, but he ought when the time and occasion arrive to re-state his views in terms of the deepest solemnity and yet without any ultimatum attached and then await a response from his associates. In other words, let him by his acts and words place his associates in the position of those who refuse to continue the Conference because of their unwillingness to live up to the terms of the Armistice. Then the President can return to this country and justify his withdrawal. He cannot justify his withdrawal any other way. Up to this time the world has been living on stories coming out of Paris that there was to be an agreement on the League of Nations. Suddenly out of a clear sky comes an order for the *George Washington* and unofficial statements of the President's withdrawal. A withdrawal at this time would be a desertion.

TUMULTY.

Cablegram

The White House, Washington,
9 April, 1919.

PRESIDENT WILSON,
Paris.

A great number of your friends here fear that the interposition of United States in matter of indemnity and reparation which is a paramount question with European nations and only of indirect interest to us will solidify the opposition of England, France, Italy, and Belgium to a league of nations. Our friends believe that any necessary sacrifices to assure a league of nations should be made. Your supporters would be happy if you could throw upon the other nations the burden of exacting indemnities and at the same time win their support to a league of nations.

TUMULTY.

Cablegram—Paris.

Received at White House, Washington,
10 April, 1919.

TUMULTY,
Washington.

President made good progress to-day by hammering ahead with his own force. His health is improving; out for a short drive this afternoon; first outing since last Thursday.

GRAYSON.

Cablegram—Paris.

Received at White House, Washington,
April 10, 1919.

TUMULTY, White House,
Washington.

Have shown your message to the President. From your side of the water your points are well taken, but he has formed his ideas through immediate contact with actual conditions on this side of the world. . . . More progress has been made in the last two days than has been made for the last two weeks. Am spending all the time I can in guiding correspondents and showing them every attention. I confer with Grasty every day. The President is working too hard following his recent illness. To know that things are going on and not properly handled, and yet be responsible for them, causes him more worry and anxiety and does more harm than actual participation. This is a matter that worries me. If his health can hold out I am still confident he will win handsomely. Am keeping as cheerful a front as possible over here.

GRAYSON.

Cablegram—Paris.

Received at White House, Washington,
April 12, 1919.

TUMULTY,
Washington.

So far as it is possible to tell amidst complexity of selfish interests things seem to be slowly clearing. President sends you his love and says keep a stiff upper lip.

GRAYSON.

Cablegram—Paris.

Received at White House, Washington,
April 24, 1919.

TUMULTY,
White House.

Thank you for your cable about Industrial Board. On the whole I think they have got into a blind alley, but I am glad you are going to obtain Hines' opinion. *Do not give yourself any concern about secret treaties. You may be sure I will enter into none.*

WOODROW WILSON.

Cablegram

The White House, Washington,
30 April, 1919.

THE PRESIDENT OF THE UNITED STATES,
Paris.

Beg to call your attention to following editorial from Springfield *Republican*. *Quote* The critical period in the peacemaking has been reached when progress can win over reaction the very least of victories only by a resolute stand of the most commanding figure in Paris. France and England cannot desert the President without branding themselves as hypocrites and ingrates. Worse things could happen than for the President to come home without a peace treaty, leaving Europe to wallow in the mire of national rivalries and hates to which reaction would sentence it for all time. There is no compelling reason why America should sign a treaty that would merely perpetuate ancient feuds and make new wars a certainty. Our chief interest in the Conference at Paris, as the President declared at Manchester, is the peace of the world. Unless that can be made reasonably sure, with Europe's sincere coöperation, the time is near when 'pack up and come home' will be America's only policy *End Quote.*

TUMULTY.

Cablegram

The White House, Washington,
8 May, 1919.

THE PRESIDENT OF THE UNITED STATES,
Paris.

In your cable you spoke of forwarding message to Congress. Have you made up your mind as to what you will discuss? Would like to suggest certain things I believe vital.

TUMULTY.

Cablegram

Received at White House, Washington,
May 9, 1919.

TUMULTY, White House,
Washington.

Happily there is no mystery or privacy about what I have promised the Government here. I have promised to propose to the Senate a supplement in which we shall agree, subject to the approval of the Council of the League of Nations, to come immediately to the assistance of France in case of unprovoked attack by Germany, thus merely hastening the action to which we should be bound by the Government of the League of Nations.

WOODROW WILSON.

Cablegram

The White House, Washington,
22 May, 1919.

THE PRESIDENT OF THE UNITED STATES,
Paris.

Great demonstration New York last night, addressed by Hughes, to protest killings in Poland, Galicia, Roumania and elsewhere. Feeling in this matter growing more intense throughout the country. Cannot something be done? It is evident that Germany is doing everything to separate the Allies. A great many newspapers in this country are worried lest you be carried away by the pleadings of Germany for a *Quote* softer peace *End Quote.* I know you will not be led astray. There is an intense feeling in the Senate in favour of the publication of the terms of the Treaty. Can anything be done to straighten this out?

TUMULTY.

Cablegram

The White House, Washington,
23 May, 1919.

THE PRESIDENT OF THE UNITED STATES,
Paris.

Mr. Taft in signed article this morning says: *Quote* Find it hard to believe that President Wilson sent sympathetic note to women who plead for Huns *End*

Quote. I think this matter of sufficient importance to be cleared up from this side. There is great deal of unrest here owing to talk in newspapers of return of German ships to Great Britain.

TUMULTY.

Cablegram—Paris.

Received at White House, Washington,
May 24, 1919.

TUMULTY,
Washington.

I think our friends in the Senate ought to be furnished very frankly with the following reason, which seems to me quite convincing, for not at present publishing the complete treaty: namely, that if our discussion of the treaty with the Germans is to be more than a sham and a form it is necessary to consider at least some of the details of the treaty as subject to reconsideration and that, therefore, it would be a tactical blunder to publish the details as first drafted, notwithstanding the fact that there is no likelihood that they will be departed from in any substantial way.

WOODROW WILSON.

Cablegram—Paris.

Received at White House, Washington,
May 25, 1919.

TUMULTY, White House,
Washington.

No one need have any concern about the return of the German ships in our possession. Full understanding has been reached about them. As for Mr. Taft's criticism, I am quite willing to be responsible for any sympathetic reply I make to appeals on behalf of starving women and children. Please give following message to Glass: You may take it for granted that I will sign the Urgent Deficiency Bill and go forward with the plans you mention in your cable.

WOODROW WILSON.

Cablegram

The White House, Washington,
26 May, 1919.

THE PRESIDENT OF THE UNITED STATES,
Paris.

Every Republican member of new Foreign Relations Committee openly opposed to treaty, a majority in favour of its amendment. Every Democratic member of Committee, including Thomas, for treaty and against separation. There is a decided reaction evident against the League, caused, in my opinion, by dissatisfaction of Irish, Jews, Poles, Italians, and Germans.

Republicans taking full advantage and liable, in order to garner disaffected vote, to make absolute issue against League. Reaction intensified by your absence and lack of publicity from your end and confusion caused by contradictory statements and explanations of *Quote* so-called compromises *End Quote*. Simonds' article appearing in certain American newspapers Sunday, admirable, explaining reasons for Saar Valley and French pact and other controversial matters.

There is a tremendous drive against League, resembling German propaganda, backed by Irish and Jews. Irish openly opposing; Jews attacking along collateral lines. Could not Lansing or perhaps White, because he is a Republican, or yourself inspire publicity or give interview explaining—officially or unofficially—the following matters:

First —America's attitude toward publication of terms of Treaty, along lines of your last cable to me.

Second —That the fourteen points have not been disregarded.

Third —The underlying reason for French pact emphasizing the point as Simonds' says *Quote* That French pact is merely an underwriting of the League of Nations during the period necessary for that organization not merely to get to work, but to become established and recognized by all nations *End quote*.

I am not at all disturbed by this reaction—it was inevitable. The consummation of your work in the signing of the Treaty will clear the air of all these distempers. Your arrival in America, your address to the Congress and some speeches to the country will make those who oppose the League to-day feel ashamed of themselves. The New York *World* had a very good editorial favouring the mandatory of Turkey.

TUMULTY.

Cablegram—Paris.

Received at White House, Washington, June 16, 1919.

TUMULTY, White House, Washington.

If Germans sign the Treaty we hope to get off the first of next week, about the 24th or 25th. It is my present judgment that it would be a mistake to take any notice of the Knox amendment. The whole matter will have to be argued from top to bottom when I get home and everything will depend upon the reaction of public opinion at that time. I think that our friends can take care of it in the meantime and believe that one of the objects of Knox and his associates is to stir me up, which they have not yet done. I may nevertheless take the opportunity to speak of the League of Nations in Belgium.

WOODROW WILSON.

Cablegram

The White House, Washington,
21 June, 1919.

THE PRESIDENT OF THE UNITED STATES,
  Paris.

The fight against the League in Knox resolution faces utter collapse. Root and Hayes here advising Republican leaders. I learned that Root is advising Republicans to vote for the League with reservations. He is advising Republicans to concentrate their forces upon a resolution of ratification, which would contain specific reservations on the Monroe Doctrine, immigration, tariff, and other purely American questions. I believe that this is the course the Republicans will finally adopt. A confidant of Mr. Taft's yesterday wanted to know from me what your attitude was in this matter, saying that Mr. Taft might favour this reservation plan. I told him I had no knowledge on the subject. It is a thing that you might consider. To me it looks like cowardice.

The American Federation of Labour adopted a resolution favouring the League of Nations by a vote of twenty-nine thousand seven hundred fifty against four hundred twenty. Andrew Furuseth led the fight against it. The resolution supporting the League contained a reservation in favour of home rule for Ireland.

TUMULTY.

Cablegram—Paris.

Received at White House, Washington,
June 23, 1919.

TUMULTY,
  Washington.

My clear conviction is that the adoption of the Treaty by the Senate with reservations would put the United States as clearly out of the concert of nations as a rejection. We ought either to go in or stay out. To stay out would be fatal to the influence and even to the commercial prospects of the United States, and to go in would give her the leadership of the world. Reservations would either mean nothing or postpone the conclusion of peace, so far as America is concerned, until every other principal nation concerned in the Treaty had found out by negotiation what the reservations practically meant and whether they could associate themselves with the United States on the terms of the reservations or not. Moreover, changes in the Treaty seem to me to belong to the powers of negotiation which belong to the President and that I would be at liberty to withdraw the Treaty if I did not approve of the ratifications. I do not think it would be wise for me to wait here for the appropriation bills. I hope to sail on the twenty-fifth or twenty-sixth and suggest that you consider the plan of sending a vessel to meet me.

WOODROW WILSON.

Cablegram

The White House, Washington,
June 23, 1919.

THE PRESIDENT OF THE UNITED STATES,
 Paris.

Your cable concerning reservations in ratification would make fine statement for the public. The country would stand back of you in this. Can I use it in this way or can I at least furnish copies to Senator Hitchcock and Mr. Taft? If you allow me to make public use of it may I change *Quote* leadership of the world *End Quote* to *Quote* a notable place in the affairs of the world *End Quote*. This in order to avoid possibility of hurting feelings of other nations. Now is time to issue statement of this kind as Lodge has practically withdrawn Knox resolution and opponents seem to be concentrating on *Quote* reservations *End Quote*.

TUMULTY.

Cablegram—Paris.
TUMULTY, White House,
 Washington.   June 25, 1919.

I am quite willing that you should make public use of my cable to you about reservations by the Senate in regard to the treaty, with this change in the sentence to which you call my attention:

Quote And to go in would give her a leading place in the affairs of the world, *End Quote* omitting also the last sentence about changes belonging to power to negotiate treaties.

WOODROW WILSON.

June 25, 1919.

Secretary Tumulty to-day gave out a message which he had received from the President, as follows:

My clear conviction is that the adoption of the Treaty by the Senate with reservations would put the United States as clearly out of the concert of nations as a rejection. We ought either to go in or stay out. To stay out would be fatal to the influence and even to the commercial prospects of the United States, and to go in would give her a leading place in the affairs of the world. Reservations would either mean nothing or postpone the conclusion of peace, so far as America is concerned, until every other principal nation concerned in the treaty had found out by negotiation what the reservations practically meant and whether they could associate themselves with the United States on the terms of the reservations or not.

WOODROW WILSON.

Cablegram from Grasty to New York Times

June 29, 1919.

Aboard the *Oklahoma.*

President's sailing from Brest most auspicious. Most beautiful weather and promise of more of same. President and Mrs. Wilson showed no ill effects from strenuous activities of past few days and while both formed sincere attachment for France, they are glad to turn faces homeward. Contrary to some reports current in America he is in excellent health. While element of novelty which entered his reception on arrival last December disappeared, there was deeper feeling manifested toward him last night in Paris than ever before. Thousands of *Quote* Vive Wilson *End Quote* came from French heart and continuous ovation. Paris showed popular recognition of leadership of American in securing peace. One very old Frenchman sprang in front of President's carriage in Champs Élysées and shouted in English: *Quote* Mr. Wilson, thank you for peace *End Quote.* That was the keynote and same sentiment was echoed in thousands of ways. Although owing to different American viewpoints, Wilson has been frequently antagonistic during this month, at end relations with other governments' heads most cordial. Lloyd George came over to Place des États-Unis last night and told President *Quote* You've done more to bring English-speaking people together than ever before˙ done by any man *End Quote.* Clemenceau looked as if losing his best friend when he said Good Bye in Invalides Station. Many representatives of smaller nations have expressed to me within past few days hope that President be able to return to Europe and continue his work of reconciliation and reconstruction, which they said nobody else in position to do or able to do so well.

GRASTY.

APPENDIX "B"

Cablegram

The White House, Washington,
16 March, 1919.

PRESIDENT WILSON,
Paris.

Former President Taft asks if he may cable to you direct, for your consideration only, some suggestions about which he has been thinking a great deal and which he would like to have you consider. He said that these suggestions do not look to the change of the structure of the League, the plan of its action or its real character, but simply to removing objections in minds of conscientious Americans, who are anxious for a league of nations, whose fears have been roused by suggested constructions of the League which its language does not justify and whose fears could be removed without any considerable change of language.

TUMULTY.

Cablegram—Paris.

Received at White House,
March 18, 1919.

In reply to your number sixteen, appreciate Mr. Taft's offer of suggestions and would welcome them. The sooner they are sent the better. You need give yourself no concern about my yielding anything with regard to the embodiment of the proposed convention in the Treaty.

WOODROW WILSON.

Cablegram

The White House, Washington,
18 March, 1919.

PRESIDENT WILSON,
Paris.

Following from Wm. H. Taft:

Quote If you bring back the Treaty with the League of Nations in it, make more specific reservations of the Monroe Doctrine, fix a term for the duration of the League and the limit of armament, require expressly unanimity of action in Executive Council and Body of Delegates, and add to Article XV a provision that where the Executive Council of the Body of Delegates finds the difference to grow out of an exclusively domestic policy, it shall recommend no settlement, the ground will be completely cut from under the opponents of the League in the Senate. Addition to Article XV will answer objection as to Japanese immigration as well as tariffs under Article XXI. Reservation of the Monroe Doctrine might be as follows:

Any American state or states may protect the integrity of American territory and the independence of the government whose territory it is, whether a member of the League or not, and may, in the interests of American peace, object to and prevent the further transfer of American territory or sovereignty to any European or non-American power.

Monroe Doctrine reservation alone would probably carry the treaty but others would make it certain. (signed) WM. H. TAFT *End Quote.*

TUMULTY.

Cablegram

The White House, Washington, 21 March, 1919.

PRESIDENT WILSON,
Paris.

The following letter from Hon. Wm. H. Taft. *Quote* I have thought perhaps it might help more if I was somewhat more specific than I was in the memorandum note I sent you yesterday, and I therefore enclose another memorandum *End Quote.*

Duration of the Covenant

Add to the Preamble the following:

Quote From the obligations of which any member of the League may withdraw after July 1, 1829, by two years' notice in writing, duly filed with the Secretary General of the League *End Quote.*

Explanation

I have no doubt that the construction put upon the agreement would be what I understand the President has already said it should be, namely that any nation may withdraw from it upon reasonable notice, which perhaps would be a year. I think, however, it might strengthen the Covenant if there was a fixed duration. It would completely remove the objection that it is perpetual in its operation.

Duration of Armament Limit

Add to the first paragraph of Article VIII, the following:

Quote At the end of every five years, such limits of armament for the several governments shall be reëxamined by the Executive Council, and agreed upon by them as in the first instance *End Quote.*

Explanation

The duration of the obligation to limit armament, which now may only be changed by consent of the Executive Council, has come in for criticism. I should think this might thus be avoided, without in any way injuring the Covenant. Perhaps three years is enough, but I should think five years would be better.

Unanimous Action by the Executive Council or Body of Delegates

Insert in Article IV, after the first paragraph, the following:

Quote Other action taken or recommendations made by the Executive Council or the Body of Delegates shall be by the unanimous action of the countries represented by the members or delegates, unless otherwise specifically stated *End Quote*.

Explanation

Great objection is made to the power of the Executive Council by a majority of the members and the Body of Delegates to do the things which they are authorized to do in the Covenant. In view of the specific provision that the Executive Council and the Body of Delegates may act by a majority of its members as to their procedure, I feel confident that, except in cases where otherwise provided, both bodies can only act by unanimous vote of the countries represented. If that be the right construction, then there can be no objection to have it specifically stated, and it will remove emphatic objection already made on this ground. It is a complete safeguard against involving the United States primarily in small distant wars to which the United States has no immediate relation, for the reason that the plan for taking care of such a war, to be recommended or advised by the Executive Council, must be approved by a representative of the United States on the Board.

Monroe Doctrine

Add to Article X.

(a) *Quote* A state or states of America, a member or members of the League, and competent to fulfil this obligation in respect to American territory or independence, may, in event of the aggression, actual or threatened, expressly assume the obligation and relieve the European or non-American members of the League from it until they shall be advised by such American state or states of the need for their aid *End Quote*.

(b) *Quote* Any such American state or states may protect the integrity of any American territory and the sovereignty of the government whose territory it is, whether a member of the League or not, and may, in the interest of American peace, object to and prevent the further transfer of American territory or sovereignty to any European or non-American power *End Quote*.

Explanation

Objection has been made that under Article X, European governments would come to America with force and be concerned in matters from which heretofore the United States has excluded them. This is not true, because Spain fought Chili, in Seward's time, without objection from the United States, and so Germany and England instituted a blockade against Venezuela in Roosevelt's time. This fear could be removed, however, by the first of the above paragraphs.

Paragraph (b) is the Monroe Doctrine pure and simple. I forwarded this in my first memorandum.

It will be observed that Article X only covers the integrity and independence of members of the League. There may be some American countries which are not sufficiently responsible to make it wise to invite them into the League. This second paragraph covers them. The expression *Quote* European or non-American *End Quote* is inserted for the purpose of indicating that Great Britain, though it has American dominion, is not to acquire further territory or sovereignty.

Japanese Immigration and Tariffs

Add to Article XV.

Quote If the difference between the parties shall be found by the Executive Council or the Body of Delegates to be a question which by international law is solely within the domestic jurisdiction and polity of one of the parties, it shall so report and not recommend a settlement of the dispute *End Quote*.

Explanation

Objection is made to Article XV that under its terms the United States would be found by unanimous recommendation for settlement of a dispute in respect to any issue foreign or domestic; that it therefore might be affected seriously, and unjustly, by recommendations forbidding tariffs on importations. In my judgment, we could only rely on the public opinion of the world evidenced by the Body of Delegates, not to interfere with our domestic legislation and action. Nor do I think that under the League as it is, we covenant to abide by a unanimous recommendation. But if there is a specific exception made in respect to matters completely within the domestic jurisdiction and legislation of a country, the whole criticism is removed. The Republican senators are trying to stir up anxiety among Republicans lest this is to be a limitation upon our tariff. The President has already specifically met the objection as to limitation upon the tariff when the Fourteen Points were under discussion. Nevertheless in this respect to the present language of the Covenant, it would help much to meet and remove objections, and cut the ground under senatorial obstruction.

Prospect of Ratification

My impression is that if the one article already sent, on the Monroe Doctrine, be inserted in the Treaty, sufficient Republicans who signed the Round Robin would probably retreat from their position and vote for ratification so that it would carry. If the other suggestions were adopted, I feel confident that all but a few who oppose any league would be driven to accept them and to stand for the League.

(End letter)

TUMULTY.

Cablegram

The White House, Washington,
28 March, 1919.

THE PRESIDENT OF THE UNITED STATES,
Paris.

Following just received from Mr. Taft: *Quote* Venture to suggest to President that failure to reserve Monroe Doctrine more specifically in face of opposition in Conference will give great weight to objection that League as first reported endangers Doctrine. It will seriously embarrass advocates of League, it will certainly lead to Senate amendments embodying Doctrine and other provisions in form less likely to secure subsequent acquiescence of other nations than proper reservation now. Deems some kind of Monroe Doctrine amendment now to Article Ten vital to acceptance of League in this country. I say this with full realization that complications in Conference are many and not clearly understood here. A strong and successful stand now will carry the League *End Quote*.

TUMULTY.

Letter from Mr. Taft.

New York, N. Y., April 10, 1919.

MY DEAR MR. TUMULTY:

We are very much troubled over the report that the Monroe Doctrine amendment to the Covenant is being opposed by England and Japan. Will you be good enough to send the enclosed to the President? We had a meeting to-day of the Executive Council of the League to Enforce Peace. Doctor Lowell and I, at the instance of the League, will be glad to have this matter presented directly to the President by cable.

Sincerely yours,
WM. H. TAFT.

HON. JOSEPH P. TUMULTY,
Secretary to the President,
The White House,
Washington, D. C.
Enclosure.

Cablegram

The White House, Washington,
13 April, 1919.

PRESIDENT WILSON,
Paris.

Following is sent at the request of Mr. Taft: *Quote* Friends of the Covenant are seriously alarmed over report that no amendment will be made more specifically safeguarding Monroe Doctrine. At full meeting of Executive Committee of League to Enforce Peace, with thirty members from eighteen states present, unanimous opinion that without such amendment, Republican senators will certainly defeat ratification of Treaty because public opinion will sustain them. With such amendment, Treaty will be promptly ratified.

(signed)WILLIAM H. TAFT
A. LAWRENCE LOWELL *End Quote*
TUMULTY.

March 27, 1919.

Admission—Paris.

For Secretary Lansing from Polk.

Following are proposed amendments to the Constitution of the League of Nations which have been drafted by Mr. Root:

First Amendment: Strike out Article XIII, and insert the following: The high contracting powers agree to refer to the existing Permanent Court of Arbitration at The Hague, or to the Court of Arbitral Justice proposed at the Second Hague Conference when established, or to some other arbitral tribunal, all disputes between them (including those affecting honour and vital interests) which are of a justiciable character, and which the powers concerned have failed to settle by diplomatic methods. The powers so referring to arbitration agree to accept and give effect to the award of the Tribunal.

Disputes of a justiciable character are defined as disputes as to the interpretation of a treaty, as to any question of international law, as to the existence of any fact which if established would constitute a breach of any international obligation, or as to the nature and extent of the reparation to be made for any such breach.

Any question which may arise as to whether a dispute is of a justiciable character is to be referred for decision to the Court of Arbitral Justice when constituted, or, until it is constituted, to the existing Permanent Court of Arbitration at The Hague.

Second Amendment. Add to Article XIV the following paragraphs:

The Executive Council shall call a general conference of the powers to meet not less than two years or more than five years after the signing of this convention for the purpose of reviewing the condition of international law, and of agreeing upon and stating in authoritative form the principles and rules thereof.

Thereafter regular conferences for that purpose shall be called and held at stated times.

Third Amendment. Immediately before the signature of the American Delegates, insert the following reservation:

Inasmuch as in becoming a member of the League the United States of America is moved by no interest or wish to intrude upon or interfere with the political policy or internal administration of any foreign state, and by no existing or anticipated dangers in the affairs of the American continents, but accedes to the wish of the European states that it shall join its power to theirs for the preservation of general peace, the representatives of the United States of America sign this convention with the understanding that nothing therein contained shall be construed to imply a relinquishment by the United States of America of its traditional attitude towards purely American questions, or to require the submission of its policy regarding such questions (including therein the admission of immigrants) to the decision or recommendation of other powers.

Fourth Amendment. Add to Article X the following:

After the expiration of five years from the signing of this convention any party may terminate its obligation under this article by giving one year's notice in writing to the Secretary General of the League.

Fifth Amendment. Add to Article IX the following:

Such commission shall have full power of inspection and verification personally and by authorized agents as to all armament, equipment, munitions, and industries referred to in Article VIII.

Sixth Amendment. Add to Article XXIV the following:

The Executive Council shall call a general conference of members of the League to meet not less than five nor more than ten years after the signing of this convention for the revision thereof, and at that time, or at any time thereafter upon one year's notice, any member may withdraw from the League.

POLK, Acting.

The first suggestion made by Mr. Root is not only substantially expressed in Article XIII of the Treaty, but almost literally, in its very text, appears in this section of the Covenant.

Mr. Root's proposition that "the high contracting powers agree to refer to the existing permanent Court of Arbitration at The Hague or to the court of arbitral justice proposed at the Second Hague, when established, or to some other arbitral tribunal, all disputes between them," etc. This is actually done by Article 13, the reference being not to the Hague or to the proposal of the Second Hague Convention, but to a court of arbitration "agreed on by the parties to the dispute or stipulated in any convention existing between them."

As will readily be seen, Mr. Root's definition of "disputes of justiciable character" is embodied literally in Article XIII of the Covenant, Mr. Root's exact language having been appropriated at the Peace Commission.

Mr. Root's second proposed amendment provided for calling "a general conference of the powers to meet in not less than two years, or more than five years," after the signing of this convention for the purpose of reviewing the condition of international law and of agreeing upon and stating in authoritative form the principles and rules thereof."

In Article XIX of the Covenant it is provided that the Assembly meet from time to time to engage in "the consideration of international conditions whose continuance might endanger the peace of the world." If it may be said that this provision of Article XIX does not make it mandatory upon the council to meet at fixed periods, for the purpose of reviewing international conditions, on the other hand it may be urged that it empowers the Assembly to advise such a review at any time, and the Council to make such review at any time and as often as the necessities might permit. "The consideration of international conditions" certainly comprehends a review of international law and a rectification of its imperfections, so that substantially the whole of this suggestion by Mr. Root is in the Covenant.

The third amendment of the Covenant suggested by Mr. Root is exceedingly interesting in several particulars. Those who would invoke the aid and sympathy of the Government of the United States in the effort for Irish freedom will observe that Mr. Root herein precludes the United States from having any interest in, or wish to intrude upon or interfere with, the political policy of the internal administration of any foreign state. Contrast this with Article XI of the Covenant, which President Wilson in a speech on the Pacific coast said was peculiarly his own and in which it is declared to be the friendly right of any member of the League to bring to the attention of the Assembly or of the Council any circumstances whatever affecting international relations which threaten to disturb the internal peace or understanding between nations, and if this may be regarded as outside the question, let it go, and turn to another significant phrase contained in Mr. Root's suggested amendment. It will be noted that nowhere in his suggested modifications of the Covenant does Mr. Root suggest any alteration whatsoever of Article X, as it stands. On the contrary, in Mr. Root's third suggested amendment he proposed to put the United States definitely on record as acceding "to the wish of the European states that this nation shall join its powers to theirs for the preservation of general peace.'"

The final proposition contained in Mr. Root's proposed third amendment is broadly cared for in Article XXI of the Covenant relating to the Monroe Doctrine, and by implication in paragraph 8 of Article XV, which prohibits any recommendation by the Council as to the settlement of the matters solely within the domestic jurisdiction of any member of the League.

It may, furthermore, be stated that the President cheerfully agreed to a reservation presented by Mr. Hitchcock, of the Senate Foreign Relations Committee, even more specifically withholding all domestic questions from the jurisdiction of the League.

Mr. Root's fourth suggested amendment proposed to permit any member of the League to terminate its obligations, under Article X, by giving one year's notice of its desire. While no such modification of Article X was made, the much broader right was given to any nation to renounce all of its obligations to the League and to terminate its membership of the League upon two years' notice at any time after joining.

The fifth suggested amendment by Mr. Root, proposing a modification of Article IX, by empowering a commission to inspect and verify, either personally or by authorized agents, all armaments, equipment, munitions, and industries relating to the manufacture of war material, does not appear to have been adopted, nor can any one rationally insist that it was essential to accept this suggestion. Article IX provides for the appointment of a permanent commission to advise the Council of the execution of those provisions of the Covenant relating to armament, equipment, munitions, etc., in the military and naval branches of industry.

A sane interpretation of this article would imply that the commission has power to inspect and verify facts, because in no other way could it possibly function.

Mr. Root's sixth proposed amendment makes it mandatory upon the Executive Council of the League to call a general conference of members to meet not less than five years or more than ten years after the signing of the Covenant for purposes of revision, etc. This modification of the Covenant was not made, but the fact that it was omitted by no manner of means precludes the exercise of that particular function by the Council. Without Mr. Root's amendment it is perfectly competent for the Council to convene such a meeting of the members of the League at any time. It might do this in less time than five years, or it might postpone the doing of it for ten years or a longer period.

APPENDIX "C"

THE WHITE HOUSE,
WASHINGTON

24 April, 1919.

PRESIDENT WILSON,
Paris.

As we see it from this distance, the selfish designs of Japan are as indefensible as are those of Italy. The two situations appear to parallel each other in their bearing upon the fate of weak and helpless nations. Would it not be an opportune time to cast another die, this one in the direction of Japan, that the whole world may know once and for all where America stands upon this, the greatest issue of the peace we are trying to make? Now is the time to use your heavy artillery and emphasize the danger of secret treaties and selfish designs of certain big nations.

TUMULTY.

Received at The White House, Washington,
11:48 A. M.

April 25, 1919.

Paris.
TUMULTY,
White House,
Washington.

Am very grateful for your message of approval about the Japanese business. It has warmed my heart mightily. The difficulties here would have been incredible to me before I got here. Your support kept me in heart.

WOODROW WILSON.

THE WHITE HOUSE,
WASHINGTON

26 April, 1919.

THE PRESIDENT OF THE UNITED STATES,
Paris.

It appears to me from this end that the Japanese demands will soon produce another crisis. If such a crisis arises, I hope you will in any statement you make emphasize again America's purpose and her unwillingness to consent to any imperialistic peace. The whole country will be with you in this

544

matter as never before.   I think that your Italian statement was the beginning of a real peace and a real league of nations.

TUMULTY.

Received at The White House, Washington,
April 29, 1919.

Paris.
TUMULTY,
White House, Washington.

Situation still difficult.   President putting up great fight against odds. Japanese claims now under discussion.

GRAYSON.

Paris.   Received at The White House, Washington.
April 30, 1919.

TUMULTY,
White House, Washington.

Japanese situation hanging by a thread.   They are in conference now. These are terrible days for the President physically and otherwise.

GRAYSON.

Received at The White House, Washington,
Paris.   May 1, 1919.
TUMULTY,
White House, Washington.

The solution of the Kiauchau question is regarded here both generally and by special friends of China, like Charles R. Crane, as remarkably favourable and fortunate considering its rotten and complicated past and the tangle of secret treaties in which she was enmeshed and from which she had to be extricated.   It is regarded as a wonderful victory for the President.   The Japanese themselves admit that they have made far greater concessions than they had even dreamed would be required of them.   The Chinese agreed that they have great confidence in their interests being safeguarded in every way and they appreciate that the League of Nations eventually will look after them.

GRAYSON.

THE WHITE HOUSE,
WASHINGTON

1 May, 1919.

THE PRESIDENT OF THE UNITED STATES,
Paris.

I have not made use of the Japanese statement but am keeping my ear to the ground and waiting.   My feeling is that an attempt to explain the compromise when no demand is made, would weaken our position instead of strengthening it. I will therefore do nothing about the Japanese matter unless you insist. It would help if I could unofficially say: First, the date of your probable return to this country; Second, whether tour country to discuss the League of Nations is possible. The adoption of the labour programme as part of the peace programme is most important, but not enough emphasis is being placed upon it. Could you not make a statement of some kind that we could use here, showing the importance of this programme as helping toward the stabilization of labour conditions throughout the world?

TUMULTY.

THE WHITE HOUSE,
WASHINGTON

2 May, 1919.

THE PRESIDENT OF THE UNITED STATES,
Paris.

Sympathetic editorial New York *World* reference Japanese settlement. I have not given out statement as yet. It does not look now as if any would be necessary.

TUMULTY.

Received at The White House, Washington,
2 May, 1919.

London.
TUMULTY,
White House, Washington.

Am perfectly willing to have you use your discretion about the use you make of what I sent you about the Chinese-Japanese settlement. Sorry I cannot predict the date of my return though I think it will be by June first. Am expecting to make a tour of the country but even that is impossible to predict with certainty.

WOODROW WILSON.

THE WHITE HOUSE,
WASHINGTON

4 May, 1919.

GRAYSON,
Care President Wilson,
Paris.

Papers here very critical of Japanese settlement. Chinese statement given great publicity.

TUMULTY.

INDEX

INDEX